Caught In Between Borders: Citizens, Migrants and Humans

Liber Amicorum in honour of
prof. dr. Elspeth Guild

Paul Minderhoud, Sandra Mantu & Karin Zwaan (eds)

Caught In Between Borders: Citizens, Migrants and Humans

Paul Minderhoud, Sandra Mantu & Karin Zwaan (eds)

ISBN: 978-94-6240-550-9

Layout: Hannie van de Put
Omslagbeeld: Sjaak van der Vooren
Bewerking banner: Carolus Grütters

Published by
Wolf Legal Publishers (WLP)
Talent Square 13
5038 LX Tilburg
info@wolfpublishers.nl
www.wolfpublishers.com

Contents

Introduction

Kees Groenendijk & Paul Minderhoud

Fascination for the Concept of Borders

Professor Guild, who started working in Nijmegen in 1997, has been fascinated by borders throughout her academic career. She gave her inaugural lecture entitled *Moving the borders of Europe* in Nijmegen in 2001, a few years before the nine Central and Eastern European countries acceded to the European Union, the largest extension in its history. From September 2009 she holds a Jean Monnet Chair Ad Personam on the subject *Reflecting on Europe's Borders: Movement of persons and the rule of law.* Her valedictory lecture of 6 September 2019 was titled *Interrogating Europe's Borders: Reflections from an Academic Career.* In her list of publications, enclosed at the end of this book, numerous publications with a central focus on borders stand out. When organizing her farewell seminar the topic was obvious as was the title chosen: *Moving the borders of Europe Revisited.* At the seminar four of Professor Guild's former PhD students (Evelien Brouwer, Madeline Garlick, Claude Cahn and Sandra Mantu) gave presentations related to borders. The written version of these presentations can be found in this book. The concluding remarks of the seminar were given by her promotores Roel Fernhout and Kees Groenendijk. And so her two decades in Nijmegen have come full circle. The other former PhD students supervised by her in Nijmegen (Daniel Wilsher, Dana Baldinger, Simon Tans, Bjarney Friðriksdóttir and Anoeshka Gehring) also contributed to this book.

The title of this *Liber Amicorum* for Elspeth therefore was rather obvious. *Caught in between borders: citizens, migrants and humans* reflects that the same person can be a citizen, a migrant or a human being within the same borders and that this categorization can change just like that. This title captures not only the academic fascination of professor Guild for borders but also, her life. Born and educated in Canada, she graduated in Greek language in Thessaloniki and then settled as a lawyer in London.

Once her academic career got shape in Nijmegen, her love developed in Paris. Years before the word Brexit was coined, she reduced its potential negative consequences by marrying a Frenchman. Living strategically at both ends of the Eurostar in London and Paris and commuting to Nijmegen on a regular basis, she was permanently crossing and caught in between borders.

Professor Guild and the Development of EU Migration Law

Elspeth started contributing to the development of EU migration law from the moment she started to practice law in London. She sent her first fax to Nijmegen in 1992: ten pages provoking us to think about how the ECJ's 1990 *Sevince* judgment on the standstill clause for Turkish workers could be the basis for the protection of self-employed Turkish migrants in Europe as well. It would take eight years before the Court of Justice in its 2000 judgment in *Savas* interpreted the standstill clause in the Protocol to the Association Agreement EEC-Turkey in the way she proposed. Her next fax was about how the Court's case law on the association with Turkey could also be useful in interpreting the 1975 EEC-Morocco Cooperation Agreement. The first reference on the clauses on migrant workers in that agreement would arrive in Luxembourg three years later.

Professor Guild contributed to the development of EU migration law in at least four different ways: first of all with her academic and other publications, secondly through her support to practising lawyers, judges and colleagues in academia, thirdly by preparing the ground for the EU legislator and, finally, by laying down the foundation for EU migration law as a separate academic discipline. We can only mention a few examples of each of those four pathways.

Rights of Individuals versus Powers of States

Over the last three decades professor Guild wrote almost three hundred articles, books, case notes, policy briefs and blogs. Her productivity and, more important, her combination of creativity, energy and wit are unique. Her 1996 compilation of and commentary on the first generation of EU instruments on immigration and asylum made the often inaccessible texts and the development of this new branch of EU law available to researchers and practitioners. In her innovative PhD, entitled *Immigration Law in the European Community*, defended in Nijmegen in 2000 professor Guild stressed the basic elements common to both the law on free movement of Union citizens and the first EU rules on migrants from outside the EU. Her study also demonstrated the unique capacity of EU law to grant enforceable rights to non-citizens even in immigration issues. The subjects of her publications changed over time from the Association Agreements and the accession of the Central European countries, to the status of long-term resident immigrants, the unhappy link between migrants and terrorism, borders and visa, Schengen (before and after 2015), citizenship and Brexit. Throughout this rich contribution professor Guild remained intrigued by and focused on two central themes . Her first focus is on how Human Rights and EU law both grant rights to non-nationals and how these rights can be enforced and developed. Her second focus is on how human beings in a marginal position (in a consulate far away, at the border, in immigration detention, or in a secret prison or a CIA rendition programme) are treated and how this treatment can be improved in order to meet minimum standards agreed in national and international law. Generally, she starts from the migrant's perspective rather than from state powers and she critically looks at efforts of states to acquire new powers or reinforce old ones with regard to non-nationals or nationals of immigrant origin on security, public order or economic grounds.

Her analysis is not limited to black letter law but relies on empirical data and on theoretical insights form sociology of migration and political sciences. Her work is a living model of how taking work done across the borders of your own discipline seriously enriches the outcome and relevance of your analysis. In recent publications on Brexit professor Guild vividly illustrated the role of law and politics in unsettling, degrading and excluding large numbers of people long settled in the UK and elsewhere in the EU. Brexit will not undo Elspeth's intensive efforts over decades linking lawyers in the UK and continental Europe. Her work in linking networks of immigration and asylum lawyers in Europe, ILPA in the UK, GISTI in France, Hohenheimer Tage zum Migrationsrecht in Germany, ASGI in Italy and the European Immigration Lawyers Conference, will continue to bear fruit.

Stimulating, Supporting and Teaching Colleagues

Professor Guild continuously stimulated practising lawyers, judges, academic colleagues, civil servants and politicians to take EU migration law seriously, by setting a good example in her own work and by supporting others. She shared her broad knowledge and expertise generously with those who asked for advice or offered it as she saw opportunities which otherwise would have remained unused. Over the years at her initiative we discussed at the Centre for Migration Law (CMR) in Nijmegen with lawyers from different EU countries having their first case on free movement or EU migration law before the Court in Luxembourg and were looking for arguments or strategies. For almost fifteen years she taught a course on EU migration law for Dutch immigration judges at the Dutch Judges Academy (SSR) several times a year. This course undeniable contributed to the fact that almost one fifth of the first 150 references to the EU Court of Justice concerning immigration and asylum were brought by Dutch courts, the Dutch references outnumbering those by German courts.

For more than a decade, Elspeth was a leading member of the Network on Free Movement of Workers (FMOW) coordinated by the Centre for Migration Law until 2014 and left a strong mark on the activities of the Network. Early on she recognized the need for cooperation with colleagues in the Central and Eastern European countries. After the 2004 accession she used her own network to find the right experts from those countries for the FMOW.

Elspeth has successfully participated in various (collaborative) research projects. She involved the Centre for Migration Law successively in a Framework 5 project on European Liberty and Security (ELISE), a Framework 6 project on the Changing Landscape of European Liberty and Security (CHALLENGE) and a Framework 7 project on Enacting European Citizenship (ENACT). Together with Cristina Gortázar Rotaeche and Dora Kostakopoulou (both contributing to this book), 'the girls' as they called themselves, she organized several Jean Monnet seminars in Madrid, Manchester and Nijmegen resulting in a book: *The Reconceptualization of European Union* Citizenship. Twice she acted as a 'founding mother' of the recognition of the CMR as a Jean Monnet Centre of Excellence.

Professor Guild also initiated at the Centre for Migration Law a very active programme hosting visiting scholars interested in European migration and asylum law and practice. The programme is still in operation and has hosted over 30 researchers from across the world (including China). One of the first visiting scholars was her PhD student Diego Acosta, who contributed to this *Liber Amicorum* and, recently, was appointed professor of European and Migration law at the University of Bristol.

Preparing the Ground for the EU Legislator and Supporting Implementation

With written and oral advice to MEPs, Commission officials, the House of Lord Subcommittee on the EU or CEPS policy briefs professor Guild contributed, often invisibly, to proposals and amendments for EU legislative instruments or policy decisions in this field. One of those activities deserves more attention. Shortly after Elspeth arrived in Nijmegen, the Council of Europe asked the CMR how the Council could best support the integration of settled immigrants. Our advice was to develop a set of common rules granting immigrants security of residence and equal treatment. The Council of Europe (CoE) committed the CMR to do a comparative research on the relevant law and its actual application in CoE Member States. Only because of Elspeth's contacts with practitioners and academics across Europe we were able to produce our report in 1998. As a follow-up Elspeth took the lead in drafting a text that later became Recommendation (2000)15 of the CoE Committee of Ministers concerning the security of residence of long-term migrants. In the meantime EU Member States decided in Tampere that the EU should take over the lead from Strasbourg and use its new competence to make binding EU law on this issue. The European Commission asked us to do a similar study on the situation in all (then) 15 Member States, which was reported in April 2000 and followed by a proposal of the Commission which resulted in Directive 2003/109 concerning the status of third-country nationals who are long-term residents. This directive reduces the risk that immigrants from outside the EU are treated as temporary guests forever. The directive grants equal treatment, strong protection against expulsion and conditional mobility within the EU. After the extension of its scope to beneficiaries of international protection, the directive covers all non-EU nationals admitted for other than strictly temporary purposes. In 2017 this new EU-residence status had been issued to 3.5 million nationals of non-EU countries. Only a few Member States (e.g. Germany, France and Belgium) still prefer to issue settled immigrants with their own, less favourable national permanent residence status.

Professor Guild was well aware that adopting an EU instrument is only the first step. She stimulated the organisation of a series of seminars at the CMR, where one year after the end of the implementation period of a new directive, academics, Commission and national officials and practising lawyers from different Member States would discuss their experiences with this directive. Each seminar was followed by a book (eight volumes appeared in this format), often with a contribution by professor Guild, which made those experiences accessible to a wider audience and contributed to the directive being taken seriously.

Laying the Foundations for EU Migration Law as a Separate Discipline

Elspeth was the first person to be appointed as tenured professor in EU migration law inside and outside Europe. Before the Amsterdam Treaty entered into force she took the initiative to found the European Journal of Migration and Law. She suggested trusted friends as members of the Editorial Board and edited the journal ever since with Paul Minderhoud, during its first years with Thomas Spijkerboer, Ryszard Cholewinski, later with Sandra Mantu (all contributing to this book). The journal's title reflected the intention to be a forum for lawyers and academics from other disciplines.

She convinced Kluwer (later Brill-Nijhoff) to publish the series Immigration and Asylum Law and Policy in Europe, which offered a wider audience for the best PhD's in the field, not only the studies she supervised in Nijmegen and London or elsewhere in Europe. It became also a platform for the studies of other young and senior colleagues. In this series, now edited together with Valsamis Mitsilegas (contributing to this book as well), since the first volume ('Security of Residence and Expulsion') between 2001 and 2019 a total of 44 volumes were published.

Professor Guild Connecting Law and Politics

Elspeth always is acutely aware of the essential role academic lawyers can play in the drafting of national and international legal standards, if they are prepared to adapt to the political agenda and to act swiftly and independently. An early example of this awareness was the Draft Resolution on national policy on admission for employment presented to the EC Ministers responsible for Immigration, the predecessor of the EU's Justice and Home Affairs Council, at their meeting on 30th November and 1st December 1992 in London. The draft purported to set out harmonised 'principles', permitting Member States to choose which principles they would find most convenient and implement them in their national law, leaving the other principles untouched. The draft explicitly excluded individual workers or employers to rely on any matter in the resolution in pursuance of their rights against a Member State. At an ILPA conference held in London later the same week, Elspeth suggested to Kees Groenendijk to do something against this 'unacceptable' plan, which would create only opportunities for states not for individuals. Thus, on Saturday morning in the empty office of Elspeth's law firm the two were writing critical comments on the draft, arguing that the resolution would open the door to 'a new guest worker system' and conflict with existing Community law and international obligations of Member States. Moreover in their eyes: 'The process is an insult to democracy.' The comments were published as a note by the Meijers Committee and ILPA. The resolution was finally adopted in a thoroughly amended form in June 1994 under the Greek Presidency. Apparently, the note had been taken seriously by the drafters.

A quarter of a century later in 2017, professor Guild was one of the first academic authors writing on the drafting of the UN Global Migration Compact. The Compact also is a set of legally non-binding norms, which potentially could disregard rights migrants acquired under binding international instruments. With the aim of damage control she mobilised a group of colleagues and asked each of them to summarize the case law of the UN monitoring bodies on one of the central human rights of migrants. Within five months she succeeded in collecting and editing the contributions and arranged for the publication of a book (*Human Rights of Migrants in the 21st Century)* which made the legal boundaries for the drafters of the Compact visible.. After the adoption of Compact, without the consent of the USA and some EU Member States, Elspeth again mobilised colleagues to write a series of blog posts on how the implementation of the Compact at the national level could best be monitored (https://rli.blogs.sas.ac.uk/themed-content/global-compact-for-migration/). It is too early to judge the effects of these academic efforts. Different aspects of the Compact are discussed in the contributions by Ryszard Cholewinski, Bjarney Friðriksdóttir and Jens Vedsted-Hansen in the final section of this book.

Importance of Her Academic Scholarship

After her dissertation professor Guild wrote three influential monographs. In *The Legal Elements of European Identity: EU Citizenship and Migration Law*, she enriched our understanding of European identity with the work of European political theorists. The role of supra-national human rights obligations in Europe and how they apply to extraterritorial action by states is the central topic in *Security and European Human Rights: Protecting Individual Rights in Times of Exception and Military Action*. It was also published in French and Hungarian. In 2009, she brought together many strands of her research in the launch of a new interdisciplinary approach to the field – *Critical Migration Studies* – in *Security and Migration in the 21st Century*. The importance of her scholarship to the academic community was honoured when Lund University bestowed on her a doctorate honoris causa in 2008. In the letter of motivation the University stated it was awarding her the honour:

> 'In the course of a rich career combining research and practice, Elspeth Guild has successfully repositioned migration law at the intersection of discourses within and beyond the legal discipline. She has offered her scholarly expertise to political institutions as well as civil society across Europe, and thereby stimulated democratic processes around the formulation of the law. Engaging with the law in its formal rigour as well as its ideational implications has been a hallmark of Elspeth Guild's scholarship, which combines empirical and theoretical strands in an exemplary and inspiring fashion.'

This book contains 33 scientific contributions by (former) colleagues, PhD students and friends of Elspeth, all of whom have a special connection with the Centre for Migration Law. The contributions are divided into five categories: borders, citizens, migrants, asylum and the global compact on migration. They reflect the versatility of the work and interest of professor Guild, who was professor of European Migration Law from 2001 till 2019 at the Faculty of Law of the Radboud University Nijmegen, the Netherlands.

Borders

The Expansion of Regional Free Movement Regimes
Towards a Borderless World?

Diego Acosta[*]

Introduction

The expansion of human rights law coupled with the explosion of regional processes of integration are the two most important phenomena that have limited states' capacity to restrict the entry of foreigners into their territory and their rights while residing within.[1] It should come as no surprise that regional agreements facilitating mobility have proliferated, and now involve around 120 countries, either at a bilateral or multilateral level.[2] For one thing, most global migration is regional, in either Europe, Africa, Asia or Southern and Central America.[3] In addition, regional instruments can be agreed on more rapidly and, in principle, introduce higher standards of protection and rights due to the more limited number of actors involved in the negotiations.[4] There is of course huge variation across regions as to degree of development of the various regional agreements, the categories of individuals entitled to mobility and equal treatment and their effective application and enforcement mechanism devices.[5]

The EU has been often considered the paradigmatic example of a functioning regional mobility framework. In the EU´s case, two features have been identified as easing implementation on the ground. First, the principles of supremacy and direct effect mean that individuals can invoke rights granted by EU law before national courts and that EU law prevails over any inconsistent domestic provision. Second, the duo Commission-Court of Justice – in their roles as overseer and supreme interpreter of EU law respectively – have facilitated the effective access to rights of those individuals exercising their free movement in Europe. Such a robust supranational component –

---

* Reader in Law, University of Bristol, UK.

1 S. Iglesias Sánchez, 'Free Movement of Persons and Regional International Organisations', in: R. Plender (ed.) *Issues in International Migration Law* (Brill, Leiden, 2015), p. 223-260.

2 V. Chetail, 'The transnational movement of persons under general international law - Mapping the customary law foundations of international migration law', in: V. Chetail & C. Bauloz (eds), *Research Handbook on International Law and Migration* (Cheltenham: Edward Elgar 2014), p. 1-74, at 35.

3 The only exceptions to this trend are North America (Canada and the USA) and Oceania (Australia and New Zealand). Please see that the reference here is to Europe and not to the European Union where more TCNs reside than EU citizens in a second Member State. See R. Bedford, 'Contemporary patterns of international migration', in: B. Opeskin, R. Perruchoud & J. Redpath-Cross, *Foundations of International Migration Law* (Cambridge: Cambridge University Press 2012), p. 17-55.

4 K. Popp, 'Regional processes, law and institutional developments on migration' in: B. Opeskin, R. Perruchoud & J. Redpath-Cross, *Foundations of International Migration Law* (Cambridge: Cambridge University Press 2012), p. 366-389.

5 See generally on this: A. Pécoud & P. de Guchteneire (eds), *Migration without Borders: Essays on the Free Movement of People* (Oxford: Berghahn Books 2007); S. Nita, A. Pécoud, P. de Guchteneire, Ph. de Lombaerde, K. Neyts & J. Gartland, *Migration, Free Movement and Regional Integration* (Paris: UNESCO 2017).

a peculiarity in comparative perspective – makes it a challenge to imagine other types of effective mechanisms of compliance and implementation in stronger inter-governmental contexts. And yet, as will be seen below, regional free movement regimes continue to expand and emerge everywhere.

Regional free movement regimes transform the meaning of citizenship and the relationship between states, their territory and foreigners.[6] Through regional migration agreements, states renounce their control over the relationship between territory and population since there is a group of non-nationals who obtain rights of entry and/or residence, coupled with other provisions on non-discrimination in terms of access to work, family reunification or, even, socio-economic entitlements. European citizenship is a reality but discussions on African or South American citizenship have been ongoing for the last few years.[7] The fact that states in all regions around the world are willing to debate and, in many instances, ratify instruments by which they renounce part of their sovereignty concerning control of the entry, residence and potential prolonged stay of certain foreigners – from regional neighbouring states – deserves further attention. This has been recognised by the Global Compact on Migration in which the word 'regional' appears more than 50 times. This liberalization may take various forms – from visa exemption to a common supranational citizenship, its common trait being that of facilitating mobility of people. Beginning in 2007, a series of books have individually analysed some of the free movement regimes at global level, but many questions merit further inquiry.[8] Following an exemplification of the proliferation of regional free movement treaties, this contribution will succinctly refer to two aspects where more research is needed. These are the motivations behind the expansion of freedom of movement and the interplay between courts and the international and the domestic legal frameworks.

A Brave New World?

A powerful narrative insists on presenting migration as a problem that is everywhere being tackled by the erection of borders – physical and legal. The media aside, even well-known and respected scholars go as far as characterising the present state of immigration regulation as a landscape where 'no new ideas are emerging', or where the

6 E. Guild, *The Legal Elements of European Identity. EU Citizenship and Migration Law*, The Hague: Kluwer 2004.

7 African Union, *Report of the First Conference of Intellectuals of Africa and the Diaspora*, 6–9 October 2004, Dakar, Senegal, Rapt/Rpt/CAID (I), Adis Ababa: African Union 2004, p. 15, paragraph 59(g), available from http://ocpa.irmo.hr/resources/docs/Intellectuals_Dakar_Report-en.pdf (accessed 8 February 2019); UNASUR, Brasilia Declaration entitled 'Towards a South American Citizenship,' Brasilia, 19–21 October 2011; see also the Andean Community and its 2015 non-legally binding Statute on Human Mobility where, for the first time, regional migrant workers are referred as Andean citizens.

8 Pécoud & De Guchteneire 2007; R. Cholewinski, R. Perruchoud & E. MacDonald (eds), *International Migration Law – Developing Paradigms and Key Challenges* (The Hague: T.M.C. Asser Press 2007); S. Nita et al. 2017. See also selected chapters in: M. Panizzon, G. Zurcher, E. Fornalé & G. Zürcher (eds), *The Palgrave Handbook of International Labour Migration. Law and Policy Perspectives* (London: Palgrave McMillan 2015).

only ones emerging point in the direction of further control and restriction.[9] This pessimistic account only offers a half truth and is unhelpful in understanding global developments. Indeed, the way in which the mobility of people has been liberalised at both the bilateral and regional level is a lesser known account, at least outside the confines of the EU's free movement of people and common supranational citizenship.[10] This is despite the fact that, as recognised by the Global Compact on Migration and its constant references to the regional level, this is possibly the most important game changer on migration regulation for the years to come. Regional migration agreements also tell us a different story about the alleged global trend of borders closure and immigration control.[11] Contradicting this accepted narrative, regional agreements open borders for at least those coming from certain countries. Examples are abundant. Already in 2007, the editors of a first volume on the subject concluded that the world was 'progressing towards more, not less, freedom of movement' of people.[12] The boom in the last 12 years is notable and more than 30 regional organisations are discussing mobility and adopting policies and legal instruments.[13] Three examples will illustrate this.

First, the MERCOSUR Residence Agreement entered into force in 2009. The agreement provides that any national from a MERCOSUR or Associate Member State may obtain a two-year temporary residence permit in another Member State by only providing proof of nationality as well as a clean criminal record for the last five years.[14] Permit holders have the right to work and equal treatment regarding working conditions, access to education for children, family reunification and other rights. According to the IOM, 2.6 million residence permits were granted in South America under the agreement between 2009 and 2016.[15]

Second, on 1 January 2015, the Astana Treaty establishing the Eurasian Economic Union (EEU) between Belarus, Kazakhstan and Russia – with Armenia and Kyrgyzstan

9 C. Dauvergne, *The New Politics of Immigration and the End of Settler Societies*, Cambridge: Cambridge University Press 2016, p. 7. Dauvergne reaches this pessimistic conclusion after only analyzing four countries in the world: Australia, Canada, New Zealand and the United States.

10 D. Kochenov (ed.), *EU Citizenship and Federalism: The Role of Rights*, Cambridge: Cambridge University Press 2017.

11 Immigration control and the relationship between security and the individual have been the subject of an important part of Guild's scholarly. See among others: E. Guild, *Security and Migration in the 21st Century*, Cambridge: Polity 2009; D. Bigo & E. Guild (eds.), *Controlling Frontiers. Free Movement into and within Europe*, Aldershot: Ashgate 2005.

12 Pécoud & De Guchteneire 2007, p. 1-32, at p. 2.

13 Nita et al. 1017.

14 Residence Agreement for Nationals of MERCOSUR Member States, Brasilia, 6 December 2002. It entered into force on 28 July 2009. The agreement applies to Argentina, Bolivia, Brazil, Paraguay and Uruguay as full Member States. Venezuela, whose membership was suspended in 2017, still needs to incorporate the Residence Agreement into its legislation before it can enter into force in the country. The Associate States that benefit from the agreement include Chile, Colombia, Peru and Ecuador. Guyana and Suriname became Associate States on 11 July 2013 but they had not adopted the Residence Agreement by 1 February 2019. An unofficial translation of the agreement can be consulted here: http://www.diegoacosta.eu/portfolio-items/unofficial-english-translation-of-the-mercosur-residence-agreement/?portfolioCats=55.

15 IOM, *Evaluación del Acuerdo de Residencia del MERCOSUR y su incidencia en el acceso a derechos de los migrantes*, Buenos Aires: International Organization for Migration 2018.

joining later – entered into force.[16] The Astana Treaty incorporates a full Section XXVI on Labour Migration. Articles 97 and 98 offer nationals of the participating states the right to work in another Member State without the need to obtain a work permit, as well as, among other entitlements, automatic recognition of educational qualifications, and equal treatment in access to medical services or education rights for the children of workers. Despite the difficulties in the implementation of certain aspects,[17] the Treaty has opened new opportunities including for example for the more than half a million Kyrgyz nationals living in Russia.[18]

Third, the African Union (AU) adopted in January 2018 its free movement of persons Protocol.[19] The Protocol, which will enter into force when ratified by 15 Member States, will facilitate migration in the region through the opening of legal paths for migration for all nationals of African countries.[20] This project could reduce irregular migration on the continent not only by eliminating irregular border crossing through the creation of a right to cross borders for all citizens of African states but also by introducing a right of residence and exercise of economic activities for such persons in any African country. It is one of the flagship projects of the African Union Agenda 2063.[21] This adds to the developments taking place in the eight Regional Economic Communities (RECs) in Africa, some of which have free movement protocols in place, such as ECOWAS or COMESA, while others have ongoing discussions to create them, such as IGAD.

Explaining the Outburst

Understanding the rationale behind the proliferation of free movement agreements is central to understanding their scope, functioning and possible replication in other regional contexts. The standard narrative where free movement of people constitutes but one of the steps to create an internal market appears unnecessarily Eurocentric. It also lacks explanatory power to understand why agreements emerge in regions where common markets are far from the main goal – even when lip service is paid to them.

---

16 For an excellent historical account see A. Leonov & O. Korneev, 'Regional Migration Governance in the Eurasian Migration System', in: A. Geddes, V. Espinoza, L. Hadj-Abdou & Brumat (eds), *The Dynamics of Regional Migration Governance*, Cheltenham: Edward Elgar Publishing 2019, p. 205-223.

17 C. Schenk, 'Labour Migration in the Eurasian Economic Union', in: A. Pikulicka-Wilczewska & G. Uehling (eds), *Migration and the Ukraine Crisis A Two-Country Perspective*, Bristol: E-International Relations Publishing 2017, p. 164-177.

18 L. Sagynbekova, *International Labour Migration in the Context of the Eurasian Economic Union: Issues and Challenges of Kyrgyz Migrants in Russia*, Working Paper 39, Naryn: University of Central Asia 2017.

19 Protocol to the Treaty establishing the African Economic Community relating to Free Movement of Persons, Right of Residence and Right of Establishment, adopted by the thirtieth ordinary session of the Assembly, Addis Ababa, Ethiopia, 29 January 2018.

20 At the time of writing the Protocol had been signed by 32 states and ratified by one, Rwanda. See https://au.int/en/treaties/protocol-treaty-establishing-african-economic-community-relating-free-movement-persons.

21 G. Mukundi Wachira, *Study on the Benefits and Challenges of Free Movement of Persons in Africa*, Geneva: African Union Commission and IOM 2018.

The example of South America is revelatory. The adoption of the 2002 MERCOSUR Residence Agreement was the result of a particular historical conjunction. Fernando Enrique Cardoso, the Brazilian President at the time, was willing to end his second and last term as Brazil's President with a personal stamp by proposing a measure to advance regional integration.[22] Thus, Brazil put forth a project for a migratory amnesty for MERCOSUR nationals on 30 August 2002, which would regularise all undocumented regional migrants through a six-month procedure. Argentina's National Migration Directorate counter-proposed to establish a permanent, rather than temporary, mechanism for MERCOSUR nationals to access residency. The timing was propitious in many respects for Argentina. It coincided with the emigration of thousands of Argentinians to Europe and the USA, thus making it easier to draw comparisons between immigrants at home and emigrants abroad. The Argentinian National Migration Directorate was pragmatic in its approach. It pointed out numerous challenges: the difficulty of patrolling a huge border with neighbouring countries, the importance of better knowledge of those who already resided within the territory for security reasons, as well as the need to offer equal treatment to regional migrants to protect indigenous workers against wage dumping and regional migrants against exploitation.[23]

In fact, the agreement's main objective, as unmistakably declared in its preamble, is to solve the situation of intra-regional migrants in irregular situations. The driving force was undocumented migration rather than the establishment of an internal market. This explains why the agreement does not provide for a right of entry—a major drawback. The individual can either regularise in the host state if he already resides there, or, alternatively, request a residence permit in the Consulate of the country to which he would like to move.

In the case of Africa, the creation of a common market is not necessarily the main driving force behind the adoption of the new Protocol on movement of persons. Indeed, the preamble makes references to other aspects such as solidarity, human rights and Pan-Africanism. Pan-Africanism is indeed an important concept that has been at the core of discussion on free movement since the 1960s and that also relates to mobility across artificial colonial boundaries.[24]

Finally, in the case of the EEU it has been argued that the geopolitical interests of Russia, and to a lesser extent Kazakhstan, play a much more important role than any internal market goal.[25] Here we would be witnessing the 'partial re-integration' of a space where labour migration is already a reality on the ground and as such recognised in this new regional organization.[26]

---

22 A. Alfonso, *Integración y Migraciones. El Tratamiento de la Variable Migratoria en el MERCOSUR y su Incidencia en la Política Argentina.* Buenos Aires: IOM 2012, p.48.

23 *Ibid.*, p. 50.

24 G. Mukundi Wachira, *Study on the Benefits and Challenges of Free Movement of Persons in Africa,* Geneva: African Union Commission and IOM 2018, p. 15.

25 C. Schenk, 'Labour Migration in the Eurasian Economic Union', in: A. Pikulicka-Wilczewska & G. Uehling (eds), *Migration and the Ukraine Crisis A Two-Country Perspective*, Bristol: E-International Relations Publishing 201), p. 164-177.

26 Leonov & Korneev 2019.

Courts and the Domestic-International Interplay

The interpretation by Courts – both regional and domestic – of not only the particular clauses pertaining to free movement of people in each regional agreement, but also of the interplay between domestic and regional norms, is central for the deepening of free movement. As Guild wrote in 2004 while referring to the European example, '[t]he power of the state to define the difference between citizens and immigrants and the rights each of them will hold, which is often considered as central to sovereignty, is less and less clearly attributable to the state.'[27] Both regional and domestic courts are taking important steps affecting our traditional understanding of sovereignty, steps that have not been duly investigated in the general literature on migration law.

When it comes to regional courts, important cases have limited state competence related to rejection of non-nationals at the border. For instance, Uganda freely accepted limiting 'her sovereignty to deny entry to persons, who are citizens of the Partner States' of the East African Community (EAC).[28] Thus, when denying entry to a Kenyan national, it is not domestic Ugandan migration law that is at stake, but rather provisions of East African Community law governing free movement. Likewise, Barbados cannot simply deny entry to a Jamaican national without offering any legitimate reasons enshrined under community law because '[i]n contradiction to foreigners in general' a Jamaican national has 'a right to enter the territory of Barbados and that of other Member States unless they qualify for refusal under the two exceptions' enshrined in the CARICOM Community law.[29]

Regional Courts have also interpreted the rights of community nationals. For example, a Colombian national was entitled to have his period of work in Venezuela taken into consideration for the purposes of calculating his pension in Colombia because an Andean Community Decision on social security guarantees this right.[30]

National courts, and their interpretation of international and regional law and its application at domestic level, emerge as crucial actors. Their importance has already been captured in recent rulings in which they have engaged with regional law with consequences for the individual.[31] For example, in a 2017 judgment,[32] the High Court in Kenya decided, together with other considerations, that Article 126 of the Treaty establishing the East African Community had been breached and thus that a Ugandan national had the right to apply to the Kenya School of Law, something prohibited to other foreigners. Whilst the Court did not go as far as the applicants, who claimed that

---

27 E. Guild, *The Legal Elements of European Identity. EU Citizenship and Migration Law*, The Hague: Kluwer 2004, p. 8.

28 East African Court of Justice, Reference No. 5 of 2011, Samuel Mukira Mohochi and The Attorney General of the Republic of Uganda, 17 May 2013, paragraph 52.

29 Caribbean Court of Justice, *Shanique Myrie v Barbados,* [2013] CCJ 3 (OJ), 4 October 2013, paragraph 50. See on this S. Caserta, 'Regional International Courts in Search of Relevance: Adjudicating Politically Sensitive Disputes in Central America and the Caribbean', 28 *Duke Journal of Comparative* & *International Law* 2017, p.59-97.

30 Andean Community's Court, Case 100-IP-2011, p. 10. The Court ruled on a very similar case and reinforced this reasoning in 137-IP-2014.

31 Colombian Supreme Court of Justice Case 35097, 6 March 2012, which references Decision 584 of 2004 on an Andean Instrument of Security and Health in the workplace.

32 High Court of Kenya at Nairobi, *Monica Wamboi Ng'ang'a & others v Council of Legal Education & 4 others* [2017] eKLR.

East Africans could not be considered as foreigners any longer in the eyes of the law since the East African Treaty defines a foreign country as one which is not part of the East African Community,[33] the importance of regional law cannot be ignored. It comes as no surprise then, that since South Sudan joined the East African Community in 2016, it is now South Sudanese nationals in Kenya who are following the judicial route to argue their right to practise law in Kenya, the same as other East African nationals from Uganda, Tanzania, Burundi and Rwanda.[34]

Whilst it is generally considered that Kenya moved from a dualist to a monist practice with its 2010 Constitution,[35] categorizations of states in these two monolithic blocks are not always helpful. [36] Rather, the central questions related to aspects of prevalence in situations of conflict between domestic and international norms or of direct applicability and effect. The professional training in international law of judges and other legal actors that could better facilitate dialogue between different legal regimes is a challenge of enormous importance for the future, one in which Professor Guild has been involved for years.

Conclusion

Hammar coined the term 'denizens' in the early 1990s to refer to those non-nationals in Europe who enjoyed several civil, social and, to a lesser extent, political rights in a territory, notwithstanding their lack of citizenship.[37] Since 1990, the number of denizens globally has multiplied. For example, being an Armenian or Kyrgyz is a legal status that has consequences and offers life opportunities beyond the established borders of Armenia or Kyrgyzstan. Indeed, some of these agreements refer to nationals from the signatory states as regional citizens, thus opening a new meaning for a word (citizenship) that has been historically associated with states. Through the proliferation of regional mobility agreements, states renounce certain capacities to exclude that have been often associated with the core of the concept of sovereignty. These new emerging modalities of membership open numerous theoretical questions about the declining role of states.[38] Developments are ongoing in many regions in the world and, despite numerous drawbacks and challenges, this represents the most important game changer in migration regulation for the years to come, one that already affects the lives and opportunities of millions.

33 Article 1, Treaty for the Establishment of the East African Community, Arusha, Tanzania, 30 November 1999.

34 *Daily Nation*, 'South Sudanese Fight to Practice Law in Kenya', 13 November 2018, available at: https://www.nation.co.ke/news/South-Sudanese-fight-to-practise-law-in-Kenya/1056-4849874-r32w39z/index.html.

35 See, in particular, Articles 2.5 and 2.6 of the 2010 Kenyan Constitution.

36 E. Denza, 'The Relationship between International and National Law', in: M.D. Evans (ed.), *International Law* (fifth edition), Oxford: OUP 2018, p. 383-411.

37 T. Hammar, *Democracy and the Nation State*, Aldershot: Avebury 1990, p. 13.

38 L. Bosniak, *The Citizen and the Alien: Dilemmas of Contemporary Membership*, Princeton: Princeton University Press 2006.

Schengen's Undesirable Aliens
Definition, Trust, and Effective Remedies

*Evelien Brouwer**

1. Schengen and the Liquidity of 'Undesirable Aliens'

In 'The Transformation of European Border Controls', Elspeth Guild and Didier Bigo use Zygmunt Bauman's metaphor of liquidity to underline that liberal economy and globalization did not result in less boundaries or a 'no borders' world, but intensified other boundaries and reshaped identities.[1] This changing nature of boundaries and identities is related to the concept of 'liquid security' which according to Guild and Bigo is modelling and channelling the travel of individuals by reading speed and comfort as forms of freedoms. In the EU of the 21st century, the meaning of borders and security became in more than one way 'liquid'. The shape of borders changed not only geographically with the expansion of the EU[2] and Schengen, but also practically, moving to the outside and even the inside of the territory. Visa lists, pre-flight checks, and new technologies allow states to check 'desirability' or admissibility of migrants at any time and any place to preserve 'security' within.[3] This 'security' may have different meanings, related to the goals of migration and border control, including: health, internal security, international relations, economic and social welfare, or even social cohesion. Furthermore, the meaning of 'security' may change due to the expanding involvement of private actors and technologies in migration and border policies.[4] Security is not only what policy or lawmakers decide that should be protected, but also a 'risk' framed by private actors or artificial intelligence.[5]

The liquidity of 'borders' and 'security' is closely connected with the decision-making of states on admission and deportability of third-country nationals, or in other

* Vrije Universiteit Amsterdam, the Netherlands.

1 Elspeth Guild & Didier Bigo, 'The Transformation of European Border Controls', in: Bernard Ryan & Valsamis Mitsilegas (eds), *Extraterritorial Immigration Control: Legal Challenges*, Leiden/Boston: Martinus Nijhoff Publishers 2010, p. 259.

2 And shrinking again, after Brexit.

3 See David Lyon, *The Culture of Surveillance. Watching as a Way of Life*, Medford (USA): Polity Press 2018, p. 36 ff, who also uses Bauman's account of 'liquid modernity'.

4 See Lucia Zedner, 'Liquid security: Managing the market for crime control', 6(3) *Criminology & Criminal Justice* 2006, p. 267-88. There is even a private enterprise with the name 'Liquid Security Solutions', selling for example CCTV cameras and monitoring, and access control systems, but also portable metal detectors and small arms ammunition.

5 See for example the press release of the European Commission on the project 'iBorderctrl' which if operational, would include the use of 'automated deception detectors' (lie-detectors) by using facial recognition technologies and border guard avatars to those seeking admission to the EU: http: //ec.europa.eu/research/infocentre/article_en.cfm?artid=49726. See further: https://www.iborderctrl.eu/.

words the framing of 'undesirable aliens'.[6] The exclusion of particular groups of persons by states or entities is nothing new. Throughout history, institutions claiming sovereignty over territory, have sought means to control the entry and exit of individuals, including their own.[7] This entails decisions based on political considerations, but also reasons of public health or economy. The question of who is to be considered 'wanted' or 'unwanted' changes over the years and is shaped by political, social, and religious events or developments of a particular time and place.[8] The sharing and mutually enforcing of decisions on 'unwanted migrants' by sovereign states in Europe is however relatively new, starting in 1995 with the use of the Schengen Information System (SIS) as one of the 'compensating measures' for the abolition of internal border controls in the Schengen area. In 2019, 26 states use SIS for the exchange of alerts on third-country nationals for the purpose of refusal of entry or stay.[9] These alerts, as we will see, can be based on national considerations with regard to public order and security.[10]

Aside from the exchange of data on 'inadmissible aliens', different measures have been developed within the EU using risk analysis or profiling to identify those to be considered as a 'risk' for the purpose of admission or stay. This means that dependent of nationality, age, country of origin, travel history, or even profession, visa authorities may decide whether or not to grant a person leave to stay in the Schengen area. For this purpose, borders increasingly function as filters, 'sorting out the desirable from the undesirable, the genuine from the bogus, the legal from the illegal, and permitting only the deserving to enter state territory'.[11] The risk analysis for deciding on the desirability of the migrant is based on data retrieved from passenger data submitted by carriers to the EU border guards[12] and EU large-scale databases. Aside from SIS, other large-scale databases are Eurodac (data of asylum seekers or persons who crossed the external borders irregularly) and the Visa Information System or VIS (data on all applicants for short term- or Schengen visa, including those whose applications have been rejected).[13]

6 I use 'undesirable aliens' in the meaning of both 'inadmissible' or 'deportable' third-country nationals. Although 'undesirable aliens' is historically a loaded word, used for example in France ('étrangers indésirables') and Germany ('unerwünschte Ausländer') to refer to former discriminatory practices of exclusion, including rejection and deportation of Jews or Roma. The definition 'ongewenste vreemdelingen' is however still used in Dutch immigration law.

7 Rutger Birnie, *The Ethics and Politics of Deportation in Europe*, PhD thesis, Florence: EUI 2019.

8 See on the criteria and (il)logic grounds of exclusion by visa lists: Elspeth Guild, 'When even Machiavelli's Prince needs a Visa – Migration, Euro-Mediterranean Relations and Intercultural Dialogue', 15 *European Foreign Affairs Review* 2010, p. 367-384; Elspeth Guild & Didier Bigo, *La Mise à l'écart des Étrangers: La Logique du Visa Schengen, Cultures & Conflits*, Paris: l'Harmattan 2003.

9 UK and Ireland have never participated in the use of SIS for the purpose of migration control, however apply SIS for law enforcement and judicial cooperation, Council Decision 2007/533.

10 Other categories in SIS II concern alerts for the purpose of surrender or extradition, or for the purpose of discreet and specific check, or on missing persons, regulated in Decision 2007/533, *OJ* L 205, 7.8.2007.

11 Bridget Anderson, *Us & Them? The Dangerous Politics of Immigration Control*, Oxford: Oxford University Press 2013.

12 Directive 2016/681 of 27 April 2016, *OJ* L 119, 4.5.2016.

13 SIS II Regulation 1987/2006 *OJ* L 381 of 28.12.2006, to be replaced by Regulation on the use of SIS for border controls 1861/2018 *OJ* L 312, 7.12.2018; VIS Regulation 767/2008 of 9 July 2008, *OJ* L 218, 13.8.2008; and Eurodac Regulation 603/2013 of 26 June 2013, *OJ* L 180, 29.6.2013.

EU laws have been adopted for the future establishment of an Entry-Exit System (recording all entries and exits of third-country nationals);[14] the European Travel and Authorisation System (ETIAS: applications for entry authorisations by visa-exempt third-country nationals)[15] and ECRIS-TCN, a central system recording third-country nationals with criminal convictions in one or more EU Member States.[16] And on top of that, the European Parliament approved in April 2019 the Commission proposal for a Regulation on interoperability.[17] This instrument will allow national authorities and EU agencies to check and compare personal information (including biometrics) which is stored into one or more of all the aforementioned databases, for both immigration and law enforcement purposes.

Decision-making at EU's borders is framed by the desire to deploy an 'almost total digital surveillance of movement within and beyond its borders' and obtain access to all personal data available.[18] As long it is clear who is 'the sovereign who hungers for data', individuals may challenge these data-driven decisions.[19] However, in the field of border and migration control, 'the sovereign' remains often invisible or hidden. A person reported in the SIS for the purpose of refusal of entry or stay, may find it problematic to counter the lawfulness or proportionality of such decision if public policy decisions of other states. When artificial intelligence or algorithms are used to define an individual as a threat to public order or security, not knowing the specific grounds of refusal hampers his or her access to effective remedies.

This contribution focuses on the use of SIS and the reporting of third-country nationals for the purpose of refusal of entry and stay, taking into account the new Regulation 2018/1861 (SIS III Regulation) adopted in November 2018.[20] Based on general principles and case-law of the CJEU, I will submit that despite the 'liquidity' of criteria to issue SIS alerts on the basis of public order and security, EU law provides some clear and more 'rigid' rules narrowing the discretionary power of states. Second, by addressing the rights of the individual at stake, we will see that Member States do have obligations to 'test trust' and to check the lawfulness of grounds for undesirability. Finally, I will emphasize the importance of the right to effective judicial protection, with regard to the use of SIS and in other cases where considerations of other states are involved in decisions on 'undesirable aliens'

14 Regulation 2017/2226 of 30 November 2017, *OJ* L 327, 9.12.2017, p. 20. See for the Commission proposal: 2016/0106 (COD).

15 Regulation 2018/1240 of 12 September 2018, *OJ* L 236, 19.9.2018.

16 Adopted by Council and Parliament in April 2019, see press release: http://europa.eu/rapid/press-release_IP-19-2018_en.htm.

17 Proposal for a Regulation on interoperability for border and visa purposes 2017/0352 (COD) and the proposal on interoperability for the purpose of police and judicial cooperation, asylum and migration, 2017/0351 (COD).

18 Octávio Sacramento, 'Schengen and the security obsession. Selective citizenship, exclusion and the ironies of control, in': Alice Cunha, Marta Silva & Rui Frederico (eds.), *The Borders of Schengen*, Brussels: P.I.E. Peter Lang 2015, p. 115-127, at p. 126.

19 Josef Ansorge, *Identify and Sort. How Digital Power Changed World Politics*, London: Hurst and Company 2016, p. 2.

20 *OJ* L 312, 7.12.2018. This Regulation entered into force in December 2018 but will only become applicable after implementing decisions of the Commission on the basis of Article 66, to be adopted no later than 21 December 2021.

2. Definition of Risk

2.1. SIS Alerts for the Purpose of Refusal of Entry and Stay and the New SIS III Regulation

In 1997, two years after SIS became operational, the European Parliament adopted a resolution expressing its concerns that the SIS, set up as 'a flanking measure' to support law enforcement agencies in the recognition of criminals, fugitives of justice and missing persons, in practice 'tends to be mainly used as a database for undesirable aliens'.[21] And indeed, in the first period SIS has been used, almost 90% of the SIS alerts on persons, concerned third-country nationals reported for the purpose of refusal of entry or stay.[22] Since 2005, this percentage gradually dropped to 53,9% in 2018.[23] This is mainly due to the increasing number of other categories of persons reported in SIS II, but also because of a decrease of the absolute number of alerts on third-country nationals in SIS.[24]

In accordance with Regulation 1987/2006, SIS alerts can be based on two grounds mentioned in Article 24 (1) (a) and (b): either a national decision based on public order or national or public security grounds, or a measure involving expulsion, refusal of entry or removal. In practice, this second category of alerts concerns mainly entry bans following return decisions in accordance with the Return Directive 2008/115.[25] The first category of public order and security grounds can be based on either a conviction of an offence by a Member State, punishable by a term of imprisonment of at least one year, or when there are serious grounds for believing that he or she 'has committed serious criminal offences or concerning whom there are clear indications of an intention to commit such offences on the territory of a Member State'. These public order and security grounds, already provided in Article 96 of the Schengen Implementing Agreement of 1990 (SIA), have been criticized for providing national authorities a wide and disproportional basis for refusal of entry and expulsion. For example, a conviction for a minor crime in one of the Schengen States, may already result into a long-term banishment from the whole Schengen territory. Furthermore, Schengen states may decide not only who is to be considered as a risk of committing a serious crime, but also what is to be considered a serious crime. The 2006 SIS II Regulation however added two restrictions with regard to the decision to issue a SIS alert. First, Article 21 SIS II

---

21 Resolution about the functioning and future of Schengen, *OJ* C 115/30, 14.04.1997 cited in Monica den Boer (ed.), *Schengen, Judicial Cooperation and Policy Coordination,* Maastricht: EIPA 1997, p. 2 and 64.

22 Evelien Brouwer, *Digital Borders and Real Rights*, Leiden: Martinus Nijhoff Publishers 2008, p. 66-70.

23 SIS II Statistics 2018, https://www.eulisa.europa.eu/Publications/Reports/SIS%202018%20statistics.pdf, published by euLISA 2019. These euLISA statistics do not provide very detailed information on the Member States submitting or using SIS alerts. More information for example can be retrieved from the 2018 statistics on the use of SIS for law enforcement purposes provided by German government to Bundestag from which it follows that France submitted the majority of alerts for the purpose of discreet and specific checks in 2018 (91.296) followed by United Kingdom (17.124) and Spain (14.335), http://dip21.bundestag.de/dip21/btd/19/073/1907365.pdf, p. 6 and 7.

24 Of the 935.497 alerts on persons in SIS II in 2018, 504.590 alerts concerned third-country nationals for the purpose of refusal.

25 This practice currently has no explicit legal basis, but is only mentioned in recital 18 of the Return Directive.

provides that national authorities must determine whether the case is 'adequate, relevant, and important enough' and second, in accordance with Article 24 (1) any SIS alert requires an individual assessment. These rules are complemented by the rules in the General Data Protection Regulation, prohibiting automated decision-making.[26]

Compared to the SIS II Regulation, the new Regulation 2018/1861 maintains in Article 24 (1) (a) and (b), the same categories of criteria for issuing alerts for the purpose of refusal of entry: those based on a threat to public policy, public security or national security, and those based on entry bans in accordance with the Return Directive, which latter category is now formally included in the Regulation. Furthermore, Article 24 (3) SIS III Regulation explicitly provides that a SIS alert based on an entry ban following the Return Directive, will only take effect when the third-country national has left the territory of the Member States or as soon as possible where the issuing Member State has obtained clear indications that the third-country national has left, this in order to 'prevent the re-entry of that third-country national'.[27] A new criterion has been added in Article 24 (2) to report alerts for the purpose of public order and security grounds, namely third-country nationals 'circumventing national law on entry or stay'. A criterion which leaves states a new discretionary power. Who is to decide what falls under the circumvention of national law on entry or stay, and does this include humanitarian aid to migrants, which in some states has become a criminal act? According to Article 24 (1)(b) of the new Regulation, the requirement of an individual assessment no longer applies for SIS alerts on the basis of the Return Directive. Furthermore, Article 21 (2) provides for an exception to the proportionality clause for SIS alerts 'related to a terrorist offence': those cases always shall be considered 'adequate, relevant and important enough'.

2.2. Criteria on 'Risk' – Case-Law of the CJEU

Despite the discretionary power of states to issue SIS alerts (and the apparent extension of this power in the new Regulation), the CJEU provided useful criteria both with regard to the scope and meaning of 'public order' and 'security' in its case-law. In *Zh. and O*, the CJEU dealt with a SIS alert based on an entry ban following a return decision on the basis of the Return Directive.[28] In accordance with the Return Directive 2008/115, when a return decision is issued to an irregular migrant, normally a period is granted for voluntary return, except if there is a risk of absconding or 'risk for public policy', in accordance with Article 7 (4) Return Directive. If no voluntary period for return has been granted, the return decision is followed by an entry ban to be reported into SIS II under the aforementioned category in Article 24 of the SIS II Regulation. For the assessment of the decision whether or not a third-country national should be granted a voluntary period of return, national courts asked the CJEU for an interpretation of 'the risk for public policy'. The CJEU held that while 'Member States essentially retain the freedom to determine the requirements of public policy in accordance with their national needs, which can vary from one Member State to another and from

26 Article 22 Regulation 2016/679 of 27 April 2016, *OJ* L 119, 4.5.2016.

27 Incorporating the criteria of the CJEU in *Ouhrami*, 26 July 2017, C-225/16, ECLI:EU:C:2017:590, para. 49.

28 CJEU 11 June 2015, C-554/13, paras 50, 59-60.

one era to another', these requirements must be interpreted strictly 'to ensure that the fundamental rights of third-country nationals are respected when they are removed from the European Union'. Furthermore, according to the CJEU, the assessment of a public order risk requires the same individual assessment as provided in the Citizen's Directive. This means that a Member State is required to assess, on a case-by-case basis, whether the personal conduct of the third-country national concerned poses a genuine, present, and sufficiently serious threat to public policy.[29] Finally, the CJEU made clear that this decision must be based on an individual examination of the case concerned and respect the principle of proportionality.[30] In *Zh. and O.*, therefore, the CJEU did not address the legitimacy of the issuing of SIS alerts in general. However, it can be argued that the aforementioned criteria on entry bans, also apply to the category of SIS-alerts issued on public order and security grounds.

Dealing with 'public security' threat and the application for a visa on the basis of the Students Directive, in *Fahimian* the CJEU found that Member States have more leeway in deciding whether an applicant represents a threat, different from the aforementioned criteria for EU citizens in Article 27 (2) Directive 2004/38.[31] Nevertheless, even in these decisions, the CJEU underlined the obligation of national authorities to 'perform an overall assessment of all the elements of that person's situation'. Refusals of visas based on public security must be based on 'an extensive knowledge of his country of residence and on the analysis of the various documents and of the applicant's statements'.[32] Therefore, even in admission cases and when public security reasons are involved, one could derive from the *Fahimian* judgment the obligation of individual assessment and substantiated decision-making. This may restrict the practical meaning of the discretionary space of Member States added in the SIS III Regulation.

3. Definition of Trust: Obligation to Consult

Although SIS II nor SIS II Regulation mention this principle explicitly, the use of SIS is based on the principle of mutual trust requiring Schengen States to enforce each other's alerts for the purpose of refusal of entry or stay.[33] In different situations, national authorities have an obligation to consult another state before issuing, respectively enforcing a SIS alert. This duty is provided in Article 25 SIA, which will replaced by Articles 27-30 Regulation 2018/1861. In *E.*, the CJEU found that an individual who has a residence permit in one Member State, may rely on Article 25 SIA and claim that the state issuing the SIS alert should consult the state of residence.[34] Here, the CJEU applied a reasoning comparable with the decisions in *Mengesteab* and *Shiri* where it found, dealing with the procedural rules for take charge or take back requests in the

29 In *E.* C-240/17, 16 January 2018. Furthermore, in para. 49, the CJEU repeated the criteria with regard to the scope and definition of 'public order' as developed in *Zh. and O.*

30 See also Ashley Terlouw, 'Voluntary Departure of Irregular Migrants and the Exception of Public Orders: The Case of *Z.ZH. & I.O. v Staatssecretaris voor Veiligheid en Justitie*', 18 *EJML* 2016, p. 126-137.

31 *Fahimian*, C-544/15, 4 April 2017.

32 Para. 40, referring to *Koushkaki* C-84/12.

33 Carlos Coelho, 'Schengen: People, Borders and Mobility', in: Alice Cunha, Marta Silva 7 Rui Frederico (eds.) *The Borders of Schengen*, Brussels: P.I.E. Peter Lang 2015, p. 21 FF.

34 C-40/2017.

Dublin system, that asylum applicants could lodge a claim on the basis of non-compliance of these rules.[35]

Articles 27-30 Regulation SIS III also include a duty for a state considering to grant or extend a residence permit to consult another state if that latter state has issued a SIS alert on the same person (Article 27). Articles 28 respectively 29, oblige a state considering to issue a SIS alert on the basis of a decision as meant in Article 24 (1), on a person who is holder of a residence permit or long-stay visa by another Member State to consult that state, or after the SIS alert has been issued and it emerges 'a posteriori' that another state granted a residence permit or long-stay visa. Different from Article 25 SIA, the Regulation 2018/1681 provides more specific rules on what happens if a consulted state does not respond or does not respond in time. According to Article 27, the consulted Member State has to respond within ten days and if it does not reply within that time limit, this implies that there are no objections for the granting or extending of the residence permit. With regard to the second category of consultation, in Article 28 and 29, the time limit of response is longer. The consulted state must inform the issuing state within 14 days, whether there are reasons to withdraw the residence permit or long-stay visa, which period in exceptional grounds maybe extended to a further 12 days on the basis of a reasoned request. As under the former Article 25 SIA, if the second state decides to maintain the residence permit, the issuing state shall not enter the alert for refusal of entry or stay into the SIS II. Article 30 deals with the situation where there is a hit on a person holding a residence permit or long stay visa. In that case the executing state must inform the issuing state of this situation; the issuing state must start the consultation procedure as meant in Article 29 and must subsequently inform the executing state of the outcome of this consultation. This provision does not prohibit the executing state to enforce the SIS alert during this information cq. consultation procedure. Article 30 merely states that the executing state must take the decision on entry of the third-country national in accordance with Regulation 2016/399 (Schengen Borders Code). With other words, even if based on a conform reading of the CJEU's rulings in *E.* and *Mengesteab*, providing the third-country national the right to claim that the information of consultation procedure should be applied, it does not provide the individual a right of entrance if the Member States fail to do so.[36]

Dealing with first admission cases, the CJEU found already in 2006 that the refusal of a visa or entry to third-country nationals who are family members of EU citizen solely based on a SIS alert without checking whether he or she presents a genuine, present and sufficiently serious threat, is in violation of EU law.[37] According to the CJEU, in these situations national authorities should use the SIRENE-network to con-

---

35 See Elspeth Guild, The EU Court of Justice rules on the Schengen Conundrum: a non-EU citizen with expulsion order in one Member State and a valid residence permit in another Member State', *EU Law Analysis*, January 2018, http://eulawanalysis.blogspot.com/2018/01/the-eu-court-of-justice-rules-on.html.

36 An example where this consultation procedure might become relevant is the *Kozlovska* case, in which Belgian immigration authorities, after expelling a Ukrainian national from their territory on the basis of a Polish SIS alert in 2018, decided in 2019 to grant her a five years residence permit, despite the fact that the Polish alert was not withdrawn. See on the situation in 2018: Evelien Brouwer, 'Schengen entry bans for political reasons? The case of Lyudmyla Kozlovska', *VerfBlog, 2018/8/30,* https://verfassungsblog.de/schengen-entry-bans-for-political-reasons-the-case-of-lyudmyla-kozlovska/.

37 C-503/03, *Commission v. Spain*, 31 January 2006.

sult the issuing state. Following the aforementioned reasoning in *Zh. and O.* and *Fahimian* one could argue this duty to consult applies to entry or visa refusals to any third-country national.

4. Definition of Rights: Access to Effective Judicial Protection

Third-country nationals reported into SIS II will generally only be informed about the existence of this report when confronted with a refusal of visa or entry, (extension of) a residence permit, or as in this case, deportation. This makes it difficult to legally challenge SIS alerts. Article 43 SIS II Regulation provides that a person may bring an action before the courts or the authority competent under the law of 'any Member State' to access, correct, delete or obtain information or to obtain compensation in connection with an alert relating to him or her. The right to appeal has been maintained in Article 54 of the SIS III Regulation, including the obligation for Member States to mutually enforce the final decisions of these courts or authorities. This means that persons reported in SIS II can start legal proceedings in any of the Schengen states and if subsequently a national court or authority in that state decides the entry ban is unlawful, the reporting state must delete the entry ban from SIS II.

Furthermore, Article 24 (4) Regulation 2018/1861 explicitly provides in a right to appeal against decision for refusal of entry and stay, stating that such appeals 'shall be conducted in accordance with Union and national law, which shall provide for an effective remedy to be requested before a court'.

Taking into account the discretionary power of Member States to report third-country nationals into SIS, especially with regard to the category based on public order and security grounds, national courts or tribunals may be reluctant or practically hampered to assess the legitimacy or proportionality of decisions issued by other states' authorities. Nevertheless, in several cases dealing with refusal of first admission or visa, the CJEU emphasized that the provided right to appeal must be read in line with Article 47 of the EU Charter.[38] Even in a field where national administrations have a wide discretionary power, Member States must ensure in their laws and practices effective judicial protection. This consideration becomes particular relevant in situations involving two or more states. When writing this contribution, two cases are pending before the CJEU which precisely address this matter. The first case, *Vethanayagam*, deals with the question in which state a visa applicant should lodge an appeal if a short term visa is refused by another state on behalf of the represented state. Article 32(3) Visa Code provides that the right to appeal must be lodged in the state taking the 'final decision'. Until now, Member States and the Commission argue that the final decision is taken by the representing state, which means that visa applicants have to lodge an appeal in another state than the state of destination, which in practice may cause many practical barriers. In her conclusion of 28 March 2019, Sharpston however argues that to ensure the right of effective judicial protection in Article 47 Charter, the represented state must be considered as the state taking the final decision, considering this state as 'natural forum' for appeal and the need to avoid 'disproportionate efforts in order to have

38 C-403/16, *El Hassani*, 13 December 2017. See also para. 45 in the aforementioned judgment *Fahimian*.

access to judicial review'.[39] The second case before the CJEU involves preliminary questions submitted by a Dutch lower court in March 2019 in two different cases.[40] These cases concern the accessibility of legal remedies if a short-term visa is refused following the objection of another Schengen state, without informing the applicant on the precise reasons or nature of the objections. Here as well, the CJEU will have to address the scope of the right to effective judicial protection in the situation that two states are involved. The conclusions of the CJEU in this latter case will be specifically relevant for the topic of this contribution, namely the refusal of admission by one state on the basis of unknown considerations of 'inadmissibility" from another state.

5. Conclusions

The obsession of policy makers with security and data surveillance is probably here to stay, including the desire to distinguish between those who are welcome and those considered as undesirable in 'Schengenland'.[41] Generally, Member States have a wide discretionary power with regard to the admissibility of third-country nationals and whether he or she is to be considered a threat for public order or security. Even if the new SIS III Regulation widened in some areas the discretionary power to issue SIS alerts on third-country nationals, this 'liquidity' of undesirability remains bound by general principles of EU law. In different cases, the CJEU stressed the principle of proportionality and individual assessment in decisions of expulsion, but also refusal of admission. Furthermore, the CJEU emphasized the right to effective judicial protection of third-country nationals in EU law, whether it concerns return decisions, visa rejection, or refusal of entry at the borders. Considering the aforementioned developments, where 'undesirability' is shaped by (often unknown) considerations from other states, and increasingly by the use of large-scale databases, risk assessment, and possibly even 'lie detectors', access to effective judicial protection will become more and more relevant.

39 Conclusion of 28 March 2019 in *Vethanayagam*, C-680/17, paras 79-81.

40 In these cases, the Schengen visa were refused by the Dutch authorities on the basis of objections of Hungary c.q. Germany in accordance with Article 22 of the Visa Code. District Court Den Haag zp Haarlem, 5 March 2019, AWB 17/15895 and AWB 18/3951 (not registered yet at the CJEU).

41 Octávio Sacramento, 'Schengen and the security obsession. Selective citizenship, exclusion and the ironies of control', in: Alice Cunha, Marta Silva & Rui Frederico (eds.) *The Borders of Schengen*, Brussels: P.I.E. Peter Lang, 2015, p. 115-127, at p. 126.

EU Borders, Fundamental Rights and Solidarity: Keeping A Close Watch

Madeline Garlick[*]

When it comes to human dignity, we cannot make compromises.
German Chancellor Angela Merkel upon the arrival of asylum-seekers in Germany, 2015

The importance of effective control of the EU's external borders is a matter on which European Union (EU) Member States agree. Beyond this, there are many questions in the realm of border management policy on which different perspectives emerge – including what effective border management entails; how should it be resourced; the role, and appropriate scope of authority of the concerned EU entities; and the relationship between national sovereignty to the Union's authority over border questions. Particularly importantly for advocates of fundamental rights, including the right to seek and enjoy asylum, a further key question is how to ensure border management is carried out consistently with Member States' international legal and Charter of Fundamental Rights obligations. This question remains highly relevant, and without a definitive answer, two decades after legal competence for border matters was transferred to EU level in 1999, alongside competence for asylum and migration.

This chapter aims to examine selected features of the development of the EU's border management policies, legislation, institutions and operational engagement, against the background of several paradoxes in Member States' approaches to the issue at EU level. With the advent of the European Border and Coast Guard (EBCG) signalling significant shifts in institutional competences and investment in border management, the chapter seeks to identify opportunities to reinforce respect for fundamental rights in EU border management, and weigh these against the risks of an increasingly intense focus on interdiction and deterrence. In conclusion, it recalls the critical importance of continuing and reinforced independent, rigorous monitoring, analysis and critique of the EU's legal framework and policies in this area, as essential means to ensure EU institutions and Member States remain mindful of their obligations and accountability for ensuring respect for fundamental rights.

* B.A. (Hons), LL.B. (Hons) (Monash); LL.M. (Cantab.), Ph.D. (Radboud University, Nijmegen). The author had the privilege of preparing her dissertation under the supervision of Professor Elspeth Guild, in the Centre for Migration Law, Faculty of Law, Radboud University Nijmegen, for which she was awarded the degree of doctorate with mention *cum laude* in 2016. She is currently Senior Legal Coordinator and Chief of Section, Protection Policy and Legal Advice, in Division of International Protection in UNHCR's headquarters in Geneva. Views expressed in this chapter are entirely those of the author and do not represent the position of UNHCR or the United Nations.

1. Borders and Free Movement: Some Manifest Paradoxes

The development of EU border policy, regulation, infrastructure and practice has followed a wide arc from States' unequivocal insistence on tight national control over national borders, through readiness to embrace and benefit from the free movement of people, initially through the Schengen area and later across Union internal borders more widely, to common regulation, integrated border management and agreement on a strengthened EBCG in early 2019.

Several paradoxes have emerged throughout this evolution. Firstly, since 1999, emphasis on States' sovereign rights to control entry to their territory has remained strong – while at the same time, EU citizens and economies have benefited greatly from the advantages of free movement of persons within the Union, and the presence of millions of non-EU citizens visiting, working and contributing to life in the Member States each year.

As a second apparent contradiction, political emphasis on untrammelled national sovereignty has been consistently firm, at least if measured by repeated reminders to publics at national level that their leaders have not ceded control over entry into their territory or exposed them to undefined security risks from unwanted arrivals. At the same time, Member States have benefited at every level from their membership of the EU and as relevant, of the Schengen area – including specifically from the freedoms established in the Union's legal framework which Member States have chosen, in the exercise of their sovereign powers, to adopt – and in particular from the free movement policies that have continued to stimulate their economies.

Third, while significant emphasis is placed in EU and national debates on stemming irregular entry, including notably for people coming from countries in and near regions of origin of refugees, statistics show that some of the largest numbers of those who are detected as irregularly present the EU are from countries which are comparatively wealthy, stable and sources of significant tourist revenue for the Member States each year.[1] Yet media and political attention fails to acknowledge these as widespread violations of immigration laws.

Finally, while EU Member States have all ratified a wide range of international human rights and refugee protection treaties, practice reveals too often a lack of readiness to ensure that the standards which exist on paper are put into effect in practice. The jurisprudence of the European Court of Human Rights (ECtHR), as well as that of UN human rights mechanisms, testifies to the shortcomings in respect for human rights in practice at the EU's external borders.[2]

1 The highest number of people detected as irregularly staying in the EU in 2018 were from Brazil, which is on the list of exempt countries in Annex II to *Regulation (EU) 2018/1806 of the European Parliament and of the Council of 14 November 2018 listing the third countries whose nationals must be in possession of visas when crossing the external borders and those whose nationals are exempt from that requirement.* See Frontex, *Risk Analysis 2019,* p. 24, https://frontex.europa.eu/assets/Publications/Risk_Analysis/Risk_Analysis/Risk_Analysis_for_2019.pdf. By contrast, the world's top refugee-producing countries are included on the EU's list of third countries whose nationals are required to obtain a visa for short stays: see Annex I, Regulation (EU) 2018/1806.

2 See, for example, ECtHR, *Hirsi Jamaa and Others v. Italy*, Application no. 27765/09, 23 February 2012, available at: https://www.refworld.org/cases,ECHR,4f4507942.htm; ECtHR *Khlaifia and Others v. Italy*, Application no. 16483/12, 15 December 2016, available at: https://www.refworld.org/cases,

Against the background of these paradoxes, border authorities and those monitoring their work face ongoing challenges in ensuring an effective balance between controlling entry at the external borders on the one hand, and providing access to territory and asylum procedures for those seeking protection on the other. Related to this, a further critical challenge lies in ensuring the fundamental rights of all those within the EU's territory, but also those at its borders and further afield within Member States' control or jurisdiction.

It can be argued that the intensive process of building up the EU's legal framework and institutions for border control has been given added momentum by reactions to the large scale arrivals in some Member States of the Union in 2015-16, often referred to as the so-called EU refugee or migrant 'crisis'.[3] At that time, while significant numbers of people arrived in some Member States, a devastatingly high number of deaths at sea were recorded along the southern coastal shores of EU Member States and other external frontiers – a grisly toll which continues to rise.[4] It also became starkly apparent that the systems in place at that time to receive and respond to asylum-seekers and other people arriving at the EU's borders were inadequately equipped to cope with the strain.[5]

2. Key Developments in EU Border Policy

Key elements of the architecture of the EU's present integrated border management system are defined in the Schengen Borders Code.[6] Highlighting the Union's collective interests in the area, the Code's Preamble states that 'border control is in the interest not only of the Member State at whose external borders it is carried out but of all Member States which have abolished internal border control'.[7] As a central aim, the Preamble affirms that '[b]order control should help to combat illegal immigration and trafficking in human beings and to prevent any threat to the Member States' internal security, public policy, public health and international relations.'[8] At the same time, the Code expresses in unequivocal terms key safeguards and provisions relating to human

ECHR,58529aa04.htm; ECtHR, *N.D. et N.T. c. Espagne*, 8675/15 and 8697/15, 3 October 2017, available at: https://www.refworld.org/cases,ECHR,59d3a7634.html ; ECtHR, *M.A. and Others v. Lithuania* (app no. 59793/17), 11 December 2018, available at: https://www.refworld.org/cases, ECHR,5c3497654.html; UN Committee on the Rights of the Child, *D.D. v Spain,* regarding Communication No. 4/2016 (Ceuta/Melilla), CRC/C/80/D/4/2016, 1 February 2019, available at: https://www.refworld.org/cases,CRC,5c73f8b64.html.

3 See Elspeth Guild, Cathryn Costello, Madeline Garlick & Violeta Moreno-Lax, *The 2015 Refugee Crisis in the European Union*, Centre for European Policy Studies (CEPS) Policy Brief No. 332, September, Brussels: CEPS 2015, http://www.ceps.eu/system/files/CEPS%20PB332%20Refugee%20 Crisis%20in%20EU_0.pdf; A. Niemann & N. Zaun, EU Refugee Policies and Politics in Times of Crisis: Theoretical and Empirical Perspectives, 56(1) *JCMS* 2018, p. 3-22.

4 UNHCR, 'Desperate Journeys: Refugees and migrants arriving in Europe and at Europe's borders, January-December 2018', Geneva: UNHCR 2019, https://www.unhcr.org/desperatejourneys/.

5 Guild et al. 2015, n. 4.

6 Regulation (EU) 2016/399 of the European Parliament and of the Council of 9 March 2016 on a Union Code on the rules governing the movement of persons across borders (Schengen Borders Code).

7 Schengen Borders Code, Preamble, paragraph 6.

8 *Ibid.*

rights, acknowledging that its provisions apply 'without prejudice to the rights of refugees and persons requesting international protection, in particular as regards *non-refoulement*'.[9]

The Visa Code[10] represents another crucial element of the EU's border management system. It permits entry without visa for short stays of some categories of travellers, which is in practice possible for nationals of many countries in the world's wealthier 'global north'.[11] Nationals of the vast majority of countries from which asylum-seekers and refugees originate are required mandatorily to hold a visa as a precondition for lawful entry.[12] Alongside this, carriers' sanctions[13] apply to impose heavy penalties on airlines, shipping companies and other private sector transporters who bring a person into an EU Member State without a visa or other evidence of lawful permission. Together, the mandatory visa requirement and imposition of carriers' sanctions have been criticised by widely-respected observers[14] for unequivocally 'expos[ing] people to risks associated with unsafe arrival in the EU', by leaving those fleeing persecution or conflict no alternative but to undertake dangerous journeys and seek to cross through unofficial border points to avoid detection. As a consequence, the means to exercise the right to asylum, as enshrined Article 18 in the EU Charter of Fundamental Rights, remains for many people inaccessible in practice.

The establishment of Frontex as the EU agency for management of operational cooperation at the Member States' external borders in 2004[15] was seen as a key development in the sphere of EU border management that would facilitate coordination among Member States' national border services, and strengthen EU border management in myriad ways. Its joint operations have provided many occasions for EU border officials to design, develop and execute together operational plans to address specific challenges at key borders. This commitment to cooperation has also been reflected consistently in EU policy documents ever since, in the European Agenda on Migration,

9 Schengen Borders Code, Article 3.

10 Regulation (EC) No 810/2009 of the European Parliament and of the Council of 13 July 2009 establishing a Community Code on Visas (Visa Code).

11 Regulation (EU) 2018/1806 of the European Parliament and of the Council of 14 November 2018 listing the third countries whose nationals must be in possession of visas when crossing the external borders and those whose nationals are exempt from that requirement, Annex II.

12 Regulation (EU) 2018/1806 of the European Parliament and of the Council of 14 November 2018 listing the third countries whose nationals must be in possession of visas when crossing the external borders and those whose nationals are exempt from that requirement, Annex I.

13 Council Directive 2001/51/EC of 28 June 2001 supplementing the provisions of Article 26 of the Convention implementing the Schengen Agreement of 14 June 1985.

14 E. Guild, C. Costello, M. Garlick & V. Moreno-Lax, *Enhancing the Common European Asylum System and Alternatives to Dublin: Study for the European Parliament's Committee on Civil Liberties, Justice & Home Affairs,* European Parliament, Directorate-General for Internal Policies, Policy Department C: Citizens' Rights and Constitutional Affairs, Civil Liberties, Justice and Home Affairs, PE 519.234, July 2015, Brussels: European Parliament 2015, available at: http://www.europarl.europa.eu/RegData/etudes/STUD/2015/519 234/IPOL_STU(2015)519234_EN.pdf, p. 18-22 at p. 18.

15 Council Regulation (EC) No 2007/2004 of 26 October 2004 establishing a European Agency for the Management of Operational Cooperation at the External Borders of the Member States of the European Union, OJ L 349, 25.11.2004.

which in 2015 spoke assuredly of 'the reality of the management of external borders increasingly being a *shared responsibility*'.[16]

While EU policy concerns all external frontiers on land, reached by air and at sea, the maritime borders have been a focus of particular attention and source of significant challenges. The Mediterranean in particular has been a scene of high tension, intrigue and tragedy for many years. In 2013, Italy launched Operation 'Mare Nostrum', a national sea border patrol operation with a focus on search and rescue for people caught in distress at sea. Over the course of 14 months, Italy deployed 900 navy personnel, as well as air force, customs police, coast guards and state police on patrol across 43,000 square km, rescued some 150,000 people, and avoided scores of tragedies and lost lives.[17] Yet the financial cost was high, at € 9 million per month, and the political cost arguably even higher. Italy emphasised stridently the view that it was patrolling and rescuing on behalf of the whole EU.[18] It could not however persuade other states to step forward and take collective responsibility for a comprehensive response, including offers for disembarkation of those rescued and responsibility for their processing, longer-term assistance and protection for refugees, and humane solutions otherwise. In October 2014, Frontex launched the new joint maritime Operation 'Triton'. However, it was amply made clear that Triton was not designed to replace Operation Mare Nostrum, and would primarily focus on border control and surveillance.[19] The limits on its effectiveness for that purpose swiftly became apparent. Statistics for drownings following the start of Operation Triton in 2015 showed that almost 1,900 people had died in the first six months of the year, over four times the total of 448 who had perished during for the same period in 2014 while Operation Mare Nostrum had been underway. Triton's engagement in rescue at sea, along with its budget and geographical scope, were subsequently expanded in 2015, but limitations on Frontex's competences prevented it from serving as a proactive Search and Rescue (SAR) operation.[20]

In subsequent years, under new political leadership, Italy dramatically changed its course on arrivals and disembarkation, refusing to allow ships carrying rescued asylum-seekers and migrants to land and disembark. In a measure diametrically opposed to the humanitarian intent of the Mare Nostrum operation, a proposal was launched in 2019

16 European Commission, *Communication from the Commission to the European Parliament, the Council, the European Economic and Social Committee and the Committee of the Regions: A European Agenda on Migration* COM(2015)240 final, 13.5.2015, p. 17.

17 Amnesty International, *Lives Adrift: Refugees and migrants in peril in the Mediterranean*, London: Amnesty International, September 2014, p. 23.

18 Statement by Prefetto Morcone, Head of the Asylum Service, Italian Ministry of Interior, Open Society Foundations meeting, Rome, March 2014.

19 European Commission, 'Statement by EU Commissioner Cecilia Malmström on Operation Triton, Brussels, 7 October 2014, quoted in S. Carrera, S. Blockmans, J-P Cassarino, S. Gros & E. Guild, 'The European Border and Coast Guard: Addressing migration and asylum challenges in the Mediterranean?', Centre for European Policy Studies, Brussels: CEPS 2017, p. 19ff.

20 V. Moreno-Lax, 'The EU humanitarian border and the securitization of human rights: the "rescue-through-interdiction/rescue-without-protection paradigm"', *JCMS* 2017, p. 1-22, at p. 10.

to criminalise boats carrying rescued people from entering Italy's territorial waters, effectively penalising shipmasters for obeying international law by responding to distress calls and saving human lives at sea.[21]

After the end of Operation Mare Nostrum and the scaling-back of national coast guard patrols in some parts of the Mediterranean, non-governmental organisations stepped into the breach. A series of ships, in larger numbers than the one or two vessels which had been active in the early 2000s, were deployed to take on the role of rescuing people from distress situations at sea. At the same time as some State-led rescue efforts were being reduced in scope, these NGO activities developed in scale and sophistication. The proactive leadership of NGOs on rescue-at-sea developed to the extent that in 2017, some 40% of rescue incidents in the Central Mediterranean were conducted with NGO involvement.[22]

The operators of these vessels nevertheless found themselves in tense situations in the face of State concerns about their actions. NGOs rescuing people and negotiating their disembarkation in the Union were seen in some quarters as creating a 'pull factor' that could encourage more to undertake the dangerous journey or, in even more extreme terms, as potentially violating prohibitions on human smuggling. Others took the view that NGOs were playing a vital role that should have been the responsibility of states in the region; yet their efforts were running counter to the objective of more effective State-led border control, as well as the goal of deterrence and denial of access to EU territory attributed by advocates to some Member States.[23] As a further apparently-linked consequence, some states began to take punitive and deterrent action against NGO vessels. Among these, in 2018, apparently at the request of an EU Member State, Panama de-flagged the rescue vessel 'Aquarius',[24] and Italy ordered the seizure of a vessel operated by against Médecins sans Frontières, alleging that their vessel had illegally dumped waste in a harbour,[25] with little apparent evidence to support the charge. In the first conviction of an NGO rescue vessel in this context, the captain of a German NGO vessel which brought migrants and asylum seekers to Malta was fined in early 2019 for irregularities in the registration of the ship.[26] These actions seemed deliberately calibrated to prevent NGOs from continuing their rescue efforts, and consequently reduce requests for disembarkation in European ports, physical arrivals in Europe, perceived pull factors and media attention to the plight of asylum-seekers and refugees facing extreme danger fuelled by desperation and fear.

---

21 Y. Maccanico, 'Analysis: Italy's redefinition of sea rescue as a crime draws on EU policy for inspiration', *Statewatch*, April 2019, https://www.statewatch.org/analyses/no-341-italy-salvini-boats-directive.pdf.

22 Council of Europe Commissioner for Human Rights, *Migration in the Mediterranean: recommendations on the protection of human rights*, Strasbourg: Council of Europe 2019.

23 See, for example, V. Moreno-Lax, 'The EU humanitarian border and the securitization of human rights: the "rescue-through-interdiction/rescue-without-protection paradigm"', *JCMS* 2017, p. 1-22.

24 *The Guardian*, '"Race against time": flag revoked for Aquarius migrant rescue ship', 2 November 2018, https://www.theguardian.com/global-development/2018/nov/02/race-against-time-flag-revoked-for-aquarius-migrant-rescue-ship.

25 *The Guardian*, 'Italy orders seizure of migrant rescue ship over 'HIV-contaminated' clothes', 20 November 2018, https://www.theguardian.com/world/2018/nov/20/italy-orders-seizure-aquarius-migrant-rescue-ship-hiv-clothes.

26 *Associated Press*, 'Malta court fines German NGO Lifeline captain', 14 May 2019, https://www.citynews1130.com/2019/05/14/malta-court-fines-german-ngo-lifeline-captain/.

The EU's border management policies have also sought to engage the efforts of States beyond the Union. As part of the 'external dimension' of EU Justice and Home Affairs policy, extensive financial assistance programmes have focussed on capacity development in neighbouring regions, including to help and incentivise North African and other countries to reinforce their border control, migration and asylum capacity. In this context, the message from the EU has been clear: neighbouring countries are expected to manage their borders effectively in ways which minimise irregular arrivals in Europe. While capacity development for the international of refugees was also part of the EU support programme, it was far less extensive than that for borders and managing irregular migration. In 2016, the EU made a statement referring to an arrangement with Turkey under which a Joint Action Plan for the support of Syrian refugees would be launched, and people arriving irregularly in the EU by boat from Turkey would be returned.[27] In this text, the aim of deterring arrivals in Europe was articulated with unambiguous clarity: '[r]esults must be achieved in particular in stemming the influx of irregular migrants.' Reservations about the risks associated with sending refugees back to a country with a nascent asylum system which maintained strict limitations on its treaty commitments to their protection were disregarded.[28] The multi-billion-Euro financial assistance package which was promised to Turkey in exchange made clear the value of such an arrangement to the EU.

Another key relationship for Europe in relation to sea arrivals has been that with Libya. In 2018, Libya declared a search and rescue zone in the international waters around its coastline, with the implication that it would take responsibility for rescue and disembarkation of people rescued from boats in distress in that area.[29] Libya has subsequently stepped up search and rescue activities, in many cases using assets, technology and training from European partners. Civil society and advocates have criticised Libya's human rights record and questioned the legality of disembarkation in the country, given clear evidence of systematic detention in conditions involving serious mistreatment and human rights violations of asylum-seekers, refugees and migrants. [30] While it is generally accepted that international law requires disembarkation of rescued persons in a 'place of safety',[31] views differ about what the concept of safety entails. Some narrow views would hold that this simply requires a location where no immediate dangers to life threaten an individual on disembarkation. UNHCR and others observe that disembarkation can only be said to have taken place in safety where the rescued

27 *Meeting of the Heads of State and Government with Turkey: EU-Turkey Statement*, 29 November 2015, available at: http://www.consilium.europa.eu/en/press/press-releases/2015/11/29-eu-turkey-meeting-statement.

28 See, for example, S. Peers & E. Roman, 'The EU, Turkey and the Refugee Crisis: What could possibly go wrong?', *European Law Analysis*, 5 February 2016, http://eulawanalysis.blogspot.com/2016/02/the-eu-turkey-and-refugee-crisis-what.html; J. Poon, 'EU-Turkey Deal: Violation of, or Consistency with, International Law?', 1(3) *European Papers* 2016, p. 1195-1203.

29 K. Santer, 'Governing the Central Mediterranean through Indirect Rule: Tracing the Effects of the Recognition of Joint Rescue Coordination Centre Tripoli', 21(2) *EJML* 2019, p. 141-165.

30 See, for example, Human Rights Watch, 'No Escape from Hell: EU policies contribute to abuse of migrants in Libya', 21 January 2019, https://www.hrw.org/report/2019/01/21/no-escape-hell/eu-policies-contribute-abuse-migrants-libya; UNHCR, 'Desperate Journeys: Refugees and migrants arriving in Europe and at Europe's borders, January-December 2018', Geneva: UNHCR 2019, https://www.unhcr.org/desperatejourneys/.

31 See Annex to the 1979 Search and Rescue Convention (SAR Convention), para 1.3.2.

person's human rights are safeguarded and, in case of an asylum-seeker, it is possible to request and receive international protection as a refugee.[32] As people disembarked must be able to enjoy safety from human rights violations. As a non-signatory to the 1951 Convention with no refugee laws, institutions or processes, and a widely-documented record of violations of the rights of refugees and migrants, Libya remains far from being a safe place for people in need of international protection.

3. Development of the European Border and Coast Guard

The Commission in 2018 issued a proposal for a Regulation on the EBCG,[33] amending and building upon the first EBCG Regulation adopted in 2016.[34] The new proposal's stated aim was to provide a 'permanent and reliable solution to ensure the Agency has the necessary capabilities to protect the EU external borders and effectively supporting returns', as part of 'a comprehensive approach on migration'.[35] It thereby aimed to increase the effectiveness of the EBCG – which continues to be known as Frontex - by covering existing gaps in the framework in place, evidently seeking to build on the experience of Frontex's past activities and its role in coordinating operational cooperation between states in relation to border control and initiatives.

Among the main changes introduced by the new proposal were a creation of a standing corps of up to 10,000 operational staff by 2020, including personnel from the Member States and, for the first time, 'statutory' Agency staff, entrusted with executive powers. More support was also envisaged for Member States on return, including with the setting up of a return management system and additional tasks allocated to the Agency, including preparation of return decisions for national authorities. The agency would also have an increased role outside EU territory, with the removal of geographical restrictions contained in the previous Regulation on carrying out actions in or involving third countries. New provisions were also foreseen on the deployment of EU migration management support teams in hotspot areas and "controlled centres" in the EU, as well as increased surveillance and contingency-planning activities. Increased financial means and the Agency's ability to acquire its own equipment were also proposed. Positively, the proposal foresaw strengthening of the internal human rights capacity by comparison with the limited resources devoted to this function in Frontex's initial structure. In general, however, the proposal continued the trajectory of policy- and institutional development in the EU towards more centralisation of border control

32 UNHCR, *General legal considerations: search-and-rescue operations involving refugees and migrants at sea*, November, Geneva: UNHCR 2019, available at: https://www.refworld.org/docid/5a2e9efd4.html.

33 European Commission, *Proposal for a Regulation of the European Parliament and of the Council on the European Border and Coast Guard and repealing Council Joint Action n°98/700/JHA, Regulation (EU) n° 1052/2013 of the European Parliament and of the Council and Regulation (EU) n° 2016/1624 of the European Parliament and of the Council*, COM(2018)631 final, Brussels, 12 September 2018 (hereafter 'EBCG Proposal').

34 European Union, *Regulation (EU) 2016/1624 of the European Parliament and of the Council of 14 September 2016 on the European Border and Coast Guard and amending Regulation (EU) 2016/399 of the European Parliament and of the Council and repealing Regulation (EC) No 863/2007 of the European Parliament and of the Council, Council Regulation (EC) No 2007/2004 and Council Decision 2005/267/EC*, OJ L 251, 16.9.2016, p. 1-76.

35 EBCG Proposal, COM (2018) 631, (n. 33 above), Explanatory Memorandum, p. 6 and 1.

and reduced scope for national-level discretion, exceptions and diluted approaches to strict border control policies.

The Preamble of the original 2016 Regulation provided that the new agency would have 'shared responsibility' with the EU Member States in the implementation of European integrated border management. It furthermore provides that '[w]hile Member States retain the primary responsibility for the management of their external borders in their interest and in the interest of all Member States, the Agency should support the application of Union measures relating to the management of the external borders by reinforcing, assessing and coordinating the actions of Member States'.[36]

These references in a Preambular paragraph, albeit non-binding, could be seen to represent a noteworthy innovation in legal terms. The idea of 'shared responsibility' raises the question of whether in case of a failure to respect legal obligations relating to fundamental rights in the course of EBCG operations, the Agency can be found responsible, alongside or separately from Member States. If so, it remains unclear by whom and how will the legal or other consequences of a violation be addressed. Furthermore, and critically, one can question whether the Agency's 'shared responsibility' puts it in any position to ensure respect for the right to asylum, given that power to grant refugee and other forms of international protection lie exclusively with the Member States.

4. Potential Opportunities – and Pitfalls

In the context of this burgeoning body of law, policy and institutional arrangements, a number of questions arise. These include that of whether these laws, policies and their application in practice have respected fundamental rights, as required by the EU Charter, as well as the principle of 'solidarity and fair sharing of responsibility among the Member States' and by being 'fair towards third-country nationals'.[37] It can also be asked whether they have served to address the practical and other challenges associated with large scale arrivals which were key factors motivating the last phase of scaled-up cooperation.

With the engagement of national border authorities in far-reaching European cooperation, should have come increased recognition of the importance of public scrutiny and accountability for conduct at borders by Member State officials. Media interest and coverage of policy and legislative developments, official statements and incidents relating to external borders has been noteworthy in its breadth and sophistication over recent years. Beyond matters likely to affect the convenience of European citizens and their freedom to travel, this analysis has also raised concerns about the impact of proposals and measures on the rights and physical safety of refugees and migrants.[38] However, in another vein, some media has focussed rather on the perceived threats to European security and territorial integrity of integrated European border

36 EBCG Regulation (see n. 34 above), Preamble, para 6.

37 *Treaty on the Functioning of the European Union,* Title V, Article 67(2); see also Article 80.

38 'EU to migrants: "go home and stay home" – Fortress Europe hardens its heart', *Politico*, 2 July 2018, https://www.politico.eu/article/europe-migration-refugees-drop-dead-angela-merkel-matteo-salvini-libya-italy-germany-refugees/.

management, potentially stoking public fears and giving support to far-right and populist narratives which misrepresent the 'threat' that refugees and migrants arriving in Europe pose to society and security in the EU.

Scrutiny has also been institutionalised to at least some extent in the border policy architecture. The establishment of the Frontex Consultative Forum on Fundamental Rights,[39] involving 15 members, including civil society organisations from across Europe, plus the EU Fundamental Rights Agency, European Asylum Support Office, Organization for Security and Co-operation in Europe and UNHCR,[40] has provided an important platform for regular dialogue between the EU border agency and observers with recognised expertise in human rights and refugee protection. The forum has included some who have been strident critics of European border policies and practice, whose participation in the forum has brought an opportunity, and arguably a responsibility, for those organisations to present constructive and realistic proposals to ensure border management respects human rights standards. It is to be hoped that the Forum's engagement has contributed to increased pressure for transparency and accountability for the implementation of EU border management policy in ways which reflect European and international standards. Yet while the committed work of the Forum is apparent,[41] its impact in practice is more challenging to assess.

In addition, the position of Frontex Fundamental Rights Officer, established as part of the Agency's structure from its inception, has provided dedicated resources for monitoring and informing internal processes and priorities. At the same time, the realistic constraints on this capacity in the past have been significant, as a single individual with limited authority in the hierarchy of the institution. The Frontex Consultative Forum has criticised the limited strength of the Fundamental Rights Office in the past.[42] With provisions adopted which aim to reinforce significantly the Fundamental Rights Officer's role under the new ECBG Regulation, it is to be hoped that this role will be in a stronger position in future to compel attention and priority to ensuring human rights safeguards are effective in practice in border management across the EU.

In principle, the potential exists to test in the courts the compatibility with European legal standards of border management policies, instruments and joint operational interventions. Title V of the TFEU, which provides the legal basis for EU measures on borders, establishes an Area of Freedom, Security and Justice which is subject to 'respect for fundamental rights'[43] as an overarching principle. Key provisions of the Charter of Fundamental Rights express unequivocal obligations which bind Member States as well as EU bodies, including the principle of *non-refoulement*[44] and the right to

39 Frontex Consultative Forum on Fundamental Rights, *Sixth Annual Report,* Warsaw: Frontex 2019, https://frontex.europa.eu/media-centre/news-release/frontex-consultative-forum-publishes-annual-report-MgLqPI.

40 For more information on its composition and operation, see: https://frontex.europa.eu/fundamental-rights/consultative-forum/general/.

41 Frontex Consultative Forum on Fundamental Rights 2019 (see above n. 39).

42 *Ibid.*, section 4.1.

43 Treaty on the Functioning of the European Union, Article 67(1).

44 European Union, *Charter of Fundamental Rights of the European Union*, 26 October 2012, 2012/C 326/02, Brussels: European Union 2012, available at: https://www.refworld.org/docid/3ae6b3b70. html, Article 19.

asylum – which is 'guaranteed' by Article 18.[45] Article 18 also demands respect for the 1951 Convention Relating to the Status of Refugees, which is centrally relevant in a border management context wherever intercepted persons request or could be in need of international protection. The *non-refoulement* principle prohibits not only removal of a person to the territory of a state where she or he faces a risk of persecution or serious harm, but also denial of entry to the territory in circumstances which would mean she or he is exposed to such a risk.[46] The ECtHR has established that the principle of *non-refoulement* and other human rights obligations apply even where European states act outside their territory.[47] These and other provisions relating to the right to life, liberty and security of the person could be invoked in proceedings before the CJEU, including on the basis of an individual complaint of violation of *acquis* or Charter standards. The law and practice of individual member States with respect to external border management has been challenged as regards its human rights compatibility in the European Court of Human Rights.[48] However, the dearth of preliminary references to the CJEU in this field raises the question of whether these legal channels are sufficiently accessible to serve effectively as legal oversight mechanisms for the EU's border policies.

The Europeanisation of border management should also have had the potential to bring a greater degree of professionalism[49] to the management of borders, including potentially most significantly in Member States with smaller civil service institutions and fewer resources to invest in management, training and oversight. The exponential growth in Frontex's budget over time, and the subsequent large allocation foreseen for the EBCG are testament to the will of the Union and the Member States to invest in effective border management. By any measure, this should allow scope for a better trained, more professional and well-managed corpus of border personnel across the spectrum of participating national border authorities. The development of communications, training curricula, tools and standard operating procedures and associated documentation to guide Frontex-led joint operations and cooperation should also have served to raise awareness of and encourage compliance with European standards, including on fundamental rights. This should be reinforced by the operation of an individual complaints mechanism, proposed by the Frontex Consultative Forum. Participation by international organisations and civil society in development and delivery of some of these tools and training materials has afforded an opportunity to ensure they reflect these standards accurately and in operationally relevant ways.

The key question, however, with regard to international protection obligations must be whether these tools and the principles are sufficient to ensure that asylum seekers and refugees can gain access to territory and to competent asylum authorities in practice in order to have their claims assessed in fair and effective procedures. Where – as in the vast majority of cases – such asylum seekers and refugees arrive at European frontiers or are intercepted *en route* without lawful permission to enter, this requires a

45 *Ibid.*, Art. 18, The formulation in Article 18, in 'guaranteeing' a right to asylum, could be seen to be stronger in its phrasing than even the right to seek and enjoy asylum in Article 14 of the Universal Declaration of Human Rights.

46 See C. Wouters, *International Standards for the Protection from Refoulement*, Leiden: Intersentia 2010.

47 *Hirsi Jamaa & Others v. Italy* (see above n. 2).

48 See above, n. 2.

49 Carrera et al. 2017 (above n. 19), p. 28.

concerned individual border official to determine that the situation requires an exception to the general duty to prevent irregular entry to the EU.[50] This is a weighty responsibility in a context in which public and political pressure weighs on national authorities to ensure large-scale arrivals do not occur again on the scale that was seen in some EU Member States in 2015. Should the assessment in an individual case be negative, and the person denied entry or 'pushed back' from EU territory, the realistic scope to challenge the decision and seek redress will be extremely limited in practice for refugees outside the EU.

Ample budgetary resources should also guarantee that European border operations are better equipped than ever in the past. There remains at least the capacity to ensure that joint operations have wider coverage and Frontex assets, or those of Member States taking part in joint operations, can respond to distress calls and ensure that lives are saved where vessels founder in the course of dangerous sea journeys.

This however necessitates a readiness on the part of Member States and the European institutions to recognise and provide scope in operational plans to address this evident need. The limits in the past on SAR capacity in the course of Frontex operations will ideally be remedied with the conferral of explicit competence for SAR on the Agency.[51] The limits and drawbacks of EU joint activities to date have been further highlighted in the course of Operation Sophia, a European Security and Defence Policy (ESDP) operation which was launched in 2015, and discontinued in 2019 without a replacement.[52] The unvarnished statistics reveal the impact of reduced presence in the Central Mediterranean of Member States as well as private vessels which are ready and able to respond to distress calls from foundering vessels, including those carrying irregular migrants and refugees. In 2015, one death occurred for every 269 arrivals in Europe via the Mediterranean from Libya; a grim total which rose to one loss per every 51 arrivals in 2018.[53] At least part of this increase is almost certainly due to a drop in the number of NGO vessels undertaking rescue in the Mediterranean across the same period, following deterrent measures taken by States.[54]

The EU treaties recall that solidarity and the fair sharing of responsibility among States are among the fundamental principles which should guide European border management, in law as well as practice. Given the evident shared interest in ensuring effective control of the Union's external frontiers, Member States have been quick to support proposals from the Commission on large-scale EU investment in border infrastructure, operations and agencies. Developments in this field have occurred with notable swiftness, by contrast with some measures in the area of asylum, where even greater sensitivities prevail and the Council and Parliament have been unable to move forward on Regulations on asylum procedures, qualification, reception and Dublin. However, solidarity and cooperation on preventing irregular arrivals have not been accompanied by agreement among States on how to deal effectively with the more limited

50 For analysis of the challenges and problems faced by border personnel in making swift decisions on admittance at points of entry, see Guild et al. 2015 (n. 3), p 20.

51 2018 ECBG Regulation, Article 4.

52 Carrera et al. 2017 (see above n. 19), p. 24ff.

53 UNHCR, 'Desperate Journeys: Refugees arriving in Europe and at Europe's borders', Geneva: UNHCR 2018, https://www.unhcr.org/desperatejourneys/.

54 See above, notes 21-24.

numbers of people who have been admitted to and sought asylum in the Union in recent years who engage Member States' international protection responsibilities. Deadlock in discussions on the Dublin Regulation has precluded agreement on its reform, notwithstanding far-reaching proposals in 2016 from the European Commission for arrangements to ensure more equitable allocation of responsibility for asylum-seekers in the EU.[55] Similarly, disagreement over responsibility for people rescued in the Mediterranean has led to acrimonious debates and significant delays in disembarkation in numerous cases.[56]

An argument could be made that if Member States were ready to agree on provisions and steps to the functioning of asylum systems, and invest political will in full implementation of their obligations, in fair sharing of responsibility for refugee protection, the demand for strict border measures would diminish. Combined with more positive migration measures such as legal migration pathways, these would offer alternatives to irregular migration, often facilitated by criminal smugglers, to people seeking entry who have a right to international protection, as well as those with a positive economic or other contribution to make in the EU. In addition, reluctance to engage in a concerted fashion on the reasons why people are forced to flee their countries of origin and come irregularly to Europe – including protracted conflict and state failure in neighbouring regions, among others – also means that border measures will inevitably address only a small part of a much wider problem.

It may be that advances on border management have served as a distraction from the internal discord among Member States on other key challenges, including that of creating a more effective system for allocating claims for protection among Member States; ensuring access to fair and efficient asylum systems, including in smaller States which have avoided large numbers so far; and building successful integration systems for both refugees and migrants, which can help maintain public goodwill and support for forward-looking migration and refugee policies.

Looking ahead, it is argued that investments in border management must be accompanied by a longer-term and holistic perspective on the challenges facing the EU, including with respect to solidarity, but also that of ensuring that asylum and migration systems can respond effectively to people who engage Member States' responsibilities. Failure to do so puts at risk Europe's commitment to an area of freedom, security and justice, but also its values and core principles more broadly. The sustainability and legality of the EU's border management policy and actions will require consistency with international legal obligations and fundamental rights, in measures which can function in practical ways. The system will require continuous scrutiny from independent, intellectually rigorous observers who are prepared frankly and fearlessly to analyse and question decisions taken and their wider impact, and voice constructively critical perspectives on both achievements made and remaining gaps.

Professor Elspeth Guild has played this role with great distinction – bringing to bear her unassailable legal knowledge, strategic insight, political judgment and direct

55 European Commission, *Proposal for a Regulation of the European Parliament and of the Council establishing the criteria and mechanisms for determining the Member State responsible for examining an application for international protection lodged in one of the Member States by a third-country national or a stateless person (recast)* COM(2016)270 final, 4 May 2016.

56 Council of Europe Commissioner for Human Rights 2019 (n. 22 above), p. 9ff.

and incisive writing. Her continued engagement in scrutiny of the EU's border management instruments and measures will continue to be as invaluable to the European Union institutions that have called upon her expertise so many times, as it remains to the States with which she has exchanged views; the civil society and international organisations which have been fortunate to have her as a partner; and the large body of students she has taught. All of these, along with the author of this piece, owe her a profound debt of gratitude and will continue to benefit from her intellectual courage and leadership.

The Border Abroad, Within and Beyond
A Rule-of-Law Based Deconstruction

*Valsamis Mitsilegas**

> 'Must living in peace … inevitably result in refusing to share it with those seeking refuge, defending it instead so aggressively that it almost looks like war?'
>
> Jenny Erpenbeck, *Go Went Gone*

> 'All my life, I have been haunted by borders – how unjust they feel when you are on the hard side, how alluring when you're on the soft side, and how surprisingly small when they crumble.'
>
> Kapka Kassabova, 'New borders will fail just as old ones did', *The Guardian*, 4 February 2017

1. Introduction

In her inaugural lecture at the University of Nijmegen, Elspeth Guild put forward a truly original and immensely influential theoretical framework to study the transformation of borders in Europe. Entitled aptly *Moving the borders of Europe*,[1] the lecture examined how in European law, the practice of borders though their control over persons has been moved beyond the borders of the physical territory of the state. By focusing on the interplay between internal and external EU borders in the Schengen area, the lecture was one of the first systematic attempts to explain the transformation of border controls via the proliferation of the actors engaged in the movement of borders though coercion – including the state, the supranational order, the private sector and individuals. As she has done consistently in her subsequent work, Elspeth brought forward forcefully the position of the individual, and the impact that the proliferation and transformation of border control has had on the rights of third country nationals. This vigilance to safeguard rights in the face of the enhancement of state power has been present in the many other strands of Elspeth's work, including migration and security,[2] and citizenship and free movement, most recently in the light of Brexit.[3] As an attempt to reflect and recognise Elspeth's enormous influence on scholarly thinking- and certainly on my thinking on migration, borders, rights and citizenship, this contribution is aimed at engaging with some of the key questions Elspeth has raised regarding the transformation of the border in Europe. The contribution will attempt to map the evolution and further proliferation of European border control, from what Elspeth has

* Queen Mary University, London, UK.

1 Inaugural lecture on the occasion of the assumption of the professorship of the CPO Wisselleerstoel at the University of Nijmegen, 30 May 2001.

2 E. Guild, *Security and Migration in the 21st Century*, Cambridge: Polity 2009.

3 E. Guild, *Brexit and its Consequences for EU Citizenship or Monstrous Citizenship*, Leiden: Brill 2016.

called 'the border abroad'[4] to the introduction of further borders 'within' the state and the Schengen area, and ultimately the construction of a border 'beyond', transcending the inside/outside dichotomy by consisting of on-going risk assessment centered on the securitisation of migration and the surveillance of mobility. The contribution aims to take the debate a step forward, by focusing on the impact of such transformation of border control not only on human rights, but on the rule of law.

2. The Border Abroad, Within and Beyond: Legal and Policy Transformations

Elspeth Guild's work has cast light on a number of paradigmatic changes in immigration control, all expressions of a profound change in the law of the border itself.[5] As Didier Bigo has noted, the notion of the border is very often considered a materialised line between two spaces.[6] This static conception of the border has been central to the emergence of traditional systems of border control. Under these systems, entry controls would take place in a specific place (the external border of the state) by checking the identification of the traveller, thus leading to what has been deemed as 'the invention of the passport'.[7] As Elspeth has noted, key in this traditional understanding is the convergence between border and territory.[8] The control of the border in these territorial terms constitutes a prime reflection of the projection of state sovereignty, by granting the state the power to decide on who is allowed entry to its territory and who is not.[9] This static conception of border control has however been challenged in recent years. Globalisation and Europeanisation have led to a profound transformation of border controls. On the one hand, and as highlighted consistently in Elspeth Guild's work, national internal borders have been replaced by – in particular for full Schengen members- by a common EU external border.[10] Yet the emergence of a 'crisis mentality' regarding the management of migration flows has led to challenges to the abolition on internal borders within the EU and the proliferation of border control *within* the EU, including by the re-introduction of border controls and by the growing use of surveillance.[11] On the other hand, the 'crisis mentality' regarding focusing increasingly upon

4 E. Guild, 'The Border Abroad – Visas and Border Controls', in: K. Groenendijk, E. Guild & P. Minderhoud (eds), *In Search of Europe's Borders*, Leiden: Brill 2002, p. 87-104.

5 V. Mitsilegas, 'The Law of the Border and the Borders of Law – Rethinking Border Control from the Perspective of the Individual', in: L. Weber (ed), *Rethinking Border Control for a Globalizing World – A Preferred Future'*, Abingdon: Routledge 2015, p. 15-32, whereupon the analysis of this framework is based.

6 D. Bigo, 'Frontier Controls in the European Union: Who is in Control?', in: D. Bigo & E. Guild (eds), *Controlling Frontiers. Free Movement into and within Europe*, Farnham: Ashgate 2005, p. 52.

7 J. Torpey, *The Invention of the Passport: Surveillance, Citizenship and the State*, Cambridge: CUP 2000.

8 Guild 2001, p. 2.

9 M. Anderson, *Frontiers: Territory and State Formation in the Modern World*, Cambridge: Polity 1996.

10 See D. Bigo & E. Guild, 'Policing at a Distance: Schengen Visa Policies', in: D. Bigo & E. Guild, *Controlling Frontiers. Free Movement into and within Europe*, Farnham: Ashgate 2005, p. 233-263.

11 V. Mitsilegas, 'The Borders Paradox. The Surveillance of Movement in a Union without Internal Frontiers', in: H. Lindahl (ed.), *A Right to Inclusion and Exclusion? Normative Faultlines of the EU's Area of Freedom, Security and Justice*, Oxford: Hart 2009, p. 33-64.

the prevention and deflection of migration flows has led to the proliferation of instances of extraterritorial immigration control.[12] Five key changes can be discerned in the in this transformation of border control.

The first change is temporal. The growing emphasis on the prevention of unauthorised entry has led to the adoption of legislation aiming at conducting border controls before an individual has reached the actual physical border. Prime examples in this context constitute the intensification of visa regimes, the imposition of passenger identification duties to carriers before travel with non-compliance leading to significant sanctions under various carriers' liability schemes and the intensification of immigration controls and surveillance before entry including on the high seas.[13] All these measures aim at preventing the flows of migrants and in particular preventing them reaching the external border of the state. This preventive dimension is inextricably linked with the second major legal change in contemporary border control, which is spatial. Border controls take place increasingly outside and beyond the territorial border aiming to prevent migrants reaching the border in the first place. States exercise border controls extraterritorially, on the high seas and on the territory of third states targeting both migrants[14] and asylum seekers.[15] The new legal mechanisms of border control described above, including the imposition of visa requirements and carriers sanctions and the exercise of border controls on the high seas or in the territory of third countries are tools of both extra-temporal and extra-territorial border control, with visa regimes being eloquently deemed to constitute part of 'the border abroad'.[16]

The third legal change in border controls involves the configuration of the actors of border control (who controls?). Border controls by state officials have been supplemented by controls resulting by the delegation of border control by the state to different actors or agencies. The first example of delegation concerns the privatisation of immigration control. The private sector is increasingly co-opted by the state to perform elements of immigration control in a move similar to what has been termed by Garland in the context of crime control the 'responsibilisation strategy'.[17] Prime examples of extraterritorial privatised immigration control are the obligations of carriers to conduct identification checks before travel[18] and the obligation of carriers to collect personal data on their passengers and transmit these data to state authorities before travel. Privatisation is coupled by a growing move towards delegation to specialised agencies, inter-agency co-operation and co-operation between various layers of intervention at national, EU and international level, backed up by the use of technology. A prime example of such agencification at EU level has been the establishment of the European Borders Agency (FRONTEX), whose primary task is the operational co-ordination of

12 V. Mitsilegas, 'Immigration Control in an Era of Globalisation: Deflecting Foreigners, Weakening Citizens, Strengthening the State', 19 *IJGLS* 2012, p. 3-60; B. Ryan & V. Mitsilegas (eds), *Extraterritorial Immigration Control: Legal Challenges*, Leiden: Brill 2010.

13 V. Mitsilegas, *The Criminalisation of Migration in Europe. Challenges for Human Rights and the Rule of Law*, Heidelberg: Springer 2015.

14 Ryan & Mitsilegas 2010.

15 M. den Heijer, *Europe and Extraterritorial Asylum*, Oxford: Hart Publishing 2012.

16 Guild 2002.

17 D. Garland, 'The Limits of the Sovereign State: Strategies of Crime Control in Contemporary Society', 36 *British J of Criminology* 1996, p. 445-471.

18 Guild 2001.

EU Member States' border controls.[19] Recent trends to militarise border control have resulted in the establishment of further layers of intervention, from the launch of defence operations by the EU (with Operation Sophia being a key example) and by organisations such as NATO.[20] The use of technology is key to the operations of new actors of immigration enforcement. As with privatisation, delegation and the establishment of cooperative arrangements result in the proliferation of enforcement mechanisms to the state border control apparatus.

The fourth major legal change in contemporary border control involves its purpose. Border control no longer serves solely as immigration control, but is also used to fight crime and terrorism. The policy link between immigration and crime at the level of EU law and policy has been highlighted by Bigo who has noted the development of an (in)security continuum transferring the security considerations of crime control to the field of migration[21] and expanded further by Elspeth Guild in her monograph on Migration and Security in the 21st Century.[22] 9/11 has transformed this insecurity continuum further, with subsequent policy and legal responses in Europe and America expressly linking – under the term 'border security' – border controls with counter-terrorism and the fight against crime.[23] Border control measures have thus been adopted and developed as security measures; criminal law is increasingly used as a tool for immigration control; and data obtained in the context of immigration and border control are also viewed as security data which must be accessible not only by immigration authorities for immigration control purposes, but also by intelligence and law enforcement authorities for security purposes.

Linked to the securitisation of migration and mobility, the fifth major legal change in contemporary border control involves the subjects of border control (who is being controlled?). While the targets of immigration control have traditionally been third country nationals wishing to enter the territory of the state exercising border controls, the conception of border control as border security has led to the law of the border being applicable to foreigners and citizens alike. Border controls aimed at the maintenance of security and based upon preventive checks and 'smart border' systems have resulted into the generalised surveillance of all passengers, whose data is transferred to national immigration and security authorities. The law of the border is thus applicable also to citizens who, along with foreigners, are under constant risk assessment by the state when they undertake every day mobility activities such as booking a plane ticket. Such risk assessment of all passengers – which has been masked under the use of terms such as 'the trusted traveller' – is justified by states as conducive to convenience and simplified controls for frequent – and trusted – travellers. However, in reality it has resulted in a global system of regulation of mobility where every passenger carries a potential risk, and where every passenger is constantly being risk-assessed. As Amoore

19 On these two trends see V. Mitsilegas, 'Border Security in the European Union: Towards Centralised Controls and Maximum Surveillance', in: E. Guild, H. Toner & A. Baldaccini (eds), *Whose Freedom, Security and Justice? EU Immigration and Asylum Law and Policy*, Oxford: Hart Publishing 2007, p. 359.

20 D. Bigo, 'The (In)securitization Practices of the Three Universes of EU Border Control: Military/Navy-Border Guards/Police-Database Analysts', 45 *Security Dialogue* 2014, p. 220.

21 D. Bigo, *Polices en Réseaux. L'Expérience Européenne*, Paris : Presses Sciences Po 1996.

22 E. Guild, *Security and Migration in the 21st Century*, Cambridge: Polity 2009.

23 V. Mitsilegas, 'Human Rights, Terrorism and the Quest for "Border Security"', in: M. Pedrazzi et al. (eds), *Individual Guarantees in the European Judicial Area in Criminal Matters*, Brussels: Bruylant 2011, p. 85.

has eloquently noted, 'the border becomes a condition of being that is always in the act of becoming, it is never entirely crossed, but appears instead as a constant demand for proof of status and legitimacy'.[24]

3. The Rule of Law Deficit in the Transformation of Border Control – Current Examples

The paradigmatic change in border control outlined thus far poses significant challenges to the rule of law. These challenges extend to both the rule of law *ex ante* (which relates to principles which are applicable in the law-making process (including legality, legitimacy, transparency and democracy); and to the *rule of law ex post*, which includes principles which are applicable after the enactment of legislation (including legal certainty, prohibition of arbitrariness and effective judicial protection including the protection of human rights).[25] This section will expand on these challenges by focusing on three current examples of transformations in border control, focusing on all three stages of the paradigm change.

3.1. The Border Abroad – Militarisation

A key development linked to extraterritorial immigration control in the EU has been the launch of the military Operation Sophia, initially launched in 2015. In terms of rule of law *ex ante,* the establishment and evolution of Operation Sophia is marked by a double democratic deficit. At EU level, a mission which involves extraterritorial immigration control has been established not under a Title V TFEU legal basis, but under a foreign policy/defence legal basis. This choice mirrors the uncritical securitisation of human smuggling in the political discourse, whereby smuggling is elevated as an existential threat against receiving states. However, it disregards the centrality of immigration control at the heart of the operation and, in terms of law-making, has been adopted under the intergovernmental framework underpinning EU CFSP action, leaving limited powers to the EU institutions, particularly the European Parliament to scrutinise its adoption and development. The democratic deficit at EU level is accentuated by a parallel democratic and rule of law deficit in international law. The development of the EU framework has been justified and legitimised by the parallel adoption of UNSC resolutions, which have operated in parallel and in conjunction with the relevant EU framework.[26] International law measures have been developed not in the form of a multilateral treaty, but in an executive framework by the UNSC. The well-founded concerns regarding the soundness and desirability of the shift of the UNSC role to

---

24 L. Amoore, 'Biometric Borders: Governing Mobilities in the War on Terror', 25 *Political Geography* 2006, p. 336-351, at p. 358.

25 On this distinction see V. Mitsilegas, 'Rule of Law: Theorising EU Internal Security Cooperation from a Legal Perspective', in: M. Rhinard & D. Bossong (eds), *Theorising Internal Security Cooperation in the European Union*, Oxford: OUP 2016, p. 109-128.

26 V. Mitsilegas 'Extraterritorial Immigration Control, Preventive Justice and the Rule of Law in Turbulent Times', in: J. Santos Vara et al. (eds.), *Constitutionalising the External Dimension of EU Migration Policies in Times of Crisis: Legality, Rule of Law and Fundamental Rights Reconsidered*, Cheltenham: Edward Elgar 2019, p. 290-308.

become a legislator which have arisen in the context of the UNSC adoption of terrorist sanctions post-9/11 apply clearly in this context.[27] UNSC resolutions adopted with minimum scrutiny have justified far-reaching EU intervention and have introduced significant changes to the rules adopted via the framework of a multilateral treaty – the smuggling Protocol to the Palermo Convention, as well as changes to operational practice at EU level. These concerns are accompanied by concerns regarding the rule of law *ex post,* in particular regarding the lack of clarity on responsibility and accountability in the activities of Operation Sophia in co-operation with national and EU actors of border control. While the recent extension of the mandate of Operation Sophia has suspended temporarily the deployment of its naval assets, the Operation will continue air surveillance and reinforcing the support of the Libyan coastguard and navy.[28] Surveillance and training operations organised by the EU and its Member States and resulting in deflection outcomes in third countries must not evade the applicability of European human rights standards and rule of law scrutiny.[29] A first step would be for the effective control test in *Hirsi* [30] to be extended to ensure clear responsibility for human rights breaches for third country operations abetted or resulting from such operations.

3.2. The Border Within – The Re-introduction of Internal Border Controls in the Schengen Area

One of the responses of EU Member States in the wake of what has been perceived as a migration 'crisis' has been to reintroduce border controls within the Schengen area.[31] Re-introduction of border controls creates additional layers of control (internal in addition to external) and is not compatible with the fundamental EU law principle of freedom of movement in a borderless Area of Freedom, Security and Justice – it creates a paradox of proliferation of control in an area without internal frontiers.[32] From a rule of law perspective, the re-introduction of border controls raises serious labelling issues under EU law, which in turn may have profound implications for the legal position and fundamental rights of third country nationals. These challenges have been vividly illustrated in the recent litigation before the CJEU, resulting in its ruling in *Arib.*[33] The case involved the re-introduction of border controls by France, during which Mr Arib was checked in the area between the border of France with Spain and a line drawn 20 kilometres inside the border.[34] Mr Arib was subsequently held in police custody on suspicion of illegal entry and was on the following day ordered to leave France and was

27 See V. Mitsilegas, 'The Global Governance of Crime: Implications for Justice and the Rule of Law', in: M. Christensen & R. Levi (eds), *International Practices of Criminal Law*, Abingdon: Routledge 2018, p. 66-86.

28 EUNAVFOR MED, *Operation Sophia: mandate extended until 30 September 2019*, Council of the EU, press release of 29/03/2019.

29 Mitsilegas 2019.

30 *Hirsi Jamaa and Others v Italy,* Application no. 27765/09.

31 For a recent overview see M. Ceccorulli, 'Back to Schengen: the collective securitisation of the EU free-border area', 42 *West European Politics* 2019, p. 302-332.

32 Mitsilegas 2009.

33 Case C-444/17 *Arib*, judgment of 19 March 2019.

34 Para. 22.

detained.[35] The main question here was the applicability in the proceedings of the EU Return Directive which has been interpreted by the CJEU as precluding national legislation such as the one in question permitting imprisonment of third country nationals in respect of whom the return has not been complete merely on account of illegal entry across the national border resulting in illegal stay.[36] France argued that in the present case the Return Directive was not applicable on the basis of Article 2(2)(a) of the Directive which allowed exceptions in cases of refusal of entry or apprehension of third country nationals at the external border - with France arguing that the re-introduction of border controls had rendered the French-Spanish border external and not internal. The CJEU disagreed. Adopting a systematic reading of the Schengen Borders Code,[37] it held that an internal border at which border control has been reintroduced by a Member State … is not tantamount to an external border for the purposes of that code.[38] Under Article 2 of the Schengen Borders Code, the concepts of 'internal borders' and 'external borders' are mutually exclusive – the very wording of the SBC therefore precludes an internal border at which border control has been reintroduced from being equated with an external border.[39] The Return Directive was thus applicable in the present case, with the CJEU following the Opinion of AG Szpunar who eloquently stated that, for the purposes of the Return Directive, 'whether an individual is intercepted near the border between France and Spain or on the Champs-Elysees is irrelevant'.[40] The CJEU ruling in *Arib* is welcome and has a double rule of law significance. It maintains the integrity, internal coherence and teleology of the Schengen space by upholding the distinction between the EU internal and external border, which bring with them distinct legal consequences. And in doing so, it brings forward the safeguards underpinning the application of the Return Directive *vis-à-vis* the draconian use of criminal law to target migrants by EU Member States.[41]

3.3. The Border Beyond – Databases and Surveillance

A major and on-going transformation in border control consists in the shift to the generalised and ongoing surveillance of mobility, blurring the boundaries between immigration control and security. The establishment and development of EU and national databases and data management agencies is key in this shift. The first step has been to 'securitise' major EU immigration databases such as SIS II, VIS and Eurodac, and, after a long period of struggle, to allow access to these databases by law enforcement authorities.[42] The second step has been to establish systems of ongoing surveillance of mobility such as an entry-exit system (EES) [43]or a European Travel Information and

35 Para. 23.
36 Case C-47/15 *Affum.*
37 *Arib*, para. 60.
38 Para. 61.
39 Para. 62.
40 Opinion of AG Szpunar, delivered on 17.10.2018, para.4.
41 V. Mitsilegas 2015.
42 For an early analysis, see Mitsilegas 2007. On the culmination of the securitisation process, see N. Vavoula, *Immigration Control and Privacy in the Law of the EU,* doctoral thesis, Queen Mary University of London, Leiden: Brill Nijhoff, forthcoming 2019).
43 Regulation (EU) 2017/2226, L 327/20, 9.12.2017.

Authorisation System (ETIAS).[44] The third step has been to extend criminal law instruments to include immigration data, with the recently agreed extension of the European Criminal Records Information System (ECRIS) to include data of third country nationals being a key example. And the fourth step (related also to the 'border within') has been to use counter-terrorism justifications to establish routine monitoring of travel of both EU and third country nationals via EU Passenger Name Record (PNR) systems (with the EU system potentially applying also to intra-EU flights).[45] Each of these initiatives individually poses significant challenges to fundamental rights, in particular privacy, data protection (in particular regarding purpose limitation) and non-discrimination. However, more acute challenges -related also to the rule of law- are posed by attempts to combine these systems and databases and to establish maximum access to data mechanisms. This is currently being attempted by efforts to delegalize and depoliticise the functions of data in border surveillance by the establishment of an EU agency responsible for managing EU databases (Eulisa[46]) and by privileging the concept of interoperability of diverse databases – a concept which was originally tabled more than a decade ago as a depoliticisation device[47] and which has appeared with a vengeance, with far-reaching Commission proposals on interoperability being recently agreed by the co-legislators.[48] Strategic litigation and ongoing efforts to ensure transparency and accountability are essential to address the rule of law challenges posed by these systems of the 'border beyond.'

4. Conclusion

The normalisation of a 'crisis mentality' with regard to migration management, the ongoing securitisation of migration and the growing reliance by policy makers and politicians on technology to solve issues perceived to be problematic have resulted in a constant realignment of the border and what constitutes border control. Inspired by Elspeth Guild's pioneering and clear-sighted work on migration management and border control, this contribution has attempted to pay tribute to her immense contribution to our thinking by drawing attention to the continuous and multi-layered transformations of border control in Europe and in casting light on the rule of law challenges they entail. Rule of law and fundamental rights red lines are essential in this attempted renegotiation of the border framed by states and the EU increasingly within a security agenda. It is these red lines, and a constant attention and focus on the migrant as an individual with agency and rights, which Elspeth's work has always reminded us to prioritise as an invaluable scholarly and moral compass.

44 Regulation (EU) 2018/1240 and 2018/1241, L 236/1, 19.9.2018.
45 Directive (EU) 2016/681, 4.5.2016, L 119/132.
46 Regulation (EU) 2018/1726 *OJ* L 295, 21.11.2018, p. 99.
47 On depoliticisation and interoperability, see Mitsilegas 2007.
48 COM(2017) 794 final (police and judicial cooperation, asylum and migration); COM(2017) 793 final (borders and visa).

The New Borders of Empire
European Migration Policy and Domestic Passenger Transport in Niger

*Thomas Spijkerboer**

In her inaugural lecture, Elspeth Guild has shown how the borders of European territories are being controlled by networks of bureaucracies and private actors, both at the external borders of the European Union and on the territory of third countries.[1] In the two decades since Elspeth made this analysis, Europe has extended the reach of its border policies even further, which are now impacting the migration policies of African countries. This paper addresses an example of this. The case study concerns the criminalisation of passenger transport inside Niger, and shows a re-internalisation of European border control – but this time European border control takes place *inside* the territory of a *third* country.

The criminalisation of domestic transportation was introduced into Nigerien law by Law 2015/36 of 26 May 2015 relating to the illegal trafficking in migrants.[2] This law was drafted with technical and financial assistance from the United Nations Office on Drugs and Crime (UNODC) in a project that was funded by Denmark and Italy.[3] UNODC mentions in this context that more than 3.000 migrants have died in the Mediterranean, and emphasises that 'criminal groups profit from these illegal activities, weakening Sahel States' ability to exert control over their territories and citizens'.[4] By using the crime control/humanitarian discourse which Europe uses to justify its border policies, [5] UNODC makes explicit what obviously is the European intention of assisting Niger with implementing the Smuggling Protocol by criminalising domestic transportation: preventing nationals of sub-Saharan countries from reaching the Mediterranean.

* Vrije Universiteit Amsterdam, the Netherlands/Lund University, Sweden.

1 E. Guild, *Moving the borders of Europe*, Katholieke Universiteit Nijmegen, Faculteit der Rechtsgeleerdheid, Centrum voor Postdoctoraal Onderwijs, Nijmegen 2001.

2 The text can be found on the UNODC website, https://www.unodc.org/res/cld/document/ner/2015/loi_relative_au_trafic_illicite_de_migrants_html/Loi_N2015-36_relative_au_trafic_illicite_de_migrants.pdf, accessed 29 March 2019.

3 UNODC, *Niger becomes the first Sahel country to legislate against migrant smuggling*, https://www.unodc.org/westandcentralafrica/en/niger-som-law.html, accessed 3 April 2019. Comp. Abdoulaye Massalaki, 'Niger passes law to tackle migrant smuggling, first in West Africa', *Reuters World News* 12 May 2015, https://www.reuters.com/article/us-europe-migrants-niger/niger-passes-law-to-tackle-migrant-smuggling-first-in-west-africa-idUSKBN0NX1M020150512, accessed 4 June 2019; I am grateful to Eric Komlavi Hahonou for pointing out this source.

4 UNODC, *Sahel Programme 2013-2017, Progress Report January 2016*, Dakar: UNODC 2017, p. 6.

5 See i.a. Paolo Cuttitta, 'Delocalization, Humanitarianism and Human Rights. The Mediterranean Border between Exclusion and Inclusion', 50 *Antipode* 2018, p. 783-803; Violeta Moreno-Lax, 'The EU Humanitarian Border and the Securitization of Human Rights: The 'Rescue-Trough-Interdiction/Rescue-Without-Protection'', 56 *Paradigm, Journal of Common Market Studies* 2018, p. 119-140.

Niger's Law 2015/36 against Migrant Smuggling

Niger's Law 2015/36 aims to prevent and combat migrant smuggling; to protect the right of people who are the object of migrant smuggling; and to promote national and international cooperation to prevent and combat migrant smuggling (Article 1). Migrant smuggling is defined as seeking to effect the illegal entry into a state of a person who is neither a national nor a permanent resident of that state, with a view to direct or indirect financial or other material advantage (Article 2). The main offences are migrant smuggling; the fabrication, procurement, provision, or possession of a false travel or identity document; as well as assistance with irregular stay. All these acts are only criminal offences if they are committed for financial gain, and they are punishable by prison terms of two to ten years or fines of 500.000 up to 5.000.000 francs CFA (approximately $ 860 to $ 8.600). Niger has a per capita income of $ 420 per year.[6]

A provision that has had a far-reaching impact is Article 20, which criminalises commercial transport companies (in Niger in practice: bus companies) who fail to verify that every passenger is in possession of the identity and/or travel documents required for the entry in the state of destination as well as in all the transit states. Such failure is punishable by a fine of 1.000.000 to 3.000.000 francs CFA ($ 1.720 to $ 5.160).[7] The price of a bus ticket from Niamey to Agadez was 27.000 franc CFA.[8]

The UN Protocol against Migrant Smuggling,[9] of which Law 2015/36 is the implantation in Nigerien law, uses a more limited notion of carrier sanctions. It obliges states party to the Protocol to adopt legislative or other appropriate measures to prevent commercial transport from being used for migrant smuggling, and in particular to oblige commercial transportation companies to ascertain that all passengers are in possession of the required travel documents required for entry into the receiving state (Article 11(2) and 11(3) Migrant Smuggling Protocol).

What is to be noted about Article 20 Law 2015/36 is that it introduces carrier sanctions on domestic transport;[10] it does not require that the trip on which a person is embarking will cross borders. This is made possible by replacing the term *receiving state* from the Migrant Smuggling Protocol by the term *state of destination or transit* in Article 20 Law 2015/36. It is conceivable that Niger itself functions as a transit state, and in that case the transport company is obliged to verify that every passenger is in

6 Source: World Bank: https://www.worldbank.org/en/country/niger/overview, accessed 16 April 2019.

7 For Niger, the minimum fine is roughly twice the per capita annual income, the maximum fine 20 times – *supra*. In the EU the fines are much lower. The per capita income in the EU was $ 33.720 in 2017 (https://data.worldbank.org/indicator/NY.GDP.PCAP.CD?locations=PL-GR-PT-DE-EU, accessed 16 April 2019), while Article 4(1) EU Directive 2001/51 prescribes minimum fines not lower than € 3.000 and maximum fines not lower than € 5.000. A 2007 study found that, at that time, only The Netherlands had introduced substantially higher fines (a maximum fine of € 16.000), Kay Hailbronner & Cordelia Karlitz, *Directive 2011/51 Synthesis Report*, Brussels: Odysseus Network 2015, http://odysseus-network.eu/wp-content/uploads/2015/03/2001-51-Carriers-Liability-Synthesis.pdf, p. 17, accessed 16 April 2019.

8 Information from 24 January 2018, http://www.iciniger.com/niger-augmentation-generalisee-prix-tickets-de-bus/.

9 UNTS 2241, p. 507.

10 I owe this insight to the presentation of Florence Boyer & Harouna Mounkaila, *Européanisation des politiques migratoires en Sahel*, Niamey: LASDEL summer school, 12 October 2018.

possession of identity and/or travel documents for Niger. In practice, this means that all passengers

- need to have a travel or identity document
- which either proves they have Nigerien nationality, or for non-Nigeriens that proves their regular presence.

In Niger, on average only 64% of all births are registered (ranging from 50% for the poorest to 89% for the richest segments of the population).[11] Of those registered, many do not have (and the poorest cannot afford) an identity document with which they are able to establish that they have Nigerien nationality. This means that substantial parts of Nigerien nationals have to be excluded from domestic transportation. Because of the Economic Community of West African States (ECOWAS) free movement law (*infra*), many non-Nigeriens have a right to be in Niger. However, as many West-Africans do not have identity documents, they are unable to prove their nationality and their regular presence in Niger. Also, often they have not crossed the Nigerien border at an official border crossing point, and if they have done so may not have received an entry stamp. Consequently, they are unable to prove their regular presence, and have to be excluded from transport in Niger.

The EU's Good Governance Support

The EU has a number of funding programmes which help, support and accompany (the terms are from policy documents mentioned below) Niger implementing its migration law and policy.

In 2012, European Union Capacity Building Mission (EUCAP) Sahel Niger was established as an element of the Common Security and Defence Policy. It was set up after the chaos following the European intervention in Libya in 2011, and sought to support the capacity building of the Nigerien security actors to fight terrorism and organised crime.[12] In July its mandate was amended so as to include the fight against irregular migration.[13] In 2015, the European Union Emergency Trust Fund (EUTF) for stability and addressing root causes of irregular migration and displaced persons in Africa was established. The purpose of the EUTF Africa is broad, namely 'to address the crises in the regions of the Sahel and the Lake Chad, the Horn of Africa, and the North of Africa.'[14] Niger is the Trust Fund's biggest recipient. EUCAP Sahel and the EUTF Africa are the two main instruments which the EU currently uses to promote good governance in, in this case, Niger.

The projects which can be related to the implementation of Law 2015/36 can be distinguished into four groups. First, there are projects in which Nigerien policy for-

11 Unicef Birth registration data November 2017, data.unicef.org, accessed 19 April 2019.

12 Article 1 Council Decision 2012/392/CFSP 16 July 2012, OJ 17.7.2012, L 187/48. EUCAP Sahel, *New CDSP mission to assist in fighting terrorism in the Sahel*, http://eeas.europa.eu/archives/csdp/missions-and-operations/eucap-sahel-niger/news/copy_20120716_ en.htm, accessed 18 April 2019.

13 Council Decision (CFSP) 2016/1172, OJ L 193/106, 19.7.2016; comp. Council Decision (CFSP) 2018/1247, OJ L 235/7, 19.9.2018.

14 Article 1(2) Commission Decision C(2015) 7293 final, 20 October 2015.

mulation is influenced – the genesis of Law 2015/36 is a prime example of that. Secondly, institutions are set up. Thirdly, the discourse of Nigerien officials and civil society is influenced through consultations and seminars where particular notions are circulated. Fourth, equipment (from border posts to vehicles) is funded. And finally, Nigerien officials are trained to apply laws such as Law 2015/36.

Institution Building

One set of activities which the EU funds are setting up a migration management bureaucracy. In 2016, the EU funded the International Organisation for Migration (IOM) for implementing its Migrant Resource and Response Mechanism (MRRM) in Niger.[15] It will support the national, regional and local authorities to implement the Migrant Resource and Response Mechanism in order to develop the Nigerien migration management capacities. More concretely, an undated power point presentation, which seems to be from 2017, refers to a specialised police unit consisting of Nigerien, French and Spanish police officers, which reinforced the operational apparatus fighting irregular migration.[16]

Discourse

The main use of a number of meetings seems to be to get Nigeriens to adopt the securitised and humanitarian discourse which the EU uses to promote its external migration policies. For example, on 4 and 5 December 2017, representatives of the Internal Security Forces, the Ministries of Justice and the armed forces of Mali and Niger met during a seminar in Niamey that was organised by the EUCAP Sahel missions in Mali and Niger. It was one form of the 'constant support of the EU in the fields of counterterrorism and irregular migration', in the words of the secretary general of the Nigerien Ministry of the Interior. The seminar discussed the state of affairs and lacunas in the cross-border cooperation between Niger and Mali. Themes addressed included cooperation frameworks, reinforcement of the presence of security forces in border and remote areas, and reinforcement of interoperability.[17]

---

15 Document d'action T05-EUTF-SAH-NE-01, https://ec.europa.eu/trustfundforafrica/sites/euetfa/files/t05-eutf-sah-ne-01.pdf, accessed 17 April 2019.

16 Direction Générale de l'Agence nationale de Lutte contre la Traite des Personnes: Rôle du Niger dans la lutte contre la traite des personnes et le trafic illicite de migrants, http://archive.ipu.org/splz-e/valletta17/gazibo.pdf, accessed 17 April 2019.

17 EUCAP Sahel, *Niger et Mali: Les Missions EUCAP Sahel au cœur des défis transfrontaliers*, 6 December 2017, https://eeas.europa.eu/csdp-missions-operations/eucap-sahel-niger/36878/niger-et-mali-les-missions-eucap-sahel-au-coeur-des-d%C3%A9fis-transfrontaliers_en, accessed 18 April 2019. The funding of this event cannot be traced to the list of contracts for the period, EUCAP Sahel Niger, *Liste des contrats de plus de 15 000 € attribués jusqu'au 31/1/2018 au titre de l'exercice Y6,* https://eeas.europa.eu/sites/eeas/files/listes_des_contrats_attribues_y6_premier_semestre_2017-2018_0.pdf, accessed 18 April 2019. Comp. IOM's regional workshops of various sorts involving Niger (two in February 2016, May 2016, June 2016, December 2016), IOM Niger country office, *Annual Report 2016*, http:// www.nigermigrationresponse.org/sites/default/files/IOM%20Niger%20Annual%20Report%202016%20FINAL%20EN.pdf, p. 15. Comp. a West-African conference on human trafficking and migrant smuggling in 2018, sponsored by Denmark and The Netherlands, UNODC, *International meeting in Niger against smuggling of migrants and trafficking in persons*, Dakar: UNODC 2018,

An example of a comparable activity addressing civil society is the workshop which took place on 21 March 2018 in Agadez. It was organised by the Association of Nigerien Women Against War, and facilitated by the National Agency in the Fight Against Human Trafficking. The general aim was to strengthen the capacity of women in the Agadez area 'towards combatting human trafficking and the smuggling of migrants, and raise awareness of related aspects'. The workshop 'was intended to help women leaders obtain a better understanding of the work done by the security forces.'[18]

Equipment

The EU also funds equipment to implement migration policy. In 2014-2015, GIZ implemented a project to construct and equip border police stations.[19] In 2016, IOM has supported the construction of border posts.[20] Furthermore, it equipped a pilot station with the MIDAS border data management system, which allows the registration of passengers and 'establishes a direct connection with police headquarters', and it has trained Nigerien officials to use the system.[21]

The EU has granted € 20 million budget support to Niger for 2016 and 2017, on the condition that it will be spent on equipment for the Internal Security Service and on the justice infrastructure.[22]

In April 2017, The EUCAP Sahel mission donated 5 four wheel drive pick-up trucks to the Nigerien police and Public Security Directorate, funded by Luxemburg. They will allow the Nigerien authorities, in the words of a high ranking Nigerien police officer, 'to better prevent and contain migration flows'.[23] In 2018, Germany, The Netherlands and Belgium funded the establishment of mobile border control units. In this way, they 'accompany Niger in controlling its borders.' The units are to be an essential

---

https://www.unodc.org/westandcentralafrica/en/2018-06-18-atelier-niamey-tipsom.html, accessed 17 April 2019.

18 EUCAP Sahel, *EUCAP Sahel Niger involves women in the Agadez region in the fight against human trafficking and the smuggling of migrants*, 29 March 2018, https://eeas.europa.eu/csdp-missions-operations/eucap-sahel-niger/42296/eucap-sahel-niger-involves-women-agadez-region-fight-against-human-trafficking-and-smuggling_en, accessed 18 April 2019. The funding of this event cannot be traced to the list of contracts for the period, EUCAP Sahel Niger, *Liste des contrats de plus de 15 000 € attribués du 1/02/2018 au 30/09/2018,* https://eeas.europa.eu/sites/eeas/files/liste_des_contrats_attribues_01_02_2018-30_09_2018_0.pdf, accessed 18 April 2019.

19 https://ec.europa.eu/europeaid/projects/renforcement-des-capacites-de-la-police-nationale-du-niger-dans-les-zones-frontalieres_, accessed 18 April 2019.

20 IOM Niger country office, *Annual Report 2016*, http://www.nigermigrationresponse.org/ sites/default/files/IOM%20Niger%20Annual%20Report%202016%20FINAL%20 EN.pdf, p. 15.

21 IOM Niger country office, *Annual Report 2016*, http://www.nigermigrationresponse.org/sites/default/files/IOM%20Niger%20Annual%20Report%202016%20FINAL%20 EN.pdf, p. 15.

22 Document d'action T05-EUTF-SAH-NE-06, p. 23, https://ec.europa.eu/europeaid/sites/devco/files/t05-eutf-sah-ne-06.pdf, accessed 17 April 2019.

23 EUCAP Sahel, *Des véhicules pour contenir les flux migratoires irréguliers*, Niamey: EUCAP Sahel, 3 April 2017, https://eeas.europa.eu/csdp-missions-operations/eucap-sahel-niger/24058/des-v%C3%A9hicules-pour-contenir-les-flux-migratoires-irr%C3%A9guliers_en, accessed 18 April 2019. From the list of contracts, it is not entirely clear which of the four contracts for vehicles concern this donation, which were acquired between 17 January 2017 and 16 march 2017, EUCAP Sahel Niger, *Liste des contrats de plus de 15 000 € attribués entre 16/7/2016 et 15/7/2017 au titre de l'exercice Y5*, https://eeas.europa.eu/sites/eeas/files/listes_des_contrats_attribues_y_5_vd_0.pdf, accessed 18 pril 2019.

actor in border zones, where state structures are not permanent.[24] Training started in March 2019, and the units should be operational by September 2019.[25]

Training

Finally, the EU funds the training of police, security and justice personnel to apply migration policy in practice. Following the adoption of Law 2015/36 which is at the heart of this paper, UNODC developed a training module for the national police and gendarmerie workshop (developed after local consultation[26] and funded by Austria[27]), which was then implemented by IOM in training sessions between 28 September and 14 October 2015 reaching more than 80 national police officers.[28] UNODC reports that, after these activities aimed at implementing Law 2015/36, the authorities seized 117 vehicles, arrested 130 suspects and repatriated 7.264 irregular migrants.[29]

Apart from law enforcers, the judiciary has also been the target of trainings. In July 2016, Nigerian judicial authorities (prosecutors and judges, including two women) received training regarding the national and international legal frameworks regarding migrant smuggling and human trafficking, including practical exercises on how to identify, investigate and prosecute these cases as well as conduct victim-friendly interviews. The project was funded by Denmark.[30] Consultations were held for developing training modules for judiciary training institutes of Burkina Faso, Mali and Niger in January 2017, funded by Denmark.[31]

This kind of training also brings together officials from different countries. On 16-18 April 2018, UNODC organised a sub-regional workshop in Niamey bringing together 32 representatives of national authorities of Mali, Morocco and Niger responsible for combatting migrant smuggling. They exchanged experiences and good practices, and did a practical exercise based on the shipwreck off Lampedusa on 3 October 2013, in which 366 migrants died. This allowed participants to work on techniques for identifying and dismantling a criminal network of smugglers, and to present a UNODC

24 EUCAP Sahel, *Le Royaume des Pays-Bas et la Mission EUCAP Sahel Niger accompagnent le Niger dans le contrôle de ses frontières*, 2 November 2018, https://eeas.europa.eu/csdp-missions-operations/eucap-sahel-niger/53874/le-royaume-des-pays-bas-et-la-mission-eucap-sahel-niger-accompagnent-le-niger-dans-le-contr%C3%B4le_en, accessed 18 April 2019.

25 EUCAP Sahel: *Compagnie mobile pour la gestion intégrée des frontières*, 18 March 2019, https://eeas.europa.eu/csdp-missions-operations/eucap-sahel-niger/60268/compagnie-mobile-pour-la-gestion-int%C3%A9gr%C3%A9e-de-fronti%C3%A8res_en, accessed 18 April 2019. 18 April 2019. From the list of contracts, it is not entirely clear which of the contracts concern this project, , EUCAP Sahel Niger: *Liste des contrats de plus de 15 000 € attribués de 1/10/2018 au 31/03/2019,* https://eeas.europa.eu/sites/eeas/files/listes_des_contrats_attribues_1er_octobre_2018-31_mars_2019_0.pdf, accessed 18 April 2019.

26 UNODC, *Sahel Programme Progress Report June 2017*, UNIDC Dakar, p. 41.

27 UNODC, *Sahel Programme 2013-2017, Progress Report January 2016*, UNODC Dakar, p. 37.

28 IOM Niger: *IOM Niger Helps Train More Than 80 National Police Officers In Document Fraud*, http://www.nigermigrationresponse.org/en/Media/Press/iom-niger-helps-train-more-80-national-police-officers-document-fraud, accessed 18 April 2019. Comp. IOM Niger country office: *Annual Report 2016*, http://www.nigermigrationresponse.org/sites/default/files/IOM%20Niger%20Annual%20Report%202016%20FINAL%20EN.pdf, p. 16-17.

29 UNODC, *Sahel Programme Progress Report June 2017*, UNIDC Dakar, p. 8.

30 UNODC, *Sahel Programme Progress Report June 2017*, UNIDC Dakar, p.43.

31 UNODC, *Sahel Programme Progress Report June 2017*, UNIDC Dakar, p. 40.

database on legislation and case law in fighting international organised crime. In small groups, the participants looked at numerous transcripts of telephone tapping of smugglers and interviews of migrant survivors in order to identify elements that would allow progress in the investigation. The project was funded by the EU.[32]

ECOWAS Free Movement

Article 59 of the ECOWAS Treaty gives citizens of the ECOWAS member states the right of entry, residence and establishment in other member states. Article 3 of the 1979 Protocol on Free Movement gives citizen of ECOWAS states the right to enter other states for a maximum of 90 days free of visa requirements. Formally, possession of a valid travel document and an international health certificate is required. Article 2 of the 1986 Supplementary Protocol requires ECOWAS member states to grant the right of residence to nationals of other member states for the purpose of seeking and carrying out income earning employment. This is conditional on possession of an ECOWAS residence card or permit.[33] In 1992, the right of establishment to settle and obtain work was implemented.[34] In practice, until 2015 border authorities accepted an ordinary valid identity card, although such a card cannot hold the immigration and emigration services' stamps. This flexible application of ECOWAS law 'is a response to the nature of the migratory exchanges that are behind the history of the region, divided by national borders regardless of the sociological and economic practices of its communities.'[35]

IOM has an ambiguous attitude towards ECOWAS free movement. Its MRRM document (*supra*)[36] mentions as an obstacle to voluntary returns of migrants from Niger that the majority of them originate from member states of ECOWAS and enjoy free movement, with the consequence that 'the Nigerien authorities are powerless to return' them (p. 4). At the same time the document claims that one of IOM's aims is to promote development through circular migration, which ECOWAS law facilitates (p. 6). In a document on the implementation of the MRRM, IOM mentions that it has engaged in institutional capacity-building, trainings and in-kind donations. It has supported the government of Niger in reducing the waiting period for the issuance of 'safe conduct' (to be understood as: assisted voluntary return) from three to one days for migrants who have no representation in Niger. The terms ECOWAS or free movement

32 UNODC, *UNODC strengthens regional cooperation in the fight against the smuggling of migrants*, https://www.unodc.org/westandcentralafrica/en/2018-04-18-atelier-tipsom-niger-avril-2018.html, accessed 17 April 2019; UNODC, *How regional cooperation between Mali, Morocco and Niger will help in the fight against migrant smuggling*, accessed 17 April 2019.

33 Aderanti Adepoju, 'Migration Management in West Africa within the context of the ECOWAS Protocol on Free Movement of Persons and the Common Approach to Migration: Challenges and Prospects', in: Marie Trémolières (ed.), *Regional Challenges of West African Migration*, Paris: OECD 2009, p. 17-48.

34 Dieudonné Ouedraogo, 'Migration and Population in West Africa', in: Marie Trémolières (ed.), *Regional Challenges of West African Migration*, Paris: OECD 2009, p. 127-142.

35 Nelly Robin, 'ECOWAS, an Area of Free Movement and First Border Post for the Schengen Area', in: Marie Trémolières (ed.), *Regional Challenges of West African Migration*, Paris: OECD 2009, p. 143-159.

36 Document d'action T05-EUTF-SAH-NE-01, https://ec.europa.eu/trustfundforafrica/sites/euetfa/files/t05-eutf-sah-ne-01.pdf, accessed 17 April 2019.

are not mentioned in the document.[37] Free movement was also not operationalized in the MRRM action document.

It has been noted by many that passenger transport within Niger has been reduced considerably since 2015. There can be little doubt that this is related to the external actions of the EU outlined above. The EU has financed a project which resulted in Niger adopting carrier sanctions on domestic transport. It has financed projects establishing the bureaucracy needed to implement this. It has promoted the circulation of discourse that sees migration as a security issue and the combat of irregular migration as a form of humanitarianism. It has equipped the new migration bureaucracy so as to be able to act on this discourse. And it has trained the bureaucracy so as to implement Law2015/36, to implement ECOWAS free movement law more strictly than had happened in the decades before, and to use the equipment effectively.

Empire

Anthony Anghie has noted that the sovereignty of Third World states is porous, and that the concept of good governance has expanded the range of domestic issues of Third World states in which states of the global North can legitimately intervene. According to his analysis, the notion of good governance is only a further recent turn in a long history in which the concept of sovereignty is made to serve the imperial aspirations of states in the global North.[38]

This is strong language, but if we look at the externalisation of European migration policy, it is not saying too much. For Niger, Europe's external action in the field of migration comes with considerable risks. Seasonal migration to and from Niger can be, and according to Nigerien observers actually is being undermined as a result of the implementation of Law 2015/36 and the stricter application of ECOWAS free movement law. For a country as poor as Niger, even a marginal negative effect is considerable. Furthermore, the confiscation of vehicles in the Agadez region which UNODC proudly mentions (*supra*) puts people out of business who have made their living by crossing the Sahara since generations. Only part of this was related to migration, and the increasingly problematic nature of their migration business was an effect of decades of European policy in the region.[39] What the newly unemployed people have to do is unclear – EU projects promising them alternative sources of income will work at the medium term only, if at all.[40] For parts of the Nigerian authorities, European migration policy has become a major source of income. In order to preserve this, they need to walk the thin line between maintaining a credible threat of further migration and sufficiently credible forms of cooperation.

37 IOM overview: *Niger 2019,* http://www.nigermigrationresponse.org/sites/default/files/IOM%20Niger%20MRRM%20Overview%202019%20-%20EN.pdf, accessed 18 April 2019.

38 Anthony Anghie, *Imperialism, Sovereignty and the Making of International Law*, Cambridge: Cambridge University Press 2004.

39 Julien Brachet, 'Manufacturing Smugglers: From Irregular to Clandestine Mobility in the Sahara', 676 *Annals of the American Academy of Political and Social Science* 2018, p. 16-35.

40 Jerôme Tubiana, Clotilde Warin & Gaffar Mahammud Saeneen, *Multilateral Damage. The impact of EU migration policies on central Saharan routes*, The Hague: Netherlands Institute of International Relations 'Clingendael' 2018.

Implementing European migration policy goes against Niger's interest in a liberal implementation of regional free movement. Europe tries to create such an interest through sticks and carrots ('conditionality'), and in fact seeks to take over control of Nigerien migration policy. In doing so, it creates division between Nigerien nationals who make a living by implementing European policy, and those whose living is being undermined by it. In the process the EU undermines ECOWAS not only by undermining free movement, but also by sidelining it institutionally.[41] It is hard to disregard the continuity with Europe's long engagement with Africa.

41 Amanada Bisong, 'Trans-regional institutional cooperation as multilevel governance: ECOWAS migration policy and the EU', *Journal of Ethnic and Migration Studies* 2018, p. 1294-1309, https://doi.org/10.1080/1369183X.2018.1441607.

Citizens

Exclusion Orders Pertaining to Union Citizens and Families: A Less Favourable Treatment?

*Pieter Boeles**

Introduction

Probably one of the least investigated issues of free movement is under what circumstances EU citizens and family members may be prohibited entry into a Member State other than their own. The instrument of an *entry ban*, regulated in the Returns Directive (Directive 2008/115), cannot be used against them, as the Returns Directive is not applicable to persons enjoying the Union right of free movement.[1] However, the Citizens' Directive (Directive 2004/38), applicable to Union citizens and their family members, mentions the possibility of an *exclusion order* under national law, which may have a similar effect as an entry ban under the Returns Directive. Principally, the measure of exclusion is subject to national law of the Member States. However, national room for manoeuver is limited by procedural guarantees in the Citizens' Directive (Articles 30-33). In this short and tentative contribution to the book in honour of Elspeth Guild, this charmingly energetic body and soul of European Migration Law, I will try to analyse what exclusion orders may mean and how they affect the freedom of movement of EU citizens and their families in comparison to the effects of the Returns Directive for third country nationals. I do not pretend completeness, I will particularly let myself led by some questions raised by some judgments of the Court of Justice.

A Terminological Exercise: What is the Meaning of the Concepts of Expulsion and Exclusion Order?

The terminology of the Citizens' Directive in this respect is not crystal clear. In the English language version of the Directive two terms, expulsion[2] and exclusion,[3] are used. A similar terminological distinction can also be found in most language version(s) that I can understand[4] but the Dutch language version only uses one term ('verwijdering') and I am not sure about how other versions deal with the distinction. Aside from this, the Directive contains no definition of the terms – which is understandable as these measures primarily fall under the scope of national law. However, there is no

* Visiting professor in the section Migration Law of VU University.

1 As defined in Article 2(5) of the Schengen Borders Code.

2 (Expulsion:) Articles 21, 28, 29, 31, 33, (expel:) 14, 27, recital 16, 22.

3 Article 32, Recital 27.

4 *French*: interdiction du territoire, éloignement; *German*: Aufenthaltsverbot, Ausweisung; *Spanish*: prohibición de entrada en el territorio, expulsion; *Italian*: divieto di ingresso nel territorio, allontanamento.

strict or consistent connection with national terminology either.[5] What is 'expulsion' and what is 'exclusion'?

It emerges from dictionary-meaning and the way the concept is used in the Directive, that an 'expulsion decision' is an administrative decision, ordering departure from the Member State. An expulsion decision is thus made before actual 'removal' as meant in Article 31(2) may take place. I will assume that an 'exclusion order' is a decision to prohibit entry, and that the term is applicable regardless of whether the person addressed is located in or outside the territory of the Member State when the order is issued. In the UK, exclusion is a measure used to prevent entry,[6] in same vein as the French 'interdiction du territoire' and the German 'Aufenthaltsverbot'.

Accordingly, an expulsion decision – containing an obligation to leave - may or may not be accompanied by an exclusion order – prohibiting entry after departure. See Article 31(4) of the Directive. Article 15 of the Directive implies that the host Member State may only impose a prohibition of entry in the context of an expulsion decision on grounds of public policy, public security or public health. Thus an 'expulsion decision' under the Citizens' Directive may mean more or less the same as a 'return decision' under the Returns Directive, and 'exclusion order' may mean more or less the same as 'entry ban'. In the *Petrea* judgment, the Court of Justice seems to consider exclusion as a specific item of expulsion:

> '[The provisions of Article 27 and 28] which cover all expulsion decisions, apply therefore in particular to exclusion decisions which are expressly referred to by Article 32 of Directive 2004/38.'[7]

My primary interest is the exclusion order. In the following part I will make a comparison between exclusion order (Citizens' Directive) and entry ban (Returns Directive).

Exclusion Order and Entry Ban: Differences and Overlaps

There are quite some differences and also some overlaps between the Citizens' Directive and Returns Directive, making a comparison into a complicated exercise:

a. An entry ban prohibits entry to the whole area of the EU-Member States (Article 3(6) Returns Directive) and that of the participating states[8], whereas an exclusion order can only prohibit entry into the Member State which issued the measure.
b. An entry ban always concerns a third country national, but an exclusion order may affect both EU citizens and their third country national family members.

5 Under UK immigration control practice, the term 'deportation' (more or less comparable with expulsion') is used when the person is still on the territory, and 'exclusion' is used when the person is already abroad. In Dutch immigration law language, it would have made sense to use 'uitzetting' and 'ongewenstverklaring' instead of one single term 'verwijdering'.
6 'Exclusion from the UK, version 2.0., Published for Home Office staff on 11 September 2018.
7 CJEU, Case C-184/16 *Petrea* [2017] para. 41.
8 Norway, Iceland, Switzerland, Liechtenstein.

c. Both an entry ban and a measure of exclusion may be accompanied by an alert in the Schengen Information System (SIS) – but only in so far as third country nationals are concerned.[9]
d. Third country nationals may be confronted with both measures, with an entry ban if and as long as the Returns Directive is applicable, but also with exclusion, namely when they are family member of an EU citizen.
e. While an exclusion order may only be issued for reasons of public policy or public security (Articles 15(3), 32 Citizens' Directive), an entry ban may (and even must) also be issued for administrative reasons, that is, when no period for voluntary departure has been granted, or if the obligation to return has not been complied with (Article 11(1) Returns Directive).
f. The duration of an entry ban must be limited, but it may exceed five years to an unspecified length of time if the third-country national represents a serious threat to public policy, public security or national security (Article 11(2)) Returns Directive). An entry ban expires automatically after lapse of time, without any need for an application to that effect.[10] The duration of an entry ban is counted from the day of departure from the territory of the EU.[11] An exclusion order is not bound to a limited period of validity and does therefore not end automatically after a certain period of time but it must be revised in any event after three years counting from the enforcement of the final exclusion order (Article 32 Citizens' Directive). In the case of the *Petrea* judgment, to be discussed in more detail below, an exclusion order was issued for a period of seven years. Under Dutch immigration law, an exclusion order may be issued for an unlimited period of time.[12]

Differences and Overlaps: Interim Conclusion

Thus, while an exclusion order is less far-reaching than an entry ban, as it only can prohibit entry into the host Member State which issued the exclusion order, and is only allowed for reasons of public policy, public security or national security, it may be issued for an unlimited period and does not end automatically by lapse of time. The mere fact that a right to revision of an exclusion is guaranteed after at least three years under Article 32(1) does not prejudge a favourable outcome of that procedure. During the validity of the exclusion order, there is no right of entry or stay into the host Member State. In the *Petrea* judgment, the Court of Justice had to deal with the case of an excluded EU citizen re-entering the host Member State without having tried to lift the exclusion order. He claimed that the competent authorities had to verify again whether the conditions set out in Articles 27 and 28 of Directive 2004/38 had been satisfied, in particular whether his conduct was still a genuine, present and sufficiently serious threat affecting one of the fundamental interests of society. The Court found this not necessary, as it follows from the very nature of an exclusion order that it remains in force as long as it has not been lifted. The mere finding that it has been infringed allows those

9 It is unclear how dual nationals, having both the nationality of an EU Member State and a third country are treated in the SIS.

10 CJEU, Case C-297/12, *Filev and Osmani* [2013] para 34.

11 CJEU, Case C-225/16, *Ouhrami* [2017] para 58.

12 Articles 67, 68 Vreemdelingenwet.

authorities to adopt a new removal decision against the person concerned. The Court also referred to Article 32(2) Citizens' Directive, categorically stating that the person affected has no right to entry while the application for revising the exclusion order is being considered.

Residence Right and Exclusion Order

In the Citizens' Directive, as interpreted in the *Petrea* judgment, the host Member State is apparently given extensive opportunity to bar access to its territory for an unspecified and even indefinite period of time once it has lawfully been assessed, at the moment of issuing the exclusion order, that the conduct of the person concerned is a genuine, present and sufficiently serious threat affecting one of the fundamental interests of society. For the Union citizen involved, the fundamental right to enter and to stay is annihilated during the whole period of validity of the exclusion order.

However, in the *K.A. and others* judgment the Court seems to adopt a different approach.[13] That judgment dealt with situations potentially covered by the *Chavez Vilchez* judgment,[14] in which third country national family members asked for family reunification with a (minor) EU citizen who never exerted the right to free movement. Though the Returns Directive – like the Citizens' Directive - allows for refusing to examine an application for residence of a third country national solely on the ground that that third-country national is the subject of a ban on entering the territory of that Member State, such a practice is not compatible with Article 20 TFEU. Under that Treaty provision, a practice of a Member State that consists in not examining such an application solely on the ground stated above, without any examination of whether there exists a relationship of dependency between that Union citizen and that third-country national of such a nature that, in the event of a refusal to grant a derived right of residence to the third-country national, the Union citizen would, in practice, be compelled to leave the territory of the European Union as a whole and thereby be deprived of the genuine enjoyment of the substance of the rights conferred by that status, is precluded.

What does that mean? Can Article 20 TFEU in a similar manner break the power of an exclusion order, even where the Citizens' Directive does not provide any leeway? Is it arguable that the *Petrea* judgment does not apply in any situation where it can be established that the Union citizen concerned would be compelled to leave the territory of the European Union as a whole? I would be inclined to answer this question in the affirmative, and not only for Union citizens of minor age, as the rights of Article 20 TFEU are given regardless of age. However it is not very likely that such a situation will arise. As the exclusion order only regards entry to the issuing Member State, the right of an EU citizen to enter other Member States – including the own Member State – remains unaffected.

But the *K.A. and others* judgment is still not exhaustively dealt with. In the third answer, the Court qualifies its first answer according to which the Returns Directive allows for refusing to examine an application for residence of a third country national

---

13 CJEU, Case C-82/16, *K.A. and others* [2018], answers 1, 2 (first [paragraph) and 3..

14 CJEU, Case C-133/15, *Chavez-Vilchez* [2017].

solely based on the existence of an entry ban. This is owed to Article 5 of the Returns Directive, which obligates Member States implementing the Directive to take due account of the best interests of the child, family life, the state of health of the third-country national concerned, and to respect the principle of non-refoulement. Under this Article it is precluded, according to the Court, to refuse dealing with a request for a residence permit of a third country national, who has previously been the subject of a return decision, accompanied by an entry ban that remains in force, without any account being taken of the details of his or her family life, and in particular the interests of a minor child of that third-country national, referred to in an application for residence for the purposes of family reunification submitted after the adoption of such an entry ban, unless such details could have been provided earlier by the person concerned.

Here again, I would be inclined to transpose this line of thought to the *Petrea* situation. The Citizens' Directive does not contain a comparable species of Article 5 Returns Directive, obligating the Member States to take due account of some expressly mentioned core humans rights. But one can hardly misunderstand the impact of recitals 5, 6, 8, 11, 20, 23, 25 and 31 of the Citizens' Directive for the obligations of Member States to maintain the unity of the family (5, 6, 8), to secure the fundamental right to free movement under the Treaty (11), to secure the right to equal treatment as the own citizens (20), to secure the principle of proportionality (23) to secure the right to a high level of legal protection (25) and to respect fundamental rights and freedoms (31). On the basis of those recitals, I would argue that a practice of consistently refusing to investigate whether an EU citizen or a family member has a right to enter and to stay in a Member State under Article 20 TFEU and the Citizens' Directive, on the sole ground that an exclusion order is still in force, is precluded if the applicant refers to new circumstances, relevant and fundamental under the Treaty and the Citizens' Directive, that could not have been provided before the issuing of the exclusion order.

Speculative as these considerations are, they do not lend themselves easily for further elaboration. So, I leave Elspeth with these unfinished thoughts on *Petrea* and *K.A.*, hoping that she will be able to do something useful with them.

Position of Third Country National Family Members

But, before concluding these reflections I would like to pay some attention to the position of family members of Union citizens who have a third country nationality. Here, I have only questions, and no answers however provisory. Above, I already noted that family members of a Union citizen may have been subject to the Returns Directive before they became a family member of a migrating Union citizen, or will again be subject to the Returns Directive once their family relationship with the Union citizen expires. What happens with a pre-existing entry ban when a third country national marries an EU citizen? Can it still remain in force, or should it be terminated? If so, is that the case before – or only after – the Union citizen uses the right to free movement? And conversely, what happens with an exclusion order of a family member when the relationship terminates, for instance by divorce or by reaching the age of adulthood or when the Union citizen loses this privileged status by some Brexit-like event? Should an exclusion order then be automatically transposed into an entry ban – with the much wider scope of prohibiting entry to the whole EU - because the applicability of the Returns Directive is no longer excluded under Article 2(3)? And what should happen with any alert with regard to these persons in the Schengen Information System (SIS)?

We do not know much about how the Court of Justice would deal with such questions. I guess that almost nobody has thought about them yet. There is still enough to do.

Extending Human Franchise
Citizenship, Migration and Human Rights

Claude Cahn[*]

Introduction

In a work from 2006, the ethicist Martha C. Nussbaum explores in detail the 'frontiers of justice' examining where our legal and social arrangements are under stress from the inherent contradictions between universality and the particular. These she locates at our arrangements concerning disability, nationality and species membership: 'Today there are three unsolved problems of social justice whose neglect in existing theories seems particularly problematic.' First, there is 'the problem of doing justice to people with physical and mental impairments.' These have 'not as yet been included, in existing societies, as citizens on the basis of equality with other citizens.' Second is 'extending justice to all world citizens, showing theoretically how we might realize a world that is just as whole, in which accidents of birth and national origin do not warp people's life chances pervasively and from the start.' Finally, we need to re-examine questions of justice in our treatment of nonhuman animals. Nussbaum argues that, for all three of these areas, classical social contract theory cannot resolve the inherent tensions.[1]

This essay in honour of Elspeth Guild examines one strand in her work, namely her efforts to explore law in the areas of migration and citizenship in the post-1989 European and global contexts. Elspeth's contribution to discussions of citizenship – and in particular her signature linkage of citizenship with questions of migration – is noted and described. The essay observes a developing willingness on Elspeth's part to push the boundaries into traditionally non-legal areas, such as examining 'identity'. It links Elspeth's work with wider developments in the field of ethics, in her identification of elements of law supporting those often apparently excluded from the legal, political or social order. It notes that Elspeth is original in this regard in her approach to law on the continent, and in particular European Constitutionality. It also notes a development in Elspeth's approach – moving in effect over time from the narrow and legal to the more expansive – paralleling developments as Europe moved from unsettled to settled as concerns free movement internally; as to ever-more-exclusionary vis-à-vis 3rd country nationals, even as the external borders have revealed themselves to be ever more porous in practice.

---

* PhD Radboud University Nijmegen (2014), www.claudecahn.net.

1 M.C. Nussbaum, *Frontiers of Justice: Disability, Nationality, Species Membership*, Cambridge: Harvard University Press 2006.

Background

I cannot entirely remember how I first came into contact with Elspeth Guild, but I believe it has something to do with a pamphlet published regularly by the Immigration Law Practitioners Association (ILPA), providing updates on EU law developments on Xerox paper, printed in incredibly small font. We had ordered the updates, for some reason, at the European Roma Rights Centre, and they were passed to me, for some reason. The year is circa 1997.

I was working on human rights issues facing Roma. This was before the major judgments of the European Court of Human Rights on Roma issues; before accession put Roma inclusion at the top of the European human rights agenda; before the Central and Eastern European accession waves; before Central and Eastern Europeans took their full place at the table of Europe. In European human rights law terms, it was also before the dam burst on the Court's jurisprudence in the 2000s – human rights was still a narrow thing, cramped and somewhat petty law.

In EU law terms, the time was post-Maastricht. What did EU citizenship mean? It was also pre-Haider, pre-Amsterdam; questions of federalism, the extent of the supranational, the balance between Union and subsidiarity were in an open, expansive, questioning phase. The term 'Fortress Europe' was a new one.

Roma had gone all over Europe. Some had been expelled from the former Yugoslavia during the conflict or had fled in advance. Ethnically cleansed, they were unable to return home viably: in the new mono-ethnic states of the dissolved Communist federations, they were welcome back nowhere. Others had abandoned gripping poverty and racist exclusion unimaginable to most western Europeans, in places such as eastern Slovakia and rural Romania, and fled west. In the open new Europe, it was unclear what law applied to a general consideration of response to their situation.

My baptism into the dilemmas of EU law came via those ILPA pamphlets. They were written in a language – competence, subsidiarity, directives, regulations, direct effect – that step-by-step brought into view the questions of a Europe struggling to find its federalist voice, and around which my now over two-decade relationship with Elspeth has taken shape. Looking back, now visible is a repeated visitation of a series of themes probed from diverse angles, which indeed form some of the most pressing questions in the areas of inclusion and just legal orders in the development of the Europe and the international system.

The Borders of Legal Orders

Although I must have actually met Elspeth at Council of Europe meetings, our first work together in depth was on a short paper on the European Court of Human Rights case *Čonka and Others v. Belgium*. *Čonka* concerned a group of Slovak Roma expelled on a plane to Slovakia by the city of Ghent, while they still had open asylum proceedings in Belgium. In order to convince the Roma concerned into coming to the police station, the authorities sent out misleading communications to the effect that they were required to come and complete further documents for their asylum requests. Belgian authorities disregarded an emergency request by the European Court to postpone the expulsion while it reviewed the case. Belgian police penned numbers on the arms of persons being expelled, a chilling and callous reminder of recent European events, particularly given the people at issue. In finding that Belgium had collectively expelled the Roma concerned in contravention of Article 4 of Protocol 4 of the Convention, the European Court arrived at its first ever finding of a violation of that provision, and it also set what has remained among its most advanced evidentiary standards for assessing the possibility of discrimination-related harms.[2]

Elspeth focussed both on other aspects of the judgment from those immediately apparent, as well as linking the ruling to other -- at first face unrelated -- jurisprudential developments. First of all, Elspeth honed in primarily on the Article 5 liberty and security of person aspect of the judgment as the more important. Within this, it is an advancement of the requirement of *bona fides* vis-à-vis foreigners which captivates her:

> The Čonka family were foreigners in Belgium. They were illegally present in Belgium. The Belgian authorities sought to detain them for the purpose of expelling them to their country of origin. However, in so doing, the Court has found that the state owes them a duty of good faith. ... Through the general principles of the Convention, the Court now finds that illegally present aliens are entitled to reliability in communications with the state. State actors are not entitled to treat them as criminals, nor are they entitled to use deception to facilitate their detention and expulsion. Respect for the individual is central, irrespective of national rules on legal/illegal presence. The right of the state to define who is lawfully present and who is unlawfully on the territory does not change the nature of the duty of good faith of the state authorities with the individual. ... Arbitrary action is no longer permitted against them on the grounds of their legal invisibility.[3]

Secondly, Elspeth links the advances of the Court's judgment in *Čonka* with the Court's (in)admissibility decision in the case of *Banković et al.*, which concerned possible culpability by 17 NATO Member States for damage caused during the 1999 bombing from the air of Serbia and Montenegro. The Court ruled the case inadmissible for reasons in particular linked to a lack of territorial control by the NATO States at the time of the military action.[4] Elspeth however holds that 'there is a much more important finding of the Court which leads towards the future of extra territorial application of the Convention. ... In the *Banković* admissibility decision, it took the opportunity to clarify where a state does engage responsibilities in its activities outside its territory. These are *inter alia* when the member State 'exercises all or some of the public powers normally exercised by that Government.' As such, 'The borders of European human rights are now under construction. ... The duty to protection and the jurisdiction to pursue violations follows control of territory. When peace-making turns into peace enforcement, the forces of European states begin to exercise public powers normally within the res-

2 '... the Court considers that the procedure followed did not enable it to eliminate all doubt that the expulsion might have been collective' (see European Court of Human Rights, Case of *Čonka and Others v. Belgium* (Application no. 51564/99), judgment of 5 February 2002, para. 61).

3 E. Guild, 'The Borders of Legal Orders: Challenging Exclusion of Foreigners', *Roma Rights Journal: Fortress Europe*, July 2002, http://www.errc.org/roma-rights-journal/the-borders-of-legal-orders-challenging-exclusion-of-foreigners.

4 European Court of Human Rights, *Decision as to the admissibility of Application no. 52207/99 of 12 December 2001 (Grand Chamber) in the case Banković and Others v. Belgium and 16 Other Contracting States.*

ponsibility of a government.' Indeed, this view presaged a wave of findings of culpability by states in the context of extra-territorial control, a wave which has not yet, as of writing completely broken.

In linking the two cases – *Čonka* and *Banković* -- Elspeth concludes that, 'the central theme of this article is the transformation of legal borders of human rights in the European context':

> My thesis is that there is an important change taking place as regards the borders of rights within Member States. As a result of *Čonka*, states are under increasing duties of good faith in respect of persons who have been classified as illegal and indeed criminals as a result of their failure to leave a state. The state's duty towards these persons extends beyond respect for their physical person but also includes reliability in communication. Thus the borders relating to who can be excluded from the duty of good faith have been transformed. At the same time, the physical borders of the jurisdiction of the Convention are also being revised. Member States may now be taking the borders of jurisdiction with them when they engage in peace enforcement operations abroad. While peace-making actions may still be beyond the scope of the Convention, once the transition has taken place between military and police, even those with military status, the European human rights duties become effective.[5]

This period saw Elspeth's wider written production in the field of European immigration law at its richest. Her academic publications on the subject are comprehensive digests of the state of EU rules on the movement of persons inside the European Union, as well as across its frontiers.[6] Nevertheless, in her work on *Čonka* and *Banković*, in effect, Elspeth gave voice in European legal terms to preoccupations in ethics which would only subsequently take shape and burst the surface, namely: how do we draw lines of solidarity and culpability? What legal distinctions do we make in the fraught question of us and them? And are these distinctions not in fact fluid, unstable, questionable, inherently suspect?

Citizens and Outsiders

Elspeth's preoccupations with the borders of legal orders either led her to – or sprang from – a deeper meditation on the nature of citizenship, nationality and, ultimately, identity. As summarized by Habermas in 1990, the context – in effect still our context now -- was '[t]hree historical movements of our contemporary period, once again in flux', that 'affect the relation between citizenship and national identity'. Habermas lists these as: the liberation of the East Central European States from Soviet tutelage; the fact that states of the European Community were, at that time 'gradually growing together, especially with the caesura that will be created when a common market is introduced in 1993', as well as the problem that 'democratic processes constituted at the level of the nation-state lag hopelessly behind the economic integration taking place at a supranational level'; and 'immigration from the poor

---

5 Guild 2002.

6 See for example E. Guild, *Immigration Law in the European Community*, The Hague: Kluwer Law International 2001.

regions of the East and South, with which Europe will be increasingly confronted in the coming years'. According to Habermas, 'This process exacerbates the conflict between the universalistic principles of constitutional democracy, on the one hand, and the particularistic claims to preserve the integrity of established forms of life, on the other.'[7]

The 1990s grappled with these dilemmas, and we are grappling with them still. At the time though, the implications of the European citizenship introduced to EU treaty law via the 1993 Treaty of Maastricht were as yet unsettled, while the remarkable advances of the international and European human rights systems were only beginning fully to unfold. The ground was thus ripe for reflections as to the meaning of belonging in an expanding and deepening Europe.

In a memorable 1996 phrase, Elspeth called citizenship and nationality the inward and outward facing aspects of the Janus face.[8] By 2004, this had evolved into book length exploration of 'the legal elements of the European identity'. *The Legal Elements of European Identity: EU Citizenship and Migration Law* is at once a wide-ranging and systematic meditation on what was at that time an as yet unsorted but emerging construction of EU citizenship and identity in EU law, a treatise at the time extending into several other aspects, including the divorce of citizenship and rights taking place in the law of the European Convention on Human Rights, as well as Europe's strained relationship with the ban on racial discrimination – and in particular the pre-1999 compelling imprint of Europe as an exclusively white and Christian polity on EU law.[9] Most extensively, the question of the possibility for non-citizens to join a polity and become fully endowed with rights is explored, on the basis of a contention that the 'three fundamental interests' of immigrants are conditions of entry in the host country and protection from expulsion; access to employment and conditions of employment; and family reunification.[10]

The post-World War II human rights revolution has at least partly cleaved rights from citizenship. These developments were elevated by the entry into force in 1976 of the International Covenants of Civil and Political Rights (ICCPR) and Economic, Social and Cultural Rights (ICESCR), changes to the substrata of international law which played out in particular following the end of the Cold War, and which established the person as a subject of international law. In Europe, the strength and vigour of the jurisprudence of the European Court of Human Rights continued to advance throughout the 1990s and into the new millennium. As a result, the system of human rights protection in Europe partially 'escapes national control'.[11]

Elspeth's signature in this discussion is among other things to situate the question of European citizenship firmly within the question of movement across borders. On

7 J. Habermas, 'Citizenship and National Identity' (1990). Reprinted in: J. Habermas, *Between Facts and Norms: Contributions to a Discourse Theory of Law and Democracy*, Cambridge, Mass.: MIT Press 1996, p. 491-492.

8 E. Guild, 'The Legal Framework of Citizenship in the European Union', in: D. Cesarani & M. Fulbrook, *Citizenship, Nationality and Migration in Europe*, Boca Raton: CRC Press 1996, p. 30-57.

9 E. Guild, *The Legal Elements of European Identity: EU Citizenship and Migration Law*, The Hague: Kluwer Law International 2004, pp.69-81.

10 *Ibid.*, p.83.

11 *Ibid.*, p.130.

the one hand, in a prolonged engagement with the government of the United Kingdom, the previously-existing European Commission on Human Rights had ruled, in the matter of *East African Asians*, that Britain's barring of UK citizens of Asian origin from immigrating to the UK from now-independent post-colonial states such as Kenya, Uganda and Tanzania constituted degrading treatment in the sense of European Convention on Human Rights Article 3. Closing the circle in the other direction, in a 1996 judgment concerning Maghrebi nationals married to citizens of a Council of Europe Member State, the European Court of Human Rights ruled in 1996 that the Article 8 right to private and family life would potentially not be infringed by expulsion from the territory of a married non-national, if the family concerned were able to live as a family somewhere else, i.e. outside Europe.[12]

Elspeth's reflections are perhaps most clearly expressed in her introduction: 'As regards identity, the fullest legal expression of inclusion is nationality; of exclusion it is expulsion with a prohibition on return. In between there is a spectrum of legal elements such as security of residence, the right to engage in economic activities, the right to equal treatment, etc. against which identity as a legal expression can be gauged. These elements are increasingly determined or circumscribed by supranational legislation. In this way, the arbiter of identity through rights is changing.'[13] Being born are 'identity rights for foreigners through human rights in Europe'.[14] It would be more than a decade before the Court itself caught up.[15]

The direct linkage of questions of migration with nationality and citizenship is by no means self-evident or given in the wider discussion of citizenship. Major strands of social science literature examining citizenship make limited if any reference to migration or migrants, instead focussing on matters wholly internal to the legal, political and social order.[16] This is similarly the case in literature on constitutionalism in diversity contexts.[17] In a field determined by the post-Maastricht establishment of European citizenship in a manner defined in direct connection with questions of free movement, as well as with the pooling of sovereignty to secure the external border, Elspeth offers the most propitious legal script possible, in a fraught and increasingly security-dominated discussion.

---

12 *Ibid.*, p.83.

13 *Ibid.*, p.15.

14 *Ibid.*, p.146.

15 European Court of Human Rights, Case of *Biao v. Denmark* (Application no. 38590/10), judgment, 24 May 2016, the first judgment of the Court finding a finding of racial discrimination in the allocation of citizenship.

16 See for example W. Kymlicka, *Multicultural Citizenship: A Liberal Theory of Minority Rights*, Oxford: Clarendon Press 1996. See also A. Shachar, 'Privatizing Diversity: A Cautionary Tale from Religious Arbitration in Family Law', 9(2) *Theoretical Inquiries in Law* 2008, Article 11: 'In discussions about citizenship, we repeatedly come across the modernist schema of privatizing identities: we are expected to act as undifferentiated citizens in the public sphere, but remain free to express our distinct cultural or religious identities in the private domain of family and communal life. Yet multiple tensions have exposed cracks in this privatizing identities formula: for instance, where precisely does the 'private' end and the 'public' begin? What happens when cultural and religious customs extend beyond the home into the spaces of our shared citizenship, such as the school, the workplace, or the voting booth?'

17 See for example J. Tully, *Strange Multiplicity: Constitutionalism in an Age of Diversity*, Cambridge: Cambridge University Press 1994.

Going Global: The Human Rights of Migrants

Many of the core issues as to the delineation of the scope of States in Europe to act on their sovereign decision in the case of non-nationals on the territory appear to have been answered by the European Court in the period up to the early 2000s. The European Union's most recent major answer to the rights of non-citizens is arguably the 2003 Directive providing requirements of equal(ish) treatment for non-EU citizens who are long-term residents. At present, most pronounced are the conditions and possibilities for European states to expel non-citizens, discussions playing out in international legal arenas, for example via recent European Court judgments on the collective expulsion of aliens; at European Union level, in efforts to revise migrant related Directive law; as well as nationally and in communities, as solidarity with foreigners vies with xenophobic populism in an increasingly acrimonious, real and symbolic struggle over the bodies of foreigners.

The large arrival of people from outside Europe in 2015 in particular urged upon the international order the need for a global response. As a result, the recent period has seen work on two Global Compacts – one concerning refugees and the other concerning migrants. Elspeth has been among a group of minds working to articulate, into this discussion, the content and scope of the human rights of migrants. The starting point for this engagement is: 'Migrants have human rights: this is a legal fact in international, regional and national law around the world. As human beings, migrants are entitled to the protection and guarantee of human rights by all States within whose jurisdiction they may find themselves.'[18] The resulting work elaborated the content of human rights law as concerns recognition before the law; rights at the border; immigration detention; irregular status; residence, termination of residence and removal; the economic, social and cultural rights of migrants; rights at work; family life; freedom of thought, belief, religion, expression and opinion; and the right to effective remedy.[19] Of note is the increasing reliance on human rights law, and – in the context of growing securitisation in Europe – a stronger, or perhaps more confident, assertion of the rights of the persons concerned than expressed in the work on *Čonka.*

Conclusion: Law and the Other: Extending the Franchise

In the course of more than two decades of discussions with Elspeth, there are a number of memorable items off the margins of the written work. These include an expressed fascination with the fact that, during one of those moments in which the UNCHR narrowed approaches to the rights of refugees to ensuring fair procedure in refugee determination, a Jesuit initiative sprang up to assist persons in fleeing Africa across the Mediterranean to Europe. In another vein, Elspeth became engaged with the liberation potential in EU free movement law, as a resident of the Banlieu might escape his social context in France by going to the UK and becoming a French chef. Looking back at

18 E. Guild, S. Grant & C.A. Groenendijk (eds), *Human Rights of Migrants in the 21st Century*, New York: Routledge, 2018, p.3.

19 *Ibid.*, p. vii-viii.

Elspeth's decades of work, one might conceive many aspects of it as bringing the challenges identified by Nussbaum in social contract theory into the terrain of law, a probing of the legal expression of those aspects which might be best used in the service of the liberation of those at the frontiers of justice.

This essay has examined only one aspect of Elspeth's rich range of work. Not explored here is the body of work on privacy, surveillance, and counter-terrorism, to name only several. In the course of this, I have to some extent cheated her rich contributions to international relations and the question of sovereignty in particular. I have chosen to look at the equality, migration and citizenship line in Elspeth's work, both because it is that with which I have been most closely in contact, but also for reasons which drew me to her work in the first place, namely that it seems to me that she has consistently striven to identify the legal expression of matters which otherwise play out in other domains: ethics, contract theory, and perhaps even theology. Said differently, Elspeth has displayed a consistent willingness to explore questions of society and polity in law, in a manner far advanced from standard legal practice, particularly in civil law jurisdictions, even as she has honed to the harder ends of black leather law. This surely is at the heart of her remarkable intellectual contributions to central questions of our age.

60 Years of European Social Security Coordination
Achievements, Controversies and Challenges

*Rob Cornelissen**

1. Introduction: Aim and Legal Basis of the EU Regulations

This year we celebrate the 60th anniversary of European coordination of social security. It was one of the first domains in which the EU was active. Regulations 3[1] and 4[2] provided for the coordination of Member States' social security systems. They protected migrant workers and the members of their families. These regulations, entered into force on 1 January 1959. They were replaced in 1972 by Regulations 1408/71 and 574/72. In 2010 Regulations 1408/71 and 574/72 were replaced by the current Regulations 883/2004[3] and 987/2009.[4] These Regulations provide, in the field of social security, a high standard of protection to European citizens who move between Member States, be it for professional or private reasons.

The objective of the social security Regulations is by nature both modest and ambitious.

The Regulations have a modest objective since they only coordinate the various social security systems, they do not harmonise them. They do not affect the freedom of Member States to determine their own systems. Member States are, in principle, free to decide who is to be insured, what benefits should be granted, how they should be calculated and for how long they should be granted.[5] The EU Regulations on the coordination of social security systems do not and cannot affect the disparities between the various systems. As the Court has underlined in its case-law, the Treaties offer no guarantee to a worker that extending his activities into more than one Member State or transferring them to another Member State will be neutral as regards social security. Given the disparities in the social security legislation of the Member States, such an extension or transfer may be to the worker's advantage in terms of social security or not, according to the circumstances.[6]

But the EU Regulations are ambitious at the same time. In fact, they have as their objective to make the right to free movement a reality by ensuring that a person is not penalised in the field of social security for having moved from one Member State to

---

* Visiting professor KU Leuven, Belgium

1 Council Regulation (EEC) 3 of 25 September 1958, O.J. 30 of 16 December 1958.

2 Council Regulation (EEC) 4 of 3 December 1958, O.J. 30 of 16 December 1958.

3 Regulation (EC) No 883/2004, O.J. L 200 of 7 June 2004, lastly modified by Regulation (EU) No 465/2012, O.J. L 149 of 8 June 2012.

4 Regulation(EC) No 987/2009, O.J. L 284 of 30 October 2009, lastly modified by Regulation (EU) No 465/2012.

5 Case C-347/10 *Salemink*, EU:C:2012:17, para. 38.

6 Case C-3/08. *Leyman,* EU:C:2009:595.

another. Social security coordination is indeed an indispensable element of free movement.

Depending on the different social and political history of each state, Member States limit the boundaries of their solidarity systems, sometimes on the basis of nationality, but mostly on the basis of territoriality.[7] In a general way this means that each state confines the scope of its national scheme by using territorial elements like working or residing in that State. The objective of the EU Regulations is to overrule the application of these criteria based on nationality and territoriality. Without such an ambition, the goal of the EU Regulations to remove all barriers in the sphere of social security, which impede a genuinely free movement, would not be met.

From day one, the Treaty included a strong legal basis for legislation in the field of coordination of social security. This legal basis is now contained in Art. 48 TFEU.

The abundant case law of the Court of Justice played an essential role in the development of the early coordination system set up under Regulation 3 into the system under Council Regulation 1408/71 and then into today's modernised Regulation 883/2004. Already in its very first judgment[8] concerning the old Regulation 3 the Court of Justice clarified that all provisions laid down in the Regulations on social security should be interpreted in the light of the objective pursued by their legal basis which aims to facilitate freedom of movement.

2. Achievements

2.1. The Pillars of European Social Security Coordination

In order to prevent different national criteria leading to conflicts of law in cross-border situations (negative conflict: a person would not be insured in any Member State; positive conflict: the person would be insured simultaneously in two or more Member States) Regulation 883/2004 contains uniform criteria to determine the applicable social security legislation. The main rule is that a person is subject to the legislation where he/she works,[9] even if his/her residence is in another Member State. However, for some categories of workers, namely posted workers[10] and workers who normally are employed in two or more Member States,[11] special rules have been created. As the Court has emphasised[12] the EU rules determining the applicable social security legislation have a binding effect. It means that national affiliation conditions (such as a residence condition) are set aside if their application is such as to deprive the conflict of law rule laid down in the Regulation of all practical effect. On the other hand the EU rules determining the applicable social security legislation have an exclusive effect:[13] a

7 R. Cornelissen, 'The principle of territoriality and the Community Regulations on social security (Regulations 1408/71 and 574/72)', 33(3) *Common Market Law Review* 1996, p. 439-471.

8 Case 75/63 *Unger,* EU:C:1964:19.

9 Article 11(3)(a) Regulation 883/2004.

10 Article 12.

11 Article 13.

12 Cases C-2/89, *Kits van Heyningen*, EU:C:1990:183, C-196/90, *De Paep*, EU:C:1991:381, C-347/10, *Salemink*, EU:C:2012:17 and C-106/11, *Bakker*, EU:C:2012:328.

13 Article 11(1).

person cannot be simultaneously be subject to the legislation of two or more Member States. However, it follows from the case-law of the Court that in some cases it is possible that a worker is also covered by the social security legislation of a Member State other than the one designated as the competent one by the Regulation.[14]

The principle of equality of treatment is one of the cornerstones of the Union. With regard to social security the right to equal treatment has found specific expression in Article 4 of Regulation 883/2004. The Court has given a broad interpretation to this principle, prohibiting not only overt discrimination based on nationality but also covert forms of discrimination which, by applying other distinguishing criteria, in fact achieve the same result.[15] It also follows from the Court's case-law under the old Regulation 1408/71 that the principle of equal treatment may require the social security institution of a Member State, when examining whether all the qualifying conditions for a benefit are fulfilled, to treat facts and events which occur in another Member State as if they were facts or events occurring in its own State.[16] This case-law is now reflected in Article 5 of Regulation 883/2004.

The aggregation of the periods of insurance completed in all Member States[17] for entitlement to benefits is a technique to put together the career of a migrant worker. In this way the Regulation guarantees that social security rights in the process of being acquired are retained. Given this purpose the aggregation provisions must be interpreted widely and cover also cases not directly governed by the letter of these provisions.[18]

The waiving of residence clauses for most cash benefits[19] reflects the principle of maintenance of acquired rights.

The rather technical and often complex coordination provisions are to be implemented by the authorities and institutions of Member States. This is possible only if there is a smooth and effective cooperation and communication between the authorities and competent institutions of the various Member States. Several provisions of the EU Regulations lay down the principles for such cooperation and communication.[20] The raison-d'être of the Administrative Commission for the coordination of social security systems[21] is to facilitate and strengthen such cooperation. The principle of good administration is reflected by the obligation for institutions to provide information to citizens in enforcing their rights and obligations and to offer them active assistance in enforcing their rights under these Regulations.[22] The electronic exchange of data between institutions (EESSI) constitutes one of the major innovations of Regulation

14 Cases C-352/06, *Bosmann*, EU:C:2008:290, C-208/07, *Von Chamier*, EU:C:2009:455, joined cases C-611/10 and 612/10, *Hudzinski*, EU:C:2012:339 and C-382/13, *Franzen*, EU:C:2015:261.

15 Cases 41/84, *Pinna*, EU:C:1986:1 and C-349/87, *Paraschi*, EU:C:1991:372.

16 Cases C-228/88, *Bronzino*, EU:C:1990:85, C-12/89, *Gatto*, EU:C:1990:89 and C-349/87, *Paraschi*, EU:C:1991:372.

17 Article 6 applies to all benefits covered by Regulation 883/2004. However, the unemployment chapter has its own specific aggregation provisions (Article 61), taking into account the specific features of the various unemployment schemes.

18 Cases C-481/93, *Moscato*, EU:C:1995:348 and C-482/93, *Klaus*, EU:C:1995:349.

19 Article 7 Regulation 883/2004. This article does not apply to '*special non-contributory benefits*'; it applies to unemployment benefits only in some specific cases.

20 Articles 76-79 Regulation 883/2004 and Articles 2-9 Regulation 987/2009.

21 Articles 71-74 Regulation 883/2004.

22 Article 76(4) Regulation 883/2004 and Article 2(1) Regulation 987/2009.

987/2009.[23] The shift from paper to electronic data exchange has required- and continues to require- intense preparatory work[24] leading to several extensions of the transitional period. This transitional period expired in June 2019[25] which means that the transmission of data between the social security institutions should now be carried out exclusively by electronic means.

2.2. Some Protection Goes Beyond Coordination

In some aspects Regulation 883/2004 provides protection which goes beyond a simple coordination, since rights are created which citizens would not otherwise have.

Article 64 facilitates geographical mobility of unemployed persons. It enables, under strict conditions and for a limited period of time, an unemployed person who receives an unemployment benefit in the competent Member State to go to another Member State in order to seek work there without losing entitlement to unemployment benefit.

Article 19 provides another example. A person who is insured for health care in one Member State and who stays temporarily in another Member State (e.g. during a city trip, family visit, holiday) is entitled to health care which becomes necessary in that other Member State as if he/she is insured in that other Member State. In order to benefit from this arrangement the person only has to show his/her European Health Insurance Card to the care provider. It is estimated that there are currently more than 218 million European Health Insurance Cards in circulation.

Article 20 enables a person who is insured for health care in one Member State to go to another Member State with the purpose to get medical treatment there, at the expense of the competent institution, provided he/she receives authorisation from that institution. If that authorisation is accorded he/she will benefit from reimbursement conditions which are far more favourable than those contained in the so-called Patients Mobility Directive.[26] As the Court has underlined in its case-law,[27] in this way Article 20 Regulation 883/2004 helps to facilitate the free movement of persons covered by social insurance and, to the same extent, the provision of cross-frontier medical services between Member States.

2.3. Virtually all European Citizens Protected

Regulation 883/2004 applies to all EU nationals who are insured under national law, whether they are employed, self-employed, students, civil servants, pensioners or indeed, non- active,[28] as well as to the members of their families and survivors, regardless the nationality of their family members or survivors. This constitutes a progress in

23 Article 4(2) Regulation 987/2009.

24 M. Fuchs & r. Cornelissen, *EU Social Security Law, a Commentary on EU Regulations 883/2004 and 987/2009,* Baden-Baden: C.H. Beck-Hart-Nomos 2015, p. 432-439.

25 However, it seems that some Member States are not yet ready to implement and integrate the necessary national infrastructure, necessitating a further extension of practical arrangements.

26 Directive 2011/24, O.J. L 88 of 4 April 2011.

27 Cases C-56/01, *Inizan*, EU:C:2003:578, para 21 and C-145/03, *Keller*, EU:C:2005:211, para 46.

28 Article 2 Regulation 883/2004.

comparison with the old Regulations which only covered economically active people and the members of their families. Regulation 883/2004 contributes to social inclusion. In fact, all EU citizens who are insured under national law are protected in the field of social security when they move from one Member State to another.

Stateless persons and refugees residing in a Member State have always been included in the personal scope of the EU social security Regulations.[29]

Members of the family and survivors cannot invoke provisions of the Regulations which are applicable solely to workers, such as the unemployment chapter.[30] But they can invoke all other provisions such as equal treatment[31] or the provisions laid down in the chapter 'family benefits'. Where an employed person is subject to the legislation of a Member State and lives with his family in another Member State, then that person's spouse is entitled, under Article 67 Regulation 883/2004, to receive a family benefit such as a parental benefit in the state of employment.[32]

2.4. Extension of Protection to Non-EU Nationals

The rules of the EU Regulations not only apply in the EU and to EU nationals but also in Norway, Iceland and Liechtenstein and to nationals of these countries, by virtue of the Agreement on the European Economic Area.[33] This agreement is a special one, since it comes close to membership, as the four fundamental freedoms are guaranteed without any notable exceptions. One of the EFTA countries , i.e. Switzerland, rejected the Agreement following a referendum. The EU and Switzerland have then concluded an agreement on free movement of persons, including full applicability of the EU social security Regulations.[34]

For a long time third-country national workers have been excluded from the protection offered by the EU social security Regulations. The explanation for this exclusion is to be found in the legal basis of the EU social security Regulations. Developments in primary law in the last two decades have paved the way for the extension of the EU Regulations to third-country nationals.[35] Regulation 1231/2010[36] now offers third-country nationals, in the field of social security, the same protection as EU citizens moving within the EU. However, this extension is subject to two conditions. In particular the condition that there should be a cross-border element between at least two Member States means that Regulation 1231/2010 does not always guarantee that third-country nationals legally residing in a Member State are treated equally as Union nationals in that Member State. Several categories of third-country nationals do have such an EU level guarantee, with some exceptions, although there is no cross-border element between Member States. This is the result either of a series of legal instruments

29 Joined cases C- 95/99 to C-98/99 and C-180/99, *Khalil*, EU:C:2001:532.

30 Case C-198/00, *Ruhr*, EU:C:2001:583.

31 Case C-308/93, *Cabanis-Issarte*, EU:C:1996:169.

32 Joined cases C-245/94, *Hoever* and C-312/94, *Zachow*, EU:C:1996:379

33 O.J. L 1 of 3 January 1994.

34 O.J. L 114 of 30 April 2002. Annex II concerns the coordination of social security schemes. It contains some special provisions for Switzerland.

35 R. Cornelissen: 'Regulation 1231/2010 on the inclusion of third-country nationals in EU social security coordination: reach, limits and challenges', 20(2) *EJSS* 2018, p. 86-99.

36 O.J. L 344 of 29 December 2010.

based on (the predecessor of) Article 79 TFEU,[37] or of the direct effect of provisions laid down in Association agreements concluded with the Maghreb countries[38] or in Decision 3/80 of the EEC/Turkey Association Council.[39] In addition, Decisions of several Association Councils are in the pipeline, guaranteeing, inter alia, equal treatment in the field of social security for workers who are nationals of the third countries concerned and who are legally employed in a Member State.

3. Controversies and Challenges

Over the years, the EU Regulations on the coordination of social security systems have been well received both by the persons covered and by the Member States. True, the Regulations are complicated, but hardly anybody would contest that they provide a high standard of protection in the field of social security for people moving across borders within the EU.

On the contrary, there have always been voices claiming that the protection offered by these Regulations, as interpreted by the ECJ, goes too far and that Member States with the highest level of social protection have to pay disproportionately favourable benefits to people covered by these Regulations. In 1988, for example, a social security professor in the Netherlands published her inaugural lecture, in which she suggested that the EU Regulations as interpreted by the ECJ constituted a threat to the residence-based social security schemes of the Netherlands.[40] Not only in the Netherlands, but also elsewhere in Europe the impression is sometimes given that the EU Regulations, as interpreted by the Court of Justice, could jeopardise the high level of protection given by the social security schemes of the 'old' Member States. Some of the issues which have been the subject of controversy over the last few years are the following:

3.1. Export of Family Benefits

According to Regulation 883/2004,[41] a person who works in one Member State and whose children reside in another Member State, is entitled to family benefits from the State of work, as if the children were residing in that State. Recently a number of 'old' Member States have requested a modification of the EU Regulations, so that that the Member State of work will be allowed to index such benefits to the standard of living

37 Directives 2003/109, O.J. L 16 of 23 January 2004, 2005/71, O.J. L 289 of 3 November 2005, 2009/50, O.J. L 155 of 18 June 2009, 2011/98, O.J. L 343 of 23 December 2011, 2014/36, OJ. L 94 of 28 March 2014 and 2014/66, O.J. L 157 of 27 May 2014.

38 Cases C-18/90, *Kziber*, EU:C:1991:36, C-58/93, *Yousfi,* EU:C:1994:160, -126/95, *Hallouzi,* EU:C:1996: 368 and C-113/97, *Babahenini,* EU:C:1998:13

39 Cases C-262/96, *Sürül,* EU:C:1999:228, C-373/02, *Öztürk,* EU:C:2004:95 and C-485/07, *Akdas*, EU:C:2011:346

40 W. Levelt-Overmars, *Halen de volksverzekeringen het jaar 2000*? (Will the Dutch residence based schemes still exist in the year 2000?), Deventer: Kluwer 1988. My critical review of her publication in *SMA (Sociaal Maandblad Arbeid)*, March 1989, triggered a rather polemic discussion between W. Levelt-. Overmars and myself, published in the May and October 1989 editions of *SMA* under the title: *Herziening van de Nederlandse volksverzekeringen in Europees perspectief.*

41 Article 67 Regulation 883/2004.

of the Member State where the children reside. The Member States concerned refer to the controversial deal that EU leaders offered to the UK[42] before the 2016 British referendum, as proof that such indexation is legally viable. The discussions on this issue are not silenced by the fact that the 2016 Commission proposal to modify Regulations 883/2004 and 987/2009[43] does not modify the existing rules on export of family benefits. This is illustrated by the fact that since 1 January 2019 Austria implements such indexation on the basis of national law.

3.2. Aggregation of Periods for Unemployment Benefits

According to Article 61 Regulation 883/2004, the application of the aggregation is subject to the condition that the person becoming unemployed has '*most recently*' completed periods of insurance or employment in the Member State where the claim for unemployment benefit is made. The philosophy behind this provision is clear: the state in which the unemployed person last worked or paid contributions should bear the burden of providing the unemployment benefit. Therefore, this condition is in line with Article 48 TFEU.[44] However, Article 61 does not specify how long the person must have '*most recently*' completed periods of insurance in the Member State where he/she became unemployed before being able to invoke the aggregation provisions. The result is a divergent implementation of Article 61 in the EU. Some Member States permit aggregation after only one day of insurance in the Member State concerned. Other Member States require a minimum period of 4 weeks (Finland) or even three months (Denmark and Belgium) before a right to aggregate past periods of insurance completed in another Member State arises. According to the 2016 Commission proposal to modify Regulations 883/2004 and 987/2009, Member States may require that someone has worked for at least three months on its territory before a person who becomes unemployed can rely on previous experience in another Member State to claim unemployment benefits. According to the March 2019 tripartite (Council, Parliament and Commission) compromise on this Commission proposal the required minimum period has been reduced to one month. Some Member States have expressed the view that this period is not long enough to ensure that the financial burden for paying unemployment benefits does not arise in situations where mobile EU workers have not yet made a significant contribution to the scheme of the host Member State.

3.3. Access to Minimum Existence Benefits for Inactive People

One of the parts of the EU Regulations that sparked most controversy over the last decade was the access to minimum subsistence benefits in the host state by economically non-active people coming from other Member States. In this context it is useful to recall that the current Regulation 883/2004 applies to all EU citizens who are insured under national law, whether they are economically active or not. For many people fears of benefit tourism are inextricably linked to the free movement of economically non-

42 Conclusions of the European Council of 18-19 February 2016 '*A New Settlement for the United Kingdom within the European Union*', O.J. CI 69 of 23 February 2016.

43 COM(2016) 815 final.

44 Case C-62/91, *Gray*, EU:C:1992:177.

active persons. The right of EU citizens to move and reside freely within the territory of the Member States is enshrined in Article 21 TFEU. Directive 2004/38[45] specifies the residence rights of EU citizens (and members of their family) who move within the EU and defines certain conditions and limitations. By virtue of Article 7(1) of this Directive the right of residence for more than three months for economically inactive persons is subject to the condition that they have sufficient resources for themselves and their family members so as not to become a burden on the social assistance system of the host Member State, as well as to the condition that they have comprehensive sickness insurance. These conditions regarding sufficient resources and comprehensive sickness insurance do not apply to workers and self-employed people.

The EU Regulations based on Article 48 TFEU apply only to legislation concerning social security (whether contributory or non-contributory). Social assistance has always been explicitly excluded from the material scope of the EU Regulations. However, a definition of the term '*social security*' or '*social assistance*' was (and is) not to be found in these Regulations. There are a number of non-contributory benefits- financed not by contributions but by taxes- which have the characteristics of social security and social assistance. It followed from the abundant case-law of the ECJ that a high number of benefits which were considered 'social assistance' by the Member State concerned actually fell within the material scope of the EU social security Regulations, with all its consequences, such as the waiving of residence clauses for entitlement to benefits. The reaction of the legislature to this case-law was to create[46] a separate coordination system for '*special non-contributory benefits'* in order to avoid their exportability. Under Article 70(4) Regulation 883/2004, the '*special non-contributory benefits'* listed in Annex X are provided exclusively in the Member State in which the persons concerned reside, in accordance with the legislation of that Member State.

A number of Member States have imposed on the entitlement to '*special non-contributory benefits*' listed in Annex X of Regulation 883/2004 for non-active people coming from another Member State the condition that they have a residence right there in accordance with Directive 2004/38. Since Directive 2004/38 and Regulation 883/2004, adopted on the same day, do not refer to each other, it became unavoidable that the ECJ had to pronounce itself on the relationship between the two legal instruments. In its famous *Brey* judgment[47] and subsequent case-law,[48] the ECJ clarified that the notion '*social assistance*' within the meaning of the Directive could comprise '*special non-contributory*' social security benefits within the meaning of Regulation 883/2004. There is nothing to prevent the entitlement to such benefits for Union citizens who are not economically active from being made subject to the requirement that those citizens fulfil the conditions for obtaining a right of residence under Directive 2004/38 of the host Member State.

---

45 Directive 2004/38, O.J. L 158 of 30 April 2004.

46 Regulation 1247/92, O.J. L 136 of 19 May 1992.

47 Case C-140/12, *Brey*, EU:C:2013:565.

48 Cases C- 333/12, *Dano*, EU:C:2014:2358, C-67/14, *Alimanovic*, EU:C:2015:597, C-299/14, *Garcia-Nieto*, EU:C:2016:114 and C-308/14, *Commission versus UK*, EU:C:2016:436.

3.4. Posting

As mentioned above, the EU Regulations contain uniform criteria to determine the applicable social security legislation. The main rule is the so-called *lex loci laboris*: a person is subject to the legislation of the Member State where he/she works. This rule is based on the idea that a migrant worker should have the same rights as a national of the host State.[49] This rule seeks to prevent unfair competition between employers who use migrant workers in a Member State and those who only use non-migrant workers. The difference in social protection level between Member States, following the 2004, 2007 and 2013 enlargements has strengthened this objective even further.

From 1959, date of entry of Regulation 3, the law of the workplace did not apply in the event that a worker is sent by his employer for a short period to another Member State to work there on the employer's behalf. It would be a severe burden on workers, employers and social security institutions if the worker was required to be insured under the social security system of every Member State to which he was posted in the course of his employment, even if such posting was of very short duration.[50] Such workers continue to be subject to the legislation of the sending State. However, in the *Manpower* and *Van der Vecht* judgments the Court has given a rather extensive interpretation of the term posting by deciding that the posting provisions also apply to a worker who is recruited with a view to being posted to another Member State. This case-law in now reflected[51] in the current Regulations.

The Court has, from the very beginning, mentioned not only the interests of the worker but also those of the employer and of the social security institutions. Initially, the ECJ underlined simplification as objective of the posting provision. However, in its 2000 *Fitzwilliam* judgment,[52] the Court ruled that the purpose of the posting provisions is '*in particular, to promote freedom to provide services for the benefit of undertakings which avail themselves of it by sending workers to Member States other than that in which they are established*'. The objective of simplification is mentioned only in the second place.

The application of the posting provisions is subject to a number of strict conditions[53] to prevent the posting provisions from being used in cases for which they are not intended. Firstly, posting has to be temporary: Article 12 Regulation 883/2004 mentions a strict maximum time limit of 24 months. Secondly, in order to avoid rotation of personnel performing the same activities, the worker may not be sent to replace a person who has completed an earlier period of posting. Thirdly, in order to reflect the goal of achieving continuity in the affiliation of the worker to the social security system of the sending Member State, the worker must have been subject to the legislation of the sending State prior to the posting. Fourthly, the worker should continue to be under the authority of the employer which posted him: there must be a direct

49 Recital 17 Regulation 883/2004. Cases C-68/99, *Commission versus Germany*, EU:C:2001:137, para 23, C-249/04, *Allard*, EU:C:2005:329, C-493/04, *Piatowski*, EU:C:2006:167.

50 Cases 19/67, *Van der Vecht*, EU:C:1967:49 and 35/70, *Manpower*, EU:C:1970:120.

51 Article 14(1) Regulation 987/2009.

52 Case C-202/97, *Fitzwilliam*, EU:C:2000:75, repeated in case C-404/98, *Plum*, EU:C:2000:607.

53 Articles 12 Regulation 883/2004 and 14 Regulation 987/2009, further elaborated in Decision A2 of the Administrative Commission, O.J. C 106 of 24 April 2010.

relationship[54] between worker and employer during the whole duration of the posting. And last, but not least, the employer should habitually carry out significant activities in the sending State. This last condition aims to prevent 'letter-box' firms from using the posting provisions.

Posting is a very sensitive issue. For some Member States and interest groups, the conditions are too strict and lead to protection of the market of the host State. For other Member States and interest groups, the application of the posting provisions lead to unfair competition and constitute a danger for the level of social protection in the host State.

Proof that the legislation of the sending State is applicable is delivered by a certificate (Portable Document A1) provided by the competent institution of the Member State whose legislation is applicable. It follows from the case-law of the Court under the old Regulation 1408/71,[55] now codified in Article 5 of Regulation 987/2009, that such document is binding for all other institutions of the Member States concerned. This means that whenever the decision of the issuing institution is contested by the institution of the place where the work is actually carried out, a (retroactive) change of the applicable legislation is not possible without the consent of the issuing institution to withdraw or to invalidate the A1 Document in question.

The Court based its case-law on the principle of cooperation in good faith laid down in Article 4(3) TEU. On the one hand, this principle requires the issuing institution to carry out a proper assessment of the facts and to (re-)examine whether all conditions for posting are fulfilled. On the other hand, the document A1 establishes a presumption that the worker is properly affiliated to the social security system of the sending Member State. It is, therefore, binding on the competent institution as well as on the judiciary[56] of the Member State in which that person actually works, even in the case of a manifest error of assessment of the posting conditions.[57] If the institution of the Member State where the work is carried out has doubts about the validity of the document or about the accuracy of the facts on which that document is based, it may start the dialogue and reconciliation procedure within the meaning of Article 5 Regulation 987/2009. However, that institution cannot unilaterally make the workers concerned subject to its own social security legislation.[58]

The dialogue procedure must be followed, even if the institution of the Member State where the work is carried out produces evidence collected in the course of a judicial investigation, that supports the conclusion that document A1 was fraudulently obtained or relied on. It is only when the issuing institution fails to take such evidence into consideration for the purpose of reviewing the grounds for the issue of that document, that a court of the Member State where the work is carried out may disregard that document. This was decided by the Court in its famous *Altun* judgment.[59] In this judgment the ECJ underlined that the principle of prohibition of fraud and abuse of rights is a general principle of EU law which individuals must comply with. However,

---

54 This notion is clarified in Decision A2 of the Administrative Commission, O.J. C 106 of 24 April 2010.

55 Cases C-148/97, *Banks*, EU:C:2000:169 en C-2/05, *Herbosch Kiere*, EU:C:2006:69.

56 Case C-2/05, *Herbosch Kiere*, EU:C:2006:69.

57 Case C-620/15, *Rosa Flusschiff*, EU:C:2017:309.

58 Case C-356/15, *Commission versus Belgium*, EU:C:2018:555.

59 Case C-359/16, *Altun*, EU:C:2018:63.

the ECJ clarified that only a national court, not a social security institution, may disregard the document concerned. In such cases, obviously the right to a fair trial must be guaranteed. A national court is only allowed to disregard such document in cases of fraud or abuse of rights. Findings of fraud are to be based on evidence that satisfies both an objective and a subjective factor. The objective factor consists in the fact that the posting conditions are not met. The subjective factor corresponds to the intention of the parties concerned to evade or circumvent the posting conditions with a view to obtaining the advantage attached to it (e.g. paying less social security contributions). The fraudulent procurement of document A1 may thus result from a deliberate action (e.g. misrepresentation of the real situation of the worker or of the employer) or from a deliberate omission (e.g. concealment of relevant information) with the intention of evading the posting conditions. In practice it will not always be easy to produce evidence supporting the subjective factor, indispensable to conclude the findings of fraud. The December 2016 Commission proposal to modify Regulations 883/2004 and 987/2009[60] contains a series of provisions aimed at fighting fraud and abuse as well as at strengthening the verification of the social security status of posted workers. This proposal is still pending before Council and Parliament.

3.5. People Normally Working in Two or More Member States

For obvious reasons, the application of the law of the workplace is not suitable in cases where a person normally pursues activities in two or more Member States. For workers with such a working pattern, other connecting factors have been incorporated in special rules. These factors are laid down in Article 13 Regulation 883/2004.

The first connecting factor for determining the applicable social security law for workers normally working in two or more Member States is the notion '*substantial part*'[61] of the worker's activities. Workers who normally work in two or more Member States and who pursue a 'substantial part' of their work in their Member State of residence are subject to the social security legislation of that State. If a substantial part is not performed in the Member State of residence, then the decisive criterion is the '*registered office or place of business*' of the employer or of one of the employers.[62]

The number of A1 documents issued for persons covered by Article 13 increased from 168.279 in 2010 to more than 1 million in 2017.[63] This is a remarkable growth within a short period of time. The share of A1 documents issued on the basis of Article 13 in the total number of A1 documents strongly increased over the last few years up to 36 % in 2017. These figures are an indication that in their search for the most advantageous social security legislation, businesses not only look at the possibilities offered by the posting provision of Article 12 Regulation 883/2004 but also at those offered by Article 13.

---

60 COM(2016) 815 final.

61 Article 14(8) Regulation 987/2009: 25% of working time or remuneration.

62 Article 13(1)(b) Regulation 883/2004.

63 F. De Wispelaere & J. Pacolet, *Posting of workers- Report on A1 Portable Documents issued in 2017,* Brussels: European Commission 2018, available on the website of the European Commission.

In fact, *'posting'* within the meaning of Article 12 is subject to the conditions and limitations explained above. This means in particular that there must be a direct relationship between the worker and employer and that the employer ordinarily performs significant activities in the Member State in which he is established. In order to be covered by Article 13, however, those conditions and limitations do not apply. In addition, there are some uncertainties how to interpret the notion *'registered office or place of business of the undertaking or employer'*, within the meaning of Article 13. In order to eliminate 'brass-plate' companies, a definition of this term is provided by Art. 14(5a) Reg. 987/2009. Unfortunately, this definition is rather vague. True, the Practical Guide[64] contains a number of criteria, but this does not exclude situations where some of these criteria are fulfilled, while others are not. Interpretation problems may arise in particular when corporate businesses with mother/daughter companies are involved. The following case, which is now pending before the ECJ,[65] may illustrates such dilemmas.

A number of European truck drivers reside in the Netherlands. They are employed by a transport enterprise established in the Netherlands. They normally work in two or more Member States and, therefore, fall under Article 13 Regulation 883/2004. They do not perform a substantial part of their activities in the Netherlands. By virtue of Article 13(1)(b) Regulation 883/2004 they are subject to the social security legislation of the Netherlands since their employer is established there. However, after a while the enterprise has engaged in outsourcing part of its operations to Cyprus. Since then it is a company established in Cyprus that recruits and pays the truck drivers concerned. The Cypriote company hires the truck drivers concerned out to the same transport enterprise established in the Netherlands. The transport enterprise claims that the truck drivers are now subject to the social security legislation of Cyprus, since their employer has its registered office in that Member State. The Dutch social security institution, however, is of the opinion that the truck drivers remain subject to the social security legislation of the Netherlands, since their real employer is the transport enterprise whose registered office is in the Netherlands. The dispute is brought before the Dutch court.

According to the findings of the Netherlands judiciary the truck drivers concerned remain de facto fully available to the transport enterprise in the Netherlands and it is the enterprise in the Netherlands which actually bears the wage costs. The Dutch court decides to refer the case to the ECJ by asking a number of preliminary questions. The first question is which of the two companies involved has to be considered as the employer of the truck drivers within the meaning of Article 13. As said before, *posting* within the meaning of Article 12 is subject to the condition that during the whole duration of the posting there is a direct relationship between the worker and employer and that the employer ordinarily performs significant activities in the Member State in which he is established. In his second question the Dutch court asks the ECJ whether these conditions should apply by analogy to the employer within the meaning of Article 13. In the event that the ECJ comes to the conclusion that the company established in Cyprus is the employer within the meaning of Article 13 and that the conditions under

64 European Commission, *Practical Guide on the applicable legislation in the European Union, the European Economic Area and in Switzerland*, Brussels: European Commission 2013, available on the website of the European Commission.

65 Case C-610/18, *AFMB Ltd.*

which employers can invoke Art. 12 do not apply to Art. 13 by analogy, then the final question is whether the objective pursued by Regulation 883/2004 is attained. In this context the Dutch court refers to recital 1 of Regulation 883/2004 and to the famous *Bosmann* judgment[66] in which the ECJ underlined that the EU Regulations based on Article 48 TFEU aim at contributing towards improving the standard of living and conditions of employment for people exercising their right to free movement. In its referring judgment the Dutch court expresses fears for abuse[67] of Article 13, since the objective of the EU Regulations is not to facilitate competitive advantages for employers. It fears circumvention of the social security legislation of the Netherlands by the companies involved by creating artificially the conditions for obtaining an advantage (level of contributions more favourable for the employer).

66 Case C-352/06, *Bosmann*, EU:C:2008:290.

67 Conclusions of Advocate-General Saugmandsgaard in case C-359/16, *Altun*, EU:C:2017:850, fn. 45.

‘I’ is a ‘We’ – *Coman*, Plural Identity and Multiple Citizenship in a Globalized World

*François Crépeau & Jean-Yves Carlier**

Any debate about dual or multiple citizenship raises many questions about the nature of citizenship itself. What is it? Why does it matter? How much should it matter? Who is and who ought to be entitled to obtain it, retain it and transmit it? In order to reflect meaningfully on multiple citizenship, one must first discuss the evolving nature of citizenship in our collective mindset and analyse its legal status.[1]

Several countries have been revising their citizenship policies in restrictive ways.[2] This seems paradoxical at a time when globalization is increasing human mobility, thereby enhancing the opportunities for, and desirability of, multiple citizenship. It seems less paradoxical, however, when one considers the intense and often acrimonious debates surrounding national identity, immigration, integration, diversity and multiculturalism that abound in settler societies such as Canada, the United States, Australia, as well as in Old World European states. The latter are grappling, on the one hand, with a supranational EU citizenship and, on the other, with the progressive recognition that they too are countries of immigration and that this has unleashed a nationalist populist backlash.

These controversies illustrate an increasing uncertainty about what it means to be a national or a citizen of one’s country. Certainly, after 9/11 and the successive terrorist attacks by both Islamist Jihadists and extreme-right anti-immigration fanatics, and with the media’s tendency to link migration, Islam, radicalism, anti-liberalism and violence, nationalist populist political actors have deployed various discursive and policy tools to mobilize collective anxiety against the ‘cosmopolitan elites’. They are promoting restrictions on the acquisition of nationality or the access to multiple nationality, as well as the ability to strip away a dual national from their Global North nationality, as a way

* François Crépeau is Professor at McGill University (Montreal, Canada); Jean-Yves Carlier is professor at the University of Louvain (Louvain-la-Neuve, Belgium).

1 About nationality and multiple citizenship, see, among many others: C. Joppke, ‘The instrumental turn of citizenship’, 45:6 *Journal of Ethnic and Migration Studies* 2019, p. 858-878; A. Tanasoca, *The Ethics of Multiple Citizenship*, Cambridge: Cambridge University Press 2018; A. Shachar, R. Bauböck, I. Bloemraad & M. Vink (eds), *The Oxford Handbook of Citizenship*, Oxford: Oxford University Press 2017; P. Spiro, *At Home in Two Countries: The Past and Future of Dual Citizenship (Citizenship and Migration in the Americas)*, New York: New York University Press 2016; S. Carrera Nuñez & G.-R. de Groot (eds), *European Citizenship at the Crossroad. The Role of the European Union on Loss and Acquisition of Nationality*, Oisterwijk: Wolf Legal Publishers 2015; D.A. Cook-Martín, *The Scramble for Citizens: Dual Nationality and State Competition for Immigrants*, Redwood City (CA): Stanford University Press 2013; Société française pour le droit international (S.F.D.I.), *Droit international et nationalité*, Paris: Pedone 2012; M. Verwilghen, ‘Conflits de nationalités. Plurinationalité et apatridie’, *Collected courses, Hague Academy*, vol. 277, Leiden : Brill Nijhoff 2000, p. 9-484 (with an abundant bibliography); A. Dionisi-Peyrusse, F. Jault-Seseke, F. Marchadier & V. Parisot (eds), *La nationalité: enjeux et perspectives*, Paris: Institut universitaire Varenne and LGDJ 2019.

2 See a high quality database at: http://globalcit.eu.

of fostering national cohesion and assuaging constructed fears of fragmentation of the national identity.

Nationalist populist voices still mount spirited rearguard reactions against the practice of multiple nationalities. A ten-year-old Canadian example: 'The practice of dual citizenship, especially among the Canadian-born, does a disservice to a country that gives us so much and asks for little in return. It needlessly conflicts our loyalties, weakens whatever sense of common purpose we have in this diverse nation of ours, and perpetuates a minimalist vision of what we owe each other and Canada as fellow citizens'.[3] A more recent American example: '… we believe that citizenship in this country should be an expression of allegiance to it, enforced not by a pledge but rather by a desire to be part of this country. Dual citizenship may have a place in American society, but the goal should be the cultivation of undivided Americans, proud of their heritage and committed to this nation.'[4]

Such assertions about the impact of dual citizenship on the relationship between the state and the citizen are commonplace enough to be presented as fact: a single allegiance would necessarily be optimal, while multiple citizenship is weakening this link. However, wholesale rejection of multiple citizenship is in worldwide decline. We therefore need a careful consideration of the validity of these claims made about nationality and multiple citizenship.

Elspeth Guild – dedicatee of this *liber amicorum* – has been interested in the question of citizenship in her publications on numerous occasions. In particular, she has deepened the notion of European citizenship, both in general terms as part of the European identity and more specifically as a 'monstrous citizenship' in the context of Brexit.[5] Beyond our modest contribution to the debate, it is a pleasure and an honour to salute the much more fundamental scholarship of our colleague Elspeth Guild and to invite everyone to read her works.

In her 2004 book on the *Legal Elements of European Identity*, she weaved together the perspectives of law and political science. Regarding the legal elements of the European identity, she underlined that 'not only must clarification be awaited from the European Court of Justice but also from the European Court of Human Rights. The decisions of the highest courts in Europe alone will not provide any final answer on European identity. The most important test is whether the people of Europe embrace the concept as it is developing and accept its legitimacy.'[6]

Building on this, we propose a two-step extension of this reflection about multiple citizenship in a global context. First, a brief analysis of a recent ECJ decision effectively shows that courts can have some influence, not so much on the construction of identities, but on their recognition in law. In this respect, the *Coman* judgment is an echo

3 R. Griffiths, 'A Long Needed Change to Citizenship Laws', *National Post* (Toronto), 16 April 2009. Online at: http://immigrationwatchcanada.org/2009/04/16/a-long-needed-change-to-citizenship-laws/.

4 'The Problem of Dual Citizenship', Editorial, *The Los Angeles Times*, 26 December 2014. Online at: www.latimes.com/opinion/editorials/la-ed-dual-citizenship-20141228-story.html.

5 E. Guild, *The Legal Elements of European Identity. EU Citizenship and Migration Law*, The Hague: Kluwer Law International 2004; E. Guild, *Brexit and its Consequences for UK and Citizenship or Monstrous Citizenship*, Leiden, Boston: Brill Nijhoff 2017.

6 E. Guild, *The Legal Elements of European Identity* 2004, p. xi.

chamber of the confrontation between the growth of multiple identities and the attempt by states to keep them under unilateral sovereign control. Second, we attempt a broader reflection on multiple citizenship as a mirror of diverse identity markers.

The *Coman* Case as an Echo Chamber of the Growth of Multiple Identities

The ECJ *Coman* judgment (2018) is a well-known decision that required Romania to grant a right of residence to a man, Mr. Hamilton, an American citizen, married under Belgian law to another man, Mr. Coman, a Romanian and American citizen.[7] It is useful to recall the facts, as they set the contemporary context of how multiple citizenship and multiple identities shape individual choices and trajectories. Mr. Coman had Romanian and American citizenship. He was studying in Romania, notably at Cuza University of Iasi. From 1997 to 2002, he was the executive director of Accept, a Romanian national human rights non-governmental organization (NGO) working for LGBT equality. While in New York, Coman obtained in 2007 a Master's degree in human rights from Columbia Graduate School of Arts and Sciences, and was the Program Director at OutRight International, where he supervised the organization's work at the United Nations. Then, along with the Baltic-American Partnership Fund, he worked for four years in grant making for civil society development in Estonia, Latvia, and Lithuania.[8] Since 2013, Mr. Coman has been director of the international human rights program of the Arcus Foundation.

In New York, he met Mr. Hamilton, an African-American American citizen. After living together in New York from 2005 to 2009, they got married in 2010 in Belgium, where Mr. Coman worked as assistant to a member of the European Parliament. This same-sex marriage was perfectly legal in accordance with Belgian law. The Belgian

7 ECJ, *Coman*, C-673/16, 5 June 2018, EU:C:2018:385. Among the commentaries, see: E. Bribosia & I. Rorive, 'Quand la Cour de justice contribue à la reconnaissance du mariage homosexuel', *Journal de droit européen* 2018, p. 344; P. Cannoot & J. Lievens, 'Zo zijn we niet getrouwd?', 26 *Rechtskundig weekblad* 2019, p. 1017-1026, at p. 1023; J.-Y. Carlier, 'Vers un ordre public européen des droits fondamentaux. L'exemple de la reconnaissance des mariages de personnes de même sexe dans l'arrêt *Coman*'. *Revue trimestrielle des droits de l'homme* 2019, p. 203; M. Fallon, 'Observations sous *Coman*', *Cahiers de l'EDEM,* June 2018; H. Fulchiron & A. Panet, 'Citoyenneté européenne, liberté de circulation et reconnaissance des situations familiales créées dans un État membre: un petit pas pour de grandes enjambées?', *Dalloz*, 6 September 2018, p. 1674; L. Gyeney, 'Sensitive Issues before the European Court of Justice – The Right of Residence of Third Country Spouses Who Became Victims of Domestic Violence as Well as Same-Sex Spouses in the Scope of Application of the Free Movement Directive (Legal Analysis of the *NA* and *Coman* Cases)', *Hungarian Yearbook of International Law and European Law* 2017, p. 211; U. Jessurun d'Oliveira, 'Het Europese Hof omarmt eindelijk het huwelijk van mensen met hetzelfde geslacht – Een stap in de goede richting', *Nederlands Juristenblad* 2018, p. 2060; É. Pataut, 'Chronique "Citoyenneté de l'Union européenne"', *Revue trimestrielle de droit européen* 2018, p. 673; A. Rigaux, 'Importantes avancées de la jurisprudence de l'Union sur le regroupement familial des couples de même sexe', *Europe*, August-September 2018, p. 7; P. Hammje, 'Obligation de reconnaissance d'un mariage entre personnes de même sexe conclu dans un Etat membre aux fins d'octroi d'un droit de séjour dérivé', *Revue critique de droit international privé* 2018, p. 816; I. Sumner, 'Groundbreaking decision or a tiny tremor? – The Court of Justice decision in *Coman*', *Nederlands internationaal privaatrecht* 2018, No. 469-471; P. Faraguna, 'L'amore vince (e l'identità nazionale perde?): il caso Coman alla Corte di giustizia', *Quaderni costituzionali* 2018, p. 711-715.

8 See: www.humanrightscolumbia.org/node/8800.

Code of Private International Law authorizes same-sex marriage if one of the two spouses 'has the nationality of a State or his habitual residence in the territory of a State whose law allows the same-sex marriage'.[9]

After that, the couple decided to settle in Romania, Mr. Coman's country of nationality. Romania refused to recognize the marriage and to grant Mr. Hamilton a right of residence for more than three months. Indeed, Article 277 of the Romanian Civil Code provides that '1. Same-sex marriage is prohibited' and that '2. Marriages between persons of the same sex concluded or contracted abroad by Romanian citizens or foreigners are not recognised in Romania.' Faced with a plea of unconstitutionality, the Constitutional Court of Romania referred thc case to the ECJ for a preliminary ruling. At stake was the interpretation of Directive 2004/38 on the right of EU citizens and their family members to move and reside freely within the territory of the Member States, as read in the light of the Charter of Fundamental Rights of the European Union.[10]

The Court answered that EU law 'must be interpreted as precluding the competent authorities of the Member State of which the Union citizen is a national from refusing to grant that third-country national a right of residence in the territory of that Member State on the ground that the law of that Member State does not recognise marriage between persons of the same sex'. It further declared that EU law 'is to be interpreted as meaning that (…) a third-country national of the same sex as a Union citizen whose marriage to that citizen was concluded in a Member State in accordance with the law of that State has the right to reside in the territory of the Member State of which the Union citizen is a national for more than three months'.

Some will criticize the Court of Justice for failing to affirm the pure and simple obligation to recognise same-sex marriage and for limiting itself to the recognition of a right of residence. Others will criticize the Court for denying a state the power to invoke its 'national identity' to impose the respect of certain values considered fundamental. The frontal opposition of these criticisms shows precisely that the Court is charting the best course, that of a narrow path of balance.

On the one hand, wishing to be modernist, the Court considers – like Advocate General Wathelet – that the spirit and letter of European secondary law leads to an evolving interpretation of the concept of spouse, regardless of gender. On the other hand, wishing to be reassuring, it refrains from undermining the national identity of Member States, 'inherent in their fundamental political and constitutional structures'.[11]

---

9 Art. 46 IPL Belgian code (Law of 16 July 2004).

10 Directive 2004/38/EC of the European Parliament and of the Council of 29 April 2004 on the right of citizens of the Union and their family members to move and reside freely within the territory of the Member States amending Regulation (EEC) No 1612/68 and repealing Directives 64/221/EEC, 68/360/EEC, 72/194/EEC, 73/148/EEC, 75/34/EEC, 75/35/EEC, 90/364/EEC, 90/365/EEC and 93/96/EEC, *OJ*, 2004, L158, p. 77, 2004, L229, p. 35 and 2005, L197, p. 34. See: C. Barnard, *The substantive Law of the EU – The Four Freedoms*, 5th ed., Oxford: OUP 2016; J.-Y. Carlier, *La condition des personnes dans l'Union européenne*, Brussels: Larcier 2007; J.-Y. Carlier & E. Guild (eds), *The Future of Free Movement of Persons in the European Union*, Brussels: Bruylant 2006; D. Martin, 'Libre circulation des citoyens dans l'Union', 03/86 *Jurisclasseur Europe* 2014.

11 In his opinion, AG Wathelet wrote: 'In fact, if it were to be considered that the concept of marriage relates to national identity in certain Member States (…), the obligation to respect that identity, which is set out in Article 4(2) TEU, cannot be construed independently of the obligation of sincere cooperation set out in Article 4(3) TEU. In accordance with that obligation, the Member States are required

To this end, the Court stresses that it limits itself to imposing the granting of a right of residence and not the recognition of same-sex marriage as such.[12]

Does this have something to do with multiple citizenship? Yes and no. Yes, first because the Court repeated its mantra from the *Grzelczyk* judgment, that 'citizenship of the Union is intended to be the fundamental status of nationals of the Member States',[13] and second because a discussion was possible on Mr. Coman's dual nationality, in view of his American nationality.[14]

No, because the recognition of same-sex marriage is not imposed because of Mr. Coman's dual Romanian-American nationality. The decision is rather based on the rights he derives, as a Romanian citizen, from the right to free movement of persons with their family members within the European Union, as well as from the mutual trust between Member States for the recognition of rights acquired in another Member State.

However, finally, again yes, this has something to do with multiple citizenship in a broad perspective. The Court expressly mentions Mr. Coman's dual nationality, the fact that he has worked in various countries and that if he is a Romanian national, he 'made use of his freedom of movement by moving to and taking up genuine residence (...) in a Member State other than that of which he is a national, and, whilst there, has created or strengthened a family life with a third-country national of the same sex to whom he is joined by a marriage lawfully concluded in the host Member State'.[15] In addition to this reference to multiple links with various countries and territories, considerations of multiple personal identities are also taken into account. Spurred on by the Advocate General, the Court takes into consideration the diversity of family and private lives in order to reject the refusal of the right of residence for the same-sex spouse, a third country foreign national. Undoubtedly, among these diversity factors to be recognized – which were openly rejected by Romania – the Court could also have underlined the fact that it was a mixed marriage from an ethnic point of view. It was not politically correct to point this out, hence the Court's silence on this point. However, it is even more incorrect to deny the role of this diversity factor, which was probably an element accentuating the radical rejection of Mr. Hamilton's long-term residence permit.

---

to ensure fulfilment of the obligations arising out of the Treaties or resulting from the acts of the institutions of the Union' (§ 40). He added that marriage and same-sex marriage 'is not something associated with a specific culture or history; on the contrary, it corresponds to a universal recognition of the diversity of families' (§ 58).

12 ECJ, *Coman*, §§ 43-46.

13 ECJ, *Grzelczyk*, C-184/99, 20 September 2001, EU:C:2001:458, § 31.

14 While it is customary to retain the nationality of the forum, it is not an obligation. The Hague Convention on Certain Questions relating to the Conflict of Nationality Laws specifies that 'a person having two or more nationalities *may be* regarded as its national by each of the States whose nationality he possesses' (art. 3). Since American nationality is the common nationality to both spouses, both having lived together for a long time in the United States, it could be considered, for Mr. Coman, a more effective nationality than the Romanian. This preference of the effective nationality over the nationality of the forum has been used, in particular with regard to the name, notably when this effectiveness is reinforced by a functional objective, such as benefiting from the effects of free movement under EU law (ECJ, *Garcia-Avello*, C-148/02, 2 October 2003, EU:C:2003:539). From this perspective, it would have been preferable for Mr. Coman to have a second nationality from an EU Member State allowing same-sex marriage, such as the Netherlands (ECJ, *Freitag*, C-541/15, 8 June 2017, EU:C:2017:432, about the name).

15 ECJ, *Coman*, §§ 40, 51.

All this can be seen as a 'medieval' citizenship, according to Dimitry Kochenov's formula, more oriented towards the furtherance of personal interests than the guarantee of collective interests. There is a general risk that 'this is a citizenship where a turn to personhood results in the limitation rather than the extension of the amount of rights associated with the status'.[16] But here, on the contrary, it results clearly in the extension of the rights, based in particular on the principle of equality, and, at the same time, it allows progress to be made towards the construction of common values. The Court's progressive interpretation recognizing the right of residence as a consequence of a valid same-sex marriage is a first step, indicative of the general direction it will take in future cases. In so doing, the Court gradually builds a European public order of fundamental rights, which participates in the development of a form of European identity.

The Court imposes on a state the negative obligation to no longer engage in specific discriminatory practices and in the rejection of multiple identities, even when that state claims that it is implementing its national public policy towards one of its own nationals. The Court is thus building a public order of inclusion, rejecting practices of exclusion. For example, in the *Coman* judgment, the aim is to include the same-sex couple in Romanian society. This is consciously done in direct opposition to the national identity claimed by the state.

Similarly, from a process-oriented point of view, it is significant that this construction is taking place in a dialogue between the Court of Justice of the European Union and the Constitutional Court of Romania. This is an example of the participation of the jurisdictions in the construction of democracy through law.[17] On the one hand, the courts have to interpret the texts drawn up by legislators, in particular with regard to general principles, by establishing a dialogue between courts and between legislative and judicial authorities. On the other hand, the participation of governments and NGOs in this kind of procedure broadens the public space for discussion. In the *Coman* case, the three governments intervening in support of Romania (Poland, Hungary and Latvia) were confronted with the opposite viewpoint of the Dutch government, but also of the NGO Accept, direct intervener in the national proceedings alongside the Coman-Hamilton couple. In other words, 'legal rules, court judgments and academic treaties may partake in the constant reconstruction of individual and collective identities', even if 'the evolution of citizens' rights will not be a linear process which will make the world a better place. Alternate takes, including retrogression and stalemates, coexist simultaneously.'[18] The construction of citizenship is the result of a combination – disruptive in time and space – of legislative, judicial and socio-political processes.

At the end of the day, one may conclude, quoting Elspeth Guild, that the *Coman* case is a good echo chamber for the fact that 'the rights of residence and equality of treatment are at the core of identity and indeed citizenship'; and that 'the right to define

16 D. Kochenov, 'The Citizenship of Personal Circumstances in Europe', in: D. Thym (ed.), *Questioning EU Citizenship*, Oxford: Hart publishing 2017, p. 51, 53.

17 R. Dworkin, *Justice for Hedgehogs*, Cambridge (MA): Harvard University Press 2011; P. Gérard, *Droit et démocratie. Réflexions sur la légitimité du droit dans la société démocratique*, Brussels: Publications Université Saint-Louis 1995; F. Rigaux, *La loi des juges*, Paris: Odile Jacob 1997.

18 D. Kostakopoulou & D. Thym, 'Conclusion: The Non-Simultaneous Evolution of Citizens' Rights', in: D. Thym (ed.), *Questioning EU Citizenship*, Oxford: Hart publishing 2017, p. 314-315.

identity is shared among (different) bodies, though the balance is changing. The nation state controls who are its nationals but remains answerable to the supranational bodies for the interpretation and definition of their rights and access to the territories. In the legal expression of the right to control identity can be found the tension of different identities and different levels of engagement on the part of individuals and states to identities. There is continuous overlap between identities, which are shared and expressed simultaneously. The appeal to one identity in law can have the effect of undermining or overruling the rights and duties associated with identity at another level.'[19]

Consequently, multiple citizenship can function as a mirror – though not without distortions – of the diversity and complexity of individual identity.

Multiple Citizenship Mirrors the Complexity of Identity[20]

One's personal identity is shaped by many features, of which nationality is only one. No one should doubt the enormity of citizenship's practical importance. One's life opportunities and the shape of one's existence are dramatically affected by whether the 'accident of birth' bestows citizenship in a stable, secure, prosperous state or in a poor, conflict-ridden, tyrannical state.[21]

While some experience their legal citizenship as their most important affiliation, others experience it as less defining than other identities, or even variable in importance depending on the context, circumstances and time. It may be pointless to demand an abstract ranking of the subjective importance of nationality, religion, gender, ability, sexuality, ethnicity, family history, education, upbringing and so many other potential factors, in constituting who one is and what matters to any one of us. It is neither necessary nor helpful to insist that one declare whether being British (for example) is always and everywhere more 'important' than being, say, female, or Scottish, or Hindu, or disabled, or an artist, or a child of Holocaust survivors, to take only a few possible identity markers.

The identities and memberships one claims as important are not necessarily coextensive with geopolitical borders. This matters in two ways. First, principles of human rights, in particular that of equality, limit the authority of states to discriminate against people under their territorial jurisdiction on the basis of citizenship or national origin: such distinction must always be justified, although justification will more easily be found in the realm of immigration law. This is the basis of the claim by so-called post-nationalists about the dwindling importance of legal citizenship.

Second, the second half of the 20th century has been characterized by the diminishing salience of nationalism as a feature of the Global North's collective political culture. Then, for many, the recognition of multiple memberships across and beyond states heralded an era where the excesses and perils of nationalism and the state system

19 E. Guild, *The Legal Elements of European Identity* 2004, p. 17.

20 In this part, several ideas and concepts originate in A. Macklin & F. Crépeau, *Multiple Citizenship, Identity and Entitlement in Canada*, 6 IRPP Study, Montreal: IRPP 2010, online: http://irpp.org/research-studies/study-no6/. The authors are indebted to Prof Macklin for agreeing with such use of the initial ideas.

21 A. Sachar, *The Birthright Lottery. Citizenship and Global Inequality*, Cambridge (MA): Harvard University Press 2009.

were leavened by relationships that transcended and extended beyond borders. In recent decades, more people now believe that it rather signals a worrisome dissolution of the ties that bind individual members of a state to each other and to their nation. Nationalist populist political forces have reclaimed the political stage and now dictate the agenda on many issues.

Allegiance to country used to be demonstrated by service in the armed forces through conscription or mandatory national service. Risking one's life for the defence of the country was recognized as the ultimate proof of national allegiance. However, this practice is slowly disappearing in the Global North where armies are becoming professionalized.

Interestingly, about 5,000 permanent resident ('green card') non-citizens enlist annually in the US military, and the US has expanded its recruitment to include temporary residents. Furthermore, the US military offers non-citizens accelerated access to US citizenship as an incentive to enlist. These trends suggest a profound attenuation of the traditional notion of military service as a duty of citizens and its replacement with a system whereby non-citizens 'earn' citizenship by undertaking a task that too few US citizens will perform voluntarily.

One possible response would be to develop a citizenship concept based on residence rather than nationality. Most social benefits have been detached from nationality and are now based on residence. One could imagine that the right to vote and thus to legitimately participate in public debates – to many, *the* essential feature of citizenship – being bestowed upon all those who reside in the country, that is, all those who are effectively subject to the laws of the country and who pay taxes there. 'No taxation without representation,' said the American Revolutionaries. Should not those who must respect the law and pay taxes have a say in how laws are adopted and implemented, and how taxes are levied and spent? For non-nationals, the residence in question would have to be defined in terms of legal status and length of stay. However, the principle would be that people who actually made the country their principal place of abode – where they work, get married, raise their children, contribute volunteer activities… – are 'part of the city' and should have a say in how it is being governed. In the end, one could have multiple national allegiances, but should exercise political rights only in the place where they spend their day-to-day life. This intellectually challenging concept would result in creating one 'citizenship of choice' for a person with multiple nationalities.[22]

Nationality would still matter as it would remain the ultimate guarantee of not being deported, but it would be decoupled from citizenship for a small percentage of the population. It has always seemed anomalous that, due to the combined effect of national citizenship laws, Italian nationals who are third generation born in Argentina (and also have Argentinian nationality) can still vote for the Italian Parliament, while many Turkish nationals who are third generation born in Germany often cannot vote for the German Parliament.

22 For a broad ethics perspective, with a charge against 'global cosmopolitanism' and with a proposal for relating voting rights to effective residence rather than nationality, see: A. Tanasoca, *The Ethics of Multiple Citizenship*, Cambridge: Cambridge University Press 2018.

Such decoupling of citizenship and nationality could have been done within the framework of European citizenship, for example, by granting European citizenship to any person legally residing in the territory of the Union for more than five years.[23] To date, this residence-based citizenship remains a utopia.[24] Until then, multiple citizenship remains a reality.

According to the *Nottebohm* judgment, the classic definition of citizenship as a nationality is: 'a legal bond having as its basis a social fact of attachment, a genuine connection of existence, interests and sentiments, together with the existence of reciprocal rights and duties'.[25] This definition of citizenship remains adapted to contemporary reality. It is more a mirror image of a person's status and affiliation than that of an allegiance. When the 'genuine connection of existence, interests and sentiments' is plural, the best legal translation of this reality is multiple citizenship.

Multiple affiliations reflect the changing nature of population growth, mobility and diversity. Many countries that were once countries of emigration are now being transformed by immigration and have come to recognize, albeit sometimes reluctantly, that their future capacity to sustain their currently aging and shrinking population, as well as the creativity and productivity of their economies, make immigration a demographic, economic and social imperative. In the settler societies of Canada, the US, Australia and New Zealand, immigration has been hitched to nation building since first contact and is now part of the collective 'grand narrative'. This narrative embodies a national identity, although this does not prevent indigenous counter-narratives, nor anti-immigration nationalist populist, or even supremacist, contestations.

Globalization enhances people's ability to sustain meaningful forms of civic, political, personal, economic and emotional attachment to more than one country, as well as to many non-state communities based on various affinities. The speed and relative ease of international travel, the possibility of transnational circulation over time, the cultural diversity of countries of immigration and the technological capacity to maintain personal contact and to remit money across vast distances, all this contributes to fostering a lived experience of multiple (if partial) belongings.

One may feel particularly linked to more than one country when one comes from a mixed background. Let us consider the Canadian-born daughter of a South Asian father and Italian-born mother who has spent her childhood in Canada. If this girl hears or speaks one or more of the languages at home, travels to India and Italy for family holidays and meets relatives in both countries, her connections to India and Italy may be different but no less 'real' than her link to Canada. She may not envisage living permanently in either country, but she may consider studying, doing an internship or working temporarily in Italy or India. It is also possible that she might meet a life partner in one or the other and decide to settle, if only for a time, in either country. This is

23 See, in honour of another distinguished colleague from the University of Nijmegen: J.-Y. Carlier, '*Incola est.* About European Citizenship', in: A. Böcker, T. Havinga, P. Minderhoud & H. van de Put (eds), *Migratierecht en Rechtssociologie, gebundeld in Kees' studies. Migration Law and Sociology of Law, collected essays in honour of Kees Groenendijk*, Liber Amicorum Prof. Dr. C.A. Groenendijk, Nijmegen: Wolf legal publishers 2008, p. 161-168.

24 One can clearly see that the resistance to such an idea comes indeed from the fact that such inclusion of many 'foreigners' in the citizenry could have an important impact on several social and political debates very much linked to 'national identity', such as on immigration and foreign policies.

25 ICJ, *Nottebohm (Liechtenstein v. Guatamala)*, 6 April 1955, Reports, p. 23.

no longer the privilege of only a rarefied elite. Mobility has been democratized and migration of large groups over time is a reality. Young people are circulating around the planet in an unprecedented manner, and those with kinship links to other countries may enjoy preferential access to the educational institutions and the labour market, even if they do not hold legal citizenship. These factors will exert an influence on the connection they feel to their parents' or grandparents' countries of origin.

This heightened mobility is reflected in literature and art. Many contemporary novels and films from around the world deal with issues relating to roots and the feeling of rootlessness after a migration process, to the transmission of cultural heritage in an era of cultural globalization and to the shifting meanings of identity and self when confronted by a diversity of national, cultural, ethnic and/or religious narratives. In contrast with the fear and loathing of 'cosmopolitanism' and the fetishization of cultural or racial purity that were the hallmark of the early 20th century and have made a comeback in the past decade, we have witnessed the emergence of an appreciation for the creative opportunities of multicultural backgrounds and for the 'creolization' of cultures and languages.

Finally, the culture of human rights and democracy has played a role in transforming our relationship to states and to traditional national grand narratives. Political stability, fundamental freedoms and economic prosperity doubtless play an important role in migration decisions. The attractiveness of any destination country rests today less on an adherence to its historical narrative (too often based on depredation, predation, colonialism, oppression, misery and violence) than on the fact that it generates enough stability and prosperity to allow people to imagine a future for themselves and their children there.

In the face of such changes in the concept of identity, one sometimes hears the complaint that some immigrants have an instrumental view of citizenship. It is argued that immigrants choose to naturalize as a consequence of a rational cost-benefit analysis that weighs the benefits of political protection, social advancement or economic advantage against the hardship of emigrating from the country of origin and satisfying citizenship requirements. This posture is contrasted against an idea that the benefits of citizenship should be accompanied by correlative duties and obligations towards the state, and further that the decision to naturalize should express a non-utilitarian embrace of the country's historical, cultural and political narrative. These objections invite at least three queries.

First, why should one require from immigrants adherence to the country's historical cultural narrative, whatever this may be, when this is not required of local-born citizens? Surely, for example, many Aboriginal Canadians do not adhere to the Canadian national grand narrative, and most Canadian-born citizens are ignorant of large chunks of it, or adhere, according to their ethnic background, to different versions of it. Similarly, the lack of specified legal obligations flowing from citizenship status applies as much to birthright citizens as to naturalized ones – for example, respecting constitutionally protected human rights or paying taxes apply to all persons under the country's jurisdiction– and is not more nor less problematic for the latter than for the former.

Secondly, are instrumental and romantic views of citizenship necessarily mutually exclusive? After all, it is not simply utilitarian to 'love' the host country because one has found there some measure of peace, security and prosperity for oneself and one's children. It is ironic that, quite often, it is those immigrants who are most courted by host states – such as investors, entrepreneurs, educated or rich immigrants – who have the most utilitarian view of citizenship acquisition, while those most despised – such as refugees and low-wage migrants – will develop the most emotional bond with their new country. As an example, it was quite comforting to see, among the hundreds of thousands of Canadians who volunteered to form groups of citizens applying for the private sponsorship of Syrian refugees in 2016-2017, many children or grandchildren of South-East Asian 'boat people' of the '80s who had been so privately sponsored in their time.

Thirdly, if one is concerned that a country's citizenship is offered 'too cheaply' to immigrants, increasing the cost of citizenship simply for that reason (by imposing stricter criteria on obtaining or retaining it) does not impede the commodification of that citizenship. It merely makes this citizenship a more expensive commodity, accessible only to those with the means to hire specialized lawyers. A country certainly has a legitimate interest in encouraging citizens to love it. However, legal rules for the acquisition or retention of citizenship are inherently limited in their capacity to guarantee, monitor or enforce the emotional attachment, personal loyalty and civic engagement that one might consider desirable traits for all citizens of the country.

Ultimately, the impact of multiple citizenship on identity, loyalty, allegiance, belonging and attachment cannot be fixed or determined objectively by appeals to a theoretical argument about what citizenship means or ought to mean. The impact can be measured only in sociological and empirical terms and will be highly variable. The experience of membership and belonging to a community, and the place of citizenship within this experience, will not be the same for all people in all places at all times. Nor can uniformity of meaning be imposed by law, be it a law that forbids an individual from acquiring or retaining a second citizenship or a law that forbids an individual from relinquishing a first citizenship.

That is not a reason for doing away with nationality or citizenship. Rather, it is a useful corrective to expansive accounts of what nationality is and to overly ambitious prescriptions about what citizenship can do.

Multiple Citizenship Benefits Countries of Immigration and Emigration Alike

In the end, allowing citizens to acquire or retain other nationalities may be to immigration countries' benefit. Conventional wisdom holds that citizenship is an important mechanism for facilitating and promoting immigrant integration, an outcome that is as important to immigrants as it is to the state's project of building and stabilizing the national community. A country of immigration that would prohibit multiple citizenship would risk the prospect of a large population of permanent residents who do not naturalize and thereby remain outside the political community because they do not wish to relinquish their other nationality.

Additionally, diasporic communities whose members have kept a nationality of origin can serve as social, political, economic and cultural integration facilitators, especially if this bridging role is recognized and fostered by the host state.

From an economic perspective, members of diasporic communities can help foster beneficial trade linkages and other economic relationships, especially if they are citizens of both countries and decide to make their dual identity a feature of their professional ventures.

From a cultural perspective, diasporic communities can also serve as intermediaries between newcomers and the host society. Multiple cultural connections will expand cultural creativity, for example in literature, film, music and cuisine.

From a diplomatic perspective, a country's influence on the international stage may increase thanks to the knowledge that citizens of diverse backgrounds may bring to the conduct of foreign relations and international trade. 'Hyphenated' citizens in the Global North may operate as personal conduits of liberal democratic values.

Countries of emigration have an additional incentive to permit dual citizenship as a means of strengthening and sustaining emotional and cultural ties among emigrants and promoting remittances and foreign investment in the countries of origin by their diasporic communities.

Recognizing that some form of common identity is necessary to enable people to live together, we are not facing a hard choice between the dissolution of any common identity in a universality that is too abstract in terms of individual rights, and the withdrawal into a myriad of single closed and separate national or communal identities. Recognizing multiple citizenship is a compromise that allows plural identities to combine individual and collective interests in our increasingly diverse societies. Multiple citizenship is, among others, one of the legal ways to translate 'I' into a 'We'.

Research Integrity, A Collective Enterprise

*Roel Fernhout**

Introduction

Since 2014, I have more or less left the field of migration and asylum law for a new challenge: research integrity. In 2013 I was appointed Confidential Advisor for Research Integrity at Radboud University and in 2014 I became the Chairman of the National Board for Research Integrity, in Dutch: Landelijk Orgaan Wetenschappelijke Integriteit (LOWI). In second instance, the LOWI decides after the Board of an institution affiliated with the LOWI about an alleged violation of research integrity. The work is very similar to my former position as National Ombudsman. There it was all about administrative integrity, nowadays research integrity is the focus point. But the manner of investigation, reporting on the findings and the method of concluding and advising are very similar.

In this respect I am unfaithful to Elspeth. In 1997 we, Elspeth, Kees Groenendijk and I, started our joint adventure that ended in 2000 in a beautiful dissertation and that co-operation lasted – with interruptions on my part – until today. An almost infinite list of scientific publications is now on Elspeth's name. As a researcher and writer you are always aware of the question of research integrity – one time more than the other – but it is always there in the background. In this contribution to the *Liber Amicorum* for Elspeth, I want to delve deeper into the issue of research integrity: what are the standards and how are they enforced. I would like to draw on the many cases that played at the LOWI.[1]

Research Integrity, Codes of Conduct

The standards for research integrity are laid down in Codes of Conduct. There are many.[2] The European Code of Conduct for Research Integrity 2017, the so-called ALLEA Code[3] and the Netherlands Code of Conduct for Research Integrity[4] which came into force on 1 October 2018 are particularly important for LOWI. The last code replaces the Netherlands Code of Conduct for Academic Practice 2004, revised in 2012 and 2014.

---

* Emeritus professor Radboud University Nijmegen, the Netherlands.

1 This contribution is based on my lectures on research integrity for Geosciences PhD students at Utrecht University (2015 and 2016) and my presentation for the PRINTEGER conference (23-8-2018).

2 See www.lowi.nl Assessment framework of LOWI.

3 Published by ALLEA – All European Academies.

4 Published by KNAW, NWO, Vereniging Hogescholen, NFU, To2 federatie en VSNU.

Remarkably, the issue of scientific integrity started already in 2001 with a memorandum of the Royal Netherlands Academy of Arts and Science[5] after a much-discussed affair (the plagiarism of prof. R. Diekstra, 1996-1998[6]). In May 2003 the National Board for Research Integrity (LOWI) was established and a code of conduct for scientific researchers was drawn up by the Association of Universities in the Netherlands, which came into force on January 1, 2005: the Netherlands Code of Conduct for Academic Practice. Nevertheless, the numbers at LOWI were still very limited. The attention for issues of research integrity is a rather recent one. It started with a serious incident, the Stapel case.[7] Diederik Stapel is a former Tilburg professor of social psychology. He was seen as a prominent Dutch psychologist, who also regularly participated in the public debate. In September 2011 his fraud came to light through complaints from his PhD students. These complaints have been investigated by a Commission. In 55 publications fraud with a very high degree of certainty was established. Strong indications of fraud were fixed by a dozen articles. There are also other publications, parts of books and dissertations, which are (almost certainly or very likely) based wholly or partly on fraudulent research. From that day on, September 2011, research integrity is a highly sensitive issue and all universities in the Netherlands declared research integrity as a top priority. Institutional codes were drafted, confidential advisors appointed and Research Integrity Committees established. And since the number at LOWI are rising.

We have seen the same with human rights codes of conduct in de past. The parallels are striking. Like human rights standards, research integrity standards are considered as granted until an incident proves the opposite. From that moment on, the codes become instrumental, living instruments and grows the public attention for issues as research integrity.

Research integrity codes are only a capstone. They are instruments of the last resort. They in itself do not bring forward adherence to research integrity standards. Therefore more is needed. Education in research integrity standards during PhD courses and during bachelor and master programmes are needed.

Research Integrity Procedures

Nevertheless, in the end the Codes of Conduct and the University Regulations for research integrity are important. The structure of the Regulations is rather simple. Everyone is entitled to file a complaint to the Executive Board of the University, with or without the Confidential Advisor. The Board send the complaint for advice to the Research Integrity Committee. The Committee considers the complaint on its admissibility and on its merits. It hears all the relevant parties and draft a report of findings and recommendation for the Board, but in the end it is the Board who decides the complaint.

5 Notitie Wetenschappelijke Integriteit, only available in Dutch.

6 J. Dijkhuis, W. Heuves, M. Hofstede, M. Janssen, A. Rörsch, *Leiden in Last. De zaak Diekstra nader bekeken.* Leiden: Elmar 1997.

7 D. Stapel, *Ontsporing*, Amsterdam: Prometheus 2012. Translation *Derailment*, available on the NRIN website (www.nrin.nl).

It is quite a step, in particular for young employees to address the Board with a complaint. For that reason the Confidential Advisor acts as a contact point for questions and complaints about research integrity. The Confidential Advisor does not take any decision on the admissibility or on the merits of the complaint. But in the event of a reasonable complaint he may mediate between the complainant and the defendant. If the mediation is not successful or otherwise he may explain the complainant how to file a complaint or offer his service to channel the complaint to the Board. If the complainant withdraws his complaint he leaves the Confidential Advisor with empty hands, even when the advisor is of the opinion that the complaint is serious. The advisor cannot take any step without the consent of the complainant. It is a fully confidential procedure.

If the Executive Board of the University declares the complaint inadmissible or rejects the complaint on its merits, the complainant, and in the case that the Board considers the complaint well founded, the defendant may address the National Board for Research Integrity (LOWI) for advice on the opinion of the Board, a kind of an appeal or second opinion procedure. But again, the decision of the LOWI is only an advice. In the end, it is the Board who decides the appeal.

Research Integrity Standards

Research integrity is still a notion in progress. It should be developed further in the case law, in particular in the opinions of the LOWI, the National Board for Research Integrity. Nevertheless, there is broad consensus that next to fabrication (entering fictitious data), falsification (falsifying data) and plagiarism (FFP), violations of research integrity will in any case be understood to mean: deliberately ignoring contributions of other authors, falsely posing as (co-) author, intentionally making incorrect use of (statistic) methods and/or intentionally interpreting results incorrectly, committing attributable inaccuracies when carrying out research and allowing and concealing misconduct of colleagues.

The developing character of the notion of research integrity is clearly illustrated by a national debate in the Netherlands on self-plagiarism or text recycling that took place some years ago. Is the extensive use by an author of the results of his earlier research findings a violation of research integrity? It is a sensitive issue, in particular when it happens without correct citations. The Royal Academy reacted with an extensive opinion in which it underlines the importance of correct citations.[8] Of course, a researcher may use his earlier findings, but he should mention the correct sources of these earlier

8 KNAW, *Correct Citation Practice*, Academy Advisory Memorandum, Amsterda,: KNAW 2014.

findings.[9] In accordance with this opinion the Code of Conduct was amended in October 2014 and the new 2018 Code of Conduct has explicitly formulated a standard in this regard.[10]

The numbers of LOWI-cases are still limited. In the early years there were none, or only one or two per year. Since 2011 (Stapel) the numbers are rising. Last year (2018) there were 29 complaints for the LOWI. Besides some very serious complaints there is an increase of manifestly unfounded complaints.

From my experience as Confidential Advisor, internal complaints from inside the university are rare. Most complaints were external, from scientists of other institutes or universities or from science journalists. From the structure of the regulations the Confidential Advisor is typically designed for internal complaints, to lower the step to launch a complaint.

Orientation of the Codes of Conduct

The original Codes of Conduct addressed only the individual researchers, not the institutions as such. Research integrity was mainly seen as an individual responsibility, not as a collective responsibility of researchers and their institutions. This was true for the first 2011 ALLEA Code and for the Netherlands Code of Conduct for Academic Practice 2004.

But it changed with the 2017 ALLEA Code and the Netherlands Code of Conduct for Research Integrity 2018. The new ALLEA Code gives attention to the research environment, what research institutions and organisations should do to promote awareness and ensure a prevailing culture of research integrity, providing clear policies and procedures on good research practices and a proper infrastructure for the management of data and research materials. Training, supervision and mentoring are important tasks for all research institutions and organisations.[11]

The new Netherlands Code of Conduct for Research Integrity 2018 formulates in its chapter 4 the institutions' duties of care for training and supervision, research culture, data management, publication and dissemination and ethical norms and procedures. Remarkably, the complaint procedures for research misconduct on the part of the researcher do not apply to the institution's duties of care. In this respect research integrity is still not a collective enterprise of researchers and their institutions.

9 Self-plagiarism played a role in LOWI-opinions 2015-02 and 2016-01 (see www.lowi.nl). An internal investigation committee of the Free University Amsterdam (VU) has accused a VU professor emeritus of (self-)plagiarism. LOWI concluded that the accused and his PhD student could not be blamed for plagiarism, but only careless source references. LOWI criticized the VU about the way in which it had dealt with the accusations and about how it had acted in the publicity.

10 Standard 41: Avoid unnecessary reuse of previously published texts of which you were the author or co-author. a. Be transparent about reuse by citing the original publication. b. Such self-citation is not necessary for reuse on a small scale or of introductory passages and descriptions of the method applied.

11 ALLEA-code 2017, par. 2.1 and 2.2.

The Bonn PRINTEGER Statement

Research integrity is inherently linked to the quality and excellence of research and science for policy. To further this agenda, the European PRINTEGER project (Promoting Integrity as an Integral Dimension of Excellence in Research) has conducted comprehensive studies on research integrity and misconduct.[12] The research of the PRINTEGER consortium shows that there is a need for increased focus and guidance on how organisations and institutions may address such issues.[13]

A Changed Perspective

To complement the existing instruments such as the ALLEA Code and the new Netherlands Code of Conduct, the PRINTEGER Statement focuses on institutional responsibilities for strengthening integrity. It takes into account the daily challenges and organisational contexts of most researchers. The statement intends to make research integrity challenges recognisable from the work-floor perspective, providing concrete advice on organisational measures to strengthen integrity. The consortium emphasises 13 key issues, elaborated in subsequent paragraphs.[14]

Dealing with Misconduct

In the short room available for me in this *Liber Amicorum* I will not deal with all the subjects of the PRINTEGER Statement but concentrate on some procedural aspects of this statement by looking at a number of recent LOWI opinions. I will focus on the following topics:

- Increasing transparency of misconduct cases (par. 9),
- Protecting the alleged perpetrators (par. 11)
- Establishing a research integrity committee and appointing an ombudsperson (par. 12), and
- Making explicit the applicable standards for research integrity (par. 13).

Increasing Transparency

The PRINTEGER Statement is very explicit in this respect. 'In order to stimulate organisations' capacity to learn from experience, there must be transparency. This means that organisations should be open about cases of confirmed research misconduct after they have been investigated, while safeguarding the legitimate rights to privacy and

---

12 www.printeger.eu.

13 E.-M. Forsberg, F.O. Anthun, S. Bailey, G. Birchley, H. Bout, C. Casonato & M. Zöller, 'Working with Research Integrity – Guidance for Research Performing Organisations: The Bonn PRINTEGER Statement', 24 *Science and Engineering Ethics* 2018, p. 1023-1034, doi:10.1007/s11948-018-0034-4.

14 Paragraphs 1. Providing information about research integrity; 2. Providing education, training and mentoring; 3. Strengthening a research integrity culture; 4. Facilitating open dialogue; 5. Wise incentive management; 6. Implementing quality assurance procedures; 7. Improving the work environment and work satisfaction; 8. Increasing transparency of misconduct cases; 9. Opening up research; 10. Implementing safe and effective whistle-blowing channels; 11. Protecting the alleged perpetrators; 12. Establishing a research integrity committee and appointing an ombudsperson; 13. Making explicit the applicable standards for research integrity.

personal data protection of individuals, as regulated in national and European laws. (...) Mandating organisations to report misconduct, and to cooperate with other organisations to collate this misconduct data, is likely to be effective in the long term.'

The need for transparency and confidentiality in dealing with misconduct are underlined in the new ALLEA Code as well, although less elaborated than in the PRINTEGER Statement. The same is true for the new Netherlands Code of Conduct for Research Integrity: 'At least in all cases where research misconduct is established, the executive board of the institution ensures that the findings of the investigation and its final judgement are made public in anonymized form'.[15]

The practice is sometimes more stubborn than these clear rules from PRINTEGER, ALLEA and the Netherlands Code of Conduct seem to suggest. Illustrative is LOWI-opinion 2016-1. In this case the Board of the Free University Amsterdam carried out an ex officio investigation, and the Board immediately (i.e. without waiting for a possible opinion from the LOWI) proceeded to make a non-anonymous publication of its decision.

LOWI ruled as follows. An *ex officio* investigation is also an integrity investigation, with the researcher finding himself in a vulnerable position. There is no reason to impose different criteria in the case of an ex officio investigation than in case of an investigation based on a complaint. There was sufficient reason to apply the guarantees in the Complaints Regulations of the Free University by analogy. In this respect it is profit that the new Code of Conduct explicitly indicates that the procedures for complaint handling have to be followed even if the institution considers it necessary to conduct an investigation on its own initiative into non-compliance with the standards for good research practices.[16]

The basic rule of the Complaints Procedure is that an anonymised summary of the findings and the opinion by the Research Integrity Committee are published. The Board deviated from this by publishing without anonymization. Nevertheless, the LOWI ruled quite lenient. Because the case had already, long before, been brought to the attention of the press with the full name being given, the Board could reasonably decide to publish without anonymization. Anonymized publication did not in fact serve a reasonable purpose any longer.

Duty of Confidentiality

The Board and other parties involved should take into account the purpose of the duty of confidentiality. In addition to a procedural guarantee for those involved, the duty of confidentiality is also required for the effective performance of duties by the LOWI to take place. The LOWI is entrusted to review a contested (preliminary) decision of the Board and advise on this. If there is a reason for it, LOWI will advise the Board to revise the decision. Thereafter, the Board takes its final decision.

Under the old LOWI Regulation, the duty of confidentiality started from the date on which the complainant submitted the complaint to the LOWI with the result that there was no formal duty of confidentiality during the period the Board published its

15 Netherlands Code of Conduct for Research Integrity 2018, par. 5.4, principle 18.
16 Netherlands Code of Conduct for Research Integrity 2018, par. 5.4, intro.

contested (preliminary) decision and the start of the LOWI procedure.[17] In the new LOWI Regulation 2018 the duty to maintain confidentiality is extended from the announcement of the (preliminary) decision of the Board to the announcement of the final decision.[18]

The duty of confidentiality, throughout the procedure, is of great importance. When allegations of violation of the principles of research integrity are prematurely made public, when no final ruling has been passed, it can be harmful to researchers and hamper further careful handling of the complaint (to the Board) or the petition (to the LOWI). Therefore, it is in the interest of all parties involved to observe the duty of confidentiality and not make any suspicions, allegations or accusations public. Even after the final decision of the Board, all Parties must continue to exercise restraint in order not to harm the original defendant and their reputation in the field. This is especially true when the complaint about violation of the principles of research integrity is unfounded. Breach of confidentiality by the representative of the Petitioner was the subject of LOWI opinion 2016-14. On 26 January 2016, the representative submitted the petition to the LOWI. In any case, from that moment, in the same way as the Petitioner, the representative, under Article 10 of the LOWI Regulation (old), was obliged to maintain confidentiality. But a few days later he addressed the matter explicitly in an interview with a newspaper and indicated that the opinion of the Research Integrity Committee of Leiden University was the main reason for submitting a petition to the LOWI. The LOWI ruled that with this interview, as published in the newspaper (and on the website of the representative), he had violated the obligation to maintain confidentiality.

In Opinion 2017-05 the Board of Leiden University decided to discontinue the complaints proceedings because the complainant had ignored an injunction to remove all online communication about the complaint within a specified period. LOWI agreed. The Board could discontinue the complaint proceeding due to (persistent) violation of the duty of confidentiality by the Complainant.

To this extent, the transparency principle of the PRINTEGER statement, ALLEA and the Netherlands Code of Conduct requires nuance. Publication of the decision of the Board must wait until the appeal period at the LOWI has expired or until a definitive decision has been made on the basis of the opinion of the LOWI. It is recommended that next to the LOWI Regulation 2018 this nuance is explicitly included in the VSNU Model Complaints Procedure Research Integrity and the resulting complaint procedure regulations of the institutions.

Protecting the Alleged Perpetrators

According to the PRINTEGER Statement researchers accused of misconduct are innocent until proven guilty. Their privacy must be protected throughout the whole investigation process in accordance with applicable legislation. In cases where accused researchers are cleared of accusations, appropriate measures must be taken to ensure that their names and reputations are not damaged or are repaired. As even unfounded

17 LOWI Regulation (old), Article 10.

18 LOWI Regulation 2018, Article 4.

complaints may cause damage to a researcher, it should be made clear that malicious complaints are a breach of research integrity.

The ALLEA Code recognizes the same principles: presumption of innocence, confidentiality of the procedures, appropriate restorative action and accusing a researcher of misconduct in a malicious way is a violation of research integrity itself. The same is true for the new Netherlands code of conduct in its paragraph 5.4 on complaint procedures.

Anonymous Complaints

What is missing in the PRINTEGER Statement and the ALLEA Code is the issue what to do with anonymous complaints. In line with the LOWI case law the new Netherlands code of conduct is clear on this issue: anonymous complaints will not be considered. However, the institution can in that case initiate an investigation on its own initiative.[19]

Leading in this respect is LOWI-opinion 2015-02. It concerned a possible violation of the principles of research integrity in which an anonymous complainant complained to the Board of Free University Amsterdam about assumed plagiarism. In essence, the LOWI deemed it undesirable for a complainant to maintain complete anonymity – meaning that no one knows the identity of the individual involved – in cases concerning possible violations of the principles of research integrity. This is in line with the Memorandum on Scientific Integrity 2001 of the Royal Netherlands Academy of Arts and Sciences, which states that 'anonymous complaints are not (and cannot be) considered'. By the way, the 2001 Memorandum is the founding document of LOWI as well.

In so far as an institution's complaint procedure allows for anonymous complaints, the LOWI considers that the Board of such an institution must proceed with great caution when exercising the competence to review (completely) anonymous complaints. The requirements of transparency, the right of defence, and the right of both parties to be heard are naturally prohibitive factors for such complaints. The interests of a complainant who wishes to remain anonymous can best be served by a satisfactory whistle-blower's system and by the undertaking to maintain confidentiality, whereby the accused and/or the Research Integrity Committee do not know the name of the complainant (in this specific case), but the Board does. In such an approach, the anonymous complainant can be held responsible for adhering to the duty of confidentiality to the same degree as the other parties involved. The Board can also hear the anonymous complainant (in this case) separately, after which the accused has the opportunity to respond (in writing) to the minutes of the hearing. That would uphold the right of both parties to be heard and the right to defence, comply with the requirement of transparency, and serve the interests of both the anonymous complainant and the accused.

In the case of LOWI opinion 2015-02, the accused (a Moroccan female PhD student) filed a report with the police for defamation. Initially, the public prosecutor refused prosecution against the anonymous complainant NN, but was forced to do so

19 Netherlands Code of Conduct for Research Integrity 2018, par. 5.4, principle 6.

by the Court of Appeal.[20] After a two-and-a-half year investigation, the public prosecution has failed to trace the identity of the anonymous complainant and has closed the case.

The accused filed a complaint with the Netherlands Institute for Human Rights as well. The Institute was of the opinion that the accused did not show that the Free University discriminated against her by considering anonymous complaints about her PhD research. But the Free University should have done more to protect the accused against media publications with a discriminatory nature.[21]

More successful was the accused in her civil procedure, a claim towards the Free University in connection with the way in which the university has dealt with the anonymous complaints. The Sub-district Court ruled that the university has acted in violation of the principle of good employment practices and has acted unlawfully towards the accused and condemned the Free University to pay compensation of euro 7.500.[22]

Establishing a Research Integrity Committee and Appointing an Ombudsperson

According to the Bonn Statement there should be an integrity committee installed at the level of the institution or at the national level.

All research organisations should also have a research integrity ombudsperson. This function should be adequately resourced, well known in the organisation, and there should be a low threshold for contacting this person. Researchers who experience research integrity dilemmas or have come into an integrity related conflict should be able to discuss their case with the ombudsperson in a strictly confidential manner.

The function of the ombudsperson should be clearly separated from a formal research integrity committee, so it is clear to researchers that contacting the ombudsperson does not imply a formal registration of a case with the committee.

The ombudsperson function could include the responsibility to continuously assess the research integrity status of the organisation, and advise on policies and action plans for strengthening the work on integrity.

The ALLEA code is not very precise on the procedures for dealing with violations and allegations of misconduct. The code is limited to the principles that need to be incorporated into any investigation process. The New Netherlands Code of Conduct is also very limited on this point. The complaint procedure is subject of the National Model Complaints Procedure for Research Integrity. This Model Regulation has been drawn up by the joint Dutch universities as a starting point and an example for the complaints procedure of each university itself. The Model Regulation provides for a research integrity committee and a confidential advisor (a sort of ombudsperson) who may not be a member of research integrity committee.

In the Netherlands it is unfortunate that the formal and material provisions on research integrity are divided over two documents, the Code of Conduct for Research Integrity and the Model Regulation.

---

20 Court of Appeal Arnhem-Leeuwarden 06-12-2015, case no. K14/1104.

21 The Netherlands Institute for Human Rights 24-07- 2015, opinion 2015-87.

22 Sub-district Court Amsterdam 25-04-2016, ECLI:NL:RBAMS:2016:2702.

The Code of Conduct is binding to the institutions that subscribe to it. This is code is already subscribed by the Royal Netherlands Academy of Arts and Sciences (KNAW), the Netherlands Federation of University Medical Centres (NFU), the Netherlands Organisation for Scientific Research (NWO), the Federation of Applied Research Institutes, the Netherlands Association of Universities of Applied Sciences and the Association of Universities in the Netherlands (VSNU). Other institutions, including private enterprises, can also subscribe to this Code.

The Model Regulation is produced by the Association of Universities in the Netherlands (VSNU) and addressed to the universities as a model for their complaint regulation but is not binding as such. For example, in the past the Free University had a complaint regulation in which the Ombudsman was a member of the Research Integrity Committee as well. In opinion 2015-02 the LOWI determined in line with the Bonn Statement that an Ombudsman or Confidential Advisor has a different role than a Research Integrity Committee and that an Ombudsman cannot therefore be a member of the committee that investigates the complaint. The Free University has amended its complaint regulation.

On the other hand, a non-university such as the Netherlands Organisation for Scientific Research (NWO) did not consider itself bound to the Model Regulation at all. In LOWI opinion 2017-12 the Applicant's complaint has been dealt with in substance by the Confidential Advisor and not by a Research Integrity Committee. The NWO Regulations do not require the involvement of a Research Integrity Committee. The LOWI has therefore found with some surprise that complaints are handled by NWO on the basis of a regulation that deviates from the prescribed Model Complaints Procedure of the VSNU on this point, and also on other points.

Making Explicit the Applicable Standards for Research Integrity

The Bonn Statement realizes that researchers are often members of disciplinary professional organisations that have research integrity guidelines that may not be completely aligned with the organisational ones. They may also engage in multi-disciplinary, multi-organisational and multinational projects and networks where there are different standards for research integrity, for instance related to authorship.

Organisations should be aware of potentially conflicting standards and must have a policy for addressing them. Project leaders should seek to specify the standards the project will follow from the very beginning; most preferably by making this explicit in a collaboration agreement. The chosen standard must be well-justified and refer to generally accepted guidelines for research integrity. This collaboration agreement should also make explicit how allegations of research misconduct will be addressed in a multi-organisational project.

The ALLEA Code is very explicit on collaborative working as well:

- All partners in research collaborations take responsibility for the integrity of the research.

  ...

- All partners formally agree at the start of their collaboration on expectations and standards concerning research integrity, on the laws and regulations that will apply, on protection of the intellectual property of collaborators, and on procedures for handling conflicts and possible cases of misconduct.

The new Code of Conduct for researchers and institutions in the Netherlands also formulates as standard for good research practice in joint research: make clear agreements about matters concerning research integrity and related matters such as intellectual property rights.

I am not aware of LOWI-opinions on collaborative working. As such collaborative working is not an issue of research integrity itself, but the need of mutual agreement on the applicable standards in collaborative working is obvious. Moreover, LOWI is not competent to advise on disputes in the field of labour law, intellectual property rights, copyright or patent law.

To Conclude

The Bonn PRINTEGER Statement has emerged from the need for increased focus and guidance on how organisations may address research integrity issues. It serves that purpose excellently. The provisions are more precise, more elaborated than in documents such as the ALLEA code and the new Netherlands Code of Conduct on Research Integrity. It differs from the other documents by its strong focus on research performing organisations. In that respect the statement is of great help. Together, the more individually oriented codes and the organisationally and institutionally oriented PRINTEGER statement ensure that research integrity is a collective enterprise of researchers and their institutions.

EU Pensioners on the Move – Perceptions of Mobility

*Anoeshka Gehring**

Introduction

The European institutions see EU citizens as important actors in the process of transforming EU citizenship into a 'tangible reality' (Stockholm Programme 2009, p. 4). By knowing and practising their EU citizenship rights, citizens are supposed to give meaning to EU citizenship which would otherwise remain a hollow concept. The mobile citizens making use of their free movement rights are seen as important driving forces in this process. They are the 'human face' of European integration (Favell and Recchi 2009). What EU citizenship means for mobile citizens themselves and how EU citizens practice and evaluate their free movement rights is generally not a central theme in reports and studies on EU citizenship. Only a few empirical studies have been conducted on this topic (cf. Ackers and Dwyer 2002, 2004; Antonsich 2008; Favell 2008; Recchi and Favell 2009; Recchi 2015).[1] This article contributes to this line of research by focussing on retirement migrants' 'lived EU citizenship' experiences.

'Lived citizenship' deals with the different ways in which social actors give meaning to and practise their citizenship (Lister, et al. 2003). In this study I will use a sociologically informed definition of citizenship in which the 'norms, practices, meanings, and identities' which citizens associate with their EU citizenship status and the rights attached to it will be central (Isin and Turner 2002, p. 4). The specific focus in this study is on how mobile citizens practice and give meaning to free movement: the 'cornerstone' of EU citizenship.

The analysis of this research is based on the experiences of a specific group of EU citizens: retirement migrants. Retirement migrants are mobile citizens who spend (part of) their retirement in a Member State other than the Member State in which they spent their working life. Traditionally, mobile workers are seen as the main actors in the European process. How 'economically inactive' mobile citizens who have reached retirement age evaluate and practise their free movement rights has received less attention. Based on qualitative fieldwork with pensioners who move after retirement from the Netherlands to Spain, this topic will be addressed. Two groups of retirement migrants

* Coordinator Stichting Vluchtelingen in de Knel. This article is based on a previously published article in '*Innovation: The European Journal of Social Sciences*'. Reference to the original article: Gehring, A. (2018). Mobile Pensioners: Retirement migrants' perspectives of EU citizenship and Free Movement. *Innovation: The European Journal of Social Sciences,* 1-16.

1 Ackers and Dwyer (2002, 2004) have conducted research into the rights attached to EU citizenship and the impact on retirement migrants' lives. Favell (2008) has conducted research into the human dimension of European integration, the practice of free movement, and mobility in an integrating Europe by focusing on what he calls 'Eurostars' who live in 'Eurocities'. Recchi (2014, 2015) and Antonsich (2008) have conducted research into the meaning of EU citizenship for citizens. Based on an innovative survey, Recchi and Favell's (2009) edited book *Pioneers of European Integration: Citizenship and Mobility in the EU* provides important quantitative insight into the different types and backgrounds of migrants using their free movement rights.

move between both countries: Dutch retirement migrants who belong to the more affluent cohort of retirement migrants, also called *lifestyle migrants* or *amenity seeking migrants,* and returning retired Spanish labour migrants who came as *guest workers* to the Netherlands and return (part of the year) to their countries of origin after retirement.

The following section of this article provides a brief overview of the development of EU citizenship and free movement. It is followed by a description of the research approach. The subsequent empirical sections discuss retirement migrants' mobility patterns and practices and the meaning attached to (free) movement. The article ends by concluding that it is important to include citizens' perspectives and practices in the debates on EU citizenship, especially when the content and potential of EU citizenship for citizens is discussed and when citizens' perspectives are used to give meaning to the concept.

EU Citizenship and Free Movement

The status of 'Citizen of the Union' has been formally enshrined in the Treaty on the Functioning of the European Union (TFEU). One of the most direct sources of rights, and the focus in this study, is free movement, which is often described as the 'cornerstone' or 'trigger' of EU citizenship (e.g. Recchi 2015). The right of EU citizens and their family members to move and reside freely on EU territory is laid down in Directive 2004/38/EC. The Directive unifies the previous legislation scattered among different Regulations and Directives and adopted conclusions from ECJ jurisprudence. Although free movement is now free for *people* and not only for *workers*, there are still some requirements for non-economically active citizens who stay more than three months and less than five years in another Member State. For stays of over three months, EU citizens and their family members (if not working) must have sufficient resources and sickness insurance to ensure that they do not become a burden on the social services of the host Member State during their stay. After a five-year period of uninterrupted legal residence, EU citizens have the right of permanent residence.[2]

Mobile citizens making use of their free movement rights, are seen as important driving forces in the process of transforming EU citizenship into a 'tangible' reality. Mobile citizens are expected to support the EU project with more enthusiasm than non-mobile Europeans, because of the experience of easy border crossing and the enjoyment of denationalized rights as EU citizens (Recchi 2015). Most of the debates on the significance of EU citizenship still focus on legal and political aspects with a top-down approach. In order to move beyond this perspective this study looks at 'lived citizenship': the meaning people attach to citizenship in their daily lives. It also sheds light on 'the ways in which people's social and cultural backgrounds and material circumstances affect their lives as citizens' (Hall and Williamson, 1999, p. 2).

2 Article 7 (1) Directive 2004/38/EC.

Retirement Migrants

In this article two groups of retirement migrants are included: Dutch retirement migrants who belong to the more general group of Northern European retirement migrants who move to the Mediterranean after retirement, and retirement return migrants who came as guest workers to a Western European country and returned to their countries of origin after retirement.

Northern European retirement migrants are often described as *lifestyle* migrants or *amenity-seeking* migrants in the literature, referring to their lifestyle and motivations for migration (King, Warnes and Williams 2000; Benson and O'Reilly 2009). Studies on Northern European retirement migrants show that Northern Europeans move to the Mediterranean in order to improve their quality of life by living in a country with a warmer and healthier climate which allows for more (outdoor) recreational activities. Studies on Northern-European retirement migrants generally frame retirement migrants as movers who do not face many obstacles when they cross borders and settle in another country after retirement (Benson and O'Reilly 2009). As will be discussed in the following sections, the idea of freedom and easy movement is also reflected in the accounts of retirement migrants themselves.

Return retirement migrants' motivations are framed in a different discourse in the literature. This discourse is less leisure focused and the mobility patterns are framed within their broader migratory history. Return retirement migrants came to Northern Europe as guest workers in the sixties and early seventies of the last century and are now retiring, or have already retired. The moment of retirement can be considered a new phase in the lives of migrants who came as guest workers to the host country. Working and earning money give meaning to guest workers' stay abroad and when, at retirement, the direct link between place of residence and income is no longer self-evident new options arise. An important new option concerns the renegotiation of place(s) of residence (Bolzman 2013, Constant & Massey 2003, Krumme 2004). The majority of the retirement migrants prefers to maintain a flexible migratory pattern due to a dual place attachment and a duality of resources (cf. Bolzman, 2013).

Studies on both Northern European as well as return retirement migration have shown that mobility after retirement is enabled by three interrelated factors (cf. King, Warnes and Williams 2000) Firstly, retirement migrants' stage in the life cycle can be associated with increased free time and the absence of work obligations. Secondly, globalisation developments such as cheap flights between the Mediterranean countries and the Netherlands and face-to-face video chat, have changed the perception of distance. And thirdly, EU free movement legislation enables retirement migrants to live their transnational lives and may create a perception of movement instead of migration for those migrants moving within the EU. These developments have made it possible for both groups of retirement migrants to: 'exploit, maintain and continue to develop residential opportunities, social networks and welfare entitlements in more than one country' (Warnes and Williams 2006, p. 1265).

Both groups of retirement migrants move at a stage in their life cycle when work obligations no longer tie them to a certain place of residence. This new stage allows them to spend (part of) their retirement in another country. Studies on Northern European retirement migration and retirement return migration show that mobile pensioners prefer to maintain a flexible mobility pattern (Bolzman 2013; Gehring 2015).

They have built up a transnational life between the country where they spent their working life and the country where they are spending their retirement (Gustafson 2008; Krumme 2004). Bolzman, Fibbi and Vial (2006) refer to the dual orientation of retirement migrants as a 'duality of resources and references'. A 'duality of resources' refers to retirement migrants' dual economic assets (pensions), family networks and broader social relationships. 'Duality of references' refers to the share of cultural and symbolic attachments between the two countries.

The amount of time spent in both countries differs per individual, but retirement migrants generally opt for seasonal migration, back-and-forth migration or (semi-)permanent migration.[3] In all situations, retirement migrants prefer to pay regular visits to both countries, as long as their health allows. In a previous study I have shown that retirement migrants' considerations for a specific migratory (and residence) pattern are often related to ways of seeking access to social security provisions, both formal and informal (Gehring 2013).

Retirement migrants thus move frequently between the country of retirement and the country in which they spent their working life. The ways in which retirement migrants refer to their mobility between countries differs and is dependent on their background. The following analysis shows that the interviewed retirement migrants speak in three ways about their mobility and (indirectly) also about free movement legislation and EU citizenship.

Research Methods

This article focuses on retirement migration from the Netherlands to Spain. It includes Dutch and Spanish retirement migrants moving or returning to Spain. Both groups of retirement migrants spent their working life in the Netherlands and moved (part of the year) after retirement. This article is based on 48 in-depth open-ended interviews, which were conducted between January 2012 and January 2013. During 2014 and 2015 several follow-up informal talks took place. Additional data was collected by participating during social gatherings and interviews with officials. The respondents were selected by purposive snowball sampling. The main criteria for selecting respondents were that the migrants were retired, in the sense that they had chosen or been required to give up paid work, and that they were spending at least six months per year in Spain.

A total of 24 interviews were conducted with Dutch retirees on the Costa Blanca in Spain: nineteen interviews with couples, two with men and three with women. 24 interviews were conducted with Spanish nationals in Andalucia, Asturias and the Ne-

3 Seasonal migrants chose to stay a long season in the retirement migrants country. Dutch retirement migrants generally chose to stay the winter months in the country of retirement (to 'overwinter') and return migrants generally chose to stay the summer months in the country of retirement so that their family members could visit them in the family home as well. The back-and-forth migrants are the migrants who chose to divide their time between both countries and spend for example 3 months in one country and then 3 months in the other country. (Semi-)permanent retirement migrants spend most of the year in the retirement country. The permanent migrants are official residents of the retirement migrants country, whereas the semi-permanent retirement migrants chose to retain their main residence in the Netherlands for a variety of reasons (see also Gehring 2016).

therlands: fourteen with couples and seven with men and three with women. The interviews were semi-structured and followed a life-history approach in which the retirement migrants were asked to talk about mobility during their working life, the decision-making process leading to (temporary) movement to Spain, the factors which influenced their preference for a certain residence and mobility pattern, and their future expectations. During the interviews retirement migrants' perspectives of (EU) citizenship were addressed directly and indirectly.

Lived EU Citizenship – Mobility and Free Movement in Practice

In this section the personal stories of retirement migrants are discussed.

Movers in the EU

Dutch retirement migrants moving to Spain describe their mobility between both countries as 'movement' instead of 'migration'. They explicitly do not see themselves as migrants. Although literature on retirement migration consistently describes the retirees as migrants, it is questionable whether this is the right term to use for the population. A semantical shift towards mobility and movement would better suit the self-descriptions of the retirees. This semantical shift ties in with the shift which has taken place within the EU. EU documents increasingly describe intra-EU movement as 'mobility' and the people as 'mobile citizens'. Although movement within the EU still, technically, takes the form of international migration, it can be done under the conditions typical of internal mobility. Recchi (2015), states therefore that mobility in the EU can be seen as migration 'in first class', without the nuisance of documents or the risks that characterize the journey and settlement of traditional migrants. In this section I will argue, that the Dutch retirees moving to Spain perceive themselves to be moving 'in first class' and can be described as 'privileged movers'.

One of the Dutch respondents who moved to Spain, Sjaak, frames his motivation to move and his perception of movement as follows:

> It is actually very simple. If you work you're bound to your work environment and if you no longer work you're free to go wherever you want. That is, so to say, the starting point and the easy part is of course the Schengen story. Thus within Europe, like we all do now, you can move wherever you want. So that was actually really clear to us: that we, after receiving our pension, when you don't have any obligations anymore in the Netherlands to an employer or family... Then, the Netherlands is not so interesting anymore, so you start to look further[...] If you don't like it there, you move back. That is possible. That is Europe. We have made that all together. [...] What I know about it, is that when you *emigrate*, the motivation is often a negative one: you can't get a job.
> *Sjaak, Dutch retirement migrant living in the province of Alicante (emphasis made by the respondent)*

EU free movement legislation, or as Sjaak states the 'Schengen story', enables his mobility and settlement in Spain. By clearly stating that he *moved* instead of *migrated* to Spain, Sjaak refers to the EU as a post-national entity in which the nuisance of borders and papers no longer exists in his perception. Instead of being a migrant who may face discrimination and other forms of disadvantage, mobile pensioners who move within Europe can be seen, and see themselves, as 'first-class', privileged, movers.

By retiring in another country, Dutch retirees often come to live in an area of the retirement country with a high number of foreigners. Living in these international environments can change the pensioners' self-understanding as citizens. Some of the Dutch pensioners express that they have transformed their national self-understanding to a more post-national or European form of identification. They explicitly feel, like the motto of the European Union, 'united in diversity'.

These pensioners provide a clear example of Favell's (2008) statement that horizons change for EU citizens who do move: 'The old nation-state-society no longer appears so inevitable as one's ultimate identity, or the framework in which to live out your life'. These Eurostars, as Favell calls EU citizens living in European global cities or free movement hubs, define their identities in relation to the international cities in which they live. This is also reflected in the accounts of the pensioners who move to Spain and who live in international environments. The Dutch retirement migrants in Spain do not live in 'global cities' but in 'global villages' where they live in an international community.

Living in an international environment and being mobile does not mean that all retirement migrants experience post-national feelings of belonging. Some retirement migrants explicitly state that, within the global village in which they live, they interact solely with other Dutch retirement migrants. These retirement migrants generally state that they do not feel united with other Europeans and consequently do not have a feeling of being European. The retirement migrants who express a more national form of identification show that mobility does not trigger a European identity per se and that by being mobile not all EU citizens support the European process with enthusiasm (see also Antonsich 2008). The differences between the interviewed retirement migrants are most often related to retirement migrants' class and educational level, as well as their language skills. Among my Dutch respondents, those who felt comfortable communicating in English and who had previous experience of living abroad during their working life, generally expressed having a more international network. Thus, although all Dutch retirement migrants refer to their mobility as a form of privileged movement, movement does not trigger identification with Europe or as a European for all retirement migrants.

First-class Migrants

Although Spanish retirement migrants move within the same space as Dutch retirement migrants who move to Spain, the narratives of both groups differ. Whereas Dutch pensioners state that they *moved* to Spain, many Spanish retirement migrants refer to themselves as migrants who *migrate* between states. They talk about their mobility as if they are first-class *migrants* instead of *movers*. Spanish retirement migrants apply a rights- based, historical narrative when talking about their mobility. This is in line with the ways in which they are reflected in the literature (Bolzman, Fibi and Vial 2006; Klinthäll 2006). By being positioned by scholars and popular media as migrants, and by migrating to the Netherlands as guest workers, Spanish retirees started to review and reflect to themselves as migrants as well.

The interviewed Spanish retirement migrants moved to the Netherlands before Spain became a member of the EU in 1986. The accession to the EU and the following developments, such as the introduction of the euro, changed the migratory experience of Spanish migrants. The Spanish retirement migrants became privileged EU citizens during their lifetime.

> We notice the [changes in Europe] of course. I am from the migrant generation, we've seen it changing. When we first came to the Netherlands we had to travel to Madrid by bus and then we took a train all the way to the Netherlands. We had to stop at each and every border and show our passport. It took us very long to get there! People were lining up. Now we just go.
> What really changed is the money. We used to have pesetas, francs and guilders when we travelled. [Now] [w]e go and come back and our children can come and visit us as well. Now it's easy in Europe and all.
> *Anna, Spanish retirement migrant living in Asturias*

The history of the Spanish retirement migrants closely follows the development of European integration in recent decades. The Spanish migrants frame their narratives on Europe in this historical perspective and in relation to the rights which they have acquired. The Spanish retirement migrants refer to the developments with regard to free movement as factors enabling their mobile life, but they also continue to explicitly describe themselves as migrants.

The EU promotes free movement and settlement as if it is similar to intra-state movement. As stated before, the EU has marked this semantically by referring to intra-EU movement as 'mobility' instead of 'migration'. The Spanish retirement migrants generally continue to refer to themselves as 'migrants' (*los migrantes*) or 'return migrants' (*los remigrantes* or *los migrantes retornados*). They came to the Netherlands as guest workers who migrated from one state and became foreigners in another state. They did not move as 'first-class' EU citizens within a space without borders. Although the legal emancipation of this group of EU citizens took place, the perception of the self has not shifted and is still rooted in the pre-EU vocabulary of migration.

Many of the Spanish migrants do not feel that they integrated well in Dutch society, because they mainly lived within Spanish communities. The assumption of the European institutions that when citizens make use of their free movement rights, greater bonds are created between Europeans and a collective European identity is boosted, is generally not reflected in the narratives of the Spanish retirement migrants. They generally did not or do not have a lot of contact with the Dutch population and they continue to feel migrants or foreigners in the Netherlands. Over the years the interviewed Spanish migrants have become transnational *migrants* who move across the borders of states and they have not changed in post-national movers.

To Conclude

Moving EU citizens are generally seen as the engine in the process of deepening European integration (Recchi 2015). Mobile citizens are seen by the European institutions as important contributors to the process of transforming EU citizenship into a 'tangible reality'. By looking at the narratives and practices of retirement migrants who move from the Netherlands to Spain after retirement, insight is provided into the diversity of the narratives of retirement migrants with regard to free movement and indirectly also with regard to EU citizenship. Retirement migrants may prefer to be mobile in similar ways, but the meanings citizens attach to their mobility are diverse and linked to their social and cultural backgrounds (Hall and Williamson 1999).

When looking horizontally at the accounts of retirement migrants, two different narratives about movement can be identified: privileged movers and privileged migrants. These narratives refer to the ways in which retirement migrants perceive themselves as mobile citizens and also as EU citizens. Although all interviewed retirement migrants are (or were) EU citizens, their perceptions of EU citizenship, and specifically free movement, differed. This is mainly linked to retirement migrants' migratory background, country of origin, country of retirement and the way in which EU citizenship was acquired.

Whereas Dutch retirement migrants explicitly refer to their EU citizenship and the rights attached to it, only some of them, mainly the higher educated retirement migrants and the retirement migrants who worked abroad during their working life, also state that they identify with Europe as a post-national entity and explicitly support the European project. The free movement rights practised by Spanish retirement migrants has not led to post-national identification per se, because they frame their narratives in a rights-based historical context by focusing on their movement as migration between national states. How EU citizenship as a 'tangible reality' is created by EU citizens practising their EU citizenship rights is thus diffuse and differs per individual. The assumption that mobile citizens are the 'engine' of European integration should therefore be nuanced in further research on EU citizenship. When analysing the influence of EU citizenship, one should take into account that the backgrounds of EU citizens are diverse and hard to capture in general and broad statistics. In-depth quantitative and qualitative research could further deepen the complex reality of EU citizenship.

Bibliography

L. Ackers & P. Dwyer, 'Fixed laws, fluid lives: The citizenship status of post-retirement migrants in the European Union', 24(3) *Ageing and Society* 2004, p. 451-475.

L. Ackers & P. Dwyer, *Senior citizenship? Retirement, migration and welfare in the European Union,* Bristol: Policy 2002.

M. Antonsich, 'EUropean attachment and meanings of EUrope. A qualitative study in the EU-15', 27(6) *Political Geography* 2008, p. 691-710.

M. Benson & K. O'Reilly, Migration and the search for a better way of life: A critical exploration of lifestyle migration', 57(4) *The Sociological Review* 2009, p. 608-625.

C. Bolzman, 'Ageing of immigrants and the question of return: New answers to an old dilemma?', in: J. Percival (ed.), *Return migration in later life: International perspectives,* Bristol: Policy 2013, p. 67-87.

C. Bolzman, R. Fibbi & M. Vial, 'What to do after retirement? Elderly migrants and the question of return', *32*(8) *Journal of Ethnic and Migration Studies* 2006, p. 1359-1375.

A. Constant & D.S. Massey, 'Return migration by German guestworkers: Neoclassical versus new economic theories', 40(4) *International migration* 2002, p. 5-38.

A. Favell, 'The new face of East-West migration in Europe', 34(5) *Journal of ethnic and migration studies* 2008, p. 701-716.

A. Favell &E. Recchi *Pioneers of European integration. Citizenship and Mobility in the EU*, Cheltenham: Edward Elgar Publishing 2009.

A. Gehring, 'Seeking access to long-term care: Legal consciousness of Dutch retirement migrants on the Costa Blanca', *3*(6) *Oñati Socio-Legal Series*, 2013, p. 1023-1040.

A. Gehring, 'Pensioners on the move: A "legal gate" perspective on retirement migration to Spain', 23(5) *Population, Space and Place* 2015, e2007.

A. Gehring, 'Dutch retirement migration to Spain and Turkey: Seeking access to healthcare across borders', *Transnational Social Review*, *6*(3) 2016, p. 326-343

A. Gehring, A. (). Mobile pensioners: retirement migrants' perspectives of EU citizenship and free movement. *Innovation: The European Journal of Social Science Research* 2018, p. 1-16.

P. Gustafson, 'Transnationalism in retirement migration: the case of north European retirees in Spain', *31*(3) *Ethnic and racial studies* 2008, p. 451-475.

T. Hall &H. Williamson, *Citizenship and community*. Leicester: Youth Work 1999.

E.F. Isin & B.S. Turner, 'Citizenship studies: An introduction', in: E.F. Isin & B.S. Turner (eds), *Handbook of citizenship studies*, London: Sage 2002, p. 1-10.

R. King, T. Warnes & A.M. Williams, *Sunset lives: British retirement migration to the Mediterranean*, Oxford: Berg 2000.

M. Klinthäll, 'Retirement return migration from Sweden', 44(2) *International Migration* 2006, p. 153-180.

H. Krumme, 'Fortwährende remigration: Das transnationale pendeln türkischer arbeitsmigrantinnen und arbeitsmigranten im Ruhestand/Continual return: Transnational circular migration of Turkish migrant workers in retirement', 33(2) *Zeitschrift für Soziologie* 2004, p. 138-153.

R. Lister, N. Smith, S. Middleton & L. Cox, 'Young people talk about citizenship: Empirical perspectives on theoretical and political debates', 7(2) *Citizenship Studies* 2003, p. 235-253.

E. Recchi, *Mobile Europe: The theory and practice of free movement in the EU*, Basingstoke: Palgrave Macmillan 2015.

A.M. Warnes & A. Williams, 'Older migrants in Europe: A new focus for migration studies', 32(8) *Journal of Ethnic and Migration Studies* 2006, p. 1257-1281.

None of the above
How the UK Voted but Didn't Decide on Brexit

*Carolus Grütters**

1. Introduction[1]

On 23 June 2016 the electorate in the UK cast their vote in a referendum on Brexit. The results showed a majority in favour of leaving the European Union. Consequently, Prime Minister David Cameron who was in favour of remaining in the European Union stepped down. Subsequently, Theresa May was elected as the new Conservative Party leader, becoming Britain's 76th prime minister.[2]

Prime Minister May who used the slogan 'Brexit means Brexit' promised to deliver Brexit. However, the Withdrawal Agreement she negotiated with the European Commission was not accepted in the British parliament.[3] The House of Commons voted three times on motions related to the Withdrawal Agreement, which was called 'May's deal'.[4] But all three times the Commons voted her deal down.[5] When she tried to arrange for a fourth vote on her deal she lost the support of her own party. Conclusively, she announced on 24 May 2019 that she was stepping down as Tory leader and therefore as prime minister, an office she had held for less than three years.

After the defeat of the government in each of the three so-called 'meaningful votes' on the Withdrawal Agreement, motions were presented that blocked a no-deal Brexit. Interestingly, all of these motions against a no-deal Brexit were passed.[6] This implied that the British parliament did not want the UK to leave the EU with May's deal but neither without a deal. As Prime Minister May stated: 'The world knows what this house does not want. Today we need to send an emphatic message about what we do want.'[7] In order to decide what alternative to May's deal would be acceptable to Parliament a series of so-called 'indicative votes' were held.[8] On 27 March 2019 a first round

---

* Centre for Migration Law, Radboud University Nijmegen, the Netherlands.

1 I have respectfully borrowed the title 'None of the Above' from the report by McLean, Spirling and Russell mentioned in footnote 28.

2 Robert Walpole is considered Britain's first prime minister (1721-1742).

3 *Draft Agreement on the withdrawal of the United Kingdom of Great Britain and Northern Ireland from the European Union and the European Atomic Energy Community*, as agreed at negotiators' level on 14 November 2018, TF50 (2018) 55, Commission to EU27, Brussels 2018.

4 According to the most authoritative work on parliamentary procedure in the UK (Erskine May, Parliamentary Practice) the so-called 1604 rule states: 'A motion or an amendment which is the same, in substance, as a question which has been decided during a session may not be brought forward again during that same session.' Thus, the propositions put forward had to be formally different. However, in practice the question remained whether the Withdrawal Agreement was accepted.

5 Commons, meaningful votes: motion 293 (15 January 2019); motion 354 (12 March 2019); motion 395 (29 March 2019).

6 Commons votes on a no-deal Brexit: 29 January 2019 (motion 312, passed 318-310); 13 March 2019 (motion 359, passed 321-278; 3 April 2019 (motion 409, passed 313-312).

7 Debate in Commons 29 January 2019.

8 As a result of an amendment tabled by Oliver Letwin (motion 373 passed 329-302, 25 March 2019).

of eight indicative votes were held. However, all of these options failed. A second round of indicative votes was held on 1 April 2019 on four of the proposals that had failed in the first round but might pass if reconsidered. Surprisingly, however, none of these alternative options passed.

Cartoon © Jos Collignon

The issue I want to investigate is what actually went wrong? Could there have been a majority for one of these proposals, and why were there so many abstentions? Successively, I'll discuss the referendum, the quantitative outcome and its perceived meaning, and the form and outcome of the 'meaningful votes' and the 'indicative votes' in Parliament, and some historical parallels with the unsuccessful voting efforts on reforming the House of Lords.

2. The Brexit Referendum

The question put on the ballot paper of the referendum on Brexit on 23 June 2016 was: 'Should the United Kingdom remain a member of the European Union or leave the European Union.' Nine days before the referendum took place, almost two hundred academics from universities in the UK led by Alan Renwick of University College London protested in an opinion in the Telegraph: 'A referendum result is democratically legitimate only if voters can make an informed decision. Yet the level of misinformation in the current campaign is so great that democratic legitimacy is called into question'.[9] The main point was that the public, i.e. the voters were being deliberately misinformed and were therefore unable to make an informed decision.

Next to the issue of misinforming the public, the Royal Economic Society reported on the referendum question itself.[10] From a scientific perspective of voting theory, Colignatus argued: 'The Brexit referendum question can be rejected as technically unsatisfactory. One could even argue that the UK government should have annulled the outcome based on this basis alone.' In short, the question is misleading. The problem is that this 'question assumes a binary choice – Remain or Leave – while voting theory warns that allowing only two options can easily be a misleading representation of the real choice.'[11] The hidden complexity in the case of the Brexit question was: what does leave actually mean? Does leave imply the adoption of another framework, such as EFTA or WTO? Will the UK remain intact or split?[12] Although heavily criticized, the Electoral Commission argued that the recommended question was clear and straightforward for voters.[13]

Cartoon © Jos Collignon

Another difference from earlier referendums in the UK was that the Brexit referendum had no clear yes-or-no question but two statements about two different issues: leave and remain. The implicit other options were, for instance: leave with a deal, leave without a deal, or remain. The referendum, for instance in Scotland on the creation of a

9 Renwick, A. *et al.*, *The Telegraph*, 14 June 2016, Opinion.

10 Colignatus, 'Voting theory and the Brexit referendum question', *Newsletter April,* Royal Economic Society, 2017.

11 Colignatus 2017.

12 Colignatus 2017.

13 United Kingdom Electoral Commission, *Referendum on membership of the European Union: Assessment of the Electoral Commission on the proposed referendum question*, September 2015.

national assembly contained the following statements: 'I agree there should be a Scottish Parliament' and 'I do not agree there should be a Scottish Parliament'.[14] Although the Brexit referendum statements were meant to be clear, the presence of other options left room for a stalemate. But even then, a deadlock was possible. One of these options is called a 'cycle'. 'Take for example three candidates A, B and C and a particular distribution of preferences. When the vote is between A and B then A wins. We denote this as A > B. When the vote is between B and C then B wins, or B > C. When the vote is between C and A then C wins or C > A. Collectively A > B > C > A. Collectively, there is indifference. It is a key notion in voting theory that there can be distributions of preferences, such that a collective binary choice seems to result into a clear decision, while in reality there is a deadlock in hiding.'[15]

A third issue was the legal consequence of the Brexit referendum. Although a referendum as such in the UK is non-binding, the government unconditionally promised to implement the result of the referendum. That was an important difference from the referendums held in Scotland, Wales and Northern Ireland in 1997 and 1998 on a form of self-government and the creation of national assemblies. The Welsh, Scottish and Northern Ireland referendums were pre-legislative and 'only' investigating whether there was support for the creation of national assemblies. These referendums also stipulated that a national assembly could only be created if supported by at least 50% of the votes and 40% of the electorate. These minimum requirements were met and the national assemblies were created in 1998 (Northern Ireland) and 1999 (Scotland and Wales). These criteria, however, were not met in the Brexit referendum. In fact, the Brexit referendum had no criteria at all for meeting certain minimum requirements.

A fourth issue related to the Brexit referendum was the composition of the electorate. The four constituent countries of the UK: England, Wales, Scotland and Northern Ireland, do not have equal terms on the right to vote. Whereas the minimum age to vote is 18 years, in Scotland 16 and 17-year-olds were allowed to vote in the Scottish independence referendum of 2014. The Electoral Commission reported positively on this expansion: 'This referendum showed that for young people, indeed for all voters, when they perceive an issue to be important and are inspired by it, they will both participate in the debate and show up on polling day'.[16] The rationale was that young people would be most affected by the outcome of a referendum and therefore should take part. However, a proposal by the House of Lords to lower the minimum age to 16 years in the Brexit referendum was rejected by the House of Commons (303-253).[17] The argument made on behalf of the government by Lord Faulks was: 'We want to avoid any allegations of interference and we fear that changing the franchise, including this particular change, could be seen as doing exactly that and could seriously undermine the legitimacy of the referendum. (…) However, we have to ask ourselves

14 The referendums in Wales and Northern Ireland contained the same type of yes-or-no statements: 'I (do not) agree there should be a Welsh Assembly', and: 'Do you support the [Good Friday] Agreement reached at the multi-party talks on Northern Ireland and set out in Command Paper 3883?'.

15 Colignatus 2017.

16 Electoral Commission, *Scottish Independence Referendum Report on the referendum held on 18 September 2014,* Edinburgh 2014.

17 House of Commons, 8 December 2015, division 144 against the Lords amendment to extend the franchise for the European referendum to 16 and 17-year-olds (303-253). The House of Lords had accepted this amendment on 18 November 2015 (293-211).

whether, in our desire to enthuse 16 and 17-year-olds, we may be in danger of placing too great a responsibility on them'.[18] Lord Tyler (Liberal Democrat) very subtly argued against this with the following rebuttal: 'Will the noble Lord tell us whether he has seen the film 'Suffragette'?[19] The argument that he has just been advancing was the argument for not giving women the vote until after the First World War and then for not extending it to those under the age of 28. Those arguments were deployed by his contemporaries, as it were, of that period'.[20]

Finally, the right to vote was limited to: British citizens, Irish citizens, or Commonwealth citizens, who were resident in the UK or Gibraltar, were registered to vote and were not legally excluded from voting. Additionally, British citizens who had lived abroad for less than 15 years were also allowed to vote. Thus, British citizens who had been living abroad for a longer period were excluded. Also excluded from voting were EU citizens resident in the UK, whereas a possible Brexit would probably have substantially influenced the legal status of these latter categories.

3. Results of Brexit Referendum

The outcome of the Brexit referendum 'stunned' the world, so it seems on reading the Washington Post or the BBC website.[21] But if one studies the polls and the comments more closely it is not improbable that a too-close-to-call prediction was overruled by a combination of wishful thinking and gamblers who simply did not believe that Brexit could really happen.[22]

The often-stated result of the referendum was that 48% voted to remain and 52% to leave the EU. However, that is not the whole picture. The first remark is that this is the overall result of the UK. If one looks at the results per country there is an interesting difference. Two countries, Scotland (62%) and Northern Ireland (56%) voted to remain, whereas the other two countries Wales (53%) and England (53%) voted to leave. One might call that a draw. However, if you include those who did not vote, either because they were not interested or because they did not know what to vote for, the picture becomes different: each of these three categories gets about a third of the votes. This also means that only 38% of the electorate voted to leave, which would not meet minimum requirements in other referendums. As mentioned above, however, there were no minimum requirements to meet in this referendum.

18 House of Lords, 18 November 2015, volume 767, c.175-176.

19 *Suffragette*, movie by Sarah Gavon (2015), on the struggle for women in 1912 in UK to obtain the right to vote.

20 House of Lords, 18 November 2015, volume 767, c.177.

21 Swanson, A., 'Five charts capture the world's stunned — and scary — reaction to Brexit', *Washington Post* 24 June 2016. Likewise, on the site of the *BBC* 24 June 2016: 'Brexit: Europe stunned by UK Leave vote'.

22 Nate Cohn, 'Why the surprise over Brexit? Don't blame the polls', *New York Times, The Upshot*, 24 June 2016.

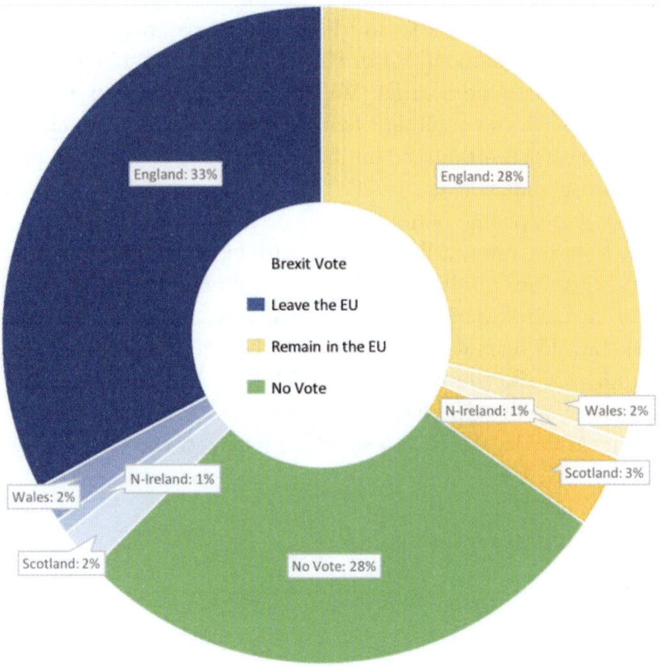

Chart 1 Brexit Vote
Sources: Centre for Migration Law; Grütters, C., E. Guild, P. Minderhoud, R. van Oers & T. Strik, Brexit and Migration, a study by the Odysseus Network requested by the EP's Committee on Civil Liberties, Justice and Home Affairs, Brussels 2018, Chart 1, p. 12; BBC <www.bbc.com/news/politics/eu_referendum/results>.

The actual differences between the number of leave voters (17.4 million) and remain voters (16.1 million) was 1.3 million: 2.7 % of the electorate of 46.5 million. Interestingly, the number of abstentions (28%) was ten times the majority of 2.7%. The results of the Brexit referendum have been analysed, for instance on the issue of age. According to the website 'Lord Ashcroft Polls' age correlates with voting behaviour: 'The older the voters, the more likely they were to have voted to leave the EU.'[23] So, if the 16 and 17-year-olds had been allowed to vote then the electorate would have increased by some 1.5 million voters. If there is a clear correlation between age and voting behaviour, it would be fair to state that three-quarters of these young voters would have voted to remain. Considering a small percentage of abstentions amongst these youngsters, probably about 1 million extra remain votes would have been cast, which would have almost closed the gap between leave voters and remain voters.

23 Lord Ashcroft Polls, 24 June 2016 <lordashcroftpolls.com/2016/06/how-the-united-kingdom-voted-and-why/>.

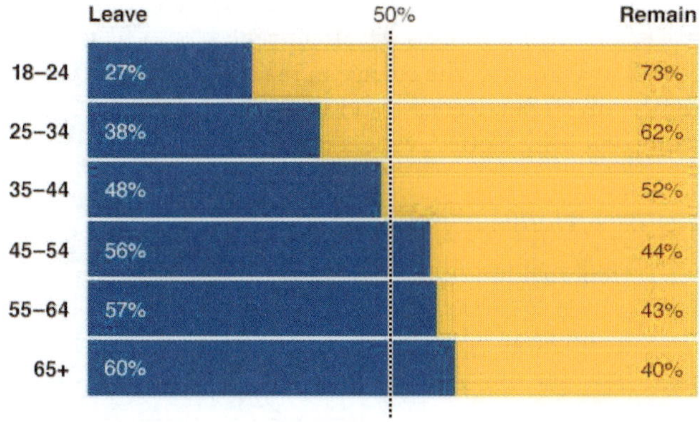

Chart 2 Age of Brexit voters
Sources: Lord Ashcroft Polls; BBC.
If we also take into account the preferences of the 3.8 million EU citizens resident in the EU and the 1.3 million British citizens who had been resident in the EU for more than 15 years, who had not been allowed to vote, one might seriously question whether the outcome of the Brexit referendum actually reflected 'the will of the people'.

4. May's Deal in Parliament

Prime Minister May tabled her deal on Brexit three times and lost these meaningful votes three times in the Commons. These results are interesting if the changes in voting behaviour are observed. First, it has to be noted that the defeat decreased: from the historical loss of 230 on the first Brexit vote (202-432), the loss was reduced to 149 in the second vote (242-391) and finally ended with a loss of 58 (286-344) in the third. Overall, one might say that each time May's deal was tabled, the results 'improved': the second vote showed a reduced gap of 81 (from 230 to 149) and the third vote reduced that gap again to 91 (from 149 to 58). Simple mathematics would have recommended having a fourth vote: another reduction of an average between 81 and 91 would have changed the defeat into a victory: 328-300. That, however, did not happen: politics never obeys the logic of a mathematical model.

Every MP who was allowed to vote did so in the first vote (15 January 2019). In this period there was a vacant seat (Newport West) so the totals did not add up to 650 but 649. The only non-voting MPs were those who never vote, i.e. the MPs of Sinn Fein (7), the Speaker (1) and his deputies (3), and the Tellers (4). Thus, the total number of votes was 634 and an absolute majority could be reached with a minimum of 318 votes. Although everyone voted in the first vote, this changed in the second and third votes. The second vote (12 March 2019) showed one abstention. The third vote (29 March 2019) showed 4 abstentions. The only abstention in the second vote came from Mr Douglas Ross, Conservative MP for Moray. Mr Ross had voted No in the first and abstained in the second. Interestingly, Mr Ross changed his mind again in the third round and voted Aye. The remaining changes comparing votes1 and 2 were not unexpected: 39 Conservatives and 1 Labour MP changed from No to Aye. The third vote showed another 41 Conservatives and 2 Labour MPs changing from No to Aye. Apart from the move of Mr Ross, 4 MPs abstained in the third vote (2 Labour, 1 SNP and 1

Independent). These changes were very effective. The ratio of the change in majority over the number of changing votes is the effectiveness ratio. This ratio varies between 0 (no effect) and 2 (maximum). The change in majority in vote 2 (81) was caused by 41 MPs; an extremely high effectiveness ratio of 81/41=1.98; vote 3 provided a change of 91 with a comparable high effectiveness ratio of 1.90.

Meaningful votes on May's deal

	Brexit vote-1 motion 293 15-01-2019	change 1-2	Brexit vote-2 motion 354 12-03-2019	change 2-3	Brexit vote-3 motion 395 29-03-2019
Ayes	202	+ 40	242	+ 44	286
Noes	432	– 41	391	– 47	344
Majority	– 230	– 81	– 149	– 91	– 58
Abstentions	0	+ 1	1	+ 3	4
subtotal	634		634		634
Others[24]	15		15		15
total	649		649		649

MPs who changed their vote; its effect on the majority; effectiveness-ratio

	change vote 1-2			*change vote 2-3*		
	Δ votes	*Δ maj.*	*ratio*	*Δ votes*	*Δ maj.*	*ratio*
all parties	41	– 81	1.98	48	– 91	1.90

Table 1 Meaningful votes on May's deal
Source: <commonsvotes.digiminster.com>

An interesting phenomenon occurred every time after these lost votes on May's deal. The Commons voted three times against a no-deal Brexit, meaning that although May's deal was voted down a majority of the Commons was against leaving the EU without a deal. These three motions were not the same, due to the '1604-rule'.[25] However, the tenor was the same: to prevent the UK leaving the EU without a deal. The first vote had a majority of 8. The second even had a majority of 43, but the third and last vote had the smallest margin possible: just one. The changes did not occur within one party. Vote 1 compared to vote 2 showed for the Conservatives: 5 moving from No to Aye; 2 from Aye to Abstention; 1 from Abstention to No; and 26 from Abstention to No. Thus, 34 Conservatives changed their mind resulting in a majority change of 33 (effectiveness ratio of 0.97). Labour was divided: 3 changed from Aye to Abstention, but another 3 changed from Abstention to Aye, an effectiveness ratio of zero. The results of the third vote against a no-deal Brexit showed 52 changes. However, of the 26 Conservatives that changed in the second vote from No to Abstention, 24 changed back in the third vote from Abstention to No. Likewise, 4 Conservatives who changed in the second vote from No to Aye, changed back from Aye to No in the third vote.

24 'Others' refers to votes which are not cast: Speaker (1), Deputy Speakers (3), Sinn Fein (7) and Tellers (4).

25 See footnote: 4.

Against a No-Deal Brexit

	vote-1 motion 312 29-01-2019	change 1-2	vote-2 motion 359 13-03-2019	change 2-3	vote-3 motion 409 03-04-2019
Ayes	318	3	321	– 8	313
Noes	310	– 32	278	34	312
Majority	8	35	43	– 42	1
Abst.	6	29	35	– 26	9
subtotal	634		634		634
Others	15		15		15
total	649		649		649

MPs who changed their vote; its effect on the majority; effectiveness-ratio

	change vote 1-2			*change vote 2-3*		
	Δ votes	*Δ maj.*	*ratio*	*Δ votes*	*Δ maj.*	*ratio*
Cons.	34	33	0.97	37	– 27	0.73
Lab.	7	1	0.14	11	– 13	1.18
LibDem.	0			0		
SNP	0			0		
remaining	4	1	0.25	4	– 2	0.50
total	45	35	0.78	52	– 42	0.81

Table 2 Against a No-Deal Brexit vote
Source: <commonsvotes.digiminster.com>

5. Indicative Votes on the House of Lords Reform

In contrast to the meaningful votes on May's deal, the indicative votes on 27 March 2019 and again on 1 April 2019 showed a different, less organised pattern of voting. Holding a series of indicative votes was meant to break a deadlock by investigating other options. In theory, it promised a way out. First, MPs could put forward their preferred alternative to May's deal to the Speaker. Second, the Speaker selected the proposals which would be debated and third, after the debate, the MPs could vote on each proposal.

This had been done before. The preamble to the Parliament Act 1911 states that the Act is a temporary measure only: 'it is intended to substitute for the House of Lords as it at present exists a Second Chamber constituted on a popular instead of hereditary basis, but such substitution cannot be immediately brought into operation'.[26] This House of Lords reform was debated several times in the Commons. However, three attempts to bring this substitution into operation failed in 1949, 1968 and most recently in 2003. This effort to reform the constitutional structure of the UK was to a certain extent comparable with the efforts to deliver on Brexit: it failed repeatedly.

26 Preamble Parliament Act 1911 (1 & 2 Geo. 5 c.13).

In 2003, eight propositions were put forward in a series of indicative votes on the House of Lords reform. These proposals varied from: (a) abolishment of the House of Lords; (b) wholly appointed; (c) wholly elected; (d-h) six different options for a hybrid House of partly elected and partly appointed peers.[27] Voting took place in a regular manner: a division was called and MPs had to walk through one of the lobbies to register their vote. Thus, the planning was that eight divisions would be called.

At the end of the day, the Commons had rejected all options: a surprising result. McLean, Spirling & Russell have written a rather interesting article on this attempt to reform the House of Lords trying to explain what Parliament did.[28] 'How, then, did the Commons come to vote against all eight options put up to it, leading itself into the contradiction of voting for the status quo by voting against the status quo?'.[29] The authors provide three hypotheses to explain the paradox. First, the loss of the abolition vote could have triggered actions from a group of MPs, which influenced the outcome of the other votes. Second, MPs did not succeed in coordinating their votes across the seven remaining options. Third, some MPs made mistakes, which made a crucial difference given the closeness of the outcome on some options.[30] The last hypothesis is illustrated by the fact that in the absence of party whips to direct the MPs into the 'correct' lobby to vote, and the fact that a number of divisions were not called, some MPs did not vote on the vote they thought they were voting on. After the division on the wholly elected option, it was expected that a division would be called to vote on the 20% elected option. However, that did not occur: The Speaker called the division off and his judgment was not challenged. Subsequently, the Speaker presented the next option and called a division on the 80% elected option. However, not all MPs were aware of that and had their no vote for what was assumed the 20% elected option registered for the 80% elected option which they actually supported. Through this mistake the 80% elected option failed (283-286); without the mistake it would have passed (287-282), and the House of Lords would have been reformed in 2003.[31]

6. Indicative Votes on Alternative Brexit Deals

Initially, 16 proposals were put forward to the Speaker of which 8 were selected. As none of the 8 proposals passed in the first series, a second series of indicative votes were held on 4 favourable options. The voting method was using ballot papers, rather than having MPs walk through one of the lobbies to register their vote. 'Some have argued that the indicative votes held on Brexit would have worked better had a different voting system been used – either "exhaustive voting", the "alternative vote", or "majority judgement".'[32] Anyhow, this method of indicative votes using ballot papers had no precedent as the 2003 votes on the House of Lords reform used 'classical'

27 These options were: 20% elected - 80% appointed; 80%-20%; 40%-60%; 60%-40%; and 50%-50%.

28 McLean, I., A. Spelling & M. Russell, 'None of the Above: The UK House of Commons Votes on Reforming the House of Lords', February 2003, *The Political Quarterly,* 2003 (84), p. 298-310.

29 McLean, Spelling & Russell 2003, p. 308.

30 McLean, Spelling & Russell 2003, p. 309.

31 McLean, Spelling & Russell 2003, p. 305.

32 Indicative votes on Brexit <https://www.instituteforgovernment.org.uk/explainers/indicative-votes> [14/5/2019].

division on each option. Four proposals as an alternative to May's deal were put forward twice: (1) Customs Union (between the UK and the EU) (Conservative); (2) Common Market 2.0 (membership of EFTA and EEA) (Conservative); (3) Public vote (to confirm any Brexit deal) (Labour); (4) Revoke Art. 50 (no Brexit at all) (Scottish National Party).

Indicative votes on Brexit alternatives

	Customs Union		Common Market		Public vote		Revoke Art. 50	
	vote-1	vote-2	vote-1	vote-2	vote-1	vote-2	vote-1	vote-2
Ayes	265	273	189	261	268	280	184	191
Noes	271	276	283	282	295	292	293	292
Majority	– 6	– 3	– 94	– 21	– 27	– 12	– 109	– 101
Abstention	102	89	166	95	75	66	161	155
Others[33]	11	11	11	11	11	11	11	11
total	649	649	649	649	649	649	649	649
MPs who changed their vote and its effect on the majority								
	Δ votes	*Δ maj.*	*Δ votes*	*Δ maj.*	*Δ votes*	*Δ maj.*	*Δ votes*	*Δ maj.*
Cons.	21	1	31	– 7	23	8	20	– 1
Lab.	8	6	58	59	8	8	31	14
LibDem.	4	– 4	4	– 2	0		0	
SNP	0		32	32	3	-1	4	– 2
remaining	5	0	13	– 9	2	0	5	– 3
total	38	3	138	73	36	15	60	8
effect.-ratio	0.08		0.53		0.42		0.13	

Table 3 Indicative votes on Brexit alternatives
Source: <commonsvotes.digiminster.com>

Next to the fact that all these options were defeated, it is clear that revocation of Art. 50, which would call off the deal completely including the ticking clock of Brexit day, was the least supported option. The majority of Noes only changed from 109 to 101. However, it took 60 MPs to get this change of 8 (effectiveness ratio: 0.13). This was caused by opposing efforts: 10 MPs changed from Aye to Abstention, but 19 changed in the opposite direction from Abstention to Aye; 3 changed from Aye to No, but 1 moved from No to Aye; and 15 from No to Abstention, but 12 from Abstention to No. One might think that such a change was caused by one of the parties. In this case, it was not. Changing one's mind in opposite directions occurred within parties. On this proposal, 20 Conservatives changed their vote resulting in a majority change of 1 (effectiveness ratio: 0.05). With Labour, a similar thing happened although less effectively: 31 votes changed the majority to 14 (ratio: 0.45).[34]

The story with the Customs Union is a bit different. Although both indicative votes failed, the majority remained very small: -6 and -3. The effectiveness ratio here was even smaller than the one for the revocation option: 0.08. It took 38 changing votes to

33 Tellers were not used.
34 10 more Labour Ayes and 4 less Labour Noes.

change the majority to 3. If this effectiveness is inspected on party level, big differences become apparent. 21 Conservatives changed their vote only influencing the majority by 1 (0.05). On the other hand, 8 Labour MPs changed their vote influencing the majority by 6 (0.75). The LibDems were very effective in this vote: 4 changing votes changed the majority to 4. Finally, 5 Independent MPs changed their vote in such a way that their effectiveness was zero. The votes on the Common Market option showed the biggest change of majority. This change of 73 was caused by 138 changing votes (ratio: 0.53). Here 31 Conservatives changed the majority to 7 (0.23), and 58 Labour MPs changed the majority to 59 (1.0) in the opposite direction. 32 SNP MPs changed the majority to 32 (1.0), and 4 LibDems caused a majority change of 2. Overall, 22% of the MPs changed their vote in an uncoordinated way. Subsequently, it still failed but the majority moved from -94 to -21. The fourth proposal in the series of indicative votes was to hold a public vote and was the only proposal by the Labour Party showing a decreasing majority from -27 to -12. This change of 15 was brought about by 36 votes (ratio: 0.42). Interestingly, this was the only vote that showed a decrease in the majority (of Noes) by all parties.[35]

Cartoon © Jos Collignon

7. So?

There was a misleading campaign, an ambiguous question, an unclear choice, a non-binding referendum on which the results would nevertheless be implemented, and an electorate whose composition was at least not optimal. So, one might seriously question whether the outcome of the Brexit referendum actually reflected 'the will of the

35 Except for the SNP that realized only one change from Aye to Abstention.

people'. Initially, it seemed implausible that all options were voted down, but it happened. In particular the number of abstentions that could have made a difference is noticeable. Most likely the absence of coordination of voting and a questionable choice for the method of the indicative votes (ballots) determined the negative results. British politics has manoeuvred itself into a deadlock. Looking back, one might say that Murphy's law applied: 'if there's any way they can do it wrong, they will'. The real question is whether British politics is able to admit that there is a crucial difference between voting and deciding.

Love Thy Neighbour II
Family Reunification and the Rights of Insiders in the CJEU Case Law

Betty de Hart[*]

1. Introduction

In 2009, I published an article on the European Court of Human Rights case law on family reunification and the right to family life (Article 8 ECHR).[1] This article focussed on the rights of insiders (citizen or permanent resident sponsors) to establish family life in their country of nationality or permanent residence with a TCN family member. It was inspired by Joseph Carens' moral principles that should guide family reunification policies of liberal states:

1. Family reunification is about the right of insiders, not outsiders;
2. In addition to their rights to family life, people also have a deep and vital interest in being able to continue living in a society where they have settled and sunk roots;
3. No one should be forced by the state to choose between home and family.[2]

These moral principles were translated into three questions that I used as an analysing tool:

1. When and how are the interests of the insider family member taken into account?
2. How are ties of the insider in the country of citizenship or residence evaluated?
3. How is the choice between home and family evaluated?

The conclusions were somewhat sobering. First, it turned out that insider family members are not always applicants before the ECtHR and even if they are, their interests receive little attention. Furthermore, although the ECtHR has acknowledged that family reunification is about the rights of insiders (*Abdulaziz*), in the balancing of interests of state versus individual, the focus is on the outsider family migrant instead. Consequently, the case law offers few clues about the roots of the insider family member in the country of residence or citizenship. Furthermore, although the Court has acknowledged that migrants may develop relationships with people in the society in which they live, it has not acknowledged that insiders develop relationships with migrants, which is seen as a threat to restrictive migration policies. Finally, the Court constructs the choice between home and family not as a consequence of state acts, but as the consequence of choices by the insider spouse. The responsibility not to disrupt family life -

---

* VU University, Amsterdam Centre for Migration and Refugee Law, the Netherlands.

1 De Hart, B. (2009). Love thy Neighbour: Family Reunification and the Rights of Insiders, *European Journal of Migration and Law, 29* (3), p. 235-252. It was republished in: De Hart, B. (2011). Love thy Neighbour: family reunification and the rights of insiders, in: Elspeth Guild & Paul Minderhoud (eds), *The First Decade of EU Migration and Asylum Law*, Leiden: Brill Nijhoff, p. 329-349.

2 Carens, J.H. (2003). Who Should Get in? The Ethics of Immigration Admissions, *Ethics and International Affairs*, 17 (1), p. 95-110.

by following the outsider to his or her country of origin - lies with the predominantly female insiders. Only in exceptional circumstances may that state have a positive obligation to make family life possible by allowing the insider to establish family life with TCN family members on its territory. These exceptional circumstances, so far, have only been applied in cases where children were involved.

In this contribution, the same three questions are used to analyse CJEU case law on Union citizens and their family reunification rights with TCN family members. A stark difference is, obviously, that CJEU case law is *always* about the insider Union citizen and his or her right to family life. Still, considering the complex, fragmented nature of the European migration law framework that does not cover so-called 'static' citizens who have not used their right to free movement, and who are seen as a 'purely internal situation' that is covered by national law, the question remains what family reunification rights they have.[3] This paper focuses on these 'static' citizens', as well as those returning home after using their right to free movement. The right to family reunification with TCN family members of the Union citizens who have used their free movement rights was already established in the 1960s, and has been expanded by the CJEU ever since, it has also become increasingly contested and problematised. As Elspeth Guild has argued, Union citizens with TCN family members have come to be seen as 'monstrous families'.[4] Although she wrote this in the context of Brexit, I suggest that the metaphor is more broadly applicable.

2. Returning Home

Surinder Singh (1992)[5]

In October 1982, Mr. Singh from India, married a British woman. After working in Germany for two years, the couple returned to the UK and started a business. Singh's residence permit as the husband of a British national was withdrawn after his wife filed for divorce in 1987. The UK claimed that national law applied and that another conclusion would enhance the danger of marriages of convenience. However, the Court found that the marriage had been genuine. The Court concluded that the national of a Member State would be withheld from using the right to free movement if s/he could not return to his or her Member State on the same conditions, especially if s/he could not take spouse and children with him or her on the same conditions as during his or her residence in the other Member State. This was the right of Community nationals on the basis of EU law to return to the home Member State. However, EU citizens could not misuse this right to circumvent national immigration laws and Member States were free to take measures to prevent such misuse.

In this case, in spite of the divorce, the focus was solely on the interests of the insider family member and her right to free movement. Consequently, the ties of the insider with the country of citizenship were not evaluated, as the issue at stake was not

3 Staver, A. (2013). Free movement and the fragmentation of family reunification rights, *European Journal of Migration and Law*, *15*(1), p. 69-89.

4 Guild, E. (2017). *BREXIT and its Consequences for UK and EU Citizenship or Monstrous Citizenship*, Leiden:. Brill Nijhoff, p. 55-67.

5 C-370/90 *Surinder Singh*, EU:C:1992:296.

the right to remain, but the right to leave. Implicitly, however, the choice between home and family was addressed, as the central starting point was that no one would be willing to leave home, if it would not be possible to return home with TCN family members. This implied that one should not be forced to choose between home and family.

Important to note is the UK's argument that allowing the Union citizen, specifically a *female* Union citizen, to return with the TCN family member to the home state would enhance marriages of convenience and endanger restrictive migration policies. Although the Court did not accept that the marriage had been fraudulent, this changed in the *Akrich* case, which will be discussed next.

Akrich (2003)[6]

The Moroccan national Akrich came to the UK in 1989 as a tourist, then applied for a student visa, that was rejected. In 1990, he was expelled to Algeria after a conviction for theft and use of a false identity card. He returned to the UK in the same way in 1992 and married a British woman, Helena, in 1996. After their application for a residence permit was refused, Helena went to Ireland to work and on his request, Akrich was expelled to Ireland to be with his wife. In 1998, they wanted to return to the UK, where Helena had found a job and a home. Helena informed the British authorities that had followed legal expert advice on the EU route. Their application for a residence permit was refused, because their stay in Ireland had only been temporary with the intention of circumventing national immigration rules.

In *Akrich*, the Court seemed to introduce the new condition that the TCN family member had to be lawfully resident in the Member State of the insider before they went to another Member State. Since Akrich had had no legal residence in the UK, he had no right to be admitted as the TCN spouse of a Union citizen who had used the right to free movement. Consequently, the use of the 'EU route', that had become a practice since *Singh* (to be discussed later), seemed effectively ended. The grounds for this decision were the violation of the migration rules by Akrich and the suspicions that the marriage was one of convenience. Although the Court ruled that the intention to make use of the right of free movement did not matter, it also stated that it could amount to abuse in cases of marriages of convenience. The AG, too, pointed to the tension between national family reunification policies concerning TCN family members that had become more restrictive and community law that granted a right to TCN family members without their being subject to national immigration law. Although the marriage had already lasted for four years, and Helena was willing to move to Ireland to be with her husband, the *Akrich* marriage was not labeled an 'authentic marriage'. Thus, the suspicion that theirs was one of convenience remained.

Metock (2008)[7]

Metock involved four couples of female Union citizen sponsors (British and one Polish) in Ireland and their African male partners whose asylum applications had failed. Their

6 C-109/01 *Akrich*, EU:C:2003:491.
7 C-127/08 *Metock*, EU:C:2008:449.

applications for admittance as a family member of a Union citizen had been rejected because the men did not have prior lawful residence in the host state and the marriages had been concluded after entering the host state.

The Court reversed its earlier decision in *Akrich*, ruling that the condition of previous legal residence only applied in cases of abuse of rights. Otherwise, if Union citizens were not allowed to lead a 'normal family life' in the host Member State, the right to free movement would be seriously hampered, even if the family members did not have prior lawful residence. The Court also decided that the date of marriage, before or after entering the Union as a TCN, did not matter. It rejected the claims put forward by several Member States that this would result in an increase in persons able to profit from a right of residence in the Community, and pointed out that such a right only existed for certain family members of Union citizens and that Member States might still check for abuse, fraud and marriages of convenience.

In this case, emphasis was put on the rights of the insider, the Union citizen and his or her right to free movement. The right to family reunification was only restricted by public order and family members mentioned in Directive 2004/38. Hence, if a Union citizen had started a relationship with a TCN unlawfully residing in the Member State to which he or she had moved, there was a right to return to the Member State of nationality on the same conditions. For those who had used their right to free movement, there was no need to choose between home and family; the need to be able to lead 'a normal family life' was put at centre stage.

However, *Metock* has remained a highly controversial decision, that has been discussed extensively at European and national levels and which Member States continue to see as an infringement of their sovereignty to control migration.[8]

3. Static Citizens

Morson Jhanjan (1982)[9]

Mrs Morson and Mrs Jhanjan, were Surinamese nationals who entered the Netherlands as tourists and overstayed. They applied for permission to reside in the Netherlands to stay with their daughter and son respectively, who were Netherlands nationals and on whom they were dependent. The son and daughter were employed, but never outside the Netherlands. The parents claimed that they should be admitted as family members of Community workers, referring to a legal expert opinion on reverse discrimination of own nationals, and claimed that they were being discriminated against on grounds of nationality. The Dutch government argued that Community law did not apply, as no borders had been crossed in order to work in another Member State. The AG argued that the right to be joined by family members derived from the freedom of movement for workers, and not from a right of residence. Hence, gaps in the right of a family to live with an individual were 'possible and perhaps inevitable'.The Court ruled

8 De Hart, B. (2017). The Europeanization of love. The marriage of convenience in European migration law. *European Journal of Migration and Law, 19*(3), p. 281-306. Lansbergen. A. (2009). 'Metock, Implementation of the Citizens' Rights Directive and lessons for EU citizenship', *Journal of Social Welfare and Family Law* 31 (3), p. 285–297.

9 Joined cases 35 and 36/82 *Morson Jhanjan*, EU:C:1982:368.

that there was no link with Community law and that the case at hand was a 'purely internal situation'.

At this point, the 'purely internal situation' was still seen as self-evident. The AG and the Court could not have foreseen how, in the future, the room of the 'purely internal situation' would be sliced off piece by piece.

Carpenter (2002)[10]

This process started with the case of Mr Carpenter, a British national who married a Filipino woman in 1996, who had no legal residence prior to her application for a residence permit as the spouse of a citizen. Mr Carpenter travelled regularly within the Union to sell advertisements, while Mrs Carpenter took care of the children from his first marriage. Although Mr Carpenter and his family never moved to another Member State to reside and work, the Court ruled that this was not a 'purely internal situation'. As a service provider, Mr Carpenter fell within the scope of EU law and could appeal to his own Member State for the right to family life his (Article 8 ECHR). Separation of the couple as a consequence of the expulsion of Mrs Carpenter would violate this right. Consequently, Mr Carpenter's freedom to provide services within the EU territory would be hampered. In the context of Article 8 ECHR, the following should be taken into account: Mrs Carpenter's behaviour had violated immigration laws, but was not considered a danger to public order; the marriage was 'authentic' (not a marriage of convenience); and their family life in which she took care of the children of the former marriage. Mrs Carpenter was acknowledged as a wife, but above all as a care provider.

As to the first question, the focus was on Mr Carpenter's right to provide services: the insider's rights not so much to reside, as the economic right to work. The British government had indicated that Mrs Carpenter merely provided 'assistance' to Mr Carpenter, but the AG argued that their arrangement was a free decision of both and there were ties between Mrs Carpenter and her stepchildren. Hence, the British government tried to put the relationship between mother and stepchildren in businesslike terms, outside the context of 'normal family life', or even to build on gendered and ethic stereotypes of docile Filipino women as 'mail order brides'.[11] However, the AG and the Court saw their family ties as genuine. The consequences of Mrs Carpenter's expulsion were put in purely economic terms: if she stayed in the Philippines, would it be possible for Mr Carpenter and his children to be economically active there? No other ties that he or the children might have had to the UK were mentioned, although Mrs Carpenter's family ties and integration into British society and culture were noted. Hence, although the focus was on the rights of the insider as an economically active Union citizen, in the evaluation of ties, the focus shifted to those of the TCN family member.

The Court's decision clearly indicated the choice between home and family that Mr Carpenter faced. Hence, the decision to deport Mrs Carpenter constituted an infringement of Mr Carpenter's right to family life, which was not proportionate to the objective pursued.

---

10 C-60/00 *Carpenter*, EU:C:2002:434.

11 Constable, N. (2006). Brides, Maids, and Prostitutes: Reflections on the Study of 'Trafficked' Women. *PORTAL: Journal of Multidisciplinary International Studies*, *3*(2), p. 1.

Chen (2004)[12]

The husband of the Chinese couple in *Chen* was director of a company based in China, but he worked frequently in the UK. During her pregnancy, Mrs Chen travelled to the UK and subsequently to Ireland, where the child was born, after which she returned to the UK. Born on Irish territory, their daughter Catherine automatically acquired Irish nationality and an Irish passport; she did not acquire Chinese nationality. Mrs Chen had intentionally given birth in Ireland for this reason, so that she could remain in the UK with her daughter. As Mrs Chen was her primary caretaker, Catherine was emotionally and financially dependent on her, while Mr Chen provided for them financially. The question of residence concerned both Catherine, as a Union citizen, and her mother, as a TCN family member. As a Union citizen, Catherine had a right of residence within the Union. According to the Court, this was not a 'purely internal situation'. Although normally the Union citizen should provide for TCN family members, it was not considered relevant that Catherine, as a minor, did not have sufficient means herself, but depended on the income of her mother, who acquired it from her husband. It was further not thought relevant that Mrs Chen had intentionally travelled to Ireland to acquire Irish nationality for her daughter and consequently a residence right as a TCN family member of a Union citizen. However, as the mother was not dependent on the child, she had not acquired such a right. Nevertheless, the Court ruled that if the TCN parent who cared for a Union citizen child was denied residence, this would take away the useful effect of the residence of the child. The residence by the child implicated that it could be accompanied by the parent-caretaker. The residence right of Mrs Chen became dependent on her daughter's.

Ruiz Zambrano (2011)[13]

This position was taken even further in *Ruiz Zambrano*, which concerned the children of Colombian parents, born in Belgium with Belgian nationality. The children's parents came to Belgium as asylum seekers and could not be returned, but were not granted asylum and had no legal residence. They did not register the children with the Colombian embassy, so the children did not acquire Colombian nationality. In order to prevent statelessness, Belgian nationality law automatically granted them Belgian nationality upon birth. The children's father was working without a work permit.

As in *Chen*, the children were the insiders whose interests as Union citizens were the central issue, while the rights of the parents as outsider family members were covered only as accessory to those interests. Their father was mentioned as having an interest to care and provide for his children. Remarkably, contrary to *Carpenter* and *Chen* where the mother-child relationship was central, the mother was not mentioned at all: whether she (also) cared for the children, or whether she was employed. She seemed to play no role at all in the children's lives.

To the ties of the insider in the home Member State, the AG argued that the right of residence contained within Article 21 TFEU was a free-standing right that could be

12 C-200/02 *Chen*, EU:C:2004:639.

13 C-34/09 *Ruiz Zambrano*, EU:C:2011:124.

exercised in the absence of movement: a right to a home and a family. In case of deportation of the father, the mother would be deported with him and the children would no longer be able to live an independent life in Belgium. Leaving Belgium with their parents, would mean uprooting them from *the society and the culture in which they were born and had become integrated,* where they lived a normal life and went to school.[14] This was the first time that the ties of the insider to the home Member State were phrased in more than mere economic terms. The father was also considered fully integrated, while the mother's integration was not mentioned. In any case, for the insider children, there was actual acknowledgement of the ties they had developed in the society in which they lived; a confirmation of Carens' second principle. Finally, the Court acknowledged the choice between home and family. The CJEU ruled that Article 20 TFEU excluded national measures that deprived Union citizens of the genuine enjoyment of the substance of the rights conferred by the status of citizenship. A refusal to grant a right to residence to a TCN family member with dependent Union citizen children would deprive them of those rights. This would lead, in the Court's view, to a situation in which those children would have to leave the territory of the Union. To the Court, the whole Union was the children's home.

Immediately after this decision, an academic debate ensued on its implications, which according to some went too far, according to others not far enough.[15] The *Chavez* decision confirmed the *Ruiz Zambrano* judgment and clarified the concept of dependence.[16] The Court ruled that the fact that the other parent, who was a Union citizen, was able and willing to assume sole responsibility for the primary care of the child was a relevant factor, but it was not in itself a sufficient ground for a conclusion that there was no dependence between the child and the TCN parent, so that the child would not be forced to leave the territory of the Union. The Court referred to the best interests of the child.

The question whether the implications of *Ruiz Zambrano* also applied to cases of adult Union citizens, was decided in two subsequent cases.

McCarthy (2011)[17]

Shirley McCarthy was a dual national, British by birth and Irish through descent from her mother, who had been living in Britain all her life. In 2002, she married George, a Jamaican national, who had no legal residence in Britain. After their wedding, the couple applied for a residence permit for George as spouse of a Union citizen. Shirley did not work and received state benefits. Whether George worked or not was not clear. Shirley had not exercised her right to free movement; her Irish nationality was put forward as the connection to EU law.

14 Par. 63 Conclusion AG.

15 See e.g. Hailbronner, K. & D. Thym (2011). Case C-34/09, Gerardo Ruiz Zambrano v. Office national de l'emploi (ONEm), Judgment of the Court of Justice (Grand Chamber) of 8 March 2011, *Common Market Law Review*, 48 (4), p. 1253-1270. Van Elsuwege, P. & D. Kochenov (2011). On the limits of judicial intervention: EU citizenship and family reunification rights, *European Journal of Migration and Law*, 13 (4), p. 443-466.

16 Case C-133/15 *Chavez Vilchez*, EU:C:2017:354.

17 Case C-434/09 *McCarthy*, EU:C:2011:277.

The AG concluded that Union citizens could not derive from Article 21 TFEU a right of residence in the home Member State if there was no cross-border element, contrary to the AG in *Ruiz Zambrano.* The AG stated that although dual nationality was relevant to the issue of law on surnames[18], this did not count for residence. In this respect, Shirley's situation did not differ from other British, single nationals who had always lived in Britain. This might result in reverse discrimination against own nationals, but that fell outside the scope of EU law. Furthermore, Shirley, who was not economically active and did not provide for herself and her family, did not even fulfil the requirements of the Union Citizens Directive. Shirley did not perform any economic activity that would be hampered by her husband's expulsion, nor were there any Union citizen children involved. There was no mention of Shirley's ties to the home state. As a final remark, the AG referred to the right to family life in Article 8 ECHR but not as a matter of EU law. The Court ruled that, contrary to *Ruiz Zambrano*, Shirley would not be obliged to leave the territory of the EU, since she was a national of the United Kingdom and had an unconditional right to remain there. Shirley's right to a home did not include a right to establish a family.

Dereci (2011)[19]

An Austrian woman had married a Turkish husband who had no legal residence in Austria. Their three minor children had Austrian nationality. Mr Dereci was refused residence because he failed to comply with the obligation to apply for residence from abroad. Mrs Dereci was the provider for the family.

The AG stated that it was unlikely that the refusal to grant Mr Dereci a residence permit would deprive his wife and young children of the enjoyment of the rights under Article 20 TFEU as Union citizens, as they were not dependent on Mr Dereci. So, apparently, the interests of the insiders rested on the notion of *dependence.* In *Ruiz Zambrano* and *Chavez*, the children were seen as dependents of the parents who cared and provided for them. This raised the question of why the *Dereci* children were not considered dependents of their father: was it because he was not a male provider? Mrs Dereci was not deprived of her right of residence in Austria and her right of free movement between Member States, together with the children who, on account of their age, would not be able to exercise that right independently. Hence, the children were considered independent of their father, but dependent on their mother. The Court decided that:

> The *mere fact* that it might appear *desirable* (...) for economic reasons or in order to keep the family together in the territory of the Union, to be able to reside with him in the territory of the Union, is not sufficient in itself to support the view that the Union citizen will be forced to leave Union territory if such a right is not granted (emphasis by author).

The phrase *the mere fact that it may be desirable* implied that insiders had no right to remain in the home Member State, or even elsewhere in the Union, with TCN family members. The choice between home and family, so vividly explained in *Ruiz Zambrano*, was being

18 C-148/02 *Garcia Avello*, EU:C:2003:539.

19 Case C-256/11 *Dereci*, EU:C:2011:734.

discarded here; not as a choice forced upon them by the state, but as a consequence of their own actions and wishes. Nevertheless, the AG explicitly mentioned the paradox that in order to enjoy family life within the Union, one had to exercise freedom of movement. If Mrs Dereci had been unable to work and thus to provide for the needs of the children, things might have been different. How could a mother of three young children, the AG pondered, provide for them without her own resources, despite her right of residence in Austria? Hence, although Mrs Dereci was married to the father of her children, in the arguments concerning her rights, she had been reconstructed as a single, unemployed mother. This again implied that if Mr Dereci had been the breadwinner of the family and Mrs Dereci had performed the classic homemaker role, things might have been different.

O, B, S and G (2013)[20]

This case further addressed the rights of Union citizens who had not left their home Member State, the Netherlands. The TCN family members wanted to remain with their Dutch sponsors in the Netherlands. In all four cases, the Dutch sponsor fell outside the scope of Directive 2004/38, although they had crossed borders within the EU, either as a worker or as a service receiver,.

The AG stated that there was no indication of marriages of convenience or abuse of rights; by now an almost obligatory statement. The cases involved were not purely internal as the right to free movement had been exercised in some way, but this did not automatically mean that there was a right of residence. As there had been border crossing in some form, the cases had to be discerned from *Ruiz Zambrano, McCarthy* and *Dereci*, where no such border crossing had taken place. As Directive 2004/38 did not apply, the AG considered Article 21 TFEU. She noted that the Netherlands had refused a right to TCN family members of own nationals, and found it 'strange' that a Member State had treated its own nationals worse than Union citizens, resulting in 'banishment' of those own nationals to other Member States. In the eyes of the AG, this did not comply with the obligation of loyal enforcement of Union law.

The AG formulated three criteria for the right for TCN family members:1. the family relationship with the Union citizen; 2. exercising the right to free movement by the EU citizen; 3. the causal link between residence of the TCN and exercising the right of free movement. If the Union citizen, after admittance of the TCN family member, moved, no longer moved or refrained from moving, this could entail a violation. Here, the move to another Member State was perceived as a choice between home and family forced upon the Union citizen. In general, a measure that forced a Union citizen to move restricted the right to free movement and violated Article 21 TFEU.

The Court ruled that residence in the host Member State must be 'sufficiently genuine' and during this residence family life must have been created or strengthened. Thus, on the one hand, the Court further limited the scope of the 'purely internal situation', while on the other hand it reaffirmed that static Union citizens had no right to family life.

20 Cases C-456 and 457/12 *O, B, S and G*, EU:C:2014:135 and EU:C:2014:136.

Concluding Remarks

The first question was: when and how are the interests of the insider family member taken into account? Obviously, in CJEU case law, the focus is always on the insider, the Union citizen although in some cases, the interests of the TCN family member are taken into account.

Secondly, the evaluation of the insider's ties with the country of citizenship is mainly put in economic terms. Only in some cases (*Ruiz Zambrano*), the society and the culture in which they were born and have become integrated are mentioned.

As to the third question, the Court takes the choice between home and family into account, largely as the consequence of state acts rather than the choice of the insider - with the notable exceptions of *McCarthy* and *Dereci*. Although there may be a right to have a home, it is not always obvious where 'home' is: the whole Union is home, but in order to claim this right, one also has to leave the home Member State.

This paradox is becoming increasingly obvious, resulting in judgments that extend the right of static citizens to family reunification, as long as some border-crossing element is involved. This approach through the loop of Union law does not solve the issue of static citizens. The notion of the 'mere desirability' to live together on the territory of the Union in *Dereci*, brings CJEU case law closer to the ECtHR case law, meaning that the couples' choice of domicile in the home Member State does not have to be respected.

The exception is Union citizen children who depend on their TCN parents, demonstrating the growing importance of children's rights in immigration law. However important this development is, it also exemplifies the exceptionality of the *Ruiz Zambrano* ruling, still leaving static Union citizens without a right to a home and a family. They remain subject to increasingly restrictive national migration polices.

Although using the EU route might seem an easy strategy for avoiding these restrictive national policies - just a 30-minute drive across the 'Love Bridge' from Copenhagen to Malmö, or hopping across the Belgian border - it does not offer a viable, durable solution. First, Member States have problematized the use of the EU route as an abuse of rights and fraud - although formally, it is not - and subjected these couples to scrutiny of both the duration and character of their stay in the other Member State, as well as the genuineness of their relationship.[21] The mistrust of 'monstrous families' of female Union citizens and their TCN husbands was continuously reinforced in the case law discussed.

Second, the use of the EU route requires substantial financial and social capital (mobility, employment, social networks, language ability), and, consequently, is not equally accessible for everyone, turning family migration into a class as well as a gender matter.[22]

21 Staver (2013), fn 3; de Hart, B. (2017). The Europeanization of love. The marriage of convenience in European migration law, *European Journal of Migration and Law*, *19*(3), p. 281-306.

22 Kofman, E. (2018), Family Migration as a Class Matter, *International Migration*, 56, p. 33-46, doi: 10.1111/imig.12433.

Cloud Agoras: Blockchain Technology, Arendt's Virtual Public Spaces and Human Mobility

*Dora Kostakopoulou**

While developments in information technology have always sparked lively debates about democratic participation and citizenship, the advent of blockchain technology promises to change the concept and nature of participatory citizenship by providing an inclusive, secure and transparent mechanism of data sharing among an unlimited number of members.[1] Blockchain participants are able to interact, share information, collaborate and have access to an incredible amount of information organised in blocks without the intervention of a centralised authority and without any reliance on a centralised platform. More importantly, everyone's copy of the distributed database will be kept updated and will be immutable; information can be added by any member of the global network, but cannot be deleted. Blockchain is thus a platform for worldwide information sharing, interaction and collaboration. As such, it has the potential to enhance political participation, trigger civic mobilisation and to provide the substratum for public action on a global scale.

Such a bottom up, participatory and size-neutral (the network could consist of billions of people) digital network does not merely offer a glimpse of what might be possible in terms of global citizenship but casts doubts on any arguments about the impossibility of global citizenship and a fair migration policy. Guild has written extensively on both throughout the decades, but the advent of blockchain simply removes three of the main obstacles for their realisation; namely, the impermeability of state borders, the size of the demos, and certain costs associated with political participation. Participants just need to have internet access in order to join a network comprising millions of citizens from diverse regions and remote locations of the globe who could be mobilised in influencing public policies and taking part in public actions.

In what follows, I will thus sidestep questions about the feasibility of global citizenship in order to examine how the new technological revolution will lead to innovations in political life and will create Hannah Arendt's public spaces of 'virtual' citizenship (section 1). In section 2, I extend this discussion to the regulation of migration and make a case for the use of blockchain technology in promoting free movement across states' borders. In the subsequent discussion, I take it for granted that blockchain is a 'game-changer' and that it *could* have significant transformative effects on societies, politics and citizenship. I use the verb 'could' because I do not wish to embrace determinism or to imply the existence of a causal relation between technology and political processes. Blockchain has the potential to transform the way we think about public spaces, citizenship, migration and political participation, but this potential can only be realised if technology is put to uses which can enhance democratic political processes.

---

* Warwick University, UK.

1 *Forum Debate on Cloud Communities: The Dawn of Global Citizenship?*, Globalcit, Florence: EUI, April 2018. (http://globalcit.eu/).

1. Virtual Public Spaces of Citizenship

Critics might object here that we do not need technological advancements in order to procure new conceptions of public space. Analyses informed by the thinking of philosophers, such as Henri Lefebvre, and geographers, such as Doreen Massey and Edward Soja, have highlighted that spaces are not given but are constructed in different ways by politics and discursive practices. Readers might recall Peter Maier's anthology on the changing boundaries of the political in the late 1980s.[2] In it, Maier mapped the blurring of the distinction between the state and civil society, while a few years later, Gilles Deleuze commented on the shifting of borders and the proliferation of political spaces within contemporary societies of control.[3] Didier Bigo and Elspeth Guild have also made distinctive contributions in this area.[4]

While all this is true, blockchain promises to realise those ideas in unprecedented ways. It also holds the promise of generating huge publics beyond (and across) geographical borders and territorially defined communities and thus of opening up new citizenship spaces. Citizenship relies on the existence of public spaces of communication, of exchange of ideas, arguments and contested viewpoints and of joint decision-making. For a significant period of time, the agoras of the direct democratic experimentation in ancient Athens became remnants of a distant past that had no chance to be replicated in the present and future. Now, virtual agoras 'containing' millions of active and activist individuals can be built onto blockchain.[5] The mythical space of a distant past becomes connected with, and re-enacted within, the contemporary world of an embodied digital network that makes citizenship a network good.[6]

This is essentially the realisation of Hannah Arendt's conception of 'virtual' public spaces. Virtual 'agoras' built on blockchain will become shared common worlds of continuous flows of speech and action, that is, spaces where people would recognise one another as equals or at least equally entitled to express their views, to 'deal only with one's peers' and to decide on common actions at national, international and global levels.[7] [6]. As Arendt had eloquently noted, the (public) space of speech and action 'can find its proper location almost any time and anywhere'.[8] By transcending topological as well as institutional accounts of the 'public space', blockchain technology not only lends credence to Arendt's conception of public space, but it also promises to open up decentralised public spaces in which all participants can be contributors, deciders and holders of institutional memories. The participants' geographical location

2 C.C. Maier (ed.), *The Changing Boundaries of the Political*, Cambridge and New York: Cambridge University Press 1987.

3 G. Deleuze, 'Postscript on the Societies of Control', *October* No. 59 (Winter 1992), Cambridge: The MIT Press 1990, p. 3-7.

4 D. Bigo, E. Guild & R. Walker, *Europe's 21st Century Challenges: Delivering Liberty and Security*, Farnham: Ashgate 2010; D. Bigo & E. Guild (eds.), *Controlling Frontiers: Free Movement into and within Europe*, Farnham: Ashgate 2005.

5 E. Isin & M. Saward, *Enacting European Citizenship*, Cambridge: Cambridge University Press 2013.

6 D. Kostakopoulou, *The Future Governance of Citizenship*, Cambridge: Cambridge University Press 2008, p. 107-110.

7 H. Arendt, *The Human Condition*, Chicago: Chicago University Press 1958.

8 *Ibid.*, p. 198.

does not matter. In an unprecedented border-transcending move, new spaces of citizenship appear 'almost any time and anywhere' as Arendt had argued. What ties all the blockchain participants together in the virtual public space of citizenship is simply their ongoing concern and active engagement.[9] These are, in reality, the characteristics that sustain all communities, be they virtual or not: members are visibly concerned about the common state of affairs and want their claims, needs, and aspirations to be heard.

This development can bring about a complete reconceptualisation of the nature of international society; non-statist ways of defining it will gain prominence. Hedley Bull's envisaged transformation of international society from a society of states to a society of peoples will be progressively realised.[10] [9]. Cloud agoras will also prompt a rethinking of communitarian ways of defining communities and international society which see society and culture as interlocked. This is because they do not rely on some form of cultural homogeneity or conformity to a majority's ideas and narratives; they rely, instead, on the coming together of strangers[11] [in order to share their concerns and information, express their interests, make demands on the political system and to articulate proposals for common action. All this is bound to give rise to interesting questions about ways of constructing political order and legitimacy in international relations and politics.

While cloud agoras have the potential of dislocating citizenship from its statist reference point and stimulating citizen involvement by delivering the affirmative requirements for an active citizenry, namely, information sharing, the exchange of ideas and preferences, capability for action and the means of exerting influence and pressure, they will not be able to resolve the 'problem of equality of voice'. Claude Lefort, Nancy Fraser, Jürgen Habermas and others have commented on the inequalities that persist in democratic public spheres. Some voices will be louder and more influential than others and women will always struggle to find time to engage even virtually. Socio-economic disparities measured in terms of education, income and occupation will also allow certain participants to easily convert their possessed resources into political involvement. The cognitive and linguistic skills for political articulations and activity are not uniformly distributed. Nor do they exist independently of individuals' socio-economic setting and geographical location across the globe.

Cloud agoras therefore will not be able to transcend the difficulties of ensuring full inclusion in the open public grid. They will certainly be more inclusionary that the existing publics, but they will still represent a stratified model of political community or public space(s). They will also have their own 'spinners', exploiters and manipulators of public opinion. I recall Jean Mansbridge's observations about the dark world of domination and manufactured invisibility of actors underpinning deliberative democracy.[12]

Although it is true that participatory parity cannot be easily achieved even in cloud agoras, it is equally true that the common world of citizenship beyond borders, states and nations would be more activist. And this is good news for democracy in general.

9 D. Kostakopoulou, 'Towards a Theory of Constructive Citizenship in Europe', 4(4) *Journal of Political Philosophy*, December 1996, p. 337-358.

10 H. Bull, *The Anarchical Society*, London: Macmillan 1977.

11 I.M. Young, 'The Ideal of Community and the Politics of Difference', 12(1) *Social Theory and Practice* 1986, p. 1-26 at p. 21-23.

12 J. Mansbridge, 'Does Participation Make Better Citizens?', 5(2) *The Good Society* 1995, p. 1-7.

It would be relatively easy for millions of blockchain members to mobilise on specific issues and to demand change in law and policy regionally, nationally and globally. It would also be more difficult for decision-making elites to ignore the voices of so many people and to pretend that they do not count or that their claims do not matter. Nor would political elites be free to resort without a second thought to political censorship, direct political pressure, limitations in the visibility of actors and projects and the adoption of marginalising strategies. The claims of cloud activists would be discussed and understood by taking into account the complexity and scale of their dissent.

Civic awakenings and political mobilisations in cloud agoras are also likely to exert influence on other public spaces that are more conventional and delineated across national and statist lines. For the boundaries of public spaces, virtual and non-virtual ones, will always be porous and issues will leak from one domain to another. The dawn of global citizenship will thus be a combination of the activation of an international or global society and of a more activist citizenship. Virtual global citizenship promises to be more virtual, in the republican sense; citizens will continually question aspects of public life, make public disclosures of wrongdoing, take an active part in public affairs and engage in regular, assertive action. By so doing, political power would be exposed to frequent challenges.

That this is good news for citizenship, democracy and politics in general cannot be denied. The virtual public space of blockchain communities will make citizens think, engage and act more critically and thus more virtually. In other words, the virtual reality of cloud agoras will have an impact on institutions and the participants themselves; it will yield pressures for more open, transparent and accountable institutions and will result in more virtuous, that is, actively engaged, citizens. Blockchain technology provides the platform for building connections, channelling ideas, inviting questioning and coordinating political action and respecting oneself and others. Whether cloud agoras will prove to be decisive public spaces and strong promoters of democratic processes that make wealth, power and privilege accountable or merely subaltern counter publics will depend on the intentions and actions of their participants. In other words, the answer to the question whether the virtual public space of global citizenship will have a decisive influence on global, regional and national public policy-making is not theoretical or scholarly; it will be a contextual one.

2. Cloud Agoras and Mobility Made Easy

A possibility that is worth exploring, here, is the use of blockchain technology to link potential 'movers', that is, individuals seeking to migrate, with those actors, be they individual or collective, who seek entrepreneurs, employees, innovators, inhabitants, consumers, tax payers, seasonal workers and so on. Because the doctrine of territorial sovereignty has been modelled upon the idea of private property ownership and, thus, of states' land ownership, states have been traditionally endowed with the power to refuse or restrict the admission of 'aliens'. Since the establishment of modern states, a few duties were seen to trump sovereign states' power to refuse entry or admission to non-nationals. Von Pufendorf and Vattel explicitly stated states' imperfect duties of mutual assistance, charity and hospitality.[13] In 1948 international law recognised the perfect duties to provide sanctuary to those facing persecution and to facilitate family reunification.[14] According to Von Pufendorf, the property owner, that is, the state, has 'the final decision on the question whether he wishes to share with others the use of his property'.[15]

European Union law progressed a step further by giving individuals the right to free movement and residence across the European Union. Initially, this right was confined to workers and persons wishing to establish themselves in another EU Member and the members of their families.[16] Subsequently, work seekers and the beneficiaries of international agreements signed by the EU and third countries benefited from free movement.[17] And in the 1990s, the institutionalisation of EU citizenship by the Treaty on European Union extended free movement to non-active economically EU citizens on the conditions that they are self-sufficient and possess health insurance.[18] Latin American countries in the new millennium enshrined in their constitution a human right to migration in the new millennium,[19] but the latter has not inspired reform in other countries yet.

In fact, most countries recognise a qualified right to migrate[20] and tend to follow the trend towards restrictive migration policies. 'Reasons of state', that is, public security, public order and public health consideration coupled with the relatively short office journey of political elites which relies on vote-hunting via a strange mix of law, politics and ideology have resulted in ad hoc reactions, incoherence and restrictive migration policies.[21]

But let us imagine millions of potentially mobile individuals connected to recruiters, be they international organisations or regions or local authorities or states seeking to address shortages in the labour markets and demographic needs, on blockchain platforms. The implications of this for the institutional design of migration policies are significant. In such cloud agoras of 'mobility made easy' through smooth interaction and coordination for the pursuit of mutual advantage, there would be little room for policies of criminalisation of migration, negative discourses dehumanising and disrespecting human beings, and, more importantly, for smuggling rings and people trafficking syndicates. The latter would simply be both unnecessary and unattractive reduced demand would make them unprofitable. In the same way that the establishment of Easyjet, and of other low cost air carriers, eliminated the need for 'middle men/women' in booking flights and seats on airplanes, a 'mobility made easy cloud agora' would

---

13 S. von Pufendorf, *De Jure naturae et gentium libri octo* (1672), New York: Oxford University Press 1934; E. de Vattel, *Law of Nations* (1758), Indianapolis: Liberty Fund 2008.

14 UDHR, Article 14(1) on the right to asylum, Article 12 and Article 16(3) (10 December 1948).

15 Von Pufendorf, *De Jure naturae*, 3.3.9. p. 364ff.

16 E. Guild, *The Legal Elements of European Identity*, The Hague: Kluwer 2004.

17 *Ibid.*

18 E. Guild, C.J. Gortazar Rotaeche & D. Kostakopoulou (eds), *The Reconceptualisation of European Union Citizenship*, Leiden: Brill Nijhoff 2014.

19 D. Acosta, *The National versus the Foreigner in South America*, Cambridge: Cambridge University Press 2018.

20 S. Benhabib, *The Rights of Others: Aliens, Residents and Citizens*, Cambridge: Cambridge University Press 2004.

21 D. Bigo, S. Carrera & E. Guild (eds.), *Foreigners, Refugees or Minorities?*, Farnham: Ashgate 2013.

impact negatively on people smuggling and trafficking industries. It will certainly be a way of making globalisation work[22] or endorsing the responsibilities of global justice.[23]

The European Union, in the future, or the Member States which currently have the competence to determine the 'volumes of admission of third country nationals to their territory to seek work, whether employed or self-employed' (Article 79(5) TFEU) could regularly advertise and update vacancies and communicate directly with interested applicants, be they high- or low-skilled, who could interact in the mobility made easy cloud agora via a mobile app. Given that mobile individuals are a self-selected group, an interactional institutional framework arranging and facilitating the journey between the place of arrival and the place of departure would reduce costs and risks for all the parties involved. More significantly, it would 'normalise' the migrant condition and by so doing reconstruct it as a human condition in global economies, diverse societies and in an increasingly interconnected world. Movement across places and countries is a natural human experience and beneficial particularly for young people who have their whole lives ahead of them and motivation to 'get ahead', to be adventurous, creative and industrious and to seek personal growth.

A 'mobility made easy' agora built on blockchain technology would revolutionalise migration law and policy. It would lift persons above, and against, migration categories as well as states of dependency. It would also result in embedding respect for fundamental rights, cosmopolitan sensibilities and would defend and protect young people, coming in the main from the Global South, from the trauma, health hazards and disrespect generated by the criminalisation of migration, the arbitrariness of discretionary decision-making and the negative public narratives about migration in the Global North. After all, we are all migrants not only in the sense of how far back we look but also in terms of accepting our mortality.

By naturalising mobility, such a development would certainly decentre the gravity given to state borders and state sovereignty. Mobility made easy cloud agoras would bind participants in mutual exchanges and mutual assistance across the globe; they would be no hierarchical distinctions among individuals on the basis of birth, residence or migration status. All participants would enjoy equality of status and have the same rights. Cloud agoras would thus exemplify a form of global egalitarianism since all individuals could potentially take part in them as equal members of a moral community of persons.

More than twenty years ago while I was trying to rethink migration policy in the EU and to devise an alternative to 'Schengenland', I suggested the establishment of migration boards in the Member States which would be institutionally linked to the European Parliament.[24] To these migration boards, municipalities wishing to revitalise their declining agricultural sector or their declining industrial plans could put forward suggestions about the recruitment, settlement and accommodation of migrants. Ethnic communities, religious organisations and other interest groups would be in a position

22 J. Stiglitz, *Making Globalisation Work*, London: Penguin 2006.

23 I.M. Young 'Responsibility and Global Justice: A Social Connection Model', 23 *Social Philosophy and Policy* 2006, p. 102-130.

24 D. Kostakopoulou, 'Is There an Alternative to "Schengenland"?', 46(3) *Political Studies* 1998, p. 886-902.

to suggest the same.[25] Such a multivocal migration policy design would be accompanied a Community Charter on migration and refugee matters furnishing the principles and guidelines for a fair and principled migration and asylum policy.[26] I had reservations about the institutional implementation of the above mentioned suggestions at that time, but I now realise that blockchain technology would equip all those actors dealing with admissions issues with direct input and effective involvement.

3. Conclusion

Communities built on blockchain would not simply be communities beyond borders. They would be global communities above state borders and this implies an orientation towards worldism or globalism. They would redefine politics and citizenship and transform spaces of vulnerability and hierarchy associated with migration into spaces where power relations are deconstructed and normalised in the service of humanity and the functional needs of diverse societies. Accordingly, identities, be they personal or collective, will be reconfigured, as Guild envisaged throughout her impactful work.[27] [26]. Borders, citizenship, equality and non-discrimination and the right to move across borders, in sum all the main foci of Guild's work would obtain a new meaning in cloud communities where human beings are respected and their abilities and talents are recognised, fostered and valued.

References

Diego Acosta, *The National versus the Foreigner in South America*, Cambridge: Cambridge University Press 2018.

Hannah Arendt, *The Human Condition*, Chicago: Chicago University Press 1958.

Seyla Benhabib, *The Rights of Others: Aliens, Residents and Citizens*, Cambridge: Cambridge University Press 2004.

Didier Bigo & Elspeth Guild (eds), *Controlling Frontiers: Free Movement into and within Europe*, Farnham: Ashgate 2005.

Didier Bigo, Elspeth Guild & Robert Walker, *Europe's 21st Century Challenges: Delivering Liberty and Security*, Farnham: Ashgate 2010.

Didier Bigo, Sergio Carrera & Elspeth Guild (eds), *Foreigners, Refugees or Minorities?*, Farnham: Ashgate 2013.

Hedley Bull, *The Anarchical Society*, London: Macmillan 1977.

Gilles Deleuze, 'Postscript on the Societies of Control', *October* No. 59 (Winter 1992), Cambridge: The MIT Press 1990, p. 3-7.

Elspeth Guild, Cristina J. Gortazar Rotaeche & Dora Kostakopoulou (eds), *The Reconceptualisation of European Union Citizenship*, Leiden: Brill Nijhoff 2014.

Elspeth Guild, *The Legal Elements of European Identity*, The Hague: Kluwer 2004.

25 *Ibid.*, p. 894-95.
26 *Ibid.*
27 Guild 2004, n. 16 above.

Engin Isin & Michael Saward, *Enacting European Citizenship*, Cambridge: Cambridge University Press 2013.

Dora Kostakopoulou, 'Towards a Theory of Constructive Citizenship in Europe', 4(4) *Journal of Political Philosophy*, December 1996, p. 337-358.

Dora Kostakopoulou, 'Is There an Alternative to "Schengenland"?', 46(3) *Political Studies* 1998, p. 886-902.

Dora Kostakopoulou, *The Future Governance of Citizenship*, Cambridge: Cambridge University Press 2008, p. 107-110.

Charles C. Maier (ed.), *The Changing Boundaries of the Political*, Cambridge and New York: Cambridge University Press 1987.

Jean Mansbridge, 'Does Participation Make Better Citizens?', 5(2) *The Good Society* 1995, p. 1-7.

Samuel von Pufendorf, *De Jure naturae et gentium libri octo* (1672).

Joseph Stiglitz, *Making Globalisation Work*, London: Penguin 2006.

UDHR, Article 14(1) on the right to asylum, Article 12 and Article 16(3) (10 December 1948).

Emer de Vattel, *Law of Nations* (1758).

Iris Marion Young, 'The Ideal of Community and the Politics of Difference', 12(1) *Social Theory and Practice* 1986, p. 1-26 at p. 21-23.

Iris Marion Young 'Responsibility and Global Justice: A Social Connection Model', 23 *Social Philosophy and Policy* 2006, p. 102-130.

The Boundaries of EU Citizenship
Reflections on Borders, Citizenship and Sovereignty

*Sandra Mantu**

Borders and EU Citizenship Seen from Critical Migration Studies

Migration, borders and sovereignty have become inseparable companions. Human mobility captured by the legal notion of 'migration' is perceived as doing something to the state, its sovereignty and accompanying understanding of membership as national. What exactly this 'something' is remains debated in scholarship but generally revolves around the demise of the nation state and accompanying 'national' forms of belonging epitomised by citizenship/nationality or, at the very least, their transformation under conditions of globalization. Elspeth's scholarship has aptly engaged with these issues and with a view to understand the role played by law in these processes. One of her main contributions has been the framing of their analysis from the perspective of the individual migrant and his/her legal standing under the label of 'critical migration studies'.[1] This is a bold and unusual move in (legal) migration scholarship, which remains concerned with the state as the main actor and object of inquiry, its right to regulate migration across its borders, the state's transformation as a result of migration, the impact of migration on inter-state relations etc. Until recently, Elspeth's interest has been the EU since it has set out a particular vision of dealing with human mobility among its Member States as a fundamental freedom – the free movement of persons – which was later refashioned as EU citizenship. Its realization rests on the idea of building an ever-closer union among the participating states with a view to create a space without internal borders in which the nationals of the Member States can move freely. Scholarship has amply debated how the effacing of internal borders rests on the hardening of EU's external borders. Elspeth has been one of the authors that have critically engaged with the notion of 'fortress Europe' as failing to capture the complexity of the border and its transformation into a filtering device; borders remain open for the bona fide migrant epitomised by tourists and businessmen, while filtering out the male fide migrants, usually the terrorists and the poor.[2] This points towards borders as polysemantic categories of inquiry and the fallacy of truth claims based on simple dichotomies of inside/outside.[3]

In this short contribution, my focus will be on EU citizenship as a site for observing and analysing the relationship between the state, borders and sovereignty. Elspeth's emphasis on the individual migrant as bearer of rights is at home within the

---

* Centre for Migration Law, Radboud University Nijmegen, the Netherlands.

1 E. Guild, *Security and Migration in the 21st Century*, Cambridge: Polity 2009.

2 E. Guild, 'Equivocal claims? Ambivalent Controls? Labour Migration Regimes in the European Union', in: E. Guild & S. Mantu (eds), *Constructing and Imagining Labour Migration. Perspectives of Control from Five Continents*, Farnham: Ashgate, p. 207-228.

3 R.B.J. Walker, *After the Globe, Before the World*, Abingdon: Routledge 2010.

EU context, even more so after the introduction of EU citizenship and the proclamation of the right to free movement as a fundamental, individual and directly effective right given by the EU to the nationals of the Member States. In relation to the EU, Elspeth's work repeatedly stresses the reversal of the traditional position of international law, where states have a sovereign right to control entry into state territory; rather, EU citizens hold a right to enter one of the other Member States and that state has a limited power to reject entry or residence.[4] This constitutes a fundamentally different starting point from where to conceptualize migration that is grounded on EU citizens' legally enforceable rights of entry and residence.

My interest in the boundaries of EU citizenship is not linked with borders as lines or spatial constructions; rather I am interested in the conceptual boundaries of EU citizenship as the sites of struggles over the ownership, matter and direction of this notion. What I want to explore here is how some of the functions of borders – to differentiate, to delimitate, to define who belongs, to include/exclude – are played out in the notion of EU citizenship. What can we learn about the notion of EU citizenship when we interrogate it from its conceptual boundaries? Who is in and who is out of the reach of EU citizenship? This interrogation builds on an on-going discussion about the nature of EU citizenship – citizenship or migration status - that Elspeth has started in the research performed by the Centre for Migration Law in Nijmegen and which we hope to continue.

Deconstructing the Relationship Between EU Citizenship and State Sovereignty

The analysis below is informed by a number of insights that for reasons of space I can only summarise here.[5] First, citizenship studies posit citizenship to be a bounded notion that relies, among others, on law to draw boundaries between those who are part of the community and those who are not. Secondly, the community is understood as a national one, while migration is seen to put pressure on the national character of membership as it constantly pushes for expansion of the community to the detriment of its cohesion. Thirdly, citizenship is a notion born out of contestation and struggles over the inclusion of parts of society into its franchise; the development of national citizenship alongside the establishment of the national state as the main form of political actor shows that these struggles can be legal, symbolic, political etc. and involve the stabilization of the fringes and of boundaries as means to ensure the viability of citizenship as a political construct. Critical legal scholars have described modern citizenship as being about the extension of the citizenship franchise to the poor as a pacifying move to ensure the stability of the social contract.[6] Finally, in this contribution I focus on legal contestation as it emerges from the jurisprudence of the ECJ in relation to EU

4 E. Guild, *The Legal Elements of European Identity. EU Citizenship and Migration Law*, Deventer: Kluwer Law International 2004.

5 S. Mantu, *Contingent citizenship. The law and practice of citizenship deprivation in international, European and national perspectives*, Leiden: Brill/Martinus Nijhoff 2015, p. 1-21; 328-346.

6 S. Mantu, 'Alternative views on EU citizenship', in: C.A. Grütters, S. Mantu & P. Minderhoud (eds), *Migration on the Move – Essays on the dynamics of migration*, Leiden: Brill/Nijhoff 2017, p. 225-246.

citizens and their claims. This approach builds on research undertaken with Elspeth in the ENACT project where we approached the ECJ as a site of citizenship enactment where understandings of what a citizen is are challenged and where EU citizenship is acted upon and constructed as the fundamental status of the nationals of the Member States.[7]

I will explore the boundaries of EU citizenship in relation to three sets of issues associated with state sovereignty and which loosely correspond to the three elements in Weber's definition of the state as encompassing a territory, a population and bureaucracy that engages in legitimate exercise of power – for my purposes here, I understand this last element as being about the governance of territory and people. These themes are also linked with some of the main criticisms voiced in scholarship around the time of the introduction of EU citizenship: its failure to include TCNs within its personal scope; its reliance on state nationality and its persistence in treating economically active and inactive mobile EU citizens differently in respect of residence and social rights. My aim is to understand if and how EU citizenship changes the exercise of sovereignty in these areas and with what consequences for EU citizens. My three areas of inquiry are:

1. control over presence on state territory – static EU citizens and TCN family members;
2. rules of membership attribution – who is/can remain a national of an EU Member State?
3. redistribution of resources as linked to the governance of people and territory – who can rely on the welfare state?

Control over Presence on State Territory

A state's right to control the presence of foreigners on its territory is seen as an attribute of state sovereignty that is recognized by international law. It is also understood as the reverse side of the national's right to be present on state territory (Article 12 ICCPR). Thus, in relation to the territory of their state of nationality, nationals enjoy a right to enter and reside that is linked to their status as nationals; to enter and reside within that same territory, foreigners require state permission. EU law grants EU citizens a right to enter and reside in another EU state (Article 21 TFEU and Directive 2004/38) and limits the possibility of the host EU state to end this right by spelling out a limited number of grounds for expulsion – public policy, public security and public health – and situations in which residence can be terminated. Moreover, EU law offers material and procedural safeguards that EU states must observe as a matter of EU law when extinguishing rights.[8] From the perspective of a state's right to control the presence of foreigners on its territory, EU citizens enjoy a position that is much closer to that of state nationals than non-EU foreigners who remain the main subject of state control. Despite the growing Europeanization of migration legislation and the adoption of

7 S. Mantu & E. Guild, 'Acts of citizenship deprivation: ruptures between citizen and state', in: E. Isin & M. Saward (eds), *Enacting European Citizenship*, Cambridge: Cambridge University Press 2013, p. 111-123.

8 S. Mantu, *Expulsion of own nationals: what implications for EU citizenship?*, Nijmegen Migration Law Working Papers Series, no. 2018/06, Nijmegen: Radboud University Nijmegen 2018.

common rules on non-EU migrants, the Member States retain a tighter grip on this latter group's access to and mobility within the EU than on EU citizens. Concerning expulsion, the ECJ has confirmed the special position enjoyed by (long-term resident) EU citizens in contrast to Turkish nationals stemming precisely from the introduction of EU citizenship and the distinctiveness of the EU project.[9]

However, the manner in which the ECJ has interpreted the Treaty and secondary law provisions on EU citizenship has led to the extension of the protection stemming from EU citizenship to TCNs in their capacity as family members of EU citizens. The ECJ has ruled that in order to enjoy family reunion with an EU citizen, it was immaterial if the TCN family member had entered the territory of the host Member State irregularly.[10] It was the position of the EU citizen exercising free movement rights that mattered and whether the family member fell in one of the categories sanctioned by EU law (Articles 2 and 3 of Directive 2004/38; Article 10 Regulation 492/2011). This jurisprudence has constantly expanded and now includes EU citizens who return to their Member State of nationality and wish to bring along a family member: where the exercise of free movement rights has been genuine and family life created or strengthened during that genuine exercise of free movement rights, the Member State of nationality must allow the family member to enter and reside with the national EU citizen as a matter of EU law.[11]

Traditionally, the application of EU citizenship provisions on free movement and residence required the person to move from her/his state of nationality; it was primarily in the territory of another EU state that EU citizenship became relevant and its rights were activated.[12] In its latest jurisprudence, the Court extends the reach of EU law to static EU citizens who have never moved. Their position in law is no longer captured exclusively by their status as nationals; it is a combination of 'national' and 'EU citizen' that dictates the legal regime applicable to their family reunification claims. As EU citizens, the nationals of the Member States may rely on the rights pertaining to that status including against the Member State of which they are a national.[13] Although Article 20 TFEU does not give autonomous rights of residence to TCNs, in certain exceptional circumstances a right of residence must nevertheless be granted to a TCN who is a family member of an EU citizen if as a consequence of such a refusal, the EU citizen would be obliged in practice to leave the territory of the EU as a whole, denying him the genuine enjoyment of the substance of the rights conferred by virtue of the status of EU citizen.[14]

Initially, it seemed that EU citizenship transforms state sovereignty over territory in respect of EU citizens but leaves intact that sovereignty when it comes to TCNs and EU citizens who reside in their state of nationality (either because they have never moved or because they have returned there). ECJ jurisprudence disproves both of these assumptions as EU citizenship expands the pool of persons over whose entry and residence the Member States can no longer claim an exclusive right of control. In its

9 Case C-371/08 *Ziebell*, EU:C:2011:809.

10 Case C-127/08 *Metock*, EU:C:2008:449.

11 Case C-456/12 *O&B*, EU:C:2014:135 ; Case C-457/12 *S&G*, EU:C:2014:136.

12 For example, the right to diplomatic protection is an exception, as it is to be enjoyed while outside the territory of the EU.

13 Case C-304/14 *CS*, EU:C:2016:674, para 24.

14 Case C-164/14 *Rendon Marin*, EU:C:2016:675, para 74; Case C-133/15 *Chavez-Vilchez*, EU:C:2017: 354.

expansion to capture EU citizens and their family members, EU citizenship creates a direct link between the EU citizen and 'EU territory' as the space within which this status and the rights attached to it are to be enjoyed.

Rules of Membership Attribution

Nationality attribution – the rules prescribing the acquisition and loss of state nationality are part of the state's sovereign right to define membership in the national community. For states, having a defined citizenry is important for asserting their external sovereignty as well as their domestic capacity to extract resources (taxes, performance of military services etc.). EU citizenship retains not only a symbolic link to state nationality, but also a functional one. Article 20 TFEU states that EU citizenship is held by the nationals of the Member States and is additional to state nationality without replacing it. Declaration no. 2 on nationality of a Member State[15] formalises the position of the Member States that view nationality as within their reserved domain (sovereignty) since EU citizenship remains dependent on the definitions supplied by the Member States concerning who is a state national for the purposes of EU law.

Although the EU has no competence in respect of state nationality and EU citizenship is an additional status, the ECJ has ruled that where nationality decisions taken by the Member States affect the rights conferred and protected by EU law, national rules have to be interpreted and reviewed in light of EU law, even if they comply with international law. In other words, the Member States must have due regard to EU law in the exercise of nationality powers.[16] The exact implications of having 'due regard to Community law' (now Union law) have been constructed on a case by case basis but at its core is the idea that the nationality rules applied by the Member States may be modified or not applied when they constitute a breach of EU law.

ECJ's inroads into state sovereignty over nationality attribution involve a delicate ballet. On one hand, the ECJ remains tributary to an understanding of nationality as an emotional bond, rather than a legal one, which translates into a cautious review of the objectives pursued by the Member States when deciding what principles of attribution to use. For example, in *Kaur*,[17] the UK could legitimately provide the exclusion of certain categories of British citizens from the scope of EU citizenship in line with its history as a colonial power without clashing with EU law. In *Rottmann*, the ECJ held that states could legitimately seek to protect public interests linked to fraudulent naturalizations by allowing for withdrawal of nationality even if this leads to loss of EU citizenship and statelessness. In *Tjebbes*[18] the Dutch state can legitimately seek to limit dual nationality in case of habitual residents abroad even if such measures lead to loss of EU citizenship. One the other hand, there is a clear recognition of the fact that loss of state nationality has EU implications that national authorities have to streamline into

15 Declaration no. 2. on nationality of a Member State annexed to the final act of the Treaty on European Union together with the decision of the Heads of State and Government, meeting within the European Council at Edinburgh on 11 and 12 December 1992.

16 Case C-369/90 *Michelletti*, EU:C:1992:295; Case C-135/08 *Rottmann*, EU:C:2010:104.

17 Case C-192/99 *Kaur*, EU:C:2001:106.

18 Case C-221/17 *Tjebbes*, EU:C:2019:189.

their nationality procedures and discuss alongside national interests.[19] Proportionality and individual assessment play a crucial role in legitimizing state nationality decisions from the perspective of EU citizenship. For individuals, the Court's position adds an extra layer of protection against loss of nationality as it requires national authorities to check compatibility with EU law as an additional element.

The most remarkable aspect of the Court's case law is the shifting point of reference in dealing with nationality: it no longer is state sovereignty, but EU citizenship as a status worthy of protection. This process starts with *Rottmann*, where the ECJ ruled that a national measure of citizenship deprivation leading to loss of EU citizenship 'falls, by reason of its nature and its consequences, within the ambit of European Union law'.[20] EU citizenship offered the Court the tools to break away from the script of international law that views nationality as an exceptional field of law within the sovereignty of the state where very little or no interference is acceptable. What happens in the EU context is that the rules no longer reflect only national interests but also EU ones and the two can diverge as EU citizenship becomes a status worthy of protection on its own. What we notice is not simply loss of state sovereignty over deciding who is a member of the national community but a transformation of sovereignty practices to include the EU level into decision making over membership attribution and the protection of the rights stemming from EU citizenship.

Redistribution of Resources

Ferrera describes the welfare state as a basic political good – an instrument serving the purpose of facilitating social cooperation, managing conflicts, sustaining generalized compliance and thus, ultimately keeping the polity together.[21] Welfare states are also territorial and bounded constructs meant to serve the national community. Despite the existence of EU rules addressing social security coordination, there is no harmonized EU welfare state; rather there are twenty-eight national welfare states. The extent to which mobile EU citizens have a right to access the welfare system of their host state and be included in the pool of persons entitled to redistribution of resources via the payment of social benefits remains a salient and contested issue. When introduced in 1992, EU citizenship was seen as relevant only for those who already enjoyed rights under than Community law measures for economically active persons (workers, self-employed or service providers), including equal treatment with nationals in the social sphere. The position of economically inactive citizens is more complex: they enjoy free movement rights but their exercise remains conditional on financial self-sufficiency, at least for the first five years before they acquire a right of permanent residence. They also enjoy equal treatment based on Article 18 TFEU and Article 24 of Directive 2004/38 but exceptions from the general rule are envisaged. The requirement for self-

19 *Ibid.*

20 *Rottmann*, para 42.

21 M. Ferrera, 'The European Social Union: how to piece it together', in: B. Vanhercke, D. Ghailani & S. Sabato (eds), *Social policy in the European Union: state of play 2018*, Brussels: European Trade Union Institute and European Social Observatory 2018.

sufficiency complicates matters further since requests for social benefits risk being interpreted as evidence of lack of resources.

In its first decade, EU citizenship underwent a process of expansion that saw the strengthening of the legal position of economically inactive EU citizens as the social rights attached to their status started to be taken seriously by the Court. According to the ECJ, EU citizens can expect to enjoy a certain degree of (financial) solidarity when exercising their free movement rights. This process started with the *Martinez Sala*[22] case and was taken further in the *Grzelczyk* case, where the court ruled that the applicable law 'accepts a certain degree of financial solidarity between nationals of a host Member State and nationals of other Member States, particularly if the difficulties which a beneficiary of the right of residence encounters are temporary'.[23] To reach this conclusion, the ECJ relied on the fact that the Maastricht Treaty had introduced EU citizenship, which was described as destined to be the fundamental status of nationals of the Member States, and a new chapter devoted to education and vocational training. The Court's expansive interpretation of the rights of economically inactive EU citizens started to slow down after the start of the economic crisis of 2008 and at the moment it can even be described as having been halted as a result of restrictive interpretations given by the Court to the rights of mobile EU citizens in cases such as *Brey*, *Dano* or *Alimanovic.*[24] The Court's recent jurisprudence emphasizes that those EU citizens who are entitled access to the welfare state must reside legally in line with the conditions set out in Directive 2004/38 - if they are not workers, self-employed or permanent residents, they need to have sufficient resources not to become a burden on the host state. In *Brey,* asking for social benefits was seen as an indication that the person does not meet the sufficient resource condition of Article 7 Directive 2004/38, while in the *Dano* case this had become a certainty.[25] This leads to the rather moot situation where social solidarity is only reserved for those who are financially self-sufficient and do not have to rely on solidarity claims.

Awarding access to the host state's welfare state as a matter of EU law remains a contested aspect of EU citizenship, especially because of its potential to undercut national mechanisms of social redistribution. Despite an expansionist jurisprudence in the area of social rights, the reach of solidarity remains different depending on the legal category under which one exercises free movement rights: EU citizens exercising mobility rights as economically active persons enjoy a larger degree of social and financial solidarity with the nationals of the hosts state than their economically inactive counterparts. The increasing politicization of EU mobility as 'poverty migration' questions the desirability of EU citizens' mobility and addresses it through the lens of EU citizens being burdens on the host welfare state. In light of these developments, one can question EU citizenship's capacity to expand the boundaries of the welfare state. Yet, notwithstanding exceptions from equal treatment for economically inactive EU citizens, jobseekers and students prior to the acquisition of permanent residence and ECJ's retreat on social solidarity, the general position that requires the inclusion of mobile EU

22 Case C-85/96 *Martinez Sala*, EU:C:1998:217.

23 Case C-184/99 *Grzelczyk*, EU:C:2001:458, para. 44.

24 Case C-140/12 *Brey*, EU:C:2013:565; Case C-333/13 *Dano*, EU:C:2014:2358; Case C-67/14 *Alimanovic*, EU:C:2015:597.

25 S. Mantu & P. Minderhoud, 'EU Citizenship and Social Solidarity', 24(5) *Maastricht Journal of European and Comparative Law* 2017, p. 703-720.

citizens into the welfare systems of their host states as a matter of EU law creates a form of social citizenship with supranational features that is not matched in international law. While ECJ jurisprudence can be seen as an expression of the failure to develop a fully-fledged normative model of welfare entitlement that completely escapes the national, EU citizenship nevertheless opens up national welfare systems towards certain categories of EU citizens and demands their equal treatment.

Conclusions

The changes brought by EU citizenship to the manifestations of state sovereignty in relation to territory, population and the welfare state point towards changing power relations between the EU and its Member States that affect the position of individuals as they become inscribed into the supranational. The traditional argument is that as a result of EU making inroads into state sovereignty, the Member States lose their sovereignty in favour of the EU, become weaker in the process and less capable of delivering their part of the social contract. In my view it is better to speak of transformation of state sovereignty as a result of EU citizenship being superimposed on state nationality. This leads to a changed relationship between the individual and the territory which s/he inhibits as well as to changed terms of engagement between the individual and the administration in relation to claiming legal identity or social rights. New sovereignty practices develop as a result of the shrinking or enlarging of EU citizenship and the fact that the borders of state nationality are not coterminous with those of EU citizenship.

The boundaries of EU citizenship are flexible enough to capture not only the mobile but also some static EU citizens and their TCN family members who can benefit from the rights of EU citizenship. While formally excluded, they nonetheless are inside the sphere of EU citizenship. EU citizenship brings along additional layers of protection in relation to family reunification or retention of state nationality that are made possible by a shift in how the holder of the right is legally constructed: no longer only a national citizen, but also an EU one. This shift requires a reframing of the boundaries between national and EU spheres of competence. These boundaries remain contingent as shown by the discussion on the welfare state and the politicization of EU mobility as poverty migration. EU citizenship encapsulates the possibility of escaping national fringes by using EU rights to overcome one's national exclusion. However, legal and political developments confront us with the disturbing possibility that when exercising EU citizenship rights the national poor do not escape their condition, instead they are transformed into 'EU poor', equally vilified and excluded. Formally included, they turn out to be in practice excluded from the ideal of EU citizenship as a citizenship status that requires equal treatment. This makes the boundary an interesting vantage point to reflect on the wider construct as there is no clear inside or outside.

What has Happened with Directive 2014/54 on Strengthening the Rights of EU Workers?

*Paul Minderhoud**

Introduction

Free movement of workers has always been a core area of interest of Elspeth. As one of the leading members of the Network on Free Movement of Workers, which was coordinated by the Centre for Migration Law until 2014, she left a strong mark on the activities of the Network. One of the most influential activities of the Network was the preparation of two reports, which provided a basis for the Commission to come up with a proposal to strengthen the enforcement of the free movement of workers in April 2013.[1] This proposal was adopted at a—for EU standards—superfast pace, within a year. On 16 April 2014 Directive 2014/54, aimed at facilitating the uniform application and enforcement of the already existing rights conferred on workers by Article 45 TFEU and by Regulation 492/2011 in the context of freedom of movement for workers, was adopted.[2] The scope of this Directive is identical to that of Regulation 492/2011 and it applies to Union workers and members of their families.

The right of free movement of workers includes the right not to be discriminated against on grounds of nationality as regards access to employment, pay and other working conditions. Regulation 492/2011 details the rights derived from free movement of workers and defines specific areas where discrimination on grounds of nationality is prohibited, in particular as regards:

- access to employment
- working conditions
- access to social and tax advantages
- access to training
- membership of trade unions and eligibility for workers' representative bodies
- access to housing
- access to education apprenticeship and vocational training for the children of Union workers
- assistance given by employment offices.

Although all these rights are present, there is a difference between formal equality (equal rights before the law) and material equality (equal outcomes, results). From a sociology of law perspective this is described as a difference between *law in the books*

* Centre for Migration Law, Radboud University Nijmegen, the Netherlands.

1 Proposal for a Directive of the European parliament and of the Council on measures facilitating the exercise of rights conferred on workers in the context of freedom of movement for workers, 26 April 2013, COM(2013)236.

2 OJ 2014 L 126/8.

and *law in action*. Directive 2014/54 aims to remove existing obstacles to the free movement of workers, such as the lack of awareness of EU rules among public and private employers and the difficulties faced by mobile citizens to get information and assistance in the host Member States. To overcome these barriers and prevent discrimination, the Directive requires Member States to:

- create national contact points providing information, assistance and advice so that EU migrant workers, and employers, are better informed about their rights
- provide appropriate means of redress at national level
- allow labour unions, NGOs and other organisations to launch administrative or judicial procedures on behalf of individual workers in cases of discrimination
- give better information for EU migrant workers and employers in general.

These measures should ensure a better application of EU law on persons right to work in another Member State and make it easier for workers to exercise their rights in practice. The Directive does not create any new rights for workers, but according to the Commission will help to ensure real and effective application of the existing legislation.

A crucial part of the Directive is dedicated to the obligation for Member States to 'designate one or more structures or bodies ("bodies") for the promotion, analysis, monitoring and support of equal treatment of Union workers and members of their family without discrimination on grounds of nationality, unjustified restrictions or obstacles to their right to free movement and shall make the necessary arrangements for the proper functioning of such bodies'.

Member States shall ensure that the competences of those bodies include: '(a) providing or ensuring the provision of independent legal and/or other assistance; (b) acting as a contact point *vis-à-vis* equivalent contact points in other Member States in order to cooperate and share relevant information; (c) conducting or commissioning independent surveys and analyses concerning unjustified restrictions and obstacles to the right to free movement, or discrimination on grounds of nationality; (d) ensuring the publication of independent reports and making recommendations on any issue relating to such restrictions and obstacles or discrimination; (e) publishing relevant information on the application at national level of Union rules on free movement of workers' (article 4).

Those bodies may form part of existing bodies at national level which have similar objectives. In that case the Member State must ensure allocation of sufficient resources to the existing body for the performance of additional tasks (recital 18).

When bodies provide assistance in legal proceedings such assistance shall be free of charge to persons who lack sufficient resources in accordance with national law or practice.

What Are Still the Main Obstacles?

The following five issues can be distinguished as providing still the main obstacles to full free movement of workers:

- Tension free movement of workers law and national immigration law;
- Equality of treatment;
- Access to employment in the public service;

- Language requirements and recognition of diploma's and qualifications;
- Frontier workers.

Tension Free Movement of Workers Law and National Immigration Law

One of the obstacles in the application of the EU rules on free movement is the lack of separation between national immigration law and the implemented free movement rules. The privileged position of EU nationals is disregarded in practice because free movement rules are integrated in general immigration law and applied by immigration officers with these national immigration rules in mind. EU workers are required to prove sufficient income (which is not correct), they are required to present documents routinely asked from third-country nationals but not required under EU law, they have to wait for their cases to be dealt with because immigration authorities give preference to other (e.g. asylum) cases, and sometimes national rules on expulsion on public order grounds are applied rather than the more strict EU public order exception.

Equality of Treatment

As a result of the economic crisis and austerity measures, national authorities have become increasingly interested in limiting access to social assistance and other benefits, including stricter scrutiny to end residence for workers. Social benefits are subject to conditions more easily met by nationals than by EU citizens (e.g. a residence condition). The Netherlands for instance introduced a language requirement in 2016 as a condition to become eligible for a social assistance benefit. Although the new requirement in theory applies to "everyone", there is an exemption for recipients of social assistance who have had eight years of education in the Netherlands. This clause exempts practically all indigenous (=non-immigrant) Dutch nationals.[3]

Access to Employment in the Public Service

There are still problems for EU workers to access employment in the public service in many EU Member States both in law and practice.[4] Article 45(4) TFEU allows for a restriction of access to certain posts in the public service to its own nationals in accordance with Article 45(4) TFEU, but the Court of Justice of the European Union (CJEU) has consistently held that this exception is to be interpreted restrictively and covers only posts which involve direct or indirect participation in the exercise of powers conferred by public law and duties designed to safeguard the general interests of the State or of other public authorities.

3 C.A. Groenendijk & P.E. Minderhoud, 'Taaleis in de bijstand. Discriminerend, disproportioneel en onnodig', 91(3) *Nederlands Juristenblad* 2016, p. 183-189.

4 P.E. Minderhoud & B. Friðriksdóttir, *Report on Posts in the Public Sector Reserved for Nationals Developments in the 27 Member States in 2009-2012* (external report), Nijmegen: Centre for Migration Law 2013.

Language Requirements and Recognition of Diplomas and Qualifications

There are continuing restrictions in some Member States regarding access to posts in several sectors (for instance academic and maritime sector) caused by strict language requirements. Another problem is that professional qualifications and experience acquired in other Member States are not taken into account or are taken into account in a different way.[5]

Frontier Workers

Special problems can still be recognised for frontier workers, who live in one Member State and work in another.[6] They often encounter difficulties with access to social entitlements and labour market support and tax issues, caused by provisions which use a direct or indirect residence requirement as a condition for eligibility. Other reported obstacles are linguistic differences, lack of information and knowledge pertaining to the legal status of frontier workers and the implications thereof, lack of mutual recognition of professional and academic qualifications and lack of cooperation between competent authorities and administrations in the various Member States.[7]

What Impact and Added Values can be Expected from the Directive?

The Directive underlines the importance of free movement of workers, even in times when this is under pressure, and faces the reality that there are still problems to tackle, despite the fact that formally equal treatment is the norm.

But in my view there are three main factors which can influence the effectiveness of the Directive in a negative way from the start.

The first problem is that the Directive, which is modeled after other Equality Directives, suffers from the same weaknesses as these other Equality Directives, and moreover lacks some of the enforcement tools of these Equality Directives.

Secondly, the success of the directive depends highly on the willingness of Member States to take this Directive seriously.

Thirdly, it is not applicable to posted workers, while this is an area where some of the most structural problems regarding discrimination on nationality occur.

---

5 U. Iben Jensen, *Analytical Note for 2013. The Language Requirements under EU Law on Free Movement of Workers*, February 2014, Brussels: European Network on Free Movement of Workers within the European Union 2014. Available at https://www.ru.nl/law/cmr/research/projects/fmow-1/thematic-analytical/.

6 Frontier workers are defined as EU citizens who work in one Member State, yet reside in another, and who return to the Member State of residence on a daily or weekly basis (Article 1(f) Reg. 883/2004).

7 Y. Jorens, P. Minderhoud & J. De Coninck, *Comparative Report: Frontier workers in the EU*, FreSsco, Brussels: European Commission, January 2015.

Same Weaknesses as Other Equality Directives

The structure and text of the provisions of Directive 2014/54 are highly similar to that of for example the Race Directive 2000/43 which implements the principle of equal treatment between persons irrespective of racial or ethnic origin.[8] An important difference is that neither the Race Directive, nor any of the other equal treatment directives cover the ground of nationality, and the Race Directive stipulates specifically states in its Recital 13 and Article 3(2) that 'This prohibition of discrimination should also apply to nationals of third countries, but does not cover differences of treatment based on nationality…'

The text of Article 3 on Defence of rights is highly similar to the text of Article 7 of the Race Directive on Defence of Rights. The same applies to Article 5 on Dialogue which corresponds partly with Article 11 Race Directive on Social Dialogue and Article 12 Race Directive on dialogue with non-governmental organizations. Article 7 on Minimum requirements corresponds with article 6 Race Directive (Minimum requirements).

Article 6 on Access to and dissemination of information corresponds with Article 10 Race Directive (Dissemination of information), but here an extra provision can be found in Article 6(2) of Directive 2014/54, which says that:

> 'Member States shall provide, in more than one official language of the institutions of the Union, information on the rights conferred by Union law concerning the free movement of workers that is clear, free of charge, easily accessible, comprehensive and up-to-date. This information should also be easily accessible through Your Europe and EURES.'

Reports monitoring the implementation of the Race Directive underline that the main challenge identified in many Member States is the lack of enforcement of anti-discrimination laws in practice, particular with regard to access to justice.[9] There is still a problem of lengthy procedures, evidence, high costs, failures in the provision of legal aid, ineffective sanctions, barriers in the form of language, issues relating to legal standing and legitimate interest.[10] For effective claiming it is necessary to have adequate access to justice, which is not always available. In this context we can refer to the so-called naming, blaming, claiming problem.[11] EU workers first have to become conscious of the fact that they are discriminated and to define the acts as such (naming). Therefore they need knowledge of the equal treatment rules but also of the facts, the context and the ability to compare their situation with the situation of others. As a second step they have to hold someone responsible for the act of discrimination (blaming) and thirdly,

8 Council Directive 2000/43/EC of 29 June 2000 implementing the principle of equal treatment between persons irrespective of racial or ethnic origin Official Journal L 180 , 19/07/2000 P. 0022-0026.

9 Report of the European Commission on the application of 2000/43 and 2000/78, 17 January 2014, COM(2014)2, p. 16.

10 Equinet, *Equality law in practice; report on the implementation of the race and general framework directives*, Brussels: Equinet 2013.

11 W.F.L. Felstiner, R.L. Abel & A. Sarat, 'The emergence and transformation of disputes: naming, blaming, claiming', *Law & Society Review* 1981, p. 613-654.

they have to start a legal procedure, which could be difficult because of fear for retaliation or worsening of the relation (claiming).

Therefore Directive 2014/54 shows characteristics of a so called 'symbol-act' which suffers from a serious lack of effectiveness in advance.[12] On the one hand this legislation seeks to strengthen the rights of workers, but on the other hand it does not provide the proper tools for enforcement of the objectives the Directive wants to achieve.

Willingness of Member States to Take this Directive Seriously

The Directive had to be implemented in national legislation by 21 May 2016. Some Member States, such as the UK and the Netherlands, have indicated from the beginning that they did not have to take many measures because all the rights of EU workers are already secured. The British government stated: 'These rights are already enforceable in the UK before the national courts and the Government considers the likely impacts of the Directive to be minor in practice'. According to the Government the Directive will not significantly affect the balance of competence.[13]

The Dutch Minister of Social Affairs said in Parliament that the Directive would not lead to much legal changes. According to the Minister and the Parliament the Netherlands is already doing a good job and the Directive will not add much.[14] He emphasized that the scope of the Directive is limited to the scope of Regulation 492/2011. Some members of parliament even questioned the necessity of the Directive in the light of the own responsibility that EU migrant workers have themselves.[15]

In order to fulfil the obligation to implement the Directive the Dutch government only issued one ministerial decree in which a part of the ministry of Social Affairs is designated with the competence to coordinate activities of already existing bodies which deal with equal treatment of Union workers, like the Dutch legal advice centres, the ombudsman, local anti-discrimination organisations and the Netherlands Institute for Human Rights (the Dutch Equality Body).[16]

According to the Dutch government the extra provision of Article 6(2) on access to and dissemination of information does not need special implementation because there is already sufficient information available on the website of the government through a special brochure: *Nieuw in Nederland* (New in the Netherlands).[17] This brochure of 20 pages provides information on the rights of workers (like labour conditions and working hours rules), but also on membership of a trade union, education, learning the Dutch language and on the possibilities of housing. This brochure has been translated in most EU languages. EU migrant workers get it when they register as a resident with the municipality in the Netherlands, which is obligatory.

---

12 V. Aubert, 'Some Social Functions of Legislation', 10(1/2) *Acta Sociologica – Contributions to the Sociology of Law* 1966, p. 98-120.

13 http://www.niassembly.gov.uk/globalassets/documents/raise/publications/2015/ofmdfm/13515.pdf.

14 *Kamerstukken II* 2012–2013, 33 635, nr. 4, p. 8-9.

15 *Kamerstukken II* 2012–2013, 33 635, nr. 4, p. 4.

16 Wijziging OMV-besluit i.v.m. implementatie richtlijn 2014/54 vergemakkelijken uitoefening vrij verkeer van werknemers, *Official publication: Staatscourant (Journal Officiel néerlandais)*; Number: 23600; Publication date: 10/05/2016; Page number: 00001-00006.

17 See www.newinthenetherlands.nl.

It can be questioned whether this minimalist approach will be seen as a sufficient way of implementation of the Directive. For instance it is not clear which body in the Netherlands is competent to deal with the issue of nationality discrimination regarding social and tax advantages.

Other Member States have taken a different position in respect of implementation. For example, Lithuania wants to use the Directive to strengthen the rights of their own Lithuanian workers in other Member States. Given the fact that Lithuania is more a sending country of workers than a receiving one this is an understandable desire. Regarding their own legislation, Lithuania has the problem that much legislation contains a permanent residence requirement which is a condition for accessing most of the social benefits. This requirement discriminates EU workers of other Member States from own nationals and has to be adapted.[18] The fact that Lithuania has changed 66 different Acts in the implementation process of this Directive raises the presumption that they have dealt with this adaptation of the residence requirement in a structural way.[19]

Not Applicable to Posted Workers

The new Directive will only apply to situations which fall under the scope of Article 45 TFEU and Regulation 492/2011. At the moment for instance in the Netherlands the more structural problems occur with Polish and Portuguese workers, who work as posted workers and fall under the scope of article 56 TFEU (freedom of services) and Directive 96/71, concerning the posting of workers (in the framework of the provision of services), which gives these workers a much lower set of rights than article 45 TFEU and Directive 492/2011 does.

A worker is 'a posted worker' when he is employed in one EU Member State but sent by his employer on a temporary basis to carry out his work in another Member State. There is an employment relation between the undertaking making the posting and the worker during the period of the posting. The core of mandatory rules on posting covers issues such as payment of minimum wages, maximum work periods and minimum rest periods, minimum paid annual leave, equal treatment between men and women and issues such as health and safety at work and includes protective measures in the terms and conditions of employment of pregnant women, of children and of young people. These workers are cheaper because they do not have to be paid the higher wages based on collective labour agreements and they fall under the lower social security and pensions systems of their country of origin, like Portugal or Poland. The issue of posting of workers seems to create more structural difficulties at this moment than the issue of free movement of workers. Posting has become one of the channels for cross-border recruitment of 'cheap' labour without reference to the rights that can be derived from EU law on genuine labour mobility.[20] Main problems are the evasion of minimum wages, abuse of payment of social security contributions and an evasion of collective agreements.

---

18 See presentations FreSsco seminar Latvia-Lithuania, Riga, 16 September 2015, http://ec.europa.eu/social/main.jsp?langId=nl&catId=88&eventsId=1042&furtherEvents=yes.

19 http://eur-lex.europa.eu/legal-content/en/NIM/?uri=celex:32014L0054.

20 J. Cremers, 'Economic freedoms and labour standards in the European Union', *Transfer* 2016, p. 149-162.

Interference of Other Developments

After the adoption of Directive 2014/54 the attention of the Commission and other (European) institutions shifted rapidly towards the introduction of other instruments or measures strengthening the position of EU workers in one way or another. The Juncker Commission which took office in November 2014 formulated other priorities. Most important in this regard are the introduction of the Social Pillar, the revision of the Posting of Workers Directive and the introduction of the European Labour Authority (ELA).

The Introduction of the Social Pillar

On 17 November 2017, the European Parliament, the Council and the Commission jointly proclaimed at the Social Summit in Gothenburg the European Pillar of Social Rights. The Pillar sets out a number of key principles and rights to support fair and well-functioning labour markets and welfare systems.[21] It is designed as a compass for a renewed process of convergence towards better working and living conditions across the Union, ensuring the citizens equal opportunities and access to the labour market, fair working conditions and social protection and inclusion. Ensuring fair labour mobility in Europe is central to this objective.[22] This Social Pillar was developed at the initiative of Commission President Juncker and promoted as the most comprehensive effort to advance the social dimension of European integration. The problem in the context of Directive 2014/54 is that the Social Pillar addresses the position of own national workers in general and not specific to the position of mobile EU workers.

The Revision of the Posting of Workers Directive

Posting of workers plays an important role in the internal market, particularly in the cross-border provision of services. The Posting of Workers Directive (Directive 96 /71/EC) and the Enforcement Directive on Posted Workers (Directive 2014/67/ EU) aim to ensure a correct balance between the freedom to provide cross-border services and the social rights of workers. While the number of posted workers continues to increase significantly, problems such as unfair practices and unequal remuneration persist.

Therefore a significant revision of the Posting of Workers Directives was proposed and adopted in July 2018. The amendments to the Posting of Workers Directive (Directive 2018/957) bring changes in three main areas: the remuneration of posted workers (making it equal to that of local workers, even when subcontracting), more coherent rules on temporary agency workers, as well as long-term posting.[23] Long-term posting (with labour law provisions of the host country to be applied) starts after 12 months (with a possible extension of six months). The overall amount of remuneration received by a posted worker must meet the level of remuneration in the host Member

21 See Proposal for an Interinstitutional Proclamation on the European Pillar of Social Rights, COM (2017) 251.

22 An overview of the European Pillar of Social Rights is available here: https://ec.europa.eu/commission/priorities/deeper-and-fairer-economic-and-monetary-union/european-pillar-social-rights_en.

23 OJ 2018 L173/16.

State (without the reimbursement of the worker's expenses) which must be published on a single national website. Host Member States can accord to posted workers the coverage of representative collective agreements in all sectors, and they must protect them against fraudulent posting. These amendments have to be implemented by the Member States before 30 July 2020. This revision of the Posting of Workers Directive introduces stricter requirements to all service providers active in transnational business, with the intent to 'create a social Europe that protects workers and stops companies from engaging in a race to the bottom', but the question remains whether this revision will be able to ensure the compromise between fair competition and the right of workers, or will it just burden transnational businesses and limit the cross-border provision of services altogether?[24]

The Introduction of the European Labour Authority

In March 2018 the Commission launched the initiative to establish an European Labour Authority.[25] The establishing of this Authority was approved by the European Parliament in April 2019 just before its mandate expired and was adopted by the Council on 13 June.[26] The European Labour Authority's objective is to help strengthen fairness and trust in the Single Market. To that effect the Authority should support the Member States and the Commission in strengthening access to information about rights and obligations in cross-border labour mobility situations and in facilitating the solution of cross-border labour market disputes or irregularities. The tasks of the Authority include:

- Facilitate access to information by individuals and employers on rights and obligations and to relevant services in cross-border labour mobility situations;
- Facilitate cooperation and exchange of information between national authorities;
- Coordinate and support concerted and joint inspections by national authorities;
- Carry out analyses and risk assessments on issues of cross-border labour mobility;
- Support capacity building national authorities through guidance, mutual learning and training;
- Mediate in disputes between Member States on the application of EU law concerning labour mobility
- Facilitate cooperation between relevant stakeholders for cross-border labour market disruptions, e.g. large scale restructuring.

The activities of the ELA will be mainly aimed at cross-border labour mobility issues at a supra national level. It will probably have more impact on the situation of posted workers than mobile workers because posted workers' employment regulation falls under multiple jurisdictions, while mobile workers' rights tends to assume a single national

---

24 www.fragomen.com/insights/blog/revision-eus-posting-workers-directive-blessing-or-curse-business..

25 Proposal for a Regulation of the European Parliament and of the Council establishing a European Labour Authority. COM (2018) 131.

26 https://www.consilium.europa.eu/en/press/press-releases/2019/06/13/european-labour-authority-council-adopts-founding-regulation/.

jurisdiction. The new Regulation also limits the possibility that the ELA launches common enforcement actions in the Member States. According to Cremers the ELA's competence to strengthen the legal capacity of the national enforcement bodies in joint and EU-wide investigations in cases of infringements or irregularities related to cross-border labour mobility needs to be reinforced.[27] The current proposal lacks teeth in his view.

Commission's Report on the Implementation of Directive 2014/54

In December 2018 the Commission published a very modest and low profile report of 10 pages on the implementation of the Directive in the Member States, fulfilling its reporting obligation under Article 9 of the Directive.[28] An important conclusion is that a number of the provisions of the Directive had already been complied with through national instruments that already existed when the Directive entered into force. Legislative amendments in many countries have been limited to transposing Article 4 on the designation of the body to promote equal treatment. A study by Jakuleviciene showed that the discretion left to the Member States in choosing these bodies responsible for the promotion, analysis, monitoring and support of equal treatment led to a situation in which only in two Member States (Germany and Ireland) a new institution has been established, while in the other Member States either the extension of the mandate of one existing body has taken place or several existing bodies together fulfill this task under the coordination of one of them (like in the Netherlands).[29] According to the Commission it remains to be seen whether these bodies cover the issue of prohibiting unjustified restriction on or obstacles to free movement in practice. Moreover, it seems no additional resources have been allocated to the existing bodies to deal with their new competences. Robust conclusions on its impact cannot be drawn at this stage but information mainly provided by the Member States should suggest that the Directive has had a positive impact for all stakeholders. According to the Commission it is difficult, if possible at all, to assess to what extent the implementation of the Directive has helped raise Union citizens' awareness of their rights regarding free movement. This is an interesting observation because this awareness raising is one of the core goals of the Directive. In short a lot remains to be done in practice to ensure the Directive's aims will be attained.

---

27 J. Cremers, 'A Single market for many Labour Markets', 9 *The Progressive Post* 2018, p. 64-65.

28 COM(2018)789. See article 9 Directive 2014/54: By 21 November 2018, the Commission shall submit a report to the European Parliament, to the Council and to the European Economic and Social Committee on the implementation of this Directive, with a view to proposing, where appropriate, the necessary amendments.

29 See L. Jakuleviciene et al., 'Institutional Models under Directive 2014/54: Advantages and Disadvantages for Free Movement of Workers and their Family Members', *European Journal of Migration and Law* 2018, p. 223-251.

Conclusion

Free movement of workers is one of the four classic freedoms on which the European Union is based. Member States have an obligation to protect this freedom to the best of their abilities. Directive 2014/54 was adopted to break through the symbolic character of the equality of rights of workers, but more has to be done to ensure that it does not become a symbolic-act itself. New initiatives like the Social Pillar and the establishment of the European Labour Authority can not only impede the effectiveness of the instruments of Directive 2014/54 but stimulate it as well. Although the start has been rather disappointing there are still chances to make a success out of Directive 2014/54. There is a challenge for governments, trade unions and NGO's to make more use of the possibilities of the Directive, a challenge for Equality Bodies to play a more (pro-)active role and a challenge for the Commission to stimulate Member States to take the Directive seriously.

Union Citizens and the European Parliament
Perception, Accessibility, Visibility and Appreciation

Henri de Waele[*]

1. Introduction

Several readers of this volume will be familiar with the caustic remark of Charles de Gaulle: 'Of course, we could start jumping up and down on our seats, exclaiming 'Europe, Europe, Europe!', but that leads to nothing and signifies nothing. (…) We should take things as they are.'[1] The present times are obviously different from those of *Le Général*, yet the average Union citizen does not necessarily maintain a higher estimation of the European institutions, nor is he likely to have abandoned all cynicism. For instance, a recent poll reveals that less than half of those questioned are satisfied with the functioning of democracy in the EU, expressing the belief that their views are insufficiently heard.[2]

Over the past fifty years, politicians have however not left things as they were, and gradually expanded the powers of the European Parliament (EP). With the entry into force of the Lisbon Treaty in December 2009, the EP finally became a fully-fledged co-legislator. In addition, it obtained a principal right of consent in the conclusion of international treaties by the EU, whereas in the past, it was largely side-lined on that front.[3]

The Parliament has been able to make full use of these new opportunities in the last decade, which could possibly have led to a correspondingly more favourable perception, and a stronger bond between the electors and the elected. After all, by virtue of their enhanced powers, the Members of the European Parliament (MEPs) were able to accomplish more for their supporters than ever before. In this light, the results of the aforementioned survey may be sorely disappointing, and require a plausible explanation. As Elspeth Guild, to whom the current *liber amicorum* is dedicated, was regularly consulted by the Parliament during her distinguished career, it seems appropriate to explore the matter further – with some of the insights perhaps feeding into future advice she may still be asked to deliver, despite her academic *otium cum dignitate* now having commenced officially.

---

* Professor of International and European Law, Radboud University Nijmegen, the Netherlands; Visiting Professor of EU External Relations Law, University of Antwerp, Belgium; Senior Fellow, Centre for European Integration Studies, University of Bonn, Germany.

1 'Bien entendu, on peut sauter sur sa chaise comme un cabri en disant "l'Europe! l'Europe! l'Europe!". Mais cela n'aboutit à rien et cela ne signifie rien. (…) Il faut prendre les choses comme elles sont', Charles de Gaulle, *Discours et messages, Pour l'Effort*, août 1962-décembre 1965, Paris: Librairie Plon 1970, p. 425.

2 European Parliament, D-G Communication, Eurobarometer, 'Democracy on the move', May 2018, p. 129 and p. 133.

3 See inter alia Art. 294 and Art. 218 of the Treaty on the Functioning of the European Union (TFEU).

The working hypothesis of the present contribution is that the limited appreciation for European democracy is partly attributable to the limited accessibility and visibility of the EP, and to the quality of the impressions that citizens get when the institution *does* makes headlines. To test the hypothesis, we shall rewind the film of the past five years, analyse the extent to which the citizen was involved or taken seriously in salient dossiers and procedures, and the likely impact thereof on his overall perception. Hereby, we successively look at the accessibility of the Parliament in the most literal sense (par. 2); the active and passive right to vote (par. 3); the right to petition and the European Citizens' Initiative (par. 4); transparency and the EU decision-making process (par. 5). A concluding section brings the key findings together and sketches a cautious way forward (par. 6).

2. Accessibility *Sensu Stricto*: The Geographical Dimension

Citizens who want to have access to Parliament in a literal sense need to head to its official place of establishment. For over 60 years, the shoe has been pinching terribly here. Once a month, the institution meets in plenary in Strasbourg. All other meetings and committee meetings take place in Brussels. The relocation circus is an absolute nightmare from a logistical perspective, not to mention the pressures put on scarce national infrastructures and the environment. The price tag is said to be EUR 114 million per year, the accumulated CO2 emissions between 11 and 19 thousand tons. This egregious waste of time, money and energy is a fact of common knowledge, producing a horrendously effective anti-advertising campaign. *Pour comble de malheur*, the Parliament's secretariat is located in Luxembourg – a detail lost on the larger public, yet reducing accessibility in a literal sense further: it renders MEPs, their staff, other staff and interested outsiders critically dependent on services located at a significantly greater physical distance than is desirable. Since the arrangement is laid down in a protocol that can only be amended unanimously, and since even the reform-minded Mr Macron has shown no inclination to give up Strasbourg, all calls to bring an end to the threefold split proved fruitless so far.[4]

For the sake of completeness, we should not neglect to mention a cunning attempt at delivering change, when the Parliament itself decided to organise two subsequent plenary sessions in the capital of Alsace, so that the caravan was at least spared one back-and-forth. In the proceedings brought by the French Government before the European Court of Justice however, the manoeuvre was condemned by the Union's judiciary, preserving the grand stasis.[5] Consequently, the negative image of the institution overall was maintained too, and one dare not speak of optimal accessibility in the most literal sense. The cumbersome geographic disposition, and the unwillingness to

4 See e.g. Cécile Barbière, 'France Continues to Block Debate on Strasbourg Seat', *EurActiv* 6 July 2017, <https://www.euractiv.com/section/future-eu/news/france-continues-to-block-debate-on-strasbourg-seat>.

5 Judgment in Joint Cases C-237/11 & C-238/11, *France v. Parliament*; for a similar challenge undertaken in the mid-1990s, see the judgment in Case C-345/95, *France v. Parliament*.

concentrate every component and activity in a single location, has also had a continuing negative impact on the approval rating of the EU as a whole.[6]

3. Accessibility *Sensu Politico*: To Choose and Be Chosen

The EP does not have a single franchise, meaning that there is no uniform arrangement for the election of the 751 MEPs. The reason lies in the fact that electoral law is still principally considered a national matter, leaving it by and large up to the Member States to decide how to shape the electoral process. Although the timing and the number of seats per country are fixed, as well as the right of both nationals and citizens from other EU Member States to cast their votes, registration rules and minimum thresholds may be maintained at a country's discretion. Remarkably, the Member State in which Elspeth is domiciled herself, the United Kingdom, has opted for a system of (qualified) proportional representation from the outset, while sticking to the first-past-the-post approach in all other elections.

The reader will be familiar with the criticism that, largely due to these national differences, 'European' elections have never actually taken place. The final result has always been a sum of the parts, with campaigns being mainly played out to domestic audiences, and each Member State designating its own factions, which eventually link in with an 'umbrella' party family. Proposals for a supranational franchise based on transversal lists, entailing that citizens across the EU could vote for at least a few candidates who do not stand in their own country, have crashed.[7] Consequently, it has neither become easier for citizens to gain access *sensu politico* in the exercise of their active right to vote, by enjoying a greater measure of control over the composition of the institution; nor has such access become easier through an extension of their passive right to vote, whereby the possibility of running in a pan-European constituency could have increased their chance of winning a seat.

In this respect, the innovation of the *Spitzenkandidaten* did not make an honest difference either: the irony is that Jean-Claude Juncker, who triumphed in 2014, failed to appear on any ballot paper – not even in his native Luxembourg. Moreover, it remains a hard legal fact that the European Council is under no obligation to appoint the person who 'won' the elections on behalf of his party family.[8] Also, the self-proclaimed 'political' Commission led by Juncker did not differ as much from its predecessors in its objectives and methods as was initially trumpeted. Besides, that peculiar task definition does not come without risks for its authority, and need not be upheld by future leaders of the institution. For this reason too, the citizen could hardly have had the feeling that,

6 Compare the aforementioned Eurobarometer, indicating that 48% of those quizzed places trust in the EU, with only 40% stating that their general impression of the Union is positive.

7 See e.g. Catherine Hardy, 'EU Parliament Rejects Transnational Lists', *Euronews* 7 februari 2018, <https://www.euronews.com/2018/02/07/eu-parliament-rejects-transnational-lists>.

8 Mattias Kumm and Kenneth Armstrong amusingly crossed swords on this issue in their contributions to the *Verfassungsblog*: see inter alia 'Why the Council is under a Legal Duty to Propose Juncker as a Commission President' and 'Why the European Council is NOT under a Legal Duty to Appoint Jean-Claude Juncker' on <https://verfassungsblog.de>.

with the Parliament as his central conduit, he managed to exert a bigger influence than before on the choices made by the EU's executive.

4. The Right to Petition and the European Citizens' Initiative

Of course, there is more to life than mobility, and in her many publications, Elspeth invariably chose to keep an eye on the position of the 'sedentary class'.[9] For those who refuse to travel to Brussels or Strasbourg, or who wish to be heard outside the election cycle, the right to petition and the European Citizens' Initiative offer interesting alternatives. Every citizen of a Member State of the Union has the option, either individually or jointly with others, to address a petition to the EP. [10] The subject however must concern the applicant directly and fall within the EU's fields of activity. The setup thus deviates from e.g. the Dutch system, wherein everyone may address the Upper or Lower Chamber with regard to every conceivable theme. In the EP, the petition is handled by a special committee of the Parliament that goes by the name 'PETI', frequently inviting applicants to elaborate 'live' on their motions.

In the last five years (2014–2018), a total of 7496 petitions were submitted. 4764 of these were declared admissible in light of the aforementioned conditions. Some of these received an individual reply, others were referred to other bodies or organs. For example, petitioner No. 1170/2015, arguing for the creation of European nuclear waste storage facilities, was ultimately re-directed to the Member State level, as the desideratum was found to lie outside the remit of the supranational institutions. Petition No. 298/2016, of which the author complained that the EU does not do enough to ensure the well-being of livestock in transit to third countries, was forwarded to the ENVI (environmental) committee. Files are also closed when the PETI committee (or, in exceptional cases, the Parliament in plenary) decides not to engage in further follow-up. This was, for example, the fate of petition No. 355/2017, the author of which called for the criminalisation of sexual acts with animals. The same was true of petition No. 2021/2014, calling for peace in Europe, and the refusal to grant asylum to religious fanatics.

A significant part of the petitions submitted has been suspended, and is open to additional signatories – often the result of there being no consensus on the most appropriate response. However, petitions equally give rise to the posing of questions to the Commission, or even to the launching of infringement proceedings against Member States, something that has also occurred in the last five years. An illustration is a series of petitions from 2016, alleging a violation of the rights of holders of maritime concessions in Italy. In addition, petitions such as No. 389/2017, of which the petitioner calls for the introduction of a 'Made in Europe' label for certain goods, have inspired (discussions about) future legislation. Therefore, to dismiss the instrument as a toothless, purely symbolic instrument would definitely not do it justice.

---

9 Take e.g. the paper *Pathways towards Legal Migration into the EU* (Brussels: CEPS 2017), which she co-edited with Sergio Carrera, Andrew Geddes and Marco Stefan, or the seminal *The Reconceptualisation of European Union Citizenship* (Leiden: Brill 2014), co-edited with Cristina Gortázar Rotaeche and Dora Kostakopoulou.

10 Currently codified in Art. 20 sub d and Article 227 TFEU and Art. 44 of the EU Charter of Fundamental Rights.

Anyone who analyses the petition register quantitatively is struck by the fact that the number of petitions seems of late to have decreased significantly. While there were still 2836 submitted in 2013, we see only half of that total being lodged in 2016, as well as in 2017. In 2018, the decline amounts to over 60%. This could boil down to incidental deviations, so that we best not sound alarm bells here without committing an exhaustive background study. Relatively less popular anyhow is the European Citizens' Initiative (ECI), which enables one million citizens from at least seven Member States to ask the Commission to prepare a legislative proposal on a specific topic.[11] If such a campaign is successful, a public hearing will take place in the Parliament. So far, only four ECIs have reached the finish line, of which only one (requesting that the right to water be properly entrenched in EU law) has triggered genuine follow-up. The initiatives to better protect human embryos, phase out animal testing and ban the use of glyphosate did not receive any notable response. Although the ECI has an undeniable potential to boost the support for the Union and its legislation, the strict procedural conditions and tight deadlines constitute serious obstacles, which have probably dimmed its attractiveness. The reforms enacted in mid-2019 are laudable, yet do not eliminate all bottlenecks.[12] In practice, one is advised not to entertain too high expectations, as neither petitions nor citizens' initiatives have ever succeeded in bridging the gap between the governing 'elite' on the one hand and 'the man on the Clapham omnibus' on the other.

5. Transparency and EU Decision-Making

Has the European *demos* perhaps gained more insight into the functioning of the Parliament and its members in recent years, or a superior access to information about the decisions it takes? It seems that the answer has to be in the negative on both counts. For instance, the rules governing the reimbursement of expenses of MEPs continue to raise questions, despite attempts to increase transparency here. A watertight oversight on how they spend the lump sum awarded for travel, accommodation, office equipment and personnel remains absent. Investigations by the Parliament's internal audit service nonetheless led to Nigel Farage and Marine Le Pen having to reimburse funds used for hiring assistants employed to carry out non-EP-related tasks. The Dutch members Judith Merkies and Annie Schreijer-Pierik shamelessly refused to justify their monthly expenses, despite being subjected to considerable pressure from their parties. Only in 2011 did the EP adopt a Code of Conduct featuring a mandatory registration of ancillary positions and financial interests. The huge variety of side-jobs and handsome remunerations cast formidable doubts on the parliamentarians' independence nevertheless. The list of 'big earners' is stunning, and many of the activities these persons undertake create at least a semblance of conflicted interests. In 2018, the practices were exposed and denounced in a detailed report by Transparency International.[13]

---

11 Art. 11 paragraph 4 of the Treaty on European Union (TEU).

12 Extensively on this Ellen Mastenbroek & Henri de Waele, 'Fulfulling High Hopes? The Legitimacy Potential of the European Citizens' Initiative', *Open Political Science* 2018, p. 75.

13 Transparency International, *Moonlighting in Brussels*, July 2018, <https://transparency.eu/wp-content/uploads/2018/07/TIEU-Moonlighting-in-Brussels-MEP-incomes.pdf>.

Initiatives to make registration of lobbyists compulsory registration were derailed repeatedly, barring citizens from acquiring insight into the influence of the latter on EU decision-making.

Traditionally, the absence of a real debating culture makes it patently unattractive for the average voter to spend time in the public gallery at Brussels or Strasbourg. In recent years, there has noticeably been more liveliness than usual, inter alia during the session in which the turbo-charged appointment of Martin Selmayr as secretary-general of the Commission was discussed, on several occasions where MEPs defended sanguine positions pro and contra Brexit, and at the historic showdown with the Hungarian Prime Minister, in which a two-thirds majority voted in favour of firing up an Art. 7 TEU sanctioning procedure. As regards the adoption of controversial international trade agreements such as the CETA, or proposed compacts on the exchange of passenger name records, the Parliament has expressed itself forcefully, and added bite to its barking.[14] The interest of the media also grew accordingly.

On the whole however, these developments appear to be the exception rather than the rule. In the vast majority of cases, any pre-existing interest of the broader public evaporates rapidly pursuant to the complexity of most topics, reducing the incentives for a kerfuffle. Another factor is likely to be the incremental popularity of the 'trilogue method', with legislation being concocted in sinister backrooms by delegations of the Commission, Parliament and Council, reducing the official decision-making procedure to a formality. Moreover, the dominant role of the Heads of State and Government in the European Council regularly confronts the only directly elected assembly with *faits accomplis* – something that is equally bound to stir up mixed feelings in the hearts and minds of the average spectator.[15] In short, looking back at the last *quinquennat*, we cannot justifiably speak of an increase in transparency, a greater (sense of) accountability, or a more open form of decision-making towards the citizen.[16]

6. Conclusions and Perspectives

In an interview in late 2018, Jan Zielonka noted the paradox that, while Parliament has over time been given more and more powers, fewer and fewer people could be bothered to vote, and Eurosceptic parties managed to win more and more seats.[17] These data underscore the citizens' unfavourable perception of the institution, of the EP's functioning, and of the EU as a whole. The present contribution proceeded from the hypothesis that the limited appreciation for European democracy is partly attributable to the still limited accessibility and visibility of the Parliament, and partly to the quality of the impressions citizens get when the institution *does* make headlines. In the previous

14 See e.g. B. Kleizen, *Mapping the Involvement of the European Parliament in EU External Relations – A Legal and Empirical Analysis*, CLEER Working Papers 2016/4, The Hague: T.M.C. Asser Institute 2016.

15 On this, see Deirdre Curtin & Päivi Leino, 'In Search of Transparency for EU Law-Making: Trilogues on the Cusp of Dawn', *Common Market Law Review* 2017, p. 1673.

16 Naturally the judgment of the General Court in Case T-540/15, *De Capitani*, should not be neglected, but a (non-absolute) duty to disclose multicolumn tables can hardly be said to have opened up the black box entirely.

17 Maria Grazyk, 'Academic: A Vision for Europe is Desperately Needed', *EurActiv* 22 November 2018, <https://www.euractiv.com/section/future-eu/interview/academic-a-vision-for-europe-is-desperately-needed>.

sections, we have looked at the extent to which Union citizens have been involved in the past five years, and taken seriously in salient dossiers and procedures. The findings seem to confirm the hypothesis. For example, we may conclude that the accessibility of the parliamentary process has not increased in a literal or technical-metaphorical sense. The 'traveling circus' remains a source of frustration, and the design of the active as well as the passive right to vote remains suboptimal. Attempts at reform stalled or failed altogether. On the same footing, both the right to petition and the European Citizens' Initiative leave many a citizen dissatisfied – a pitiful conclusion, but *prima facie* supported by a numerical analysis. Various scandals surrounding the use of public funds, and well-founded suspicions of conflicts of interests fuel the dissatisfaction further. To this, we must unfortunately add the byzantine structure of the decision-making and the shady role of lobbyists. The less frequent moments when the Parliament pops up in the news positively are probably insufficient to counter the cascade of dubious habits, defective procedures and bad publicity. Although the European Ombudsman's proactive stances are to be applauded, her critical reports on e.g. 'Selmayrgate' or the lack of transparency in trilogues serve to confirm the negative perceptions – certainly if such damning assessments do not manage to effect lasting changes in policy, law and practice.[18]

Should we then, in accordance with the advice of Charles de Gaulle in 1965, cling to our seats, and take things as they are? First of all, it deserves emphasis that the picture does not necessarily look rosier nowadays with regard to the confidence citizens place in their *national* parliaments. In comparison though, due to the opacity of the subject-matter that is usually discussed there, the EP will always experience a greater difficulty in appealing to the imagination of the masses.

In terms of solutions, the introduction of a coalition–opposition model has often been touted to make the system more transparent and intelligible. The elections in mid-2019 brought us a bit closer to that ideal, producing a larger 'anti-EU bloc'. It is doubtful however whether the setup truly heightens the interest of the citizens, or makes them feel that their concerns and interests will be addressed better. In a globalised world, a stagnant Europe can never be a Europe that protects. Fostering disagreement merely prompts the vicious circle of a Union that is less effective than before, suffering an additional loss of legitimacy exactly because of its waning prowess.

That the EP does not possess a general right of initiative, and is dependent on the Commission's willingness to propose new legislation, continues to puzzle the outsider and the layman alike. While no miracles are to be expected from Treaty amendment here, it would be a major step in the right direction of a mature parliamentary architecture. However, if the other deficiencies flagged in this chapter are not addressed simultaneously, European integration will not be rid of its discontents anytime soon.

Arguably, the main challenge lies not in the pushing through of drastic institutional innovations, but in the devising of targeted communication strategies in order to build a solid case for such innovations, and to sell them convincingly afterwards. After all, the distance between voters and their elected representatives decreases the easier it

18 See 'Recommendation of the European Ombudsman in Joint Cases 488/2018/KR and 514/2018/KR on the European Commission's appointment of a new Secretary-General', 31 August 2018, respectively 'Decision of the European Ombudsman setting out Proposals following her Strategic Inquiry OI/8/2015/JAS concerning the Transparency of Trilogues', 12 July 2016.

becomes for the former to stay in touch with the latter, and so long as the latter take care to explain their every (in)action to the former. Social media are perhaps *the* modern tools for improving the perception, accessibility, visibility and appreciation of the Parliament. When deployed cleverly, they might even help to shore up the image in the United Kingdom of the EU's most democratic institution – something that is sure to please the person this *liber* seeks to honour.

Migrants

The Strangers: Security, Estrangement and Migrants

*Tugba Basaran**

> 'If wandering is the liberation from every given point in space, and thus the conceptional opposite to fixation at such a point, the sociological form of the "stranger" presents the unity, as it were, of these two characteristics. This phenomenon too, however, reveals that spatial relations are only the condition, on the one hand, and the symbol, on the other, of human relations.' (Simmel 1950)

The stranger is not defined by movement, but comes into existence in a social relationship. In this relationship, the stranger is a paradoxical figure of physical proximity, but social distance (Marotta 2012). Written by Georg Simmel in 1908, the stranger probes into the production of social and symbolic boundaries (Lamont and Molnar 2002), social relations and social distance. The figure of the stranger is the starting point for our analysis. This article queries how the stranger becomes a stranger. The common assumption is that particular groups of people are classified as 'strangers', due to physical characteristics, due to religion or due to provenance. In this article, however, I want to engage with the construction of the stranger as a result of purposeful state intervention – or in other words, estrangement policies intended to create social distance at physical proximity.

Estrangement is as an integral component of the state's security measures, but much disregarded component of security research. Estrangement, the creation of social and emotional distance at spatial proximity, a social distance that produces the stranger, is an intended and core component of security measures, intended to socially isolate securitized populations. Estrangement policies can be found in a number of historical and contemporary formations, deployed during war, as part of anti-terrorism policies, but also for migration. Social distance contributes towards emotional distance, disengagement and indifference, authorizing the public to look away from the suffering of strangers under conditions of security. This provides the very possibility of state and public violence without public interference. Violence that would usually be condemned is permitted towards the stranger.

The questions at stake in examining estrangement policies, that is the intended creation of social distance as a product of the political and legal interventions in the name of security are: How do liberal societies securitize social interactions? How do they create the stranger, as a figure of spatial proximity, but social and emotional distance? Particularly, how is legal authority deployed to shape social relations and interactions? How are contemporary law, legal institutions and public policies involved in the contemporary production of estrangement policies? And what are the legal strategies deployed to create and maintain social distance? The formation of the stranger in

* University of Cambridge, UK.

liberal democracies provides an important vantage point for understanding contemporary forms of violence in liberal democracies and sheds light on the relation between politics, law and society in liberal democracies.

1. Legalized Estrangement

Estrangement, the creation of social distance, is an integral element of security. Estrangement polices, however, are widely disregarded in scholarly works. When discussing security, law and violence, state violence, is routinely conceptualized as a direct form of violence. Here violence is examined as the relationship between the ruler and the ruled, the sovereign and its subjects. This conception is inherent both to classical political theory from Hobbes to Rousseau as well as contemporary theory from Benjamin to Agamben (Agamben 1998; Austin 1991; Arendt 1986; Hobbes 1996; Benjamin 1978). The focus here is on public violence, that is state agents, institutions and their direct effects, including military violence, policing violence, but also legal violence. In a similar vein, critiques of state violence focus on the rights of the individual, on the relation between security and liberties to counter public violence. The effective securitization of particular groups cannot take place, however, without complementary estrangement measures.

Security measures require the governing of the public, of third parties, to induce a conforming conduct of the general populations governed. They require the regulation of the conduct of non-state actors, the public in their various private and professional functions, whether doctors, taxi drivers, fishermen or by-passers. The state seeks to govern commercial, social and even humanitarian interactions between the public and securitized populations. It strives to survey, control and manage the relations of a variety of public actors, whether individual actors, private corporations or civil society organizations, with the stranger.

As a security strategy, legal institutions of estrangement emerge most visibly under conditions of war and conflict. Many security strategies strive to isolate opponents by punishing civilian interactions and, thus, withdrawing access to essential resources of survival, including medication, accommodation and provisions. Haphazard to the motives of interaction, whether out of humanitarian intentions or political solidarity, these strategies claim the inseparability of the armed forces from their civilian support base and promote an approach, which could best be described, as guilt by association. Any association with the enemy is open to scrutiny and penalty under the presumption of a concealed bond with the enemy. This enemy approach is deployed in colonial wars, occupations, as well as anti-terrorism strategies and genocides and targets all social relations, including for profit and not-for profit relations, family and public relations. Even the humanitarian space is often not exempted from efforts to isolate the enemy.

Contemporary anti-terrorism and criminalization efforts equally employ estrangement policies. One of the most widely used prohibitions is that of 'material support or resources' to groups designated as Terrorist Organizations (18 USC 2339).[1] In the US, the material support clause criminalizes activities, including training, expert advice, service and personnel.

1 For an updated FTO list, see http://www.state.gov/j/ct/rls/other/des/123085.htm.

> 'The term "material support or resources" means any property, tangible or intangible, or service, including currency or monetary instruments or financial securities, financial services, lodging, training, expert advice or assistance, safehouses, false documentation or identification, communications equipment, facilities, weapons, lethal substances, explosives, personnel (1 or more individuals who may be or include oneself), and transportation, except medicine or religious materials.' (18 USC 2339 A).

A variety of human rights organizations contend that these 'material support provisions violate the First Amendment as they criminalize activities like distribution of literature, engaging in political advocacy, participating in peace conferences, training in human rights advocacy, and donating cash and humanitarian assistance, even when this type of support is intended only to promote lawful and non-violent activities' (CCR). It imposes 'guilty by association' and provides discretionary powers to law enforcement.

Law's capacity to regulate social relations and generate estrangement at physical proximity is also crucial to various historical forms of segregation. Segregation relies on the regulation of lawful and unlawful social relations. Various types of segregatory regimes, including apartheid, colonialism, slavery and anti-Semitic regimes, regulated social relations at physical proximity, sought to provide social distance within a close interactional unit. These extended to all types of daily social interactions amongst members of the society with laws targeting physical contact between Jews and non-Jews in Nazi Germany (Nuremberg laws 1935), or rendering unlawful for blacks and whites to play together or in company with each other games, such as cards, dice, dominoes, checkers, pool or billiard (Alabama 1930). These estrangement measures that had as their concern the direct regulation and penalization of social interactions were naturally embedded in and complemented by various other types of laws for upholding segregatory regimes that targeted public institutions, but also regulated the conduct of private companies, i.e. separate accommodation and seating to be provided in private establishments. Segregatory regimes provided for severance of the majority of social relations, with core forms of lawful contact limited to specific economic relations, and reduced the human – at best – to an economic factor, surplus populations, whose economic value comes along with economic disposability.

Even though these examples are different in very significant aspects, they have a common foundation in estrangement: the intended disabling of social relations. Estrangement towards the enemy presupposes the curtailment of all interactions; estrangement towards labour requires the curtailment of most, but not all interactions. In both, relations to estranged populations are suspect and governed meticulously. Common to the various forms of estrangement as a security approach is the intent of withdrawing support, isolating the securitized subject and thus rendering him/her vulnerable and under the comprehensive control of the state. These legal institutions of estrangement remain central to contemporary liberal democracies, as both wartime and peacetime strategies. Estrangement, the creation of social distance, continues to be an integral part of security, with severe legal and social penalties for violations hereof.

2. Legal Estrangement, Irregularity and Everyday Relations

Estrangement remains an important policy for liberal democracies in dealing with irregular migrants. The governing of social relations is conducted directly by rendering everyday interactions necessary for living in a society unlawful and providing sanctions towards facilitating or assisting the stranger. Estrangement policies towards irregular migrants encompass a wide range of third parties, including individuals, companies, professional groups, but also non-profit organizations. The profile and motives of these third parties for wanting to interact with irregular migrants are varied, ranging from solidarity for activists and human rights defenders, to humanitarianism for humanitarian organizations and individuals, to commercial motives for employers, landlords and transport companies. Then, there are those who are incidentally confronted with the irregular migrants, bypassers who may meet irregular migrants in need without further motives attached and may act in the moment. Estrangement policies target, regulate and control the variety of these third parties and seek to govern their conduct.

Sanctioning of social relations takes place through various means, including both laws as well as practices of law. The framework for sanctioning social relations between irregular residents and the regular residents is provided by a variety of laws targeting different areas of social interaction. The targets are natural and legal persons. It is difficult to identify a core corpus of estrangement laws, but estrangement relies on a number of laws diffused and dispersed across various areas, including criminal law, administrative law and civil law, but also a variety of different legal regimes ranging from smuggling to labour relations. In the following I shall provide an overview of the variety of social relations of the subject in irregular situation that are regulated and rendered unlawful. I shall illustrate in the following, as an example, the sanctioning of social relations in Europe analysing legal restrictions on social relations, including labour relations, commercial relations, social relations and humanitarian relations:

First, labour relations: These are sanctions for employers, such as The Employer Sanctions Directive 2009/52/EC that specifically targets the employment of non-EU nationals and provides for minimum common standards on sanctions and other measures, including criminal penalties against employers. Even before this Directive, the employment of irregular migrants was – even if not criminalized – considered unlawful, leading to the employment of irregular labourers in informal markets as manual labour, primarily in agriculture, construction, domestic work and the catering industry. Due to the ban on wage relations, both for the irregular labourers as well as the regular employers, they render the irregular wage earners vulnerable to exploitation.

Second, commercial relations: Many types of commercial relations are prohibited. As such the Facilitation Directive 2002/90/EC (OJ L328/17 and OJ L328/1) equates for-profit interactions with irregular migrants to criminal offences. The Facilitation Directive provides for criminal offences for aiding unauthorized entry, transit and residence. Any for-profit interaction, whether as a taxi driver for border crossing or for renting accommodation is criminalized. The Facilitation Directive closely follows international anti-smuggling legislation prohibiting the facilitation of unauthorized entry, transit and residence for profit and anti-trafficking laws prohibiting the recruitment, transportation, transfer, harbouring or receipt of persons for the purpose of exploitation (United Nations Convention against Transnational Organized Crime – UNTOC 2002). The Facilitation Directive goes beyond these, however, by also criminalizing non-profit interaction for transport and accommodation, allowing Member States to punish families having irregular relatives, parents and husbands to staying with them (see also French case law). Another important tool for sanctioning commercial relations is the Carrier Sanctions Directive Sanctions (Art. 26 of Schengen Convention, supplemented by Directive 2001/51), which provides penalties for transporting irregular migrants, including sanctions against airlines and travel agencies.

Third, social relations: Duties to report constitute obligations of public and private service providers to report the presence of irregular migrants. These provisions are usually under civil law and include healthcare professionals, social workers, and teachers. Public service providers, such as schools, medical facilities, police and courts may have duties to report. Irregular migrants are hesitant to claim any services or to ask for their rights. Basic social services are only available to lawfully residing persons, with unlawful person having no or greatly inferior access. Reporting and sanctions hereto, or 'the active participation of a vigilant public' has not received sufficient interest (Walsh 2014). In the US, this emerged with Proposition 187 (California 1994), later ruled unconstitutional, that denied irregular migrants all social services by requiring teachers, doctors and social workers to report irregular residents. A number of exclusionary ordinances have taken its place across the US (Walker and Leitner 2011).

Sanctions for labour, commercial and social relations are part of third sector strategies of policing, which combine delegation and deputization of policing functions to the private sector with strategies to involve ordinary citizens in providing for security. As part of neoliberal approaches to policing and the regulatory state, policing increasingly takes place by compelling and convincing citizens and the private sector to assist the state's agents (Braithwaite 2000), 'more than self-discipline and care, citizens are made responsible for regulating the conduct of others' (Walsh 2014). Formal institutions delegate crime control to the civil society, private actors and citizens. The state enlists companies, communities and citizens in its effort to govern security, countering the monopolization of crime control by state institutions. Policing works through the capillaries of the society. As Garland pointed out long time ago, formal institutions of crime control and criminal justice are embedded and joined with a variety of social institutions and informal social controls, however '[t]oo often our attention focuses on the state's institutions and neglects the informal social practices upon which state action depends' (Garland 2001: 6). Civil society actors are engaged in 'preventing and controlling legal transgressions' and to regulate 'access to public goods, spaces, and institutions' (Walsh 2014).

Fourth, humanitarian relations: given the restrictions of commercial and social relations, it is probably not surprising that this also effects humanitarian relations. Over the last two decades an increasing number of laws and regulations have been devised with the intention of discouraging humanitarian assistance to irregular migrants. Under specific legal provisions, humanitarian assistance can even be criminalized (see Basaran 2014). The Facilitation Directive, for example, provides only an *optional* humanitarian exception clause for member-states, but even if the distinction between for-profit and non-profit acts is provided in law (see, for example, UNTOC 2000), various court cases, but also fines prove that what would usually be regarded as humanitarian act, can be penalized when it is extended towards irregular migrants. This includes prosecution of rescue at sea under smuggling clauses, as in the case of *Cap Anamur* (2009) or *Morthada/El Hedi* (2009) in Italy, but also charges for contempt of public officials in France or public littering for providing for water bottles in the US desert (Basaran 2014). Not only humanitarian acts, but also humanitarian actors and humanitarian subjects are regulated under conditions of security.

Estrangement can take multiple formations. Apart from the explicit regulation of social relations that render some everyday activities and interactions unlawful, as highlighted above, estrangement is the creation of a mindset and sentiments through techniques of law that render relations to the stranger different from other types of relations. It is the result of law and legal institutions that shape the mindset and sentiments of the governed towards particular populations. This also includes various subtle legal techniques that produce and shape social relations and social distance, and create the stranger. These legal techniques are ordinary tools of laws, such as the production of legal identities, the production of legal spaces, legal borders and legal regimes for particular populations. These include the labelling, criminalization and securitization of particular populations as alien, illegal or terrorist and by that the creation of the social category of the stranger and the production of legal and political discourses of threat. They also include governing techniques, including spatial, technological and legal ways of governing the conduct of populations as to shape social relations under conditions of security, such as the differential sets of rights and protections guaranteed to irregular migrants, the legal set-up of different set of detention and expulsion regimes.

The discriminatory nature of estrangement policies is concealed as a normality of law in form of legal norms. For estrangement policies, whether they explicitly render certain relations unlawful or implicitly curtail relations by providing a specific mindset and sentiments, it is especially their potential for norm setting that is significant. The discriminatory nature of many estrangement policies is located in the very distinctions created by normalizing a certain thought and culture as a norm.

3. Concluding Thoughts on Estrangement and Liberal Democracies

Governing of security takes place through society (Foucault 1991; Dean 1999), by governing social relations. The public is rendered passive by policy and practice that strategically punishes, criminalizes and hence reduces public interaction with the securitized. Equally, however, the society is rendered active as delegated policing forces, as to survey and report. The intended effect of social distance is the creation of the stranger. Security as estrangement, the creation of social distance, the securitization of social relations, is an intended and core component of security measures.

In seeking to control societies, law takes an important role in regulating social relations. In an effort to socially isolate securitized populations, severe administrative and criminal sanctions are foreseen for interactions with securitized populations, punishable by fines and imprisonment. Liberal democracies strive to ban interactions between the public and the securitized through laws that restrict not only collaboration, but in wider sense also any kind of social interaction, whether out of humanitarian concern, social solidarity, commercial interest or due to unintended consequences of accidental encounters. Almost any interaction is rendered suspect, perceived as possibly aiding and abetting the securitized population. With social relations discouraged, the precondition for indifference to the fate of securitized population is established. The very possibility for security acts is created through public indifference, uncaring about the suffering of others, seeking to abstain from politics, unwilling to observe, witness, and unwilling to engage. Estrangement policies seek to limit interactions, as to hinder relations of empathy and solidarity and facilitate indifference and disengagement by the public.

Estrangement policies and the formation of the stranger provide an important vantage point for understanding contemporary forms of violence in liberal democracies. They illustrate how law is complicit in creating social, emotional and moral distances, in authorizing spaces for discrimination and foreclosing spaces of solidarity and dissent. Estrangement policies provide for legal norms, and by that also authorize cultural norms, that allow for differential treatment of securitized populations. A societal devaluation of particular lives becomes legally authorized, as even humanitarian acts become suspicious and are open to criminalization. Violence that would usually be condemned is permitted towards the stranger. Estrangement policies demonstrate the liberal character of violence, how antipathy and discrimination in liberal societies is induced, authorized and justified by law and legal institutions.

References

Agamben, Giorgio, *Homo sacer: Sovereign power and bare life* (Trans. Daniel Heller-Roazen), Palo Alto, CA: Stanford University Press 1998.

Arendt, Hannah, *The Origins of Totalitarianism*, London: Verso 1986 [1951].

Austin, Sarat & Thomas R. Kearns, 'A Journey Through Forgetting: Toward a Jurisprudence of Violence', in: Austin Sarat and Thomas R. Kearns (eds), *The Fate of Law*, Ann Arbor: University of Michigan Press 1991.

Basaran, Tugba, 'The curious state of the Good Samaritan: Humanitarianism under conditions of security', *Governing Borders and Security* 2014, p. 61-75.

Basaran, Tugba, 'The saved and the drowned: Governing indifference in the name of security', 46(3) *Security Dialogue* 2015, p. 205-220.

Basaran, Tugba & Elspeth Guild, 'Mobilities, ruptures, transitions', in: Tugba Basaran, Didier Bigo et al., *International Political Sociology: Transversal Lines*, New York: Routledge 2016, p. 272-285.

Benjamin, Walter, 'Critique of Violence', in: Peter Demetz (ed.), *Reflections*, New York: Schocken 1978 [1921].

Bodin, Jean & Julian H. Franklin, *Bodin: On Sovereignty*. Cambridge: Cambridge University Press 1992.

Braithwaite, J., 'The New Regulatory State and the Transformation of Criminology', 40(2) *British Journal of Criminology* 2000, p. 222-238.

Dean, Mitchell, *Governmentality: Power and Rule in Modern Society*, London: Sage 1999.

Foucault, Michel 'Governmentality', in: G Bruchell, C. Gordon and P. Miller (eds), *The Foucault Effect: Studies in Governmentality*, Chicago: University of Chicago Press 1991 [1978], p. 87-104.

Garland, David, *The Culture of Control: Crime and Social Order in Contemporary Society*, Chicago: University of Chicago Press 2001.

Hobbes, Thomas, *Leviathan*, London: A&C Black 2006.

Lamont, Michèle & Virág Molnár, 'The study of boundaries in the social sciences', 28(1) *Annual review of sociology* 2002, p. 167-195.

Marotta, Vince, 'Georg Simmel, the stranger and the sociology of knowledge', 33(6) *Journal of Intercultural Studies* 2012, p. 675-689.

Simmel, Georg, 'The stranger', from Kurt Wolff (Trans.), *The Sociology of Georg Simmel*, New York: Free Press, 1950, p. 402-408.

Tilly, Charles, 'War making and state making as organized crime', in: Peter B. Evans, *Violence: A reader*, New York City, NY: New York University Press 1985, p. 35-60.

Walker, Kyle E. & Helga Leitner, 'The variegated landscape of local immigration policies in the United States', 32(2) *Urban geography* 2011, p. 156-178.

Walsh, James P., 'Watchful Citizens: Immigration Control, Surveillance and Societal Participation', 23(2) *Social & Legal Studies* 2014, p. 237-259.

Addressing the Root Causes of People Forced to Move
Creating an International Model for People Voluntarily on the Move

Cristina Gortázar Rotaeche[*]

1. People on the Move

The globalization that our society has been experiencing for decades has had major consequences on the phenomenon of international migration[1] Migratory movements are a complex process that can only be correctly analysed from a multidisciplinary perspective; they are movements whose directions, destinations, returns or circularity depend on so many factors that it is easier to speak of 'migrants' than of 'immigrants' and 'emigrants'.

Migration has completely penetrated the daily lives of our industrialized society: one migrant serves us coffee, another is our partner, another might be our superior at work. The second and following generations of these migrants generally acquire the nationality of the country of residence (whether or not they lose their nationality of origin), thus turning today's societies into multicultural ones. If properly managed, such multiculturalism can unquestionably become a strength for the society able to manage it. In this regard, one of the pending subjects of western societies during the remaining decades of the 21st century is the appropriate conversion of multicultural societies into intercultural societies,[2] societies that have been enriched in their human, cultural, economic and symbolic capital.

What has been described above is not impossible, although it is complex. The fact, for example, that some of the architects of recent terrorist attacks in European capitals are European citizens, as well as being the descendants of immigrants, constitutes reliable proof of the failure of integration policies in certain immigration-receiving societies. We are living through difficult times, but we must not falter in the construction of societies that are increasingly fair, respectful of the Rule of Law and of the fundamental rights of the human person whilst at the same time being safe and peaceful. The way is not paved, but the path is made by walking.

If we shift our focus away from industrialized societies, we notice that a considerable number of international migrations take place between developing countries (38%), with only 35% of them from developing countries to developed countries (the

* Comillas Pontifical University, Madrid, Spain.

1 In 2017, approximately 258 million people were international migrants; 3.4% of the world's population. These figures represent an increase of 49% since 2000. A DESA. (2017): Trends in International Migrant Stock: The 2017revision. (United Nations database, POP / DB / MIG / Stock / Rev.2017, New York, United Nations, Department of Economic and Social Affairs, Population Division).

2 N.Meer, T. Modood & R. Zapata-Barrero (Eds), *Multiculturalism and Interculturalism: Debating the Dividing Line,*. Edinburgh: Edinburgh University Press 2016.

remaining international migrations, therefore, move between developed countries).[3] As for refugees (international migrants with international protection status),[4] it is important to remember that 85% of them are staying in developing countries.

The demographic impoverishment of Western societies leads them to foster an increase in migration (the 'd' pull effect), while the weakness of democracy and development (the '2ds' push effect) of many emitting societies mean that international migration flows tend to increase towards economically stronger societies, those which are thriving in democratic and developmental terms. For the receiving societies, these '2ds' as push effects imply a great many irregular and disordered migrations. What is wrong? Even though it is not the only one, perhaps the most relevant cause is the scarcity of accessible legal channels for potential migrants. This is not reasonable as Western countries should encourage (or import) demographics, and export democracy and development. To this end, among other tasks, they must empower emerging countries economically, by liberalizing the procedures regulating the entry of their products into developed countries; they must also make co-development viable and prevent the brain drain from sending to receiving countries. In addition, remittances sent by immigrants to their countries of origin sometimes have a high cost; the host societies should regulate the transparency of these transactions and seek to reduce their costliness (a proposal included in the 2030 Agenda for Sustainable Development).

According to co-development theory[5], migration has positive effects on the development of countries of origin, since migrants send remittances that are invested there whilst helping to create or consolidate the network with diasporas, which encourages free mobility or circular migration and thereby the development of the sending countries. Co-development is presented as a 'win-win-win', or triple win situation: the country of origin wins, the country of destination wins, and so does the migrant him- or herself. Naturally, this would only be entirely true under the kinds of laboratory-like conditions that rarely prevail. In practice, the co-development formula is still far from being a plausible reality.[6]

As already mentioned, it is essential that receiving States provide legal channels for immigration so as to avoid irregular and disorderly migrations. Such channels would turn a vicious circle (more irregular immigration, more restrictions and controls) into a virtuous one (greater legal access, more orderly immigration and better integration). The key is to promote mobility by ensuring security. It is not an easy task.

---

3 UNPD, *World Population Prospects*, New York: United Nations, Department of Economic and Social Affairs, Population Division 2017.

4 In 2017, there were more than 68.5 million refugees. Of these 68.5 million people, only about 25.4 million are recognized refugees or asylum seekers, and the remaining 43.1 million are forced internally displaced persons (who have crossed an international border). UNHCR, *Global trends in forced displacement in 2017*, Geneva: UNHCR 2018.

5 S. Nair, *Rapport de bilan et d´orientation sur la politique de codéveloppement liée aux flux migratoires*, Mission Interministérielle Migrations/Codéveloppment, Paris: Ministère des Affaires Etrangères 1997, http://www.ladocumentationfrancaise.fr/var/ storage/rapports-publics/984000139/0000.pdf

6 C. Gortázar Rotaeche, 'The constant link between migration and sustainable development: the 2030 Agenda and the "leave no one behind" principle', in: C. Urbano de Sousa (Ed.) *The relevance of migration for the 2030 Agenda for Sustainable Development*, Lisbon: Universidade Autónoma de Lisboa 2019, p. 29-32.

2. Recognising Protection Status for All *People Forced to Move*

In principle, for the legal sciences there exist only nationals, foreigners or stateless persons. Thus, for example, a Canadian who joins a powerful multinational company as financial director is as much a foreigner in Spain as a Sub-Saharan who has managed to enter Spain irregularly after a months-long, life-risking journey. But are these situations really sociologically comparable? The answer is surely negative. The Canadian businessman is an 'invited' non-national whose life in the country of arrival will probably be well organized.

The Sub-Saharan is a migrant and also, in principle, a migrant in an irregular situation.

Let us suppose that his name is Abdul and that he left Mauritania to arrive in Spain following a difficult, risky journey. Abdul is not persecuted, and his life is not at immediate risk, however, he considers that, as the only male in the family, he must undertake the migratory journey to assist with the urgent needs of his sisters and to take care of his mother. He is not, in principle, eligible for international protection status in Spain (either because of refugee status or subsidiary protection status), and neither, under Spanish law, is he a candidate for an extraordinary residence permit. Abdul would be an immigrant in an irregular situation.

Let us also imagine that there is another male in the family, the younger brother of Abdul's father. His name is Ousmane, and for years he has been travelling to the Central African Republic, where he has joined a Christian religious community. Since 2013 the political situation in the Central African Republic has been critical and Christians - especially in the capital - are in danger as they are subjected to persecution by radical Islamist groups. Ousmane's conversion to Christianity makes him a likely target of these radical Islamists. And let us suppose, finally, that Ousmane manages to travel to Chad[7] and from there, on a possibly forged visa, that he flies to Paris, where he applies for international protection. Ousmane is a refugee and France should study and recognise his refugee status according to the 1951 Geneva Convention and the EU *Qualification* Directive (2011).[8] Ousmane's irregular entry into France, coming from the country of persecution, is not an obstacle to the recognition of his international protection status and cannot be sanctioned (as stated in Article 31 of the 1951 Geneva Convention and the EU *Asylum Procedures* Directive[9]).

It is important to point out that, in our example, both Abdul and Ousmane have entered Spain and France irregularly. Both have fundamental rights that must be scrupulously respected, but Ousmane also has the absolute right not to be returned to the country of persecution or risk, nor to any other country that in his opinion might return

7 For the purposes of my example I consider that Chad is not a safe country for Ousmane. Therefore, it must be considered as coming from the place of persecution.

8 Directive 2011/95 / EU of the European Parliament and of the Council of 13 December 2011, which establishes rules regarding the requirements for the recognition of third-country nationals or stateless persons as beneficiaries of international protection, to a uniform status for refugees or for persons entitled to subsidiary protection and the content of the protection granted (recast), *Official Journal of the European Union* L 337/9, December 20, 2011.

9 Directive 2013/32 / EU of the European Parliament and of the Council of June 26, 2013 on common procedures for the granting or withdrawal of international protection (recast), *Official Journal of the European Union* L 180/60, June 29, 2013.

him to the country of persecution or risk to his life and integrity (the principle of *non-refoulement*). He also has the right to a fair and effective process under which his refugee (or subsidiary protection) status can be proven. It is certainly not easy to prove a refugee status, or indeed other analogous status offering such protection, which is why there exist people who, though deserving of international protection, live among us as mere migrants and without the essential protection, for example, of non-return to the country of persecution or generalized violence.

So far, we have sought to visualize the differences between, on the one hand, a migrant in an irregular situation with no apparent grounds for international protection under current International Refugee Law (IRL), and a migrant who, having entered the country of destination irregularly, has the right to international protection in the State where he or she arrives. All refugees are immigrants, but not all immigrants are refugees.

Nonetheless, the migrant-refugee classification is often unfair. Under current IRL, refugees and other persons with special international protection (in the EU, subsidiary protection) can claim privileged international status in relation to other migrants. But there are many forced migrants who lack such protection, and it is timely to make a plea for the international protection of all those people who are moved forcibly, even when their motives are not covered by the 1951 Geneva Convention or other instruments on international protection. My claim is that international protection should be available to all those people who leave their country of origin for serious reasons completely beyond their control, and where it is inhumane to force them to return. Unfortunately, this is not the line of thinking or action of those governments and institutions that have come to create a strict duality between refugees and misnamed 'economic immigrants', a policy that leaves many forced migrants stranded within the latter group.

I seek an answer to the following question: What is the reason for the existence of IRL? In the current state of its development, IRL understands that, in cases of refuge, the State of origin has ceased to protect the person either willingly or unwillingly; that the State-citizen bond has been broken; and that the person has been left helpless and, therefore, that international law builds a new protection status for them as refugees. On the other hand, International Migration Law (IML) assumes that in the cases of these human movements, the State-citizen bond continues but that these people voluntarily migrate to find a better life. The difficulty lies in the narrowness with which the current IRL defines the causes giving rise to refugee status, a status that applies primarily to the person with a well-founded fear of persecution for reasons of race, religion, nationality, membership of a particular social group or political opinion, and provided that the person has managed to leave the country of persecution. This definition, provided by the 1951 Geneva Convention, cannot be adapted to the assumptions of asylum seekers existing in current international society. In several regions of the world, efforts have therefore been made to provide international protection for refugees from war and flagrant and massive violations of human rights; among these efforts, we find the aforementioned subsidiary protection. However, international protection has not yet been extended to cover refugees from climate, development projects, natural disasters, severe poverty, etc. And, of course, neither does it embrace those so-called internally displaced people who have not yet managed to cross an international border. In order to manage forced human movements, expanding the content of the IRL is therefore a necessary, though not sufficient, condition.

3. Avoiding the Root Causes of *People Forced to Move* and Creating an International Model for *People Voluntarily on the Move*

No one can ignore that the efforts of the international community must be aimed at addressing the root causes of forced migration. This is the key. There is still much work to be done, and the consequences of not appropriately attending to it are potentially catastrophic. In addition to reducing and, if possible, eliminating the causes of forced migrations, we must create an international model for the management of voluntary migrations in general. Migrations managed as an option, and not as a necessity, are the most effective tool for the reduction of inequalities within and among the member states of the international community and are also key to the reduction of poverty.

The year 2016 represents two milestones for the future management of migrations. On 1 January 2016, the 2030 Agenda for Sustainable Development entered into force. This agenda designs a plan to achieve seventeen Sustainable Development Objectives (SDOs) over a period of fifteen years, and establishes 169 concrete goals to that effect. Also, on September 19 of the same year, the New York Declaration for Refugees and Migrants was adopted. This was the starting point for the preparation of two global compacts to be negotiated within a period of two years: one of the pacts, promoted by the special representative for International Migrations, deals with Migrations, and the other, entrusted to the United Nations High Commissioner for Refugees, with Refugees. Both Pacts encourage voluntary (soft law) commitments on the part of the state and the other actors, together with a system of periodic accountability aimed at ensuring progress in the effective fulfillment of their commitments.

The relationship between the 2030 Agenda and the Global Compacts demonstrates once again the essential relationship between migration and sustainable development. But this beneficial relationship between the two realities can occur only if the appropriate policies are implemented by the various actors - not only the sovereign states- and with appropriate coordination at the global, regional, national and local levels. Our fingers are crossed.

Hearing Children in Court Proceedings in Migration Cases, Towards Recommendations

*Josine Krikke & Dana Baldinger**

1. Introduction: The Best Interests of the Child at the Heart of the Decision

Recent European jurisprudence and recent decisions of the United Nations (UN) Committee on the Rights of the Child emphasize that in any decision concerning migration where a child is involved, the best interests of the child are of paramount importance, must be investigated thoroughly and placed at the heart of the decision. From the *El Ghatet* (ECtHR), *E. Secretary of State of Security and Justice* (CJEU), *Chavez-Vilchez* (CJEU) and *C.E v. Belgium* (UN Committee on the Rights of the Child) judgments and decisions the following conclusions may be drawn. First of all, in migration cases involving a child, the particular background and present situation of the child must be considered in a thorough and careful manner. Superficial considerations do not suffice. Factors to be examined are the school situation, the age and maturity of the child, his or her physical and mental health and special needs.[1] In its judgment in *El Ghatet*, (2016), the ECtHR considered that it is up to the domestic courts to secure the guarantees set forth in Article 8 of the ECHR, to take into account the child's best interests and to make sure that these best interests are sufficiently reflected in the reasoning of the court.[2] The responsibility for investigating the life of the child concerned is thus not only the task of the administrative decision making body but certainly the task of the domestic courts.

The actual situation of the child concerned can be investigated in different ways. One way is to speak with the child concerned. It is, in fact, a right of children to freely express their views in all matters affecting them. According to Article 12 of the Convention on the Rights of the Child, States Parties shall assure to the child who is capable of forming his or her own views the right to express those views freely in all matters affecting the child, the views of the child being given due weight in accordance with its age and maturity. According to the second paragraph of Article 12, the child shall in particular be provided the opportunity to be heard in any judicial and administrative proceedings affecting the child, either directly, or through a representative or an appropriate body, in a manner consistent with the procedural rules of national law. Article

* Josine Krikke works at the District Court of Amsterdam in the administrative law section as a legal expert and court clerk. Dana Baldinger is a judge at the Council of State (Raad van State), the second instance court of appeal for migration cases and other administrative law cases. This article reflects the personal opinions of the authors and does not necessarily reflect the stances of the District Court of Amsterdam or the Raad van State.

1 The list of factors is not exhaustive but only illustrative. It is helpful to consider the material rights laid down in the Convention on the Rights of the Child as the 'interests' of the child, such as family life, education, health care, leisure and recreation, protection by the state when a child cannot live at home, etc.

2 ECtHR, *El Ghatet v. Switzerland*, 8 November 2016, no. 56971/10, paras. 47, 53.

24 of the EU Charter of Fundamental Rights similarly recognises the right of the child to express its views freely and imposes an obligation to take these views into consideration in matters which concern the child.

Based on our daily judicial work, we have the impression that national courts in the Netherlands dealing with migration cases do not always abide by this obligation. Often, we do not offer children concerned in migration cases the opportunity to talk freely to the court. Sometimes we do allow children who are brought along to the court room by a parent to speak to the court, but we lack appropriate standards for doing so. We think that we should be able to do better in this respect. With that aim in mind, below we will first explore what the right of the child to be heard exactly entails. In doing so, we will focus on hearing children in court proceedings. We will discuss the stances of both European Courts (the CJEU and the ECtHR) on hearing children in court. After that, we will shift our focus to the position of the UN Committee on the Rights of the Child. This Committee has developed a set of highly elaborated recommendations on the right of the child to be heard in matters affecting him or her and, importantly, also on hearing children in court. We will conclude this article by formulating a number of recommendations for national judicial practice.

2. Hearing Children in Court: The Stance of the CJEU

Article 24 of the EU Charter of Fundamental Rights reads as follows:

> '1. Children shall have the right to such protection and care as is necessary for their well-being. They may express their views freely. Such views shall be taken into consideration on matters which concern them in accordance with their age and maturity.
> 2. In all actions relating to children, whether taken by public authorities of private institutions, the child's best interests must be a primary consideration. [...].'

This provision is of general applicability and not restricted to particular proceedings. At present no case-law of the CJEU exists on the right of the child to be heard in proceedings concerning migration. However, in the case of *Joseba Andoni Aguirre Zarraga versus Simone Pelz*,[3] which concerned proceedings instigated by a parent following abduction of the child to another State by the other parent, the CJEU elaborated on what the right of the child to be heard entails. In this case a German court asked the CJEU whether it could enforce the order to return the child to Spain even if the child's rights had been infringed in the proceedings resulting in that order. The Spanish judge had not obtained the child's current views and was therefore unable to take account of those views in its judgment concerning the custody rights in respect of the child. Furthermore, the German court observed that the efforts made by the Spanish court to hear the child were inadequate.[4] In its judgment the CJEU took the stance that the right of the child to be heard under Article 24 of the Charter refers to the child having not the right, but the opportunity, to be heard. It is not an absolute right. In some cases it can be in the best interests of the child not to hear the child. The domestic courts

3 CJEU, *Joseba Andoni Aguirre Zarraga v. Simone Pelz*, 22 December 2010, C-491/10 PPU.
4 *Ibid.*, para. 35.

have a degree of discretion here. If, however, a national court decides it is necessary to hear the child concerned, measures should be in place ensuring that the child has an genuine and effective opportunity to express its views. The CJEU ruled as follows:

> '(...) Accordingly, while remaining a right of the child, hearing the child cannot constitute an absolute obligation, but must be assessed having regard to what is required in the best interests of the child in each individual case, in accordance with Article 24(2) of the Charter of Fundamental Rights. (...) Whilst it is not a requirement of Article 24 of the Charter (...) that the court of the Member State of origin obtain the views of the child in every case by means of a hearing, and that that court thus retains a degree of discretion, the fact remains that, where that court decides to hear the child, those provisions require the court to take all measures which are appropriate to the arrangement of such a hearing, having regard to the child's best interests and the circumstances of each individual case, in order to ensure the effectiveness of those provisions, and to offer to the child a genuine and effective opportunity to express his or her views.'[5]

As said above, this case concerned proceedings instigated after parental abduction of a child to another Member State. However, as Article 24 of the Charter is of general applicability and not restricted to any particular type of proceedings, it may be argued that the reasoning adopted by the CJEU in this decision can be transposed to migration cases. That would mean that in proceedings concerning migration, national courts have a degree of discretion and may, in cases at hand, decide to hear the child concerned. In doing so, the court enables the child to participate in the proceedings and exercise influence on the decision to be taken. Next to that, by hearing the child involved, the court may obtain direct valuable information about the actual life of the child. If a national court decides it is necessary to hear the child concerned, measures should be in place ensuring that the child has an genuine and effective opportunity to express her/his views

3. Hearing Children in Court: The Stance of the ECtHR

The ECtHR has placed the right of a child to be heard in court proceedings under the procedural limb of Article 8 of the ECHR by requiring that the applicant be sufficiently involved in the decision-making process.[6]

As an applicant has to be involved in the decision-making process, hearing of the person concerned can be necessary. This depends, however on the specific circumstances of the case. In several custody related cases, the ECtHR has ruled that Article 8 of the Convention does not encompass an obligation to always hear a child in court. It is up to the domestic courts to assess the evidence before them and to decide whether or not a child has to be heard. The courts have to take into consideration the specific

5 *Ibid.*, paras. 62-64.

6 See for example ECtHR, *Z.J. v. Lithuania*, 29 April 2014, no. 60092/12, para. 100; ECtHR, *Leonov v. Russia*, 10 April 2018, no. 77180/11, para. 67.

circumstances of the case, having due regard to the age and maturity of the child concerned. For example, in its judgment in the case of *Sahin versus Germany*[7] the ECtHR held that

> 'As regards the issue of hearing the child in court, the ECtHR observes that as a general rule it is for the national courts to assess the evidence before them, including the means used to ascertain the relevant facts (see Vidal v. Belgium, judgment of 22 April 1992, Series A no.235-B, pp. 32-33, §33). It would be going too far to say that domestic courts are always required to hear a child in court on the issue of access to a parent not having custody, but this issue depends on the specific circumstances of each case, having due regard to the age and maturity of the child concerned.'[8]

The case of *Sahin* is an interesting one as the issue of whether or not to hear the child in court was one of the main issues of the complaint under Article 8 of the Convention. In the *Sahin* case, the German national court had refused the applicant, a father of a girl born out of wedlock, access to this child because contact would not be in the child's best interests. The relations between the parents were very strained and contacts would, as a result, take place in an emotionally very tense atmosphere. Relying on an expert psychological opinion, the national German courts did not hear the child as hearing it was considered to be harmful for her. Applicant Sahin lodged a complaint to the ECtHR that Article 8 had been breached because of the denial of access to this child and because his child had not been heard. In its judgment of 11 October 2001,[9] the ECtHR held that the competent national courts, when refusing the applicant's request for a right of access, had relied on relevant reasons in finding that, having regard to the strained relations between the parents, contact was not in the child's best interests. Turning to the procedural requirements inherent in Article 8, the ECtHR found that the failure to hear the child in court had entailed insufficient protection of the applicant's interests in the access proceedings. The ECtHR concluded that, in these circumstances, the national authorities had overstepped their margin of appreciation, thereby violating the applicant's rights under Article 8 of the Convention. On 9 January 2002 the German Government requested that the case be referred to the Grand Chamber, contending that the Chamber should not have found a violation of Article 8 of the Convention. The Grand Chamber considered that it was satisfied that the German courts' approach was reasonable in the circumstances and provided sufficient material to reach a reasoned decision on the question of access in the particular case. On the question whether the child should or should not have been heard by the German national court, the Grand Chamber ruled that in the specific circumstances of the case, the decision of the court not to hear the child had been reasonable:

> 'In this connection the Court notes that the child was about three years and ten months old when the appeal proceedings started, and five years and two months at the time of the Regional Court's decision. The expert reached her conclusion, namely that a right of access without prior contact to overcome the conflicts between the parents was not in the child's interests, after

7 ECtHR, *Sahin v. Germany* [GC], 8 July 2003, no. 30943/96.
8 *Ibid.*, para. 73
9 ECtHR, *Sahin v. Germany*, 11 October 2001, 13279/05 13279/05.

> several meetings with the child, her mother and the applicant father. Consulted on the question of hearing the child in court, she plausibly explained that the very process of questioning entailed a risk for the child. Such a risk could not be avoided by special arrangements in court. (…) the Court is satisfied that the German courts' procedural approach was reasonable in the circumstances. The Court can therefore accept that the procedural requirements implicit in Article 8 of the Convention were complied with.'[10]

However, from later case-law it can be established that if a question of fact plays an important role in the proceedings, hearing the child can be of crucial importance. In the case of *Jucius and Juciuvienė v. Lithuania*[11] the applicants alleged an infringement of Article 8 in that the national Lithuanian courts awarded custodianship of their two orphaned nieces, with whom they had lived for three years, to the children's paternal grandparents. On the question whether or not the girls should have been heard in court, the ECtHR considered as follows:

> 'Thus the proceedings were of crucial importance for the applicants and involved the assessment of their character as well as the motives and the wishes of the girls. In the Court's view, this was a question of fact which could not be adequately resolved on the basis of the case file. In such circumstances, where evaluations of this kind played such a significant role and where their outcome could be of major detriment to the applicants, it was essential to the fairness of the proceedings that the appellate court hold a hearing and afford the applicants and the girls an opportunity to be heard and fully participate in order to ensure the best interests of the orphaned children in the future.'[12]

So far, the ECtHR has not had an opportunity to express its position on the right of the child to be heard in migration cases. However, as the general principles and notions about the right of the child to be heard, as developed in the case law mentioned above, form part of the procedural limb of Article 8, it may be argued that they are just as relevant and applicable in migration cases where Article 8 of the Convention is invoked and where children are involved. It may therefore be argued that the notion of discretion of the domestic courts to decide whether or not to hear children in cases at hand, and the notion that hearing children becomes more important when questions of fact and evaluation of the facts are disputed, are applicable to migration cases. Another argument for this conclusion would be that in the case law of the ECtHR the concept of the 'best interests of the child' was first developed in custody related cases and then expanded to migration cases.[13]

10 ECtHR, *Sahin v. Germany* [GC], 8 July 2003, no. 30943/96, paras 73-77.
11 ECtHR, *Jucius and Juciuvienė v. Lithuania*, 25 November 2008, no. 14414/03.
12 *Ibid.*, para. 31
13 ECtHR, *El Ghatet v. Switzerland*, 8 November 2016, no. 56971/10, paras. 46, 47.

4. Hearing Children in Court: The Stance of the UN Committee on the Rights of the Child

As said above in section 1, according to Article 12 of the Convention on the Rights of the Child, States Parties shall assure to the child who is capable of forming his or her own views the right to express those views freely in all matters affecting the child, the views of the child being given due weight in accordance with its age and maturity.

General Comment No. 12 of 20 July 2009 states that this right of children to be heard and taken seriously constitutes one of the fundamental values of the Convention.[14] Although the term participation itself does not appear in the text of Article 12, the right to be heard strongly reflects the notion of participation, which includes information-sharing and dialogue between children and adults based on mutual respect.[15] The child has the right not to exercise this right. Expressing views is a choice of the child, not an obligation. States parties have to ensure that the child receives all necessary information and advice to make a decision in favour of her or his best interests.[16] The Committee emphasizes that Article 12 imposes no age limit and discourages States parties from introducing age limits either in law or in practice which would restrict the child's right to be heard in all matters affecting her or him. Research has shown that the child is able to form views from the youngest age, even when s/he may be unable to express them verbally.[17] It is not necessary that the child has comprehensive knowledge of all aspects of the matter affecting him or her, but that he or she has sufficient understanding to be capable of appropriately forming her or his own views on the matter. The child has the rights 'to express those views freely', meaning that the child can express her or his views without pressure and can choose whether or not she or he wants to exercise the right.[18] Article 12 stipulates that simply listening to the child is insufficient; the views of the child have to be seriously considered when the child is capable of forming her or his views.

Importantly, Article 12, paragraph 2, specifies that opportunities to be heard have to be provided in particular 'in any judicial and administrative proceedings affecting the child'. The Committee has emphasized that this provision applies to all relevant judicial proceedings affecting the child, without any limitation. It specifically mentions as examples care and adoption, separation from parents, unaccompanied children, asylum-seeking and refugee children.[19]

According to the UN Committee, implementation of Article 12 requires five steps to be taken in order to effectively realize the right of the child to be heard in a formal judicial proceeding.[20] First, the child needs to be informed about his or her right to be heard and about the impact that his or her expressed views will have on the outcome.

---

14 *General Comment No. 12* of the UN Committee on the Rights of the Child, CRC/C/GC/12, 20 July 2009.

15 *Ibid.*, para. 3.

16 *Ibid.*, para. 16.

17 G. Lawson, *The evolving capacities of the child*, Florence: Innocenti Research Centre, UNICEF/Save the Children 2005.

18 *Ibid.*, para. 22.

19 See the list of examples in para. 32 of *General Comment No. 12*. The list of types of procedures is much longer but the types of procedures mentioned here are the relevant ones in migration law.

20 These five steps are described in *General Comment No. 12*, paras. 41-46.

The child must be adequately prepared before the hearing, providing explanations as to how, when and where the hearing takes place and who the participants will be. The views of the child in this regard have to be taken into account.[21] Second, the hearing has to be encouraging and enabling. It should have the format of a talk rather than a one-sided examination. Preferably, a child should not be heard in open court, but under conditions of confidentiality.[22] Third, if the child is capable of forming her or his own views in a reasonable and independent manner, the judge must consider the views of the child as a significant factor in resolving the case. Good practice for assessing the capacity of the child must be developed. Fourth, the judge has to inform the child of the outcome of the process and explain how her or his views were considered. This feedback is a guarantee that the views of the child are not only heard as a formality, but are taken seriously. The feedback may prompt the child to insist, agree, make another proposal, or file an appeal or complaint. Fifth, complaint procedures and remedies need to be available for violations of Article 12. Remedies and procedures must provide reliable mechanisms to ensure that children are confident that using them will not expose them to risk of violence or punishment.

Importantly, *General Comment No. 12* contains a specific paragraph about the right of the child to be heard in immigration and asylum proceedings.[23] This paragraph states that children in immigration and asylum proceedings are in a particularly vulnerable situation. For this reason it is urgent to fully implement their right to express their views on all aspects of the immigration and asylum proceedings. In the case of migration, the child has to be heard on his or her educational expectations and health conditions. In the case of an asylum claim, the child must additionally have the opportunity to present his or her reasons leading to the asylum claim. The Committee emphasizes that these children have to be provided with all relevant information, in their own language, on their entitlements, the services available, including means of communication, and the immigration and asylum process, in order to make their voice heard and to be given due weight in the proceedings. A guardian or adviser should be appointed, free of charge, for unaccompanied minors. Asylum seeking children may also need effective family tracing and relevant information about the situation in their country of origin to determine their best interests. Particular assistance may be needed for children formerly involved in armed conflict to allow them to pronounce their needs.

The case of *C.E. v. Belgium*[24] (2018) was already mentioned above in section 1. As this case concerns migration, it is highly relevant and illustrative for our topic. In its decision on this case, the Committee not only concluded that Articles 3 and 10 were

21 In the Netherlands in civil family law cases a special, child-adequate invitation letter is sent to the child. In this letter the child is informed about the case and about his or her right (not obligation, but right) to speak with the judge.

22 In the Netherlands in civil family law cases there is no judicial consensus about confidentiality of the hearing. Judges of the first instance court hear children confidentially and make a brief summary of this hearing which is shared with all the parties to the case, whereas the full verbatim report of the hearing is put into the file in a closed envelope which is accessible only for the judge and court clerk but not for the parties. At appeal level (second instance), the judges share the full report of the child hearing with the parties.

23 *Ibid.*, paras 123, 124.

24 UN CRC, *C.E. v. Belgium*, 27 September 2018, CRC/C/79/D/12/2017.

violated. Next to these violations Article 12 was considered to be breached by the Belgian authorities as the child concerned, a five-year old girl, had not been heard in the proceedings. The Committee considered as follows:

> 'With regard to the authors' claims based on Article 12 of the Convention, the Committee notes the State party's arguments that C.E. was 1 year old at the time of the first decision and 5 at the time of the second, that she was not capable of forming her own views and that the need to allow a child to express his or her views would not be justified for the purposes of applying the rules for granting residence permits. The Committee points out, however, that Article 12 imposes no age limit on the right of the child to express her or his views, and discourages States parties from introducing age limits either in law or in practice that would restrict the child's right to be heard in all matters affecting her or him. It is not necessary that the child has comprehensive knowledge of all aspects of the matter affecting her or him, but that she or he has sufficient understanding to be capable of appropriately forming her or his own views on the matter It also notes that any decision that does not take into account the child's views or does not give their views due weight according to their age and maturity, does not respect the possibility for the child or children to influence the determination of their best interests. The fact that the child is very young or in a vulnerable situation (e.g. has a disability, belongs to a minority group, is a migrant, etc.) does not deprive him or her of the right to express his or her views, nor reduces the weight given to the child's views in determining his or her best interests. (...). The Committee observes in this case that C.E. was 5 years old when the second decision on the authors' application for a humanitarian visa was made and that she would have been perfectly capable of forming views of her own regarding the possibility of living permanently with the authors in Belgium. The Committee does not share the State party's view that it is not necessary to take the views of a child into account in proceedings conducted to determine whether he or she should be issued a residence permit, quite on the contrary. The implications of the proceedings in the authors' case are of paramount importance for C.E.'s life and future, insofar as they are directly tied to her chances of living with the authors as a member of their family.[25]

5. Towards Recommendations for Hearing Children in National Courts in Migration Cases

Below, we will provide some ideas on how the recommendations of the UN Committee on the Rights of the Child may be implemented in national judicial practice.

Our first recommendation would be to seek guidance in established civil practice. In the Netherlands, in civil cases concerning children, such as cases about custody, access, guardianship etc., it is established practice that the judge speaks with the child concerned. There is a specific basis to do so as Article 809 of the Dutch Civil Procedural Code specifies that in cases concerning children the judge hears the child. In general, in civil cases children younger than 12 are only heard in exceptional circumstances. The District Court of Amsterdam is also hearing children between 8 and 12 years old in specific cases. Although Article 12 of the UN Convention on the Rights of the Child contains no specific age limit, the ECtHR, CJEU and the UN Committee

25 *Ibid.*, paras. 8.6-8.9.

on the Rights of the Child have all ruled that the age and maturity of the child should be taken into account when deciding whether or not to hear the child. As the age of 12 years old can be regarded as sufficiently mature to understand proceedings, we recommend to hear children of 12 years and older in all circumstances. The question whether to hear children younger than 12 should be decided on a case by case basis.

Our second recommendation would be to draw up a standard letter in which the child concerned in a migration case is informed about the case and is informed about the right he or she has to speak to the judge if he or she wishes to do so. This letter should provide explanations as to how, when and where the hearing takes place and who the participants will be. It should be formulated in a child-friendly way and be of an inviting nature. The letter should also make clear the that the views of the child count and that the judge therefore finds it important to speak with the child.

Our third recommendation regards the court hearing itself. The hearing has to be encouraging and enabling. It should have the format of a talk rather than a one-sided examination. A child should preferably not be heard in open court, but rather in the setting of a talk. As to the recommendation of the UN Committee on the Rights of the Child that the hearing should be confidential, we would recommend to keep the session where the child speaks with the judge indeed small-scale and low key, with the number of persons present limited to the child, the judge, the court clerk and, if the child is very young or the child wishes so, a parent or caretaker or social worker who is directly connected to the child. After the hearing all parties to the proceedings shall be provided with a brief summary of the hearing. The child should be informed about this.

Our fourth recommendation would be to develop good practice for hearing children. Judges should receive regular training in hearing children, preferably provided by experts who work with children like specialized psychologists. Having a small pool of specialized judges who have experience in hearing children might be better than letting all judges hear children.

Our fifth recommendation would be that the judge informs the child of the outcome of the proceedings and explains how her or his views were considered. This feedback is a guarantee that the views of the child are not only heard as a formality, but are taken seriously. In an ideal world the judge will write a separate, child friendly summary of his or her decision. And make sure that the child will receive this decision.

6. Conclusion

In section 1 of this contribution we expressed our concern that national courts in the Netherlands dealing with migration cases do not always abide by the obligation imposed by Article 12 of the UN Convention on the Rights of the Child and Article 24 of the EU Charter on Fundamental Rights to provide children with the opportunity to freely express their views in court proceedings concerning them. Sometimes we do allow children who are brought along to the court room by a parent to speak to the court, but we lack appropriate standards for doing so. In other cases, we do not hear the children concerned at all. We think that we should be able to do better. With that aim in mind we have explored what the right of the child to be heard exactly entails, with a particular focus on this right in court proceedings. We have discussed the stances of both European Courts (the CJEU and the ECtHR) on hearing children in court and discovered that both Courts have developed some general principles on this issue. These general principles have been developed in other contexts than migration but we have argued that they are also applicable to migration cases. We have then moved on to explore the position of the UN Committee on the Rights of the Child on the issue of hearing children in matters affecting them, again with a particular focus on court proceedings, and have discovered that this Committee has developed a set of highly elaborated recommendations on the right of the child to be heard in matters affecting him or her, including recommendations specifically for hearing children in court proceedings. The Committee has stressed the importance of the right of the child to be heard in migration and asylum proceedings as children involved in such proceedings find themselves in a particularly vulnerable situation. We have concluded by formulating a number of recommendations for national judicial practice. We hope that this contribution can and will serve as a starting point for discussions on the issue of hearing children in court in migration cases and can serve as a beginning of developing standards and good practice.

Dear Elspeth, Dana would like to end with a personal word of gratitude. Elspeth, you taught me to treat developments in international and European law in a holistic way and draw lessons from them for my daily judicial work. It was so inspiring to be your PhD student. After every meeting with you and Kees I felt so encouraged to move on. Thank you so much for all your time, patience and confidence in me. I will always burn a candle for you in the cathedral of my heart.

A 'Guildian' Analysis of The Equivocal Trusted Sponsorship under EU Labour Migration Law

*Tesseltje de Lange**

This contribution applies a 'Guildian' analysis of the institution of the trusted sponsor in the European Union and its Member States. A Guildian analysis is to place the migrants' perspective central.[1] Elspeth Guild studied power relations between states, third parties and migrants with an eye for the 'professional futures of the individuals involved'.[2] The Guildian analysis considers the extent to which the individual labour migrant 'alone can regulate his or her life in accordance with clear rules with a degree of security as to the consequences of any particular choice or action'.[3] This analysis is applied to the instrument of trusted sponsorship, or recognized employer, which is incorporated in two Directives and one proposed Directive on highly skilled migration of third-country nationals coming into the EU. These Directives are on the entry of Students, Researchers and some others,[4] the Intra-Corporate Transfers Directive[5] and the proposed recast of the Blue Card Directive.[6] I will give some insights into the drafting history with respect to the concept of the trusted sponsor in each Directive, the requirements for trusted sponsors, the costs and benefits that come with being a trusted sponsor and, most relevant to the Guildian analysis, the consequences of a failing trusted sponsor for the migrant.

Other perspectives on labour migration are those of the host state, which has to secure its labour market from imbalances resulting from unwanted migration *and* might need to cure labour market shortages. The interest of an individual European Union Member State does not necessarily coincide with the European Unions' point of view, for one because labour markets are not equally needing of migrant workers throughout

---

* University of Amsterdam.

1 E. Guild, *European Community Law from A Migrant's Perspective*, PhD Radboud University Nijmegen, Nijmegen: GNI 2000.

2 E. Guild, 'Equivocal Claims? Ambivalent Controls? Labour Migration Regimes in the European Union', in: E. Guild & S. Mantu, *Constructing and Imagining Labour Migration. Perspectives of Control from Five Continents*, Farnham: Ashgate 2011, p. 207-228 at p. 223.

3 Guild 2000, p. 314.

4 Directive on the conditions of entry and residence of third-country nationals for the purposes of research, studies, training, voluntary service, pupil exchange schemes or educational projects and au pairing, 2016/801/EU of 11 May 2016

5 Directive 2014/66/EU of the European Parliament and of the Council of 15 May 2014 on the conditions of entry and residence of third-country nationals in the framework of an intra-corporate transfer.

6 Directive 2009/50/EC of 25 May 2009 on the conditions of entry and residence of third-country nationals for the purposes of highly qualified employment.

the Union. Obviously, there is a business perspective to have readily available the workers needed to deliver.[7] Both Member States and businesses may be competing for the same international talent, or Member States compete over businesses whereby easy access to labour migrants is a 'country branding' tool. Another perspective is that of the country of origin, which may benefit from labour migration through remittances or so called brain circulation.[8] This is not some futuristic artificial intelligence concept where brains are linked into a circuit,[9] but, in the words of Vertovec, an alternative discourse to the much feared brain drain; brain circulation describes labour migration 'within transnational networks of skilled workers… throughout an international arena (such as Indian IT workers who work, at one time or another, in Singapore, Australia and the USA, as well as in India)... The idea is to accept the fact that skilled persons may want to migrate for career development, while seeking to encourage the skilled migrant's return, mobilization or association with home country development.' The circular perspective does aim to limit the migrants' freedom to decide on saying yes or no.

The study by Noronha, D'Cruz and Ul Lateef Banday[10] shows how Indian IT workers embed in the Netherlands (of whom many live in Amstelveen, also called 'Mumbai on the Amstel'[11]) are internationally wanted highly skilled labour migrants. However, they can see their freedom of choice and action restricted through migration law or their employers' instrumental use of it. Noronha et al. describe how, for instance, employers make their Indian staff return to India before they have a full five years of employment, to avoid access to permanent residence and independency from their employer in their professional aspirations. The question addressed in this chapter is to what extent the instrument of the trusted sponsor or recognised employer allows the individual labour migrant to regulate his or her own life? I will argue that the instrument of trusted sponsorship is an equivocal instrument of facilitating and controlling large scale skilled labour migration. It is an enabler of labour migration. But also, and for this I will mainly use the Netherlands as an example, the instrument can seriously limit the migrants' room for individual choices and actions.[12]

7 For a business perspective see S. Ramasamy, *The Role of Employers and Employer Engagement in Labour Migration from Third Countries to the EU*, OECD Social, Employment and Migration Working Papers, No. 178, Paris: OECD Publishing 2016, http://dx.doi.org/10.1787/5jlwxc0366xr-en.

8 S. Vertovec, *Transnational Networks and Skilled Labour Migration*, WPTC-02-02, Ladenburg, 14-15 February 2002, Transnational Communities Programme, Oxford: Oxford University Press 2002.

9 See for instance SF-novel by Steve Toutonghi, *Join*, New York: Soho Press 2016.

10 E. Noronha, P. D'Cruz & M. Ul Lateef Banday, 'Navigating Embeddedness: Experiences of Indian IT Suppliers and Employees in the Netherlands', *Journal of Business Ethics* 2018, p. 1-19, published online: https://doi.org/10/1007/s10551-018-4071-3.

11 *Financieel Dagblad*, 'Mumbai aan de Amstel barst uit zijn voegen', 21 april 2019.

12 The UK opted out of the EU labour migration directives discussed here. However, the so called points based system in use in the UK uses a similar instrument or 'permissive action' (T. de Lange, 'The privatization of control over labour migration in the Netherlands: in whose interest?', *European Journal of Migration and Law* 2011-2, p. 185-200) with employers having control over the migration management process. The UK government (as the Dutch) generated considerable revenues from the sponsorship fees (F. Jurje, 'The EU's External Labour Mobility and Trade – a Multilayered Governance Approach?', in: S. Carrera, L. den Hertog, M. Panizzon & D. Kostakopoulou (eds), *EU External Migration Policies in an Era of Global Mobilities: Intersecting Policy Universes*, Leiden: Brill Nijhoff 2019 (in the Immigration and Asylum Law and Policy Series edited by E. Guild & V.Mitsilegas), p. 218-219.

Three EU Directives and the Trusted Sponsor

Students, Researchers and Some Other Directives

Directive 2016/801/EU of 11 May 2016 sets conditions of entry and residence of third-country nationals (meaning non-EU nationals) for the purposes of research, studies, training, voluntary service, pupil exchange schemes or educational projects and au pairing (SRD). I focus on students and researchers. Member States may approve hosting organisations for all of these categories, but for au pair bureaus.[13] The original Commission proposal provided the option to approve a hosting organisation only for researchers.[14] The extension of the concept of approved sponsor beyond the researchers was the result of the political negotiations.[15] Setting up such a procedure for others than researchers followed, amongst others, from Amendment 57 of the European Parliament concerning fast-track procedures.[16] As a possible alternative to state approval of the sponsor up front, an amendment suggested host entities to be registered in an accreditation system, in order to facilitate future application procedures.[17] Indeed, obligatory (private) accreditation is, in other domains of administrative law, a common tool to select 'good' government partners and the recognised sponsor shows some similarities to an accreditation systems.

Member States are given the discretion to provide for an approval procedure in accordance with procedures set out in the national law or administrative practice.[18] EU law does not set any conditions or limitations as to the characteristics of the sponsor. Applications for approval shall be made in accordance with those procedures and be based on their statutory tasks or corporate purposes as appropriate and on evidence that they conduct research. The reference to national law or administrative practice leaves the Member States a wide margin of discretion in the design of an approval procedure, if designed at all. The Directive does however require Member States to grant an organisation an approval for a minimum period of five years. Only in exceptional cases, may it be for a shorter period. Although the Directive does not articulate grounds for approval it does give facultative and non-limited grounds for refusal to renew or for withdrawal of the approval where, in the case of for instance research organisations.[19] Member States may require migrants, their family members, or host entities to pay fees for the handling of notifications and applications. The level of such fees shall not be disproportionate or excessive.[20]

---

13 Article 15. Au pairs are not to be made subject to trusted sponsors because they are prone to abuse (preamble 23). Apparently, the Commission takes the view that highly skilled migrants are abuse resistant. As the work of Noronha et al. (2018) shows, this does not always hold true.

14 See for the proposal document COM(2013) 151 final – 2013/0081 COD) of 26 March 2013. The previous Researchers Directive 2005/71 included the obligation to recognize an institution, article 5.

15 Brussels, 5 April 2016, COM(2016) 184 final, 2013/0081(COD), Communication from the Commission to the European Parliament pursuant to Article 294(6) of the TFEU. Political agreement was reached between co-legislators at the trialogue meeting of 17 November 2015, and was endorsed by COREPER on 25 November 2015, and by the LIBE Committee on 30 November 2015.

16 Statement of the Council's Reasons, 11 March 2015, Doc. no. 14958/2/15 REV 2 ADD 1, p. 9-10.

17 Amendment 86 by MEP Hélène Flautre (Greens) suggesting an alternative Article 15 par. 1 a.

18 Article 15 SRD.

19 Article 9 SRD.

20 Article 36 and Preamble 4 SRD.

The benefits of the approval are in the fast track application procedure, which is still long: 60 days instead of the standard 90 days.[21] If applying to stay with an approved institution, the applicant shall be exempted from presenting to the Member States' authorities one or more of the documents or evidence of their address in the Member States, their health insurance, payment of handling fees,[22] proof of having sufficient resources to cover subsistence costs without having recourse to the social assistance system, as well as return travel costs. The assessment of these requirements is left to the host institution. The host will need to check for the availability of sufficient resources based on an individual examination of the case and shall take into account resources that derive, inter alia, from a grant, a scholarship or a fellowship or a valid work contract or a binding job offer. The approved research institution, in part, takes on the role of migration authority.

The approved status can be withdrawn, for instance, when the organisation no longer conducts research, when it has not covered the costs of return of a migrant or when it failed to inform the authorities on time of the finalization of the research (and hence provide a reason for withdrawal of the residence permit of the migrant researcher). Where an application for renewal has been refused or where the approval has been withdrawn, the organisation concerned may be banned from reapplying for approval for a period of up to five years from the date of publication of the decision on non-renewal or withdrawal.[23] Sanctions against host entities who have not fulfilled their obligations under the Directive shall be effective, proportionate and dissuasive.[24] Member States have again been granted a rather wide margin of discretion to determine in their national law the sanctions and consequences of the withdrawal of the approval or the refusal to renew the approval for the existing hosting agreements, as well as the consequences for the researchers concerned. From a migrant rights perspective this is a missed opportunity for the EU to set minimum standards on the protection of researchers, students and other wanted highly skilled migrants against their dependence on 'failing' institutions. Possibly article 33 (on proportionate sanctions) can be read as to be precluding sanctions that disproportionally hurt the migrant, but other than that, the Directive is silent on the migrants' legal position *vis-à-vis* the Member State in case the host fails to comply. The obligation to publish a list of approved institutions is relevant here as well: according to Dutch case law the migrant can check the list regularly to see if his or her institution is still compliant and his or her residence permit is not at risk.[25] I doubt migrants check such lists on a regular basis. Its availability provides false security for the migrant.

21 Article 34 SRD.
22 Article 35 SRD.
23 Article 9 par. 3 SRD.
24 Article 33 SRD.
25 This follows from Dutch Council of State 30 November 2017, JV 2018/71 with note Marcel Reurs, ECLI:NL:RVS:2017:3294. The Dutch list is available at: https://ind.nl/Paginas/Openbaar-register-erkende-referenten.aspx.

Intra-Corporate Transferees Directive

The ICTD applies to third-country nationals admitted in the framework of an intra-corporate transfer as managers, specialists or trainees. This Directive sets the standards for their temporary labour migration of a maximum of three years, or one year for trainees. It's most important asset is that it provides for some intra-EU Mobility.[26] Member States may also set up a simplified procedure for multinationals which have been recognised for that purpose, again in accordance with their national legislation or administrative practice.[27] The recognition must be regularly assessed, an instruction missing in the SRD. Member States may require the payment of fees for handling of all applicants in accordance with the Directive, which fees shall not be disproportionate or excessive.[28]

Once recognised, the multinational is facilitated with simplified procedures relating to the issuing of intra-corporate transferee permits, permits for long-term mobility, permits granted to family members of an intra-corporate transferee, and visas. Simplification shall include at least the applicant's exemption from presenting some of the evidence and a fast-track admission procedure allowing intra-corporate transferee permits and permits for long-term mobility to be issued within less than 90 days. Without success EP suggested that fast track meant that a decision should be at taken within 45 days, but that suggestion was dropped during the negotiations.[29] The recognition also imposes certain obligations on the multinationals, again obligations not imposed on the hosts of researchers or students: they shall notify to the relevant authority any modification affecting the conditions for recognition within 30 days.[30] Obviously, this requires a proper administration of project and human resources management. Apart from the fees and administrative obligations, the recognized sponsor is at risk of administrative sanctions. Member States *must* provide for *appropriate* sanctions, including revocation of recognition, in the event of failure to notify the relevant authority. In the event the multinational would lose the status of a recognised sponsor, the transferred TCN migrant worker is not protected however and is likely to lose his or her residence permit. Likely, but not definitely. Any decision to withdraw or to refuse to renew an intra-corporate transferee residence permit shall take account of the specific circumstances of the case and respect the principle of proportionality.[31] Because the ICTD requires the multinational to declare it will take care of the return of the transferee, no right to a search period for another job in the country where one is stationed is provided for.[32]

A Guildian analysis of this Directive would, in general, leave us with a sour taste because it does not present the migrant as an actor. The ICTD only allows for temporary migration of otherwise wanted highly skilled people and only as an 'asset' of the

26 On this see Á. Töttős, 'Negotiations in the Council', and other chapters in: P. Minderhoud & T. de Lange, *The Intra Corporate Transferee Directive*, Oisterwijk: Wolf Legal Publishers 2018, p. 5-18

27 Article 11 ICTD.

28 Article 16 ICTD.

29 Council Document 5771/14, Amendment 69.

30 Article 11(8) ICTD.

31 Article 8 ICTD.

32 Article 5(1) under c) sub iv ICTD.

multinational corporation, moved (and returned) across the globe, at the multinationals will. Albeit probably paid well (although, given the hours they might be asked to work, maybe not even so). Originally, the Directive prescribed that the Member States check on the financial health of the multinational, in order to secure continued payment of the transferees.[33] But all prescriptions regarding the recognition, which might be considerate of migrant rights, were deleted along the way. What remains creates an equivocal migration management tool, with fast tracks however in which the migrant is not 'alone' to regulate his or her life. Security of residence following any particular choice or action by the migrant under the Directive is low, this is for the multinational to decide on. In the Dutch case, the migration authorities prefer for these migrants to stay on. If the migrant and a recognised employer so desire, they can switch into a national highly skilled migrant status.

Proposed Recast Blue Card Directive

Finally, let me address the Blue Card Directive (BCD). The BCD sets standards for the admission of highly qualified and well earning third-country nationals. Its recast was submitted on 7 June 2016 and, nearly three years on, is still under negotiation.[34] The foreseen obligation to redesign national schemes for highly skilled into a blue card scheme, appears to be a deal breaker.[35] The proposed recast has a wider scope than the original BCD. While the 'current' Blue Card builds on the traditional demand-driven labour migration model, the recast allows for more hybrid labour migration schemes: it introduces a job search period, which is a typical supply-driven model. It is also expected to introduce a new the concept of a recognised employer to provide for fast track procedures. According to the proposal, the recognition procedure is to be regulated at national level. Again, such procedure must be transparent and not entail disproportionate or excessive administrative burden and costs for employers. The benefit is a fast tracked procedure (30 days maximum) and it has less evidence requirements.[36]

Sanctions against its abuse are required and where the employer has been sanctioned for the employment of illegally staying TCN pursuant to Directive 2009/ 52/EC (on employer sanctions), this may be a reason to be excluded from recognition as a trusted sponsor. Interestingly, if the status is refused or withdrawn this does *not* mean the Blue Card residence permit may be refused or is no longer valid, it only means that the application or renewal of that EU Blue Card will be done through the more traditional, more time consuming, procedures. It would make the procedure more of an administrative burden for the employer but would *not* jeopardize the migrants' opportunity to enter and remain with this employer as a highly qualified migrant worker.

From a migrants' perspective, the BCD recast would be an important improvement compared to the current Dutch highly skilled migration scheme, which today

33 T. de Lange, 'Concluding Remarks. Is the Intra-Corporate Transfer Directive Welcoming International Talent?', in: P. Minderhoud & T. de Lange, *The Intra Corporate Transferee Directive*, Oisterwijk: Wolf Legal Publishers 2018, p. 163-164.

34 Proposal for a Directive on the conditions of entry and residence of third-country nationals for the purposes of highly skilled employment of 7 July 2016 COM(2016) 378 final2016/0176 (COD).

35 PART 1/2 FITNESS CHECK on EU Legislation on legal migration Brussels, 29 March 2019 SWD(2019), 1055 final, p. 45-46.

36 Article 12 BCD-recast proposal.

offers no serious alternative in case the recognised employer falls short. In the Dutch case, a withdrawal of the recognition of the employer means illegality for all the highly skilled TCN employed by that sponsor, unless the migrants find a new recognised employer, within three months. In practice we have seen cases where it took more than three months for the TCNs *to find out* their employer was no longer recognised, although, like with the research institutions, a list of recognised sponsors is made public. This happened in cases of mergers, take overs and the alike, where the employees were transferred to another legal entity within a group, but the employer had forgotten to obtain recognised sponsorship status for the new entity. Hence, the TCNs had no time to find another employer.[37] Once a residence permit was obtained again, they had a 'gap', meaning they did not have continuous legal residence and thus the counting of years before eligibility for permanent residence started from scratch and they were, again for five years, tied to an employer with trusted sponsor status. So much for their future professional freedom. This is obviously equivocal treatment of the otherwise so sought after highly skilled labour migrants. In Sweden the law was changed to avoid revoking the residence permit of the wanted labour migrants due to their employers lack of compliance.[38] From a migrants' perspective, the proposed BCD recast offers more protection, the recognition covers fast tracking procedures and less control but doesn't tie the worker to the employer as the Dutch trusted sponsorship does. Also, the mobility right incorporated in the BCD, which allows BC holders to move to another Member State without losing entitlements to long term residence, provides room for taking control over ones migratory and professional ambitions. Although, according to Noronha, Indian IT workers are not prone to collectivisation,[39] their collective call for an agreement on the recast BCD (or strike if it remains disagreed upon?) would possibly make for a powerful action of migrant workers in the EU.

Some Final Thoughts

To conclude, let me start by pointing out that few EU Member States have actually implemented a procedure for the recognition of employers and fast tracking procedures for their wanted migrant workers. Spain, Slovakia, Italy and the Netherlands have it. France has been said to contemplate its use.[40] The recently proposed German labour migration law offers expedited procedures based on an agreement between the employer and the German immigration authorities.[41] This been said, I come to four final thoughts using the 'Guildian' analysis of the design of the recognised employer, or trusted sponsor, and whether the individual labour migrant 'alone can regulate his or her life in accordance with clear rules with a degree of security as to the consequences

37 Dutch Council of State 30 November 2017, *JV* 2018/71 with note Marcel Reurs, ECLI:NL:RVS:2017:3294.

38 P. Herzfeld Olsson, 'Transposing the ICT Directive into Swedish Law – A Company Friendly Exercise', in: P. Minderhoud & T. de Lange, *The Intra Corporate Transferee Directive*, Oisterwijk: Wolf Legal Publishers 2018, p. 139-154, at p. 142.

39 Noronha et al. 2018.

40 J. Antoons, A. Ghimis & C. Sullivan, 'The Intra-Corporate Transfer Permit and Mobility in the European Union: The Business Perspective', in: P. Minderhoud & T. de Lange, *The Intra Corporate Transferee Directive*, Oisterwijk: Wolf Legal Publishers 2018, p. 67-84, at p. 78.

41 Proposal Fachkräfteeinwanderungsgesetzes13 March 2019, par. 81a (p.35).

of any particular choice or action'. Firstly, any demand-driven labour migration scheme with work permits could be said to allow for an employer to have power over the migrant worker, hence, little is decided on 'alone' when work permit requirements or the like apply. All schemes discussed are mainly demand driven. Secondly, the recognised sponsorship under the ICT and the SRD and practice in the Netherlands, *increase* the migrants dependency on the host. The BCD, as it now stands as well as the proposed recast, offers more room to manoeuvre individually. It is, thus, a pity that it isn't agreed upon yet. Thirdly, one must consider that highly skilled and well paid migrant workers are commonly perceived as not so vulnerable, able to hire a lawyer to advise them and able to check a website listing recognised employers. But having them rely on their employer for all information on, and application for, their migration status implies a high risk of abuse. And such abuse occurs. Future sponsorship systems should hence require, in some more detail, Member States to take responsibility for the wanted highly skilled migrants. Fourthly, and somewhat to the contrary of the previous conclusion, the trusted sponsorship, as an equivocal instrument of migration control, is a very important tool in stepping up labour migration into the European Union, not just in fast tracking procedures, but in allowing larger numbers of labour migrants to arrive without too much political upheaval. Both final points go to the heart of the Member States' obligation to provide worker protection, an obligation that cannot be neutralised by the States' privatisation of labour immigration control. The trusted sponsorship schemes should not exacerbate the migrants' dependence on the employer. They should provide *just* fast track procedures, not instead of but as a free to choose alternative to otherwise also well-functioning, but lengthier, regular procedures. There should be nothing equivocal about that. As such, the procedure should provide the migrant an interesting opportunity for a true Guildian 'professional future' in which the migrant 'alone can regulate his or her life in accordance with clear rules, with a degree of security as to the consequences of any particular choice or action'.

Migration Rights, EU Law and International Trade Agreements

Revealing Gates for Business in Fortress Europe

*Simon Tans**

Under the supervision of Elspeth Guild I have written my dissertation in one of the many fields which she specialises in, migration rights derived from EU law and WTO law. In specific, she has created my main research path, moving beyond the realm of international trade law and to investigate in detail the consequences of international trade agreement provisions for the autonomy of states concerning migration and access to the labour market. Both in relation to the chapters I had to write and to various conferences I attended where she acted as discussant, I was always awed by the ease in which she managed to move discussions to a broader view. It invariably left me with new ideas to develop regarding my own research. In this contribution, I will do just that, use one of Elspeth's conclusions and practically apply it. I will focus on one specific example of Elspeth's research interests, access for the economically active to an EU Member State's market.

Essentially, access to the EU Member State's market can be divided into two main systems. First, EU law itself grants access to EU nationals on the basis of the internal market provisions. The second system consists of access rights granted to third-country nationals.[1] Additionally, a third group of beneficiaries may be identified on the basis of agreements with specific third countries which in essence provide similar rights to the nationals of these states as is granted to EU nationals.[2] This group clearly belongs to the first system, as they have comparable access as EU nationals have.

Access for third-country national workers is based on secondary legislation, for instance the Blue Card Directive and the Seasonal Workers Directive.[3] Access for third-country national service providers can be based on specific directives, such as the Intra-Corporate Transferee Directive, and it can be derived from various international

* Simon Tans is assistant professor in EU and international law at the Radboud University Nijmegen, the Netherlands.

1 E Guild, 'Questioning Temporary Migration Schemes in the EU', in: S Carrera, A Geddes, E Guild and M Stefan (eds), *Pathways Towards Legal Migration into the EU*, Brussels: CEPS 2017, p. 42; E Guild, 'Intra-Corporate Transferees: Between the Directive and the EU's International Obligations', in: P. Minderhoud & T. de Lange (eds), *The Intra Corporate Transferee Directive. Central Themes, Problem Issues and Implementation in Selected Member States*, Oisterwijk: Wolf Legal Publishers 2018, p. 65.

2 E. Guild, 'Equivocal Claims? Ambivalent Controls?' ,in: E. Guild & S. Mantu (eds), *Constructing and Imagining Labour Migration*, Aldershot: Ashgate Publishing 2011, p. 214.

3 Directive 2009/50/EC on the conditions of entry and residence of non-EU nationals for the purposes of highly-qualified employment; Directive 2014/36/EU of the European Parliament and of the Council of 26 February 2014 on the conditions of entry and stay of third-country nationals for the purpose of employment as seasonal workers.

agreements signed by the EU.[4] The EU's secondary legislation initiatives are based on the model provided by the General Agreement on Trade in Services (GATS), which in itself also provides access rights for third-country national service providers. The GATS provided the EU with a model system to regulate trade in services, for instance with former Soviet States.[5] More recently, various Free Trade Agreements (FTA) signed by the EU continue to provide access to the EU market for service providers from specific third countries such as Canada and Japan.[6] Interestingly, while much attention is granted to this new generation of FTA, earlier EU agreements already contain rules on movement rights for service providers.

For instance, rights for Intra-Corporate Transferees (ICT) are provided in agreements with Algeria, Armenia, Azerbaijan, Georgia, Kazakhstan, Kyrgyz Republic, Moldova, Russia, Ukraine, Uzbekistan and Jordan.[7] Elspeth emphasizes that these international agreements, 'though largely ignored by states and to a great extent unknown to lawyers' do have legal consequences. One of the reasons why such agreements are not taken as seriously as for instance the implementation of a specific EU directive, is the fact that these agreements often do not have direct effect, as is clear from case law and as is now added in the agreements themselves as well.[8] Yet, Elspeth explains that in relation to rights for ICT, it is the ICT Directive, which is intended to provide a basic level of access and protection to third-country national ICT, that essentially provides a specific legal argument for those wishing to utilize the just mentioned international agreements. As is the case with other types of secondary legislation addressing (temporary) movement rights for third country nationals in relation to labour or service provision, the ICT Directive specifically provides that it applies 'without prejudice to more favourable provisions of' bilateral and multilateral agreements'.[9] As such, it is the secondary legislation that actually ensures the necessity for a Member State to correctly apply the international agreement. If the ICT Directive contains a more onerous provision than an international agreement, this onerous provision should be set aside. This should simply be a matter of *pacta sunt servanda*, yet ignoring the international agreement is no longer a matter for international law only. Due to the ICT Directive EU legislation turns this into a legal obligation based on EU law. The same applies to other directives containing a similar clause.

When we practically apply Elspeth's reasoning to for example the EU – Algeria Agreement, the result is interesting. The ICT Directive provides various conditions in relation to ICT. For instance, the ICT Directive states that evidence must be provided in relation to the prior-employment of the ICT (at least three, up to twelve uninterrup-

4 The international trade agreements under discussion here expressly avoid any form of labour mobility; Directive 2014/66/EU on the conditions of entry and residence of third-country nationals in the framework of an intra-corporate transfer.

5 Guild 2018, p. 57.

6 The Comprehensive Economic and Trade Agreement between the EU and Canada (CETA) and the EU-Japan Economic Partnership Agreement.

7 Guild 2018, p. 59.

8 S. Tans, *Service Provision and Migration*, Leiden: Brill 2017, p. 260-263; see for instance CETA, Article 30.6.

9 Article 4(1) under b ICT Directive; Guild 2018, p. 66.

ted months immediately preceding the date of the ICT) in the home state by the company relying on the ICT provisions.[10] This simply was not specifically included in the EU – Algeria Agreement, yet, that agreement does provide the condition that ICT is conditional on 12 months prior employment.[11] Demanding proof (ICT Directive) and simply imposing a condition of 12 months prior employment (EU - Algeria) should in my opinion not be seen as more onerous, specifically as the EU – Algeria Agreement also indicates that the ICT should be 'in accordance with the legislation in force in the host country of establishment'. This last condition nevertheless is included to ensure that measures of the host state applying in a specific service sector, can be imposed on the ICT from Algeria. I am not convinced that such language also applies to the example of demanding proof as required by the ICT Directive.

I find the ICT Directives requirement of evidence 'that the third-country national will be able to transfer back to an entity belonging to that undertaking or group of undertakings and established in a third country at the end of the intra-corporate transfer' a bit more tricky. It is evident that the EU-Algeria Agreement addresses temporary movement only, as such, the Algerian ICT will no longer have any legal ground based on the international agreement to stay within the host Member State. Yet demanding proof in advance is something quite different.[12] Similarly, the ICT Directive requires 'evidence that the third-country national has the professional qualifications *and experience* needed in the host entity to which he or she is to be transferred (…)'.[13] This again may be read in the EU-Algeria Agreement provision dealing with ICT, yet required experienced is not listed there. True, being a manager or a specialist probably means that the required experience will be there in the first place, yet the EU-Algeria Agreement simply speaks, in relation to specialists, of 'uncommon knowledge essential to the establishment's service, research equipment, techniques or management. The assessment of such knowledge may reflect, apart from knowledge specific to the establishment, a high level of qualification referring to a type of work or trade requiring specific technical knowledge, including membership of an accredited profession'.[14] I am not convinced that an Algerian ICT can be required to provide evidence of experience necessary for the specific activity required in the branch office in the host state. Essentially, uncommon knowledge should in my opinion be sufficient.

What is evident is that since the signing of the first agreements including service mobility related rights (the GATS itself and the aforementioned EU Agreements with former Soviet Union states), the legal language used in secondary EU legislation and modern FTAs is far more detailed, in particular in relation to conditions and evidence.[15] Providing a practical example of the argument made by Elspeth demonstrates that such

10 ICT Directive Article 5(1)b.

11 EU-Algeria Agreement, Article 33(2).

12 ICT Directive Article 5(1)(c) IV.

13 ICT Directive Article 5(1)(d) IV, emphasis added.

14 EU-Algeria Agreement, Article 33(2)b.

15 On variations in language used in GATS commitment and more modern FTAs, the EU-CARIFORUM Agreement and CETA in specific, see: S. Tans, 'Trade Commitments in GATS, EU-CARIFORUM and CETA, and the Inclusion of Blanket References to Entry, Stay, Work and Social Security Measures', in: S. Carrera, A. Geddes, E. Guild & M. Stefan (eds), *Pathways Towards Legal Migration into the EU*, Brussels: CEPS 2017, par 16.7; Note that the Ukraine should be exempted from the list above as the EU-Ukraine Agreement as the original agreement was replaced with a modernized version in 2016.

details may become problematic if formulated too stringently. It leads me to one of the main point of this line of Elspeth's research. During a conference held by the author she referred to the oddity of FTAs consistently providing rights for private parties while at the same time such agreements prohibit any possibility to rely on such rights. During another conference she remarked that the implementation of trade agreements should be left to trade, not the home office. It is exactly that which in my opinion is what has happened to more stringently formulated modern counterparts, they are increasingly addressing concerns over immigration and access to the labour market. Yet, that is the sole purpose of trade agreements, business and trade require movement. It is trade agreements that provides gates for such movements and it is up to practitioners to use them and Member States to allow them to be used.

'They Only Use the Opportunities Provided by the Law'
Chapters from the History of Ukrainian-Hungarian Migration Relations

*Judit Tóth**

1. Introduction

Between 1993 and 2015, a total of 843,000 people acquired Hungarian citizenship, of which 708,000 were after the introduction of the simplified naturalisation, from 2011 onwards. Between 2011 and 2015, only 61,000 became Hungarian citizens within the border, i.e. they claimed naturalisation as living or settled there, while others asked for and acquired Hungarian citizenship and an old-age pension without Hungarian residence. In late 2017, the number of persons who acquired Hungarian citizenship via simplified naturalisation reached one million. But when and why do naturalised people want to move to Hungary? Let's look at just a few elements of this, on the basis of the available data.

Investigative journalists have found that in 2018, only 256 cases were prosecuted and 1,032 were investigated for citizenship abuse and corruption,[1] although, for many years, the frauds were known in this field.[2] In 2014, the State Secretary for Ethnic Politics acknowledged[3] that the government knew about naturalisation-related fraud, namely that Hungarian citizenship was being obtained with false documents by many Ukrainians and Russians, including thousands of criminals and dubious figures among the one million newly naturalised people.[4] Such abuse is still ongoing, and in the case of illegally acquired citizenships, so far withdrawals and several measures have been taken to exclude the possibility of abuse. For example, multi-lingual flyers inform prospective applicants that both language proficiency and personal submission of an application are prerequisites for a positive application review. The Secretary did not say that over 623,000 applicants requested simplified naturalisation between 2011 and

* University of Szeged, Hungary.

1 Állampolgársági csalások, [Citizenship Frauds] *Index*, 5 March 2019.

2 Corruption cases in accelerated naturalisation were released in the press, e.g. bribery for accepted naturalisation application was 700 EUR, *HVG,* 9 January 2014. For the 'non-speakers' story see Thorpe, N.: Hungary creating new mass of EU citizens. *BBC,* 7 November 2013, Subotica; *MTI,* 11 April 2015; *MTI,* 13 May 2015; *MTI,* 9 January 2014; *MTI,*5 November 2014; *HVG,* 6 September 2014. The method of abusive cases is analysed in *Népszava,* 15 July 2013; *HVG,* 24 April 2013; *Index,* 16 September 2014 and 17 September 2014.

3 Elismerte az államtitkár az állampolgárságos csalásokat, [The Secretary acknowledged the citizenship frauds] Index, 16 September 2014.

4 Megvan az egymilliomodik honosított külhoni magyar, [There is the one millionth naturalised outlander Hungarian] *MTI,* 16 December 2017.

2014, but that the due diligence authorities did not have enough human resources to properly process the requests of the arrivals, so only 20,867 applications were rejected.[5]

The simplified naturalisation[6] was introduced in 2011, and it has been a hotbed of corruption since then. Why? Because the non-Hungarian citizen, whose ancestor was Hungarian or likely to be of Hungarian origin, is eligible to be preferentially naturalised, if there is no public-security objection against him, and his Hungarian language proficiency is proved. It is not regulated how applicants' language skills are checked, the evidence of Hungarian origin submitted, as well as the history of the applicant living for safety in another country. All naturalisation procedures in Hungary are essentially 'secret' because there is no right of access to the documents, no regular decision is made, which would explain the reasons for the decision. There is no remedy against this decision. Therefore, new and more recent corruption cases are emerging. For example, in 2015, the National Defence Service filed a complaint against 48 people because three administrators of the Public Administration and Electronic Public Services Office issued Hungarian passports and other personal documents to foreigners who were not entitled to such documents.[7]

2. Abusive Naturalisation

About 100-120 thousand ethnic Hungarians live in Trans-Carpathia. They usually have all the documents needed for naturalisation, all they have to do is fill in the online form and then send it personally to a Hungarian office. They do not even have to leave Ukraine, because they can work on paper at the local Hungarian consulates, at most, they have to take a citizenship oath in Hungary. Applicants are required to attach two photographs to the naturalisation application and the ID card data sheet. For 1,000-1,500 EUR, criminals can make their own Hungarian passport with photos and fingerprints, and travel freely anywhere in the world, for example without visas to 151 countries. All of this made for the ethnic Hungarian minority that is considered as vulnerable. And who are those taking a new identity for themselves? Those, who have nothing to lose.

In Ukraine, the business of Hungarian citizenship has been booming for several years: if the age and gender of the fraudster fit those who have already acquired Hungarian citizenship, anyone can take a completely new Hungarian identity, passport and new life with him anywhere in the EU. How? Because there is no photograph on the naturalisation application document, and the fraudster is asking for a passport or ID card with his own photo and fingerprints at a Hungarian government office. According to the locals, the method was taken over from the Romanians by the dealers. The poor (the Roma, the sick, the unemployed with debt) sold their naturalisation records (profiles) in almost every village along the border, although they received only € 120-180 from the intermediaries. The Ukrainian and Hungarian investigative bodies also discovered a series of frauds. Thus, in the region near the border, the personal information

5 Több ezer orosz bűnöző kaphatott magyar állampolgárságot, [Several thousand Russian criminals might acquire Hungarian citizenship] *Index*, 26 January 2018.

6 Art.4(3) in the Act LV of 1993 on Hungarian Citizenship amended by the Act XLIV of 2010.

7 Citing Gyulai, G. (Hungarian Helsinki Committee) in Állampolgárság i csalások, [Citizenship Frauds] *Index*, 5 March 2019.

of the submitter is checked at the time of making the passport, but there is always a careless or corrupt administrator in Budapest or elsewhere, who prepares the photo and fingerprints and passes the form for the passport without checking the submitter's data. The deal is focused on the local wealthy and respectable people, not the Ukrainian or Russian mafia. Mayors, pastors, and local entrepreneurs manage this for their community, while getting rich. After the introduction of simplified naturalisation, if a rich Russian or Ukrainian wanted to acquire citizenship, he sought the Ukrainian mafia, which forged counterfeiting and corruption for the naturalisation of the person for € 5-30,000. This is a more cumbersome operation that is more expensive and risky. The naturalisation and passport administration installed at the Budapest Government Office in 2017 has been modified, and it requires comparing the photo attached to the naturalisation application with the photograph in the applicant's passport.[8] But this does not include ex-post verification of documents issued in the past.

According to the Prosecutor General's inquiries into the naturalisation and establishment of long-term migrants from Ukraine[9] by the end of January 2019, 370 cases had been investigated by the police, of which 60 are still pending. In 156 cases, charges have been made and are in court. Courts have delivered judgments in 108 cases for fraud, document abuse, corruption, and giving false information. In general, they are involved in criminal proceedings

a) for the most part, applicants for citizenship do not speak Hungarian, yet the administrator has approved the language proficiency, because often the other person (who plays this role for money, the intermediary), who speaks Hungarian, has applied instead of the applicant;
b) other cases involve the use of the legally acquired Hungarian citizenship document by another person (he sold the right of application to the entitled person by exchanging the appropriate photographs) to obtain the Hungarian passport;
c) the third type of violation is the fictitious proof of residence in Hungary, which is often confirmed by the owner of the house or apartment in question, even though the alien is not resident there and, according to the certificate, false information has been entered in the inhabitants' address register.

Also reported was that sentences of between two to five years of imprisonment were given to two offenders in a naturalisation case involving a total of 51 accused persons; ten were given suspended jail sentences, and regarding 39 people, fines were imposed. As the Prosecutor General summed up, the two organizers were dual citizens (Ukrainian and Hungarian) who, in 2014, provided help in acquiring Hungarian citizenship to people who did not speak Hungarian, and their photos were attached to the passport application, while in Hungary, well-known pseudo-applicants participated in the procedure. Only one verdict was issued in 2019 on this case.[10] Three non-Hungarian speaking persons were arrested in the middle of a naturalisation oath ceremony in a corruption case, together with the mayor and the clerks in the Eastern region of Hungary.

---

8 Ezrével jutnak hamis magyar személyazonossághoz ukrajnai csalók, [Thousands of Ukrainian fraudsters get Hungarian identity] *Index*, 21 February 2017.

9 General Prosecutor's Response (NF 333/2019/25-II.) to Vadai Á. MEP, February 2019.

10 Két vádlott letöltendő börtönt kapott egy honosítási perben, [Two defendants were sentenced to serve imprisonment in a naturalisation lawsuit] *Index*, 11 April 2019.

The court also found guilty the notary of a village in the border county and his companion for helping Ukrainians to acquire Hungarian citizenship: he was sentenced to three years' imprisonment, and his companion to one year of imprisonment for accepting bribes. They had been asked by their Ukrainian acquaintances to help them acquire Hungarian citizenship, although, they did not meet the legal requirements. The clerk assumed the task for 500 EUR per person, and in 11 cases took over the naturalisation applications from his partner. He issued a receipt for the money he received in ten cases, with a stamp that was not official.[11]

There were zero withdrawals of citizenship in 1993–2012, according to the OIN statistics, but the accelerated naturalisation has changed this solid statistic. A rise in the withdrawal of citizenship from naturalised persons in an accelerated procedure has been observed as Table 1 indicates. The first withdrawal of citizenship from Mr. Jenő Lacko brought a surprise, so the public was briefly informed by the President of the Republic.[12] His Hungarian nationality was obtained through the accelerated/preferential naturalisation procedure: he misled the authority by providing false or untrue data on his identity (name and birth data), and the Minister of the Interior proposed the withdrawal to the President. His abusive conduct was made public after his citizenship oath had been taken. The decision entered into force on the day of publication and his citizenship ceased on the same day, while not affecting his Ukrainian citizenship. The press release contained no explanations of the decision, so the press investigated how the upgraded speed of the naturalisation process contributed to the public security risks because the authority had no proper time for individual checking and risk analysis of applicants. According to the official explanation, the withdrawal was based on Art 4. and Art 9. of the Act on Nationality.

Table 1: Withdrawal of citizenship (naturalisation decision within ten years of acquisition)[13]

Year	*Citizenship*	*Minors*	*Total*
1993-2012	--	--	0
2013-2019 (April 10)	Russian/Ukraine: 97 (56%)	23	174
	Yugoslav/Serbian: 57 (33%)		
	Romanian: 18 (10%)		
	Spanish: 2 (1%)		

This meant that either security requirements (clean criminal records) were missing or that the applicants' Hungarian language knowledge or information on Hungarian ancestors had been manipulated. The police have launched criminal investigations into

11 Fejenként 500 euróért intézett magyar állampolgárságot ukránoknak egy szabolcsi jegyző, [A notary in Szabolcs arranged for Hungarian citizenship for Ukrainians for EUR 500 per person], *Narancs*, 13 December 2017.

12 *Magyar Közlöny*, [Official Gazette] 13 July 2013. Resolution of the State President No. 339 of 2013, and *MTI*, 29 September 2015.

13 Author's calculation on the basis of resolutions by the President of the State, published in the Official Gazette (Magyar Közlöny).

receiving bribes from applicants and for counterfeiting documents against at least eight officials in parallel.

2. Pensioners' Mobility

The number of Russian and mainly Ukrainian citizens, who applied for a pension in Hungary, increased significantly after 2012, i.e. the migration of pensioners to the border area was detected at first. The Soviet-Hungarian Agreement on Social Care, concluded in 1962,[14] was named by the Russian Federation and Ukraine as the legal successor of the Soviet Union. Russian/Ukrainian citizens, as well as family members of any nationality, if they were employed in Russia/Ukraine or in Hungary (acquiring social insurance period) and reside in Russia/Ukraine or Hungary may apply for social insurance benefits (old-age and survivors' pensions, accident annuities, mining fees, invalidity benefits, sickness, maternity and family benefits). According to the main rule, the state, in which the applicant was employed, pays the benefits, but if (s)he has moved from Ukraine to Hungary, then the Hungarian authority has to determine and cover the benefits.

Upon request, the pension insurance authority obtains the missing employment documents, but the applicant's identification documents or authentic copies have to be attached, which are also translated by the proceeding authority. The applicant must be resident in Hungary at the time the application is submitted, i.e. long-term migrant status or Hungarian citizenship is required together with a registered address in Hungary. If the applicant has worked only in the USSR/Russia/Ukraine, but never in Hungary, the average earnings are calculated by taking into account the average salary for the same job, with the appropriate qualification, in Hungary, at the time the pension is determined. A pensioner can receive the benefit (by bank transfer or by post) from the Hungarian pension fund as long as (s)he resides in Hungary. If someone has already moved to Hungary as a pensioner, (s)he must resign from the Ukrainian pension scheme, and apply for a pension in Hungary on the basis of Hungarian legislation. The lifetime stay of the applicant in Hungary can be checked at any time during or after the procedure (by the Treasury or the Government Office).[15]

According to the Agreement, the monthly average amount of expenditure paid by the Hungarian pension fund, and the number of applicants/eligible persons is growing[16] as Table 2 proves. Unfortunately, it is not possible to calculate mechanically the total pension expense on the basis of the December data, as the individual payments are continuously started during the calendar year. It can only be estimated, but it takes at least EUR 15-35 million per year.

---

14 Presidium's Law-Decree No. 16 of 1963 on promulgation of the Agreement of the People's Republic of Hungary and the Federation of Soviet Socialist Republics on the Cooperation in the Field of Social Care (concluded on 20 December 1962) and its Executive Ministerial Decree No 7 of 1964, August 30 (MüM)

15 National Treasury https://nyugdijbiztositas.tcs.allamkincstar.gov.hu

16 Written answers to Kiss, László and Korózs, Lajos MEP by the state secretary from the responsible ministry (EMMI, Hiv. szám: K/8813, Országgyűlés Hivatala) 24 February 2016.

Table 2: Implementation of the Soviet-Hungarian Social Security Agreement[17]

Year	Expenses in December (EUR)	Applicants	Pension holders
2006	1 522 222	763	423
2007	2 027 888	897	870
2008	2 257 693	867	1298
2009	2 250 000	851	1714
2010	2 483 637	981	2132
2011	2 621 429	1242	2599
2012	2 789 655	1210	3043
2013	3 016 892	1125	3591
2014	3 214 286	1 579	4408
2015	3 603 226	2 283	7 873
2016	4 193 549	n.d.	9 288

In Hungary, the average old-age pension is three to five times more than the average Ukrainian pension.[18] Moreover, free medical care and free public transport accompany a pension provided in Hungary. It is understandable why Hungarian citizenship or the long-term migrant status is attractive to Ukrainian citizens: they can obtain a much higher pension together with other social advantages. This goes hand in hand with home purchases, production of residence and employment documents, bank account contracts, and administrative mobility, as well as all-encompassing corruption, especially in one of the poorest regions, near the Ukrainian border.

However, in October 2012, the Pension Insurance Directorate organized a Hungarian-Ukrainian pension advisory day for interested Ukrainian citizens, on how to claim pensions guaranteed by the Hungarian state, while the right to benefit from the Hungarian disability pensions was taken away,[19] on grounds that the pension fund would be unsustainable. For financial stabilization the government planned to save HUF 217 million out of the total HUF 330 billion on their disability pensions by the end of December 2013. In this atmosphere, it is understandable that the pensioners and disabled people in Hungary have watched jealously the 15 million pensioners in Ukraine, and wondered how many more could come. In the press, it has been reported that pension payments were stalling in Ukraine, which also encouraged the choice of a Hungarian pension. That is why (anecdotal) information has spread: 80 percent of applicants submitted documents detailing high earnings that were hard to believe, and most applicants were in senior positions, so they counted on receiving an advanced Hungarian pension. Administrators had no authority to examine the authenticity of the documents. A nurse working in the Emergency Department of the Town Hospital (Kisvárda) for 30 years has said that on average, a hundred people come from Ukraine every day for Hungarian citizenship proceedings, while the elderly also claim a Hungarian pension. According to people living along the border, pregnant mothers also come

17 Source: ONYF, EMMI (Pension Fund, Ministry of Welfare).

18 Kelet-Magyarország, *[East Hungary] 3 March 2016.; Szabolcs Online,* 3 March 2016.

19 With retroactive effect by the Act CXCI of 2011.

for free medical treatment, including Hungarian-Ukrainian and Russian-Ukrainian mothers.[20]

Applicants can submit documents containing false data without any problems, as the Hungarian authorities do not know the level of the previous Ukrainian wages. The authenticity of the address is not verified, although, it is easy to obtain a certificate of Hungarian residence for good money. The majority of pensioners are not living in Hungary continuously. On the Ukrainian black market, almost all existing papers can be obtained: driver's license, graduation certificate, language exam, diploma and documents certifying employment in Ukraine. The press has long been saying: acquiring Hungarian citizenship also means new voters, and the government party needs all their votes, so they make gestures from the public finance through the provision of pensions. It is unlikely that the Hungarian authorities are simply helpless, but it is not in the interests of the ruling party to tighten up the conditions for obtaining a Hungarian pension. Some politicians, in the hope of gaining some political benefit, are bringing together Hungarians from the kin-state with Hungarians living beyond the border, because the inhabitants will get fewer pensions.[21]

Bolsakov, Oleksiy, Head of the Foreign Pensions Department in the Trans-Carpathian County Office of Ukraine's Pension Fund, said that between 2009 and 2017, 5,646 people in the region had discontinued their pension in Ukraine, and applied for it in Hungary. In 2015, 3,793 citizens of working age moved from Ukraine to Hungary, and they asked for proof of their employment in Ukraine, for the Hungarian pension application. These numbers are therefore severely different from the data above in Table 2. According to the government party, this is only a pseudo-problem: pensions paid under the Agreement do not account for half a percent of the total pension fund spending, whereas the number of pensioners in Hungary is 2.1 million. In the discourse, it explains why the press is full of lies about the fact that some of the ten thousand Trans-Carpathian pensioners are destroying the pension fund. On the other hand, it is estimated that 40,000 workers, mostly from Trans-Carpathia, whose upbringing and education did not cost a penny to the Hungarian state, are legally employed in Hungary. They replace the chronically absent workforce, and pay all kinds of contributions and taxes. That is why a project management office was established in Budapest with the support of the Ministry of National Economy, and it has been operating since 2017 to manage the employment of Ukrainian workers in Hungary. As a result, in August 2017, there were already 6,300 Ukrainian workers in the Hungarian labour market. It is estimated that about two hundred thousand Ukrainians will work and pay contributions in Hungary within two years. Therefore, if the political opponents were to think positively, it would be noticed that most Ukrainians had established a permanent address in their country, fleeing from the Ukrainian-Russian war, in order to avoid military service in the army. Another compelling reason for employment is that the acquisition of Hungarian citizenship is not enough for the mobile Ukrainian people to work, because a Hungarian registered address, ID card, tax ID and health insurance certificate are also needed, and they are based on each other. In spite of the fact that many of

20 Ukrán nyugdíjasok tömegesen lépik át a magyar határt [Ukrainian pensioners crossing the Hungarian border, en masse], http://www.pestmegyei-hirhatar.hu.

21 Ukrán-magyar határmenti nyugdíj biznisz, [Ukrainian-Hungarian Pension Business at the Border], *Városi Kurír*, 4 December 2017.

them are Hungarian (dual) citizens, they are still unable to settle in Hungary. Although there are rumours that for a monthly sum of HUF 5,000 someone can certify his/her residence in Hungary, the strict controls have already 'stopped the abusive practice'.[22]

Really, did it? In recent years, the population of villages has grown by thousands of people in the region near the Ukrainian border, and the village of Kispalád, which had a 151 percent increase in population, stands out among them. There are houses in the village, where more than 90 Ukrainian citizens have been registered as resident in the address register, besides the original residents, although, the owner has never seen these 'residents' across the border. However, many official notifications in the box indicate that these addresses have been given to the authorities. Due to the false declarations, two reports were filed at the city police station (Fehérgyarmat), and now they are investigating the abuse of public documents.[23] Sale prices of one-and-a-half-room apartments in the border settlements increased one and a half times, but the apartments for sale were not advertised for long. In 2017, in the border regions, 195 inspections were carried out at the request of the Social Insurance Authority. On this basis, the disbursement of pensions was terminated in 17 cases. The audit also included the submission of new applications, of which the pension claims of 61 applicants were denied. At the beginning of February 2018, two government officials were arrested in Hajdúdorog, who, according to the suspects, had assisted two Ukrainian citizens in obtaining false documents.[24]

But there was news that an apartment of 50 square metres was officially inhabited by hundreds, and 120 in another, and of course there are many residents who do not speak Hungarian; that is, certainly not a Hungarian minority. If you really need a Hungarian registered address, you will find it on the Internet for HUF 40,000. The migration of pensioners not only improved the demographics in the border regions (for example, the population in Szabolcs-Szatmár-Bereg County increased by at least 23 thousand, despite the significant emigration), but also increased the number of those entitled to vote. For instance, in the past six years, the number of persons entitled to vote has doubled in Beregsurány, Botpalád, and Lónya, and the number of voters has tripled in Kispalád.[25] And these voters are loyal: the locals tell them for whom to vote (for example, the local mayor), and they vote without knowing the actual political environment.

Following the questions by the parliamentary opposition, the Foreign Minister tried to reassure the public and reported on bilateral negotiations. The government was reviewing the Agreement on social care with Ukraine.[26] He denied that many Ukrainians set up a home address in Hungary in order to receive a larger pension. It was also not true that the rules on cooperatives[27] had been amended, so that the leaders of the

22 Lass, G., A nagy nyugdíjhazugság, [The big pension lie], *Demokrata,* 10 March 2018.

23 Nyomoznak az ukrán-magyar nyugdíjbiznisz miatt, [There is an investigation due to the Ukrainian-Hungarian Pension Business], *hvg.hu*, 22 December 2017.

24 Utánajártak: ilyen a nagy ukrán nyugdíjbiznisz, [Inquired: how the big Ukrainian Pension Business at the Border looks like] *HírTV,* 1 December 2017.

25 300 ezres nyugdíjat szerezhetnek olyanok, akik nem is Magyarországon élnek, [HUF 300,000 pension could get by those, who do not even live in Hungary], *24.hu*, 1 December 2017.

26 Szijjártó utánanéz az ukrán nyugdíjak ügyének, [Szijjártó will inquire the Ukrainian pension case], *Hír Tv*, 18 January 2018.

27 Act LXXXIX of 2017, which amended Act X of the 2006 on Cooperatives.

government party group would have a greater influence over cooperatives of pensioners. However, it appears that the Ministry of National Economy has provided half a billion HUF support to the Ukrainian Labour Recruitment/Job agency, and several applications have been received for cooperatives formed by pensioners. Already one hundred of such cooperatives have been formed, including the East Neighbours' Cooperative as part of a network of companies linked to union leaders.[28]

In 2009, a proposal to modernize the Agreement was completed. The draft treaty with the Ukrainian side on social benefits has been pending since 2012, which includes the principle of proportionality for establishing pensions. In other words, instead of applying the old territorial pension claim, there will be a pro rata pension calculation, i.e. if an employee has worked in several countries, each party will only pay its own share of the pension.[29]

What should be done to adjust the Hungarian pension of a Ukrainian retired person, who has moved to Hungary, to his or her last job before retirement or to the longest term? This was the subject of a lawsuit between a pensioner and the social security authority. The case was adjudicated by the Supreme Court, and then by the Constitutional Court, on the basis of a request for a review of the norm.

The Constitutional Court established that the first sentence of Article 6 (2) of the Ministerial Decree regulating the implementation of the Agreement was unconstitutional, and had therefore been annulled. It further stated that the first sentence of this paragraph was no longer applicable to a case pending before the Supreme Court, and other forums.[30] The applicant moved from Ukraine to Hungary on 20 November 2012. From 14 April 2009 until 30 June 2015, she received a retirement pension established by the Ukrainian social security authority. As of 1 July 2015, the Hungarian social insurance authority was asked to establish an old-age pension, and by the decision of 30 December, the authority determined the old-age pension in the amount of HUF 147,010 per month, based on the longest job held by the applicant.

The social security institution of the second instance changed the decision at first instance, and established an old-age pension of HUF 124, 720 for the applicant from the same date, because it had had no opportunity to take into account the average salary of the applicant's last job. In fact, from January 2015, Hungarian law provided that the wage earned by a pension claimant for the longest period of time must be taken into account in the calculation. Thus, the calculation was based on the applicant's job as an official administrator, not as a commercial director. However, eligibility was applicable from April 2009, meaning that the Hungarian pension rules at that time should have been applied by the authority. Therefore, the Labour Court annulled the decision of the social security authority and ordered the authority to conduct a new procedure. In the Supreme Court proceedings, it was considered that the Hungarian law[31] in force at the time of the establishment of the benefit should be applied, subject to the provisions of the Decree implementing the Agreement.

---

28 *HírTV*, 3 December 2017.

29 http://www.refradio.eu/radio/sion/mutat/562/.

30 Constitutional Court's decision, No. 15 of 2018, 8 October.

31 Act LXXXI of 1997 on Old-age Pension and its Executive Government Decree No. 168 of 1997, 6 October.

The Constitutional Court held that there was a contradiction between the rules in force and that the Government Decree took precedence over the Ministerial Decree on the application of the Agreement, and therefore annulled the relevant provision of the latter. It also rendered the protection of legal certainty as set out in the enacting terms. In other words, the Ukrainian pensioner had to get a lower pension,[32] but still, the Hungarian wage is attractive, especially if it is spent in Ukraine.

Conclusions

Ukraine is one of the countries most affected by the migration policy of the Hungarian government. Not only as a neighbour, but also because ethnic-based nation-building policies have contributed to tensions between the two countries. Citizenship regulation (preferential naturalisation) and the granting of Hungarian pensions to Ukrainian citizens are used to build a mass base supporting the government. On the one hand, the aim is to obtain new government votes by securing the voting rights of new citizens and to preserve voters who sympathize with ethnic policies. According to the government, citizenship, the authenticity of the Hungarian passport, the erosion of EU legal loyalty and EU citizenship are not a high price to pay for that.

The growth of corruption cases, crimes, and vulnerability of the poor, polarizing the public, and infringement of EU law by accelerated naturalization procedures, uncontrolled regulatory procedures[33]- these all are blocking the progress of Ukraine's European and security integration. But there is a higher price for this policy: according to information from the Department of Homeland Security, at least 65 out of 700 passport holders from fraudulent procedures have entered the United States, and at least 30 have remained there while the American authorities try to find and deport them. The US government considered this to be a serious problem that would change the status of Hungary in the Visa Waiver Programme. In April 2018, DHS staff travelled to Budapest and made it clear to the Hungarian government that if they did not solve the problem, Hungary would be expelled from the Visa Waiver Programme.[34]

This fairly complicated public power game was summed up by an ordinary voter:

> 'it is not popular among the locals to be the city leader who is openly in favour of the Trans-Carpathian pensioners. Because the Ukrainian state is incapable of providing a human life worthy of the Trans-Carpathian Hungarians, they only use the opportunity provided by law.'[35]

32 Kulcsár, A., Alkotmánybírósági döntés ukrán nyugdíjügyben, [Constitutional Court decision in a Ukrainian pension case], *Magyar Idők*, 9 October 2018.

33 Tóth J., Challenged Public Security by Non-resident Nationals, *Magyar Rendészet,* 2017/5. 51—66.

34 Pethő, A. & J. Hudson, *The Washington Post – Direkt* 36, 10 May 2018.

35 Lass, G., A nagy nyugdíjhazugság, [The big pension lie], *Demokrata,* 10 March 2018.

Thinking Fast and Slow
Migration Decision-making and Political Crises

*Dan Wilsher**

Introduction

Elspeth Guild has always been a scholar of movement across disciplines. This piece seeks to move deftly from psychology to jurisprudence in considering fairness in migration decision-making. States have legal obligations to provide some form of due process in most cases of immigration refusals. This ranges from 'basic' consultation to full-blown suspensive appeals. This paper uses Daniel Kahneman's distinction between 'fast' and 'slow' decision-making[1] to model due process in migration cases. In the UK context, it looks at how negative framing of groups of migrants saw them being allocated to faster decision-making processes. Whilst facilitating speedy political responses to crises, such allocation decisions have increasingly been questioned during judicial proceedings on fairness and reliability grounds.

Deciding Fast and Slow in a Moving World

The international movement of people across borders takes place on a vast, industrial scale in the modern era of globalisation. For the UK alone, around 75 million people cross the external border annually. As for most developed nations, this movement is generally *authorised* and is based on simple rules of administration to facilitate entry. Following Kahneman's distinction in relation to psychological thinking between rapid, rule-based decision-making ('system 1' thinking) and more considered, deliberative decision-making ('system 2' thinking), we can see their analogues in migration control. As Kahneman puts it: 'System 1 operates automatically and quickly, with little or no effort and no sense of voluntary control.' By contrast, 'System 2 allocates attention to the effortful mental activities that demand it, including complex computations. The operations of System 2 are often associated with the subjective experience of agency, choice and concentration.'[2] He observes that for reasons of efficiency, System 1 is essential and, generally, works well for many situations.

In migration control terms System 1, which we can call *Semi-automated movement facilitation,* is based upon group coding and minimal administrative discretion. This governs the vast majority of movement and is based upon simple rules located in, for example, visa exemptions, Schengen open-borders rules, standardized questionnaires and points-based visas. The creation of such categories often emerges from diplomatic

---

* The City Law School, London
1 D. Kahneman, *Thinking, fast and slow*, London: Penguin 2011.
2 Ibid.,, 20-21.

interactions and international reciprocal agreements with other developed (or emerging) economics designed to promote trade, services or investment. Refusals are proportionately rare and the consequences generally modest. There is thus little need nor obligation for deep due process protections.

System 2, which we can call *human rights migration determination,* governs those seeking to stay or enter based upon humanitarian or human rights grounds. The emergence of the main categories here, such as refugees, resulted from historic agreements designed to re-integrate displaced persons, not to facilitate or encourage movement as such. These cases are much fewer as industrialized States seek to impede migrants' (largely drawn from less developed countries) ability to make such applications. For those that do apply, however, legal constraints often provide a minimum level of due process to each individual before a negative decision can be issued. This represents Kahneman's more deliberative thinking. Negative decisions here are quite common. This full system of due process (including suspensive appeals) is expensive and slow. System 2 can also become overwhelmed if numbers increase sharply beyond current capacity.

Summary: System 1 and System 2

Semi-automated Movement Facilitation (System 1)
- Simple
- Large scale
- Routine and Less Consequential
- Automated or rule-based
- Speedy
- Negative decisions rare
- Due process limited and non-suspensive

Human Rights Migration Determination (System 2)
- Complex
- Small scale
- Momentous and Highly Consequential
- Human discretion prominent
- Slow
- Negative decisions quite common
- Due process extensive and suspensive

Contesting the Boundary between System 1 and 2

This is of course a simplification. Some groups may fall between Systems 1 and 2, showing a mixture of features. Political evaluations become important in deciding which system to allocate them to. For asylum-seekers of nationalities with low-success rates, governments may conclude that removing such persons will not have serious consequences for them. In these cases, negative decisions are not merely 'quite common', but may verge on 100%. Despite this, legal and practical constraints prevent the use of the simple automated rules of System 1. Each person must be interviewed personally and country research must be conducted. Adverse points must be put to them. We can see here an emerging 'System 1.5' which lies somewhere between the two approaches – a slimmed down due process.[3]

In practice, at the political level, such evaluations have relied upon different types of objective evidence relating to, for example, country reports on human rights.[4] An assessment is then sometimes 'confirmed' by the low success rate of such claims. The group may come to be perceived in negative terms as abusive or manifestly unfounded. There is a danger of confirmation bias in such an approach.[5] This may lead to a higher risk of error. There are other methods by which negative framing of groups arise which we will explore below. These include exposure of a scandal within the system indicating that a group has been granted status wrongly or they are dangerous. Even if there is a strong quantitative basis for concluding that a group of cases is indeed one broadly without merit, there may be a level below which due process cannot fall before it is deemed inherently unfair. In the constitutional allocation of power, the judiciary generally determines what the minimum content of fairness requires.

In summary, there are three critical issues that arise. First, the *categorization question;* how does the political branch define groups as 'abusive', 'dangerous' or 'without merit', so as to justify taking them out of System 2? Unreliable classification obviously gives rise to error-risk. Second, even if the categorization is apparently objectively reasonable, the abbreviated system may be so qualitatively unfair that it does not meet basic rule of law standards. This is the *fairness question.* Entering into the fairness question is the third issue of the *gravity of consequences question*: our assessment of what fairness requires is strongly influenced by the potential consequences of error. This in turn is comprised of an appreciation of the risk of error multiplied by the gravity of consequences of error.

The Emergence of System 2 and Due Process in UK Migration Law

Migration cases were at the root of the evolution of public law fairness principles in the UK. In the landmark decision in 1967 in *HK (an infant)* the Court of Appeal ruled that when the Commonwealth son of a resident Commonwealth citizen was refused entry to the UK for settlement because of doubts about him being a minor, there was a duty to act fairly in disclosing the reasons for that doubt to afford an opportunity to rebut it.[6] Ensuring due process was of 'vital importance to the immigrants since their *whole future* may depend upon it.'[7] [italics added] This ruling was later extended to all immigrants, not simply those from the Commonwealth. The court's, somewhat vague,

3 For an example, see Directive 2013/32/EU of the European Parliament and of the Council on procedures for granting and withdrawing international protection. Articles 10-24 set out the basic guarantees surrounding the administrative phase. For the suspensive appeal right and the limitations thereon in inadmissible or unfounded cases see Article 46.

4 The test in Directive 20013/32/EU is that there is 'generally and consistently no persecution' in that country.

5 Kahneman 2011, p. 80-81.

6 *Re H.K. (an infant)* [1967] 2 QB 617.

7 633 D-E.

reference to the serious consequences of migration decisions appears to have influenced its imposition of a duty to consult. A focus upon gravity of consequences points towards a need for System 2 thinking.

Ongoing struggles over how far Executive migration decisions should be subject to deeper judicial scrutiny resulted in 1983 in the House of Lords judgement in *Khawaja*[8] with its bold assertion of the general equal status of immigrants and citizens. Although the case was brought within habeas corpus, because the claimants were detained, it was actually far wider in its confirmation that the rule of law applied to immigrants. As Lord Scarman said '[h]abeas corpus protection is often expressed as limited to "British Subjects". Is it really limited to British nationals? Suffice it to say that the case law has given an emphatic No to the question. Every person within the jurisdiction enjoys the equal protection of our laws…'. The *Khawaja* decision came to be seen as a marker for the judiciary to be alert to excessive executive autonomy in decision-making over immigrants.

The courts' assertion of the right to fairness in judicial review cases was however of limited value without an appeal right on the merits. The 1969 Immigration Appeals Act was thus an important milestone which created important new rights to an in-country merits-based appeal to an adjudicator against refusals of leave to enter[9] or remain when a person was lawfully in the UK. There was also an onward appeal, with leave, to the Immigration Appeal Tribunal. These rights were soon afterwards reproduced for aliens and Commonwealth citizens (both now termed immigrants) under the 1971 Act.[10] The grounds of appeal were quite broad, even before the human rights era, comprising error of law, breach of the Rules and wrongful exercise of discretion.

The significant omission related to in-country rights of appeal for irregular migrants and those refused leave to enter. Amongst these two groups, even those who feared persecution or other violations of human rights had only the remedy of judicial review until these omissions were corrected in 1993[11] (for asylum) and 1999 (for human rights).[12] These expansions were necessary as the judicial review system itself became overburdened by asylum cases. Thus, by 1999, the UK had developed a deep system of scrutiny in immigration cases that mirrored many of the elements set out in System 2. Notably this extended to cover temporary migrants such as students and work-permit holders. System 1 meanwhile covered those much larger numbers arriving without visas for temporary purposes. Since that high-water mark, for political and administrative reasons which we explore below, there has been an almost complete reversion from System 2 into a hybrid System 1.5. Ironically, the appeal system has been reduced to just the last two types of case that were added: asylum and human rights.

---

8 *Khawaja v. Secretary of State for the Home Department* [1983] UKHL 8

9 Refusal of leave to enter attracted an in-country right of appeal only if the person possessed a valid entry clearance. S13.

10 Part II.

11 Asylum and Immigration Appeals Act 1993 s8.

12 Immigration and Asylum Act 1999 s65.

Thinking Faster – The Turn Towards System 1.5

This trend had already been trailed in 1998 when, with asylum claims rising to 46,000, a media perception of crisis saw the Blair government introduce a detained 'fast-track' application system for 'straightforward' asylum cases. These were those where a decision could be expected to be made quickly after a screening interview. Appeal rights were unaffected and so the change was not a fundamental shift away from System 2 but it was a clear forerunner. The change was upheld by the courts as fair because lawyers were provided, the time-table was flexible and there was a discretion to remove complex cases from the system.[13] With the appeal right preserved, the risk of error was further mitigated. The fairness question was thus resolved in the government's favour. By contrast, later cases saw two instances in which countries' placement upon a white list (with truncated appeal rights) were struck down by the courts. These were rare examples of when the categorization question was directly overturned by the courts. They found that the test of 'no serious risk of persecution' could not be satisfied based upon an objective assessment of the human rights records of the countries concerned.[14]

As asylum claims reached a new (UK) record of 80,000, the Blair government went further in 2003 with the introduction of 'super-fast track' appeal procedure rules which were combined with fast-track applications. These required both decisions and for appeal hearings to be arranged within a few days and to be decided shortly afterwards. Applicants were initially selected for the system based upon being drawn from five nationalities found to have low success rates – in effect a 'white list'. A contemporary challenge to the system in the higher courts focused only on the truncated Home Office first-decision stage and found it broadly compatible with fairness looking at the qualitative aspects of the system.[15] Refusal rates of 99% were viewed by the Court as not necessarily indicative of inherent unfairness because the white-list itself was not challenged. The political context was not mentioned but the high-profile of the asylum crisis at the time cannot be under-estimated. The detained fast-track remained in place unchallenged despite concerns over its expansion to all male asylum-seekers and the high failure rate for those in the system compared to similar cases outside it.[16]

Years later in 2014-15, the same system was reviewed again by the judiciary. The context had changed (asylum applications were below 30,000) and the political focus

13 *Saadi v. Secretary of State for the Home Department* [2002] UKHL 41.

14 *R v. Secretary of State for the Home Department exp Javed* [2001] 3 WLR 323 challenging the vires of the designation of Pakistan as such a country under s1 of the Asylum and Immigration Act 1996. The Court was prepared to adopt a rigorous approach: 'Although rational judgment or evaluation was called for from the Secretary of State, what had to be evaluated was the existence of a state of affairs. Whether that state of affairs pertained was a question of fact' (per Lord Phillips MR at para. 56) The designation of Jamaica was struck down because of the high risk to gay people there. See *R (app JB (Jamaica) v Secretary of State for the Home Department* [2014] 1 WLR 836.

15 *R (on app of Refugee Legal Centre) v. Secretary of State for the Home Department* [2004] EWCA Civ 1481. 'It is limited to single male applicants from countries which are believed by the defendant to be those where in general there is no serious risk of persecution.' (Para.2)

16 Detention Action, *Fast-track to Despair*, London: Detention Action 2011, which shows how the 'white-list' was expanded and ultimately all cases could be considered within the fast-track.

had moved decisively toward EU and other economic migrants. Appeals were successful in around 10% of cases. Now it was found the operation of both the Home Office and Tribunal stages were in fact unlawful. New evidence provided by an NGO showed that, in practice, detainees were unable to consult promptly with lawyers to adequately prepare claims and appeals in the short time allowed.[17] Applicants also had to point out the weaknesses in their cases in order to attempt to secure adjournments. The courts held that, based upon these qualitative factors, the system was inconsistent with basic fairness. The risk and gravity of error were obvious given that, in asylum cases, credibility of the applicant is usually in issue and that gathering evidence is complex. Between 7% and 18% of asylum claims (up to 4,000 cases a year) had been put through these procedures and so tens of thousands of applicants may have been affected before the system was declared unlawful.[18] The judicial correction was more readily possible in a changed political environment. The fast-track procedures had achieved their political goals long before they were declared unfair.

After managing the asylum crisis, by 2005 the Labour government was already facing new criticism about rising economic migration. The White Paper[19] that year proposed a new points-based grouping visas into 'Tiers' (for workers, students etc) and requiring migrants to show certain levels of skill or qualification to earn points.[20] This created a system of detailed mandatory requirements that moved away from the old system of administrative judgement. This in turn lessened the need for a merits-based appeal system because differences of view between officials and judges were less likely. As a consequence, the Tribunal's jurisdiction to allow appeals against points-based refusals was excluded entirely for entry clearance cases and for most leave to remain cases (those where new evidence was filed with the Tribunal).[21] This was an attempt to move immigration decisions towards System 1, as matters of routine administration, not requiring a System 2 rooted in deliberative justice. The lack of discretion meant that the risk of error was reduced and there was a system of internal review to mitigate any residual risk.

These changes toward simplified immigration decision-making (as opposed to that in protection cases) philosophically paved the way for the abolition of the statutory appeals system (in 2014 by the Conservative government) for all but human rights or protection cases.[22] A failure to follow the Home Secretary's own Immigration Rules is

17 R *(on app of Detention Action) v. Secretary of State for the Home* Department [2014] EWCA Civ 1634 *and* R *(on app of Detention Action) v. Lord Chancellor* [2015] EWCA Civ 840.

18 Home Office, Immigration Statistics.

19 Home Office, 'Controlling our borders: making migration work for Britain: five year strategy for asylum and immigration' Cmd 6472, February 2005. 'The movement of people and labour into the UK remains vital to our economy and our prosperity.' Prime Minister Tony Blair from the Introduction.

20 Tier 1 allowed entry or stay without a specific job offer for more qualified migrants. Tier 2 was the general work-permit scheme. The system required an applicant to meet a number of hard-edged rules relating to both substance and evidence. Thus financial requirements were set at exact figures (not left to judges to decide on what was 'adequate') and had to be proved by exact documents filed with an application (three months bank statements). An adjunct was the reduction in the role of judges because the failure to satisfy one of these rules meant an appeal was bound to fail. The jurisdiction of the Tribunal to admit new evidence not filed with an application was also limited by statutory amendment. The Points-based system has remained ever since and has not been challenged in the courts.

21 See NIAA 2002, s85(4) as amended by s19 UK Borders Act 2007.

22 S19 Immigration Act 2014.

now subject only to internal administrative review – an *ex post facto* form of consultation. This hollowing out of the appeal rights marks a move from System 2 towards System 1.5 for the majority of immigration cases. An increased risk of uncorrected error, inherent in removing statutory appeals, was considered a justified political choice given the more objective points-based approach and the need to prevent delay and abuse. The higher courts had given some comfort to the government's approach by having already indicated (a) that refusals to extend leave for immigrants on temporary visas did not inherently engage their Article 8 ECHR rights[23] and (b) that an out-of-country appeal was an adequate remedy in such cases, so precluding the availability of judicial review proceedings in-country.[24]

Letting Fairness Back In – The Return of System 2

Since 2014, the courts have in engaged in a series of conflicts with government over the move from System 2 towards quicker, less deliberative and non-suspensive processes. In each instance, the government identified a category of migrants with characteristics justifying their allocation outside System 2 into much reduced due process systems. For the courts however, the fairness issue, when combined with cases engaging Article 8 ECHR (the risk and gravity of error) have led to a reassertion of System 2 thinking. In a further development, the categorization issue has also become more contested by the courts.

Political tension has smouldered in the UK over the deportation of foreign criminals for many years but it had peaked in 2006-7, at which time the Labour government introduced 'mandatory' deportation. The Courts later endorsed a codified system which meant that Article 8 ECHR claims would not readily prevent deportation.[25] A political step to further resolve the issue was taken in 2014 when the government introduced powers to certify this group of cases so that appeals could only be brought once the appellant had left the UK. Whilst written consultation occurred prior to final deportation orders being issued, appellants could not attend their appeal hearings. The Supreme Court landmark decision ruled in *Kiarie*[26] that, given the nature of such appeals would require live evidence from the deportee, the absence of video-links meant that it was inherently unfair to execute deportations before appeals were heard. The risk of error was substantial. Furthermore, the Article 8 ECHR claims made by the appellants based upon long-residence and family life, provided a sufficient gravity of consequences of error. The Court noted that Article 8 included procedural rights to be able to vindicate claims made under it. Thus for both common law and ECHR reasons, the Court strongly reaffirmed the importance of access to justice for this class of appellants who had been framed in quite negative terms in the prevailing political discourse.

The *Kiarie* principle was taken further in the Educational Testing Services ('ETS') scandal cases. This situation arose from a TV show in February 2014 which revealed

23 *Patel v. The Secretary of State for the Home Department* [2013] UKSC 72.
24 *Secretary of State for the Home Department v. Lim* [2007] EWCA Civ 773.
25 *Hesham Ali v. The Secretary of State for the Home Department* [2016] UKSC 60.
26 *Kiarie v. The Secretary of State for the Home Department* [2017] UKSC 42.

cheating at two centres where foreign students took English tests that were sent to the Home Office to secure further leave. The ETS company's checks concluded that 34,000 tests conducted between 2011-2014 were invalid.[27] The Home Office, after checking the processes, relied upon these third-party findings to revoke the students' visas and issue removal decisions. These decisions were often unappealable due to the loss of appeal rights. The volume of cases meant that consultation would have been very onerous. System 1 systems were deployed because the Home Office was faced with a crisis where significant abuse had indeed occurred on a large scale. Quite soon however there emerged significant disputes about the scientific validity of the testing process and thus the reliability of the group identified as dishonest was contested.

The Upper Tribunal in the main one of its rulings[28] agreed that there were serious doubts and uncertainties about the methodology used to construct the group. Thus the categorization question was seriously probed. This said, in the end, the Tribunal concluded that the general evidence of cheating and a specific finding by ETS that a person's test had been found invalid was sufficient to satisfy the initial *evidential* burden to raise an issue of fraud. The Tribunal thus did not invalidate the group construction as such. An applicant must thereafter put forward an explanation or alternative account, but the legal burden of proof remained on the Home Office throughout. They had to disprove the appellant's evidence on the balance of probabilities. A review by the National Audit Office found that of around 10,000 people who chose or managed to appeal, around 40% were successful.[29] This data is complex because sometimes students won on other issues, but it is clear that the construction of the ETS group as abusive and the use of System 1 procedures to rapidly revoke their leave was subject to a not insignificant risk of error.

Turning to the fairness question in the ETS cases, the Court of Appeal[30] relied upon the *Kiarie* principle to hold that, because the issues turned upon their credibility, these students needed to participate in their hearings whether by way of judicial review or appeal in-country. The risk of error was otherwise tangible. They should not be required to leave the UK to appeal as this would not constitute an effective remedy. The court noted that, even though they were short-staying students, the finding of cheating would mean that they could not re-enter the UK for a set period. This gravity of consequences was sufficiently severe that an in-country remedy was appropriate, even for those who had not made Article 8 claims as such.

The final example provides another illustration of the importance of fairness, particularly in cases where an immigrant has their honesty impugned as part of an effort to deal with a pattern of abuse by a group. In 2015 the Home Office[31] began to share data with the tax authorities. This revealed that some migrants ('Tier 1' cases) had given higher figures for their earnings from self-employment to the Home Office than they

27 National Audit Office, Investigation into the response to cheating in English language tests, HC 2144 Session 2017–2019 24 May 2019, Fig.1 for a time-line.

28 *SM and Qadir v. Secretary of State for the Home Department* (ETS – evidence – burden of proof) [2016] UKUT 229 (IAC).

29 *Ibid.*, 24.

30 *Ahsan v. The Secretary of State for the Home Department [2017] EWCA Civ 2009.*

31 For the background, see Review of application by Tier 1 (General) migrants refused under paragraph 322(5) of the Immigration Rules. Home Office, November 2018.

had in their tax claims. The Home Office concluded that, based upon reasonable evidence, there was a systematic pattern of such behaviour involving over one thousand cases. As a result, when these applicants applied for settlement later on, they were refused on the basis that they had either filed false information to the Home Office or were of bad character in filing false tax returns.[32] The processing was rapid and based principally upon the data alone. For many of the applicants, the only available remedy was judicial review. The Court of Appeal ruled that detailed prior consultation with the applicant was a prerequisite of fairness both at common law and because the case also engaged Article 8 ECHR.[33] The Home Office could not simply base its conclusion of dishonesty upon the discrepancies alone without putting the allegation to the applicant. Furthermore, based upon the *Kiarie* principle, the applicants were entitled to in-country appeals and/or judicial review hearings on the merits of their refusals. In short, a full System 2 process was required.

Conclusions

System 1 thinking is appropriate for many migration decisions on grounds of efficiency and consequences. As the risks of error rise and the consequences are more severe, it is important to look towards System 2. Courts have had a significant role in both scrutinizing the creation of groups but more importantly in looking at inherent fairness. The removal of most statutory appeal rights in 2014 further highlighted this role, not just in Article 8 cases, but more widely as a rule of law issue. The most recent ETS and Tier 1 scandals reveal interesting features of the interaction between the construction of groups, fairness and the gravity of consequences for migrants. In both instances, there was strong evidence of abuse which justified serious and swift action against the group. This said, the dangers of error and its serious consequences were underestimated. Reliance upon System 1 thinking was too strong once the group had been identified. For these groups at least, fairness in the administrative and judicial systems – in effect System 2 thinking – were necessary and, indeed, important in revealing the potential for error. The political context was less demanding because, unlike during asylum crises, these scandals did not have such a high political profile. The courts were more ready to scrutinize both the reasonableness of the group construction and the fairness issues.

32 R *(on the application of Khan) v. Secretary of State for the Home Department* (Dishonesty, tax return, paragraph 322(5)) [2018] UKUT 384 (IAC).

33 *Balajigari v. The Secretary of State for the Home Department* [2019] EWCA Civ 673. 'For all of those reasons, we have come to the conclusion that where the Secretary of State is minded to refuse ILR on the basis of paragraph 322 (5) on the basis of the applicant's dishonesty, or other reprehensible conduct, he is required as a matter of procedural fairness to indicate clearly to the applicant that he has that suspicion; to give the applicant an opportunity to respond, both as regards the conduct itself and as regards any other reasons relied on as regards "undesirability" and the exercise of the second-stage assessment; and then to take that response into account before drawing the conclusion that there has been such conduct' (para. 55).

Asylum

Asylum Exclusion Provisions & Terrorist Acts Involvement
The Sum of All Fears

*Marie-Laure Basilien-Gainche**

Introduction

Counter-terrorism law and refugee law see their respective fields join in Article 12(2)(c) of the Directive on standards for the qualification of third-country nationals or stateless persons as beneficiaries of international protection, for a uniform status for refugees or for persons eligible for subsidiary protection, and for the content of the protection granted, the so-called Qualification Directive (QD).[1] This provision reflects at a regional level the international provision captured in Article 1(F) of the 1951 Geneva Convention relative to the status of refugees (CSR): this Convention does not apply to any person with respect to whom there are serious reasons for considering that he has been guilty of acts contrary to the purposes and principles of the United Nations.[2] Article 12 QD (both Directive 2004/83 and Directive 2011/95) lists the grounds for exclusion from refugee status, that correspond to points (b) and (c) of Article 1F CSR. The second paragraph of Article 12 QD states that 'a third country national (TCN) or a stateless person is excluded from being a refugee where there are serious reasons for considering that': 'a) he or she has committed a crime against peace, a war crime, or a crime against humanity'; 'b) he or she has committed a serious non-political crime outside the country of refuge prior to his or her admission as a refugee [...], even if committed with an allegedly political objective'; 'c) he or she has been guilty of acts contrary to the purposes and principles of the United Nations as set out in the Preamble and Articles 1 and 2 of the Charter of the United Nations.' The third paragraph of Article 12 QD extends that exclusion to 'persons who incite or otherwise participate in the commission of the crimes or acts' mentioned in the previous paragraph.

What is the purpose of these asylum exclusion provisions that are present at both international and European level? As the Court of Justice of the European Union puts it in its decision *B. & D.*,[3] the aim 'is to maintain the credibility of the protection system provided for in accordance with the 1951 Geneva Convention' (para. 115), by 'excluding from refugee status persons who are deemed to be undeserving of the protection

---

* University Jean Moulin Lyon III, Lyon, France.

1 Council Directive 2004/83/EC of 29 April 20014 on minimum standards for the qualification and status of third country nationals or stateless persons as refugees or as persons who otherwise need international protection and the content of the protection granted, and its recast Directive 2011/115 of the European Parliament and of the Council of 13 December 2011.

2 EASO, *Exclusion: Articles 12 and 17 Qualification Directive (2011/95/EU). A Judicial Analysis*, Valletta: EASO 2016, 110 p.

3 CJEU, GC, *Bundesrepublik Deutschland v. B. & D.*, cases C-57/09 & C-101/09, 9 November 2010, EU:C:2010:661.

which that status entails and of preventing that status from enabling those who have committed certain serious crimes to escape criminal liability' (para. 104). The UN Security Council even adopted Resolution 2178 (2014) which called upon States, in conformity with international law and international refugee law (inter alia), to ensure that refugee status is not abused by perpetrators, organisers or facilitators of terrorist acts. The point can be summed up simply: 'The status of terrorist and refugee are legally incompatible and mutually exclusive'.[4]

Yet such asylum exclusion provisions are not without raising issues or causing dangers. As long as there is no general definition in international law or European law of *terrorism* or *terrorist*, domestic legislations can exploit the qualification of terrorism to fight against opposition, human rights defenders, refugees, migrants, etc. The threat is not hypothetical while the EU norms tend to assimilate refugees and terrorists. An illustration is offered by the Eurodac database of the fingerprints of asylum seekers: this database, that is actually used to register all the TCNs arriving in the hotspots and irregularly crossing the Schengen external borders, can be accessed by all police authorities under the fight against terrorism,[5] and could be employed to fight against irregular migration[6] which is considered both as the top priority in the fight against criminality[7] and as an objective of general interest.[8] That is why great attention must be paid to three different elements to ensure the due and fair application of the asylum exclusion provisions, so as to avoid discriminatory political drifts and human rights infringements: the terrorist nature of the considered acts and facts must be genuine (1); the involvement of the TCN concerned in the above-mentioned terrorist acts has to be effective (2); the aftermath of the application of the asylum exclusion provisions needs to be assessed (3).

4 Stephen Coutts, 'Terror and Exclusion in EU Asylum Law Case', *European Law Blog*, 3 March 2017, http://europeanlawblog.eu/2017/03/03/terror-and-exclusion-in-eu-asylum-law-case-c-57314-lounani-grand-chamber-31-january-2017/

5 Regulation (EU) No. 603/2013 of the European Parliament and of the Council of 26 June 2013 on the establishment of 'Eurodac' for the comparison of fingerprints for the effective application of Regulation (EU) No 604/2013 establishing the criteria and mechanisms for determining the Member State responsible for examining an application for international protection lodged in one of the Member States by a third-country national or a stateless person and on requests for the comparison with Eurodac data by Member States' law enforcement authorities and Europol for law enforcement purposes, and amending Regulation (EU) No 1077/2011 establishing a European Agency for the operational management of large-scale IT systems in the area of freedom, security and justice

6 European Commission, *Towards a reform of the Common European Asylum System*, COM(2016)197, 6 April 2016, p. 9.

7 According to the different EU policy cycles on serious and organised crime (2010-2013, 2014-2017, 2018-2021), one of the cross-border threats Europol and Member States' law enforcement authorities have to cope with is the fight against illegal immigration. This one has been identified by Europol and approved by the Council as one of the priorities that Operation Action Plans have to deal with.

8 CJEU, *Sophie Mukarubega*, case C-166/13, 5 November 2014, EU:C:2014:2336 & CJEU, *Khaled Boudjlida*, case C-249/13, 11 December 2014, EU:C:2014:2431. Marie-Laure Basilien-Gainche & Tania Racho, 'Quand le souci d'efficacité de l'éloignement l'emporte sur l'application effective des droits fondamentaux', *Lettre Actualités Droits Libertés, La Revue des droits de l'homme*, 18 November 2014, DOI: 10.4000/revdh.957.

1. The Nature of Terrorist Acts: The Seriousness of the Purposes and Threats

In order to understand what terrorist acts can be, it is useful to look at the CJEU jurisprudence. In its decision *B. & D.*,[9] the Court states that 'exclusion from refugee status on one of the grounds laid down in Article 12(2)(b) or (c) of Directive 2004/83 [...] is linked to the seriousness of the acts committed, which must be of such a degree that the person concerned cannot legitimately claim the protection attaching to refugee status under Article 2(d) of that directive' (para. 108). The 'seriousness of the acts' is detailed by the Court that describes them as 'characterised by their violence towards civilian populations' (para. 81). Yet the gravity of the crimes to which these terrorist acts correspond, and the intensity of the violence toward civilians they entail, do not only define the nature of the considered acts; they also by themselves imply such significance and severity that authorities 'cannot be required to undertake an assessment of proportionality' as far as they provoke the application of Article 12(2) (para. 109). This element is of great importance as it induces a limited intensity of the requirements the national authorities have to satisfy when excluding a TCN from the scope of international protection on these grounds. Another implication of the serious nature of the acts consists in their disqualification as political 'even if committed with a purportedly political objective': they will 'be regarded as serious non-political crimes within the meaning of point (b) of Article 12(2) of Directive 2004/83' (Para. 81). Nevertheless, the aims terrorist acts pursue are not neglected, as they are regarded as being 'contrary to the purposes and principles of the United Nations' on the ground of Article 12(2)(c) QD: this is recalled by the CJEU, which refers to Resolutions 1373 (2001) and 1377 (2001) of the UN Security Council relating to measures combating international terrorism. These two resolutions consider that not only acts of terrorism, but also financing, planning, preparing, inciting and supporting such acts are contrary to the purposes and principles of the Charter of the United Nations.

UN Security Council Resolution 2178 (2014) in point 5 enounces an even wider approach to these acts, as it encapsulates 'the recruiting, organising, transporting or equipping of individuals who travel to a State other than their States of residence or nationality for the purpose of the perpetration, planning, or preparation of, or participation in, terrorist acts or the providing or receiving of terrorist training, and the financing of their travel and activities'. A similar trend of enlarging the scope of terrorism by expanding the number of offences designated as terrorist can be noticed at EU level. Article 1 of Council Framework Decision 2002/475/JHA on combating terrorism (FDCT) introduced a common definition of terrorist acts: those are acts carried out intentionally that 'given their nature and context, may seriously damage a country or an international organisation, where committed with the aim' of 'seriously intimidating a population'; or 'unduly compelling a government or international organisation to perform or abstain from performing any act'; or 'seriously destabilising or destroying the fundamental political, constitutional, economic or social structures of a country or an international organisation'. This approach by the purposes is supplemented by three lists of terrorist offences: a first (very long) one of the terrorist offences considered as such (Article 1); a second one of offences relating to terrorist groups that encapsulates the fact of directing or participating in such an organisation (Article 2); and a third list

9 CJEU, GC, *B. & D.*, cases C-57/09 & C-101/09 (n. 3).

of offences related to terrorist activities by inciting, recruiting, training (Article 3); all being extended by Council Framework Decision 2008/919/JHA. Yet the proposal for a Directive on Combating Terrorism enlarges the definition of terrorist acts and offences, considering the additional protocol of the Council of Europe on the prevention of terrorism adopted in May 2015 as implementing some normative provisions of the UNSCR 21278 (2014), which the EU signed on 22 October 2015.[10] For instance, the proposal criminalises the financing of terrorist acts even in the absence of any link to specific terrorist acts, the training for terrorist purposes and the travelling abroad to participate in the activities of a terrorist group.

2. The Involvement of TCNs: The Effectiveness of Their Implication in Terrorist Acts

Yet questions must be raised concerning the effective involvement in the considered terrorist offences that is needed to trigger the asylum exclusion clauses. Does the fact that a TCN applying for asylum was member of an organisation listed as terrorist automatically mean that s/he must be excluded from refugee status? Does the intentional participation in the activities of a terrorist group automatically imply the application of the asylum exclusion clauses? In the *B. & D.* decision, the CJEU answers in a negative way to such interrogations, as the exclusion from international protection is 'conditional on an individual assessment of the specific facts, making it possible to determine whether there are serious reasons for considering that, in the context of his activities within that organisation, that person has committed a serious non-political crime or has been guilty of acts contrary to the purposes and principles of the United Nations' (para. 94).[11] The Court even proposes a non-exhaustive list (the expression 'inter alia' is explicit) of the elements that must be taken into account: 'the true role played by the person concerned in the perpetration of the acts in question; his position within the organisation; the extent of the knowledge he had, or was deemed to have, of its activities; any pressure to which he was exposed; or other factors likely to have influenced his conduct' (para. 97). To sum up, before considering the use of the asylum exclusion clauses, it is necessary to realise 'a full investigation into all the circumstances of each individual case' (para. 93), in order to prove that the TCN applying for international protection 'has been involved in terrorist acts with an international dimension' (para. 84). The Court asserts indeed that 'the mere fact that the person concerned was a member of such an organisation [on the list forming the Annex to Common Position 2001/931 because of its involvement in terrorist acts] cannot automatically mean that that person must be excluded from refugee status' (para. 88).

Nevertheless, the *B. & D.* decision affords Member States significant leeway, when asserting that exclusion from refugee status under Article 12(2)QS is not 'conditional upon the existence of a present danger to the host Member State', because 'the grounds for exclusion at issue were introduced with the aim of excluding from refugee status

10 COM(2015) 625 final, 2 May 2015. The consolidated text of the proposal is available on Statewatch website: http://statewatch.org/news/2016/nov/eu-council-c-t-directive-consolidated-text-14238-16.pdf.

11 CJEU, GC, *B. & D.*, cases C-57/09 & C-101/09 (n. 3).

persons who are deemed to be undeserving of the protection' (para. 104). This margin offered to national authorities appears to be quite worrying when deployed as it is in the *Lounani* case.[12] Lounani had been convicted for providing logistical support to the Moroccan Islamist Combatant Group (an organization listed as terrorist by the UN Security Council), as he had provided material resources or information and had participated actively in the organization of a network for sending volunteers to Iraq. Yet 'no finding was made that Lounani personally committed terrorist acts, or instigated such acts, or participated in their commission' (Para. 65): in other words, Lounani was not directly involved in terrorist acts. The CJEU reaffirms the impossibility of excluding automatically on the ground of a criminal conviction in line with its jurisprudence in *B. & D.*, yet considering such a conviction to be of 'particular importance' for the individual assessment that must be performed (para. 78). Moreover, according to the Court, the application of the asylum exclusion clauses established in Article 12 QD 'cannot be confined to the actual perpetrators of terrorist acts', following henceforward the opinion of Advocate General Sharpston who insists on explaining with forceful argumentation why the scope of the asylum exclusion clauses should not be limited to the offences listed in Article 1 FDCT.[13] The scope of Article 12 QD 'can also extend to those who engage in activities consisting in the recruitment, organisation, transportation or equipment of individuals who travel to a State other than their States of residence or nationality for the purpose of, inter alia, the perpetration, planning or preparation of terrorist acts' (Para. 69). If this position sounds logically and normatively founded, the expansion of the scope of the asylum exclusion clauses it implies is all the more disturbing since it refers to the Security Council resolutions: first the qualification of MICG as a terrorist group, and second the interpretation of the asylum exclusion clauses (para. 66). Hitherto the content of the Security Council resolutions has been highly political and harshly controlled, meanwhile it deploys 'an aggressively preventative approach towards the suppression of terrorist activity through the disruption of the peripheral acts involved in the organisation and funding of terrorism'.[14] Some concerns appear hence, relative to such an apprehension that opens the way to creating the perverse precognition system Philip K. Dick describes in *Minority Report.*[15]

3. The Aftermath of the Asylum Exclusion: The Point of No Return?

Two different situations can be examined. The first one concerns the case of a TCN who has lodged an asylum application, and who is regarded as a danger to the security of the host Member State or has been convicted by a final judgment for a particularly serious offence which is assessed to constitute a serious threat to the host community. The national authorities are assumed then to reject the asylum application, according to Article 13 QD which demands respect for the requirements established in Chapter III (so in Article 12). The second situation deals with the case of a TCN who has already

12 CJEU, GC, *Lounani*, case C-573/14, 31 January 2017, EU:C:2016:380.

13 Opinion of Advocate General Sharpston delivered on 31 May 2016, EU:C:2016:380, para. 45-58.

14 Coutts 2017.

15 On the numerous questions this decision raises, see Steve Peers, 'Foreign fighters' helpers excluded from refugee status: the ECJ clarifies the law', *EU Law Analysis*, 31 January 2017, http://eulawanalysis.blogspot.com/2017/01/foreign-fighters-helpers-excluded-from.html.

obtained an international protection status and who is considered to be or to have been involved in alleged terrorist acts. The national authorities are supposed to revoke the granted status: either the refugee status – Article 14 QD – or the subsidiary protection – Article 17(3) QD. There is an issue at stake here. Are the Member States compelled to refuse or revoke the protection? In other words, it must be asked whether there is a duty or an option to not protect, whether there is a possibility for the national authorities to offer the considered TCN more favourable treatment. The wording of Article 14 QD makes a distinction: the revocation of the international protection is mandatory if the considered TCN 'should have been or is excluded from being a refugee in accordance with Article 12' (Article 14(3) QD); the revocation is only discretionary 'when: a) there are reasonable grounds for regarding him or her as a danger to the security of the Member State; b) having been convicted by a final judgment of a particularly serious crime, constitutes a danger to the community of that Member State' (Article 14(4) QD). If Member States are used to being offered by EU law the possibility to introduce or retain more beneficial standards, the reservation enounced in Article 13 QD precludes them from having in their domestic legal order provisions that grant refugee status to persons who are excluded from that status pursuant to Article 12. As the CJEU states in its *B. & D.* decision, national authorities may grant protection in application of their national law (for discretionary considerations or for humanitarian reasons) to such a TCN who falls under this EU asylum exclusion clause, 'provided that that other kind of protection does not entail a risk of confusion with refugee status within the meaning of the directive' (Para. 121). However, it is difficult to imagine the cases in which this national protection would neither fall within the scope of that Directive nor infringe the system established by this very norm (para. 120).

Nevertheless, even if a TCN's international protection application or status is rejected or revoked because of the application of the asylum exclusion clauses, some provisions still apply that prevent national authorities from returning her/him to a country where s/he would face a real risk of torture or other inhuman or degrading treatment. The UN Security Council adopted Resolution 1624 (2005), which reaffirms that it is imperative to combat terrorism in all its forms, and stresses that States must ensure that any measures taken to combat terrorism comply with all their obligations under international law; such measures should be adopted in compliance with, *inter alia*, refugee law and humanitarian law. Some international and regional human rights protection obligations hence remain that require national authorities to guarantee the principle of *non-refoulement.* Particularly relevant are Article 3 of the European Convention on Human Rights (ECHR)[16] and Article 4 of the EU Charter of Fundamental Rights (EUCFR) that enshrine the prohibition of torture, inhuman or degrading treatment or punishment, as well as Article 19 EUCFR that explicitly proclaims the principle of *non-refoulement.* Yet these provisions, whose scope is wider than the one provided by Articles 32 and 33 CSR, induce the absolute and non-derogable nature of the principle, so much

16 ECtHR, *Soering v. United Kingdom*, application No 14038/88, 7 July 1989, para. 85 seq.; *Cruz Varas v. Sweden*, application No 15576/89, 20 March 1991, para. 69 seq.; *Vilvarajah v. United Kingdom*, application No 13163/87, 30 October 1991, para. 107 seq.

so that no exemption is allowed even on the ground of the personal behaviour (including direct involvement in terrorist acts) of the considered TCN.[17] Pursuant to Article 21(2) QD nonetheless, the obligation of *non-refoulement* that national authorities have to respect can be waived when 'there are reasonable grounds for considering the TCN in question to be a danger to the security' of the host Member State, or when s/he has been 'convicted by a final judgment of a particularly serious crime' and thus 'constitutes a danger to the community of that Member State'. Therefore, even though the CJEU considers that 'the act of excluding a person from refugee status pursuant to Article 12(2) does not necessarily imply the adoption of a position on the separate question of whether that person can ultimately be removed to his/her country of origin',[18] the similarity of the wording in Articles 12 and 21 QD seems to imply a quasi-mechanical possibility for the national authorities to adopt removal orders against the TCN excluded from the international protection scope.

Conclusion

The examination of the manner in which counter-terrorism law and refugee law meet in EU law via Article 12 QD underscores some trends that reveal how perilous the criminal law and asylum law conjunction is from a human rights protection perspective. The potential indefinite extension of the definition of terrorist acts, the uncertain limitation of the direct involvement in international terrorist acts, the ambiguous implications of the obligation of *non-refoulement*, all these both political and normative dynamics, proclaim the primacy of an alleged security perspective that involves the embrittlement of the guarantees of fundamental rights, even of those enshrined as absolute and non-derogable.

17 ECtHR, *Chahal v. United Kingdom*, Application No. 22414/93, 15 November 1996, para. 79 seq.; *Ahmed v. Austria*, Application No. 25694/96, 17 December 1996, para. 40 seq.; *H.L.R. v. France*, Application No. 24573/94, 29 April 1997, para. 35; *Saadi v. Italy*, Application No. 37201/06, 28 February 2008, para. 127; *Sufi & Elmi v. United Kingdom*, Application No. 8319/07, 28 June 2011, para. 212.

18 CJEU, GC, *B. & D.*, cases C-57/09 & C-101/09, para. 110.

Hungary, In Front of Her Judges

Boldizsár Nagy[*]

Invocation

Few persons (if any) are more interested in justice than Elspeth Guild. Refugees, citizens, societal security, fairness of social services, borders, illiberal governance and the many ailings of the EU are all in the limelight of her inexhaustible attention.

Our dialogue over the last, almost four decades, has touched upon all of them (and hopefully will extend for many more years to come). The optimism of the early nineties may be more coloured by now, but the determination to resist and fight back when our shared values are under attack has not dwindled an inch.

And fight we must.

So it may be justified to confront the threatening phenomena, even though writing about the Refugee Law Reader or the commentary to the Global Compact on Safe and Orderly Migration and other projects I had the privilege to share with her, would be more rewarding. But justice comes first (not America, Britain or Hungary)!

This brief contribution will look into the question of how the two courts of Europe and other major players have reacted to the gradual dismantling of a functioning refugee regime and the poisonous discourse accompanying it and to the threats against those assisting asylum seekers. So „justice' is understood both in a legal and a moral sense, as the goal of righting wrongs, as offering legal and moral remedy. Space limitations require that judgments of national courts affecting Hungary (like transfer decisions in Dublin cases) will be left beyond the scope of this study.

The Strasbourg Mirror

The European Court of Human Rights (ECtHR) has decided six cases of asylum seekers' human rights complaints against Hungary, all after 2010 when the Fidesz – Christian Democratic People's Party alliance – came to power. In *Lokpo and Touré v. Hungary,*[1] *the applicants claimed* that their five months long detention (still under the previous government[2]) violated Article 5 (1)[3] of the European Convention on Human Rights (ECHR).[4] The subsequent cases also related to the detention of asylum seekers. These

* Central European University, Budapest, Hungary.. See www.nagyboldizsar.hu.

1 Application no. 10816/10, judgment of 20 September 2011.

2 The reason for including the case is that the it was already the Orbán government that was notified of the case on 25 August 2010. It could have settled, but instead 'adopted' the behaviour of the preceding government.

3 The applicants also claimed breaches of Articles 5 (4) and 13, but the Court did not rule on those.

4 Convention for the Protection of Human Rights and Fundamental Freedoms Rome, 4 November 1950.

were: *the Al-Tayyar Abdelhakim* case,[5] the *Said* case,[6] the *Nabil* case,[7] the *O.M.*[8] case and finally the *Ilias and Ahmed* case.[9] *Ilias and Ahmed* – unlike the other cases – was not limited to a breach of Article 5 (1) of the ECHR, but also entailed a claim based on Article 3 concerning the treatment by the Hungarian authorities in the transit zones at the Hungarian-Serbian border and the threat of ill-treatment if returned to Serbia. Whereas in the first three cases the Court established the violation by a majority votes, all the judgments since 2015 were unanimous.

There is another set of thirteen cases, not available in HUDOC yet, which involve the starving of 21 individuals. In all these cases the Court granted interim measures in 2018 and 2019, ordering the restoration of food provision to rejected asylum seekers, who are nevertheless detained in the transit zone after an expulsion order that for practical reasons cannot be implemented.[10]

The detention cases were responding to three distinct types of detention. The first four revolved around the then applicable rules on detention of Act no. II of 2007 on the Admission and Right of Residence of Third Country Nationals (Third Country Nationals Act /TCNA/) read in conjunction with Act no. LXXX of 2007 on Asylum (Asylum Act). In *Lokpo and Touré*, *Abdelhakim*, *Said and Said* the asylum seekers were held in aliens law detention with a view to deportation and were not transferred to open reception centres, even when the asylum case entered the in-merit phase after admissibility was established. That was seen by the applicants as a breach of section 55 of the Asylum Act:

> 'If the refugee authority proceeds to the substantive examination of the application and the applicant is detained by order of the immigration authority, the immigration authority shall release the applicant at the initiative of the refugee authority.'

The refugee authority systematically refrained from initiating their release, therefore the applicants were held continuously even during the substantive examination of their case. The ECtHR did not decide whether the refugee authority was under an obligation to initiate the transfer (as claimed in each case by the applicant) or simply had the discretionary right to do so (as stated by the government.)

The Court's line of argument was elaborated in *Lokpo and Touré* and taken over – in the form of long quotes – in *Abdelhakim* and *Said and Said.* The key observation is that 'lawfulness' and 'a procedure prescribed by law' cannot be limited to the adopted rules of the state. The Court assumes that the ECHR includes express or implied general principles and requires a certain quality of the national law, which must be 'compatible with the rule of law' (*Lokpo and Touré*, § 18) and has to follow the purpose of Article 5 of the Convention that no person be deprived from their liberty in an arbitrary

5 Application no. 13058/11, judgment of 23 October 2012.
6 *Hendrin Ali Said and Aras Ali Said v. Hungary*, application no 13457/11.
7 *Nabil and others v. Hungary*, application no. 62116/12, judgment of 22 September 2015.
8 Application no. 9912/15, judgment of 5 July 2016.
9 Application no. 47287/15, Chamber judgment of 14 march 2017, Grand Chamber judgment pending at the time of writing the manuscript.
10 For more detail see: Hungarian Helsinki Committee, *Hungary Continues to Starve Detainees in the Transit Zones Information update by the Hungarian Helsinki Committee* 23 April 2019, Budapest: HHC 2019, https://www.helsinki.hu/wp-content/uploads/Starvation-2019.pdf, accessed on 15 June 2019.

fashion (§ 21). The detention is arbitrary if it is not executed in good faith, is not closely connected to the purpose of preventing unauthorised entry or if the place and conditions of detention are not appropriate and, lastly when the length of the detention exceeds that reasonably required for the purpose pursued (§ 22). A motive that ought to pervade any decision on asylum seekers is introduced in para 22: asylum seekers have not 'committed criminal offences but [are] aliens who, often fearing for their lives, have fled from their own country'.

The breach of Article 5 (1) f was established partly by the fact that the five months long detention was not proportionate to the aim pursued (§ 23), partly by the fact that detaining persons simply because the refugee authority failed to initiate their freeing 'verges on arbitrariness' and the lack of an 'elaborate reasoning' of the detention decision deprived it from lawfulness (§ 25). In all the three cases the Court refrained from examining the appropriateness of the judicial remedy required by Article 5 (4).

The balance so far: the ECtHR found in three subsequent cases that the detention of asylum seekers as practiced in Hungary in around 2010 was not compatible with the rule of law, verged on arbitrariness and was unlawful because of the lack of elaborate justification of the detention.

In *Nabil* the argument differed slightly as the rule on freeing the detained asylum seeker was removed from the Asylum Act, but the Third Country Nationals Act still required that detention be terminated when 'it becomes evident that the expulsion or transfer cannot be executed' (Section 54 (6) b).

Decided in the fall of 2015, *Nabil* showed more sympathy towards a state subject to large scale of arrivals. The Court accepted, that a detention may be with a view to deportation even if there is a pending asylum case (§ 38), repeated the *Saadi* doctrine,[11] according to which

> '[... U]ntil a State has 'authorised' entry to the country, any entry is 'unauthorised' and the detention of a person who wishes to effect entry and who needs but does not yet have authorisation to do so can be, without any distortion of language, to 'prevent his effecting an unauthorised entry' (Nabil, § 27 quoting Saadi, § 65).

It refrained from addressing the odd argument of the Hungarian Government, according to which there are two meanings of the term 'safe third country', one for asylum cases and a more restricted one for the 'immigration perspective" trying to argue that from the immigration perspective Serbia was safe (§ 25).

The question of *Nabil* was when detention is justified under the second limb of Article 5 (1) f. The Court stressed that detention is lawful only if deportation or extradition proceedings are in progress and are conducted with due diligence and there is true prospect of executing the deportation. A further requirement is that there be no national rule that prohibited deportation pending a decision on asylum (§§ 29, 38 and 35). The Court based the finding of breach on the new consideration that the domestic courts ought to have investigated – as prescribed by the TCNA – whether there was an actual risk of absconding, whether alternatives to detention were available and lastly whether the expulsion eventually could be enforced (§ 41).

11 *Saadi v. the United Kingdom* [GC], application no. 13229/03, judgment of 28 January 2008.

Nabil confronted Hungary with the rigidity of its practice that systematically refrained from looking for alternatives to detention even though that was required by Section 54 (2) of the TCNA.

The second type of case is *O.M.,* with a new legal institution in the centre: the asylum detention as introduced by Section 31/A of the Asylum Act in 2013. By implication the case could also have been a test of the recast Reception Conditions Directive,[12] as by 2014 the relevant rules on detention were transposed. The Court evaded the challenge to assess the compatibility of the Reception Conditions Directive rules on detention with the taxative list in Article 5 (1) of the ECHR. Instead, it only examined the nature of the obligation under Article 5 (1) b justifying detention.[13] The Government's argument implied in essence that all the grounds of detention, as formulated in the Reception Conditions Directive and transposed into Section 31/A of the Asylum Act, constituted such obligations.

The Court refused that implicitly and explicitly. The implicit rejection took the form of recalling the eight general principles guiding the interpretation of Article 5 (1) b.[14] As the conditions permitting asylum detention in Hungary went beyond them, they had to fail. In the explicit refusal of the Government's defence the Court remarked that the applicant 'made reasonable efforts to clarify his identity and nationality: there is no indication that he did not fully cooperate with the authorities'. As Hungarian law did not expressly require documentary evidence of identity and nationality no obligation justifying detention was identified, especially, as the Court also noted the lack of any effort to find alternatives to detention or to assess the case 'in a sufficiently individualized manner' (§§ 51-2).

In the context of detention, *O.M.* pointed out that the systematic detention of asylum seekers as an administrative measure under the Asylum Act is untenable. The practice contradicted the strict principles defining the conditions in which Article 5 (1) b could serve as the basis of detention. The Court did not recognise that the EU or Hungary would be entitled to expand permissible grounds for detention (which they, in fact, did). The judgment revealed the bad faith of the system when requiring an identity document not available to the asylum seeker, and presuming the risk of absconding without even trying to apply alternatives to detention. It also revealed the reification of the asylum seeker by not providing sufficiently individualised assessment of the risk of flight.

---

12 Directive 2013/33/EU of the European Parliament and of the Council of 26 June 2013 laying down standards for the reception of applicants for international protection (OJ L 180, 29.6.2013, p. 96-116).

13 'The lawful arrest or detention of a person for non-compliance with the lawful order of a court or in order to secure the fulfilment of any obligation prescribed by law.'

14 The eight principles based on O.M. §§ 42-3:
- there must be an unfulfilled obligation incumbent on the person concerned,
- the arrest and detention must be for the purpose of securing its fulfilment,
- detention must not be punitive in character,
- as soon as the relevant obligation has been fulfilled, detention must end,
- the enforced obligation must be interpreted narrowly,
- the detention must be truly necessary for the purpose of ensuring its fulfilment,
- no milder means are available and applicable,
- a balance must be struck between the importance in a democratic society of securing the immediate fulfilment of the obligation in question and the importance of the right to liberty.

The only example of the third type of cases is *Ilias and Ahmed*, in which a Grand Chamber judgment has not yet been adopted, albeit the hearing was held more than a year ago. The case scrutinised yet another form of detention, that occurring in the transit zones established by Hungary at the Hungarian-Serbian border in 2015.[15] First, the Court refuted the Government's claim that confinement in the transit zone is not detention (and therefore Article 5 (1) ECHR does not apply), as the detained people were free to leave the zone towards Serbia. The Court found that since leaving the zone could only occur if asylum claims were abandoned and since Serbia never consented to their irregular entry into its territory, 'confinement to the transit zone amounted to a *de facto* deprivation of liberty' (§ 56). In the standard examination of lawfulness of the measure, the Court listed not only the national rules but, referring to the Asylum Procedures Directive, also noted that EU law demands that no asylum seeker be detained for the sole reason that he or she is an asylum applicant (§ 64). As the border procedure according to Section 71/A of the Asylum Act is based on the legal fiction that the procedure in the transit zone is conducted before admission, the right to stay in the territory of Hungary otherwise guaranteed by Section 5 (1) a of the Asylum Act is denied. People are detained in the transit zone without a formal decision on the detention and without separate legal remedy addressing the detention.

According to the judgment, the 23 day detention took place 'without any formal decision of the authorities and solely by virtue of an elastically interpreted general provision of the law .... no special grounds for detention in the transit zone were provided for in Article 71/A.' (§ 68). That made the confinement of the asylum seekers arbitrary and a breach of Article 5 (1) f (§ 69).

It is a systemic failure of Hungarian asylum law, one can add, as the rules are applicable to everyone in the transit zone. In fact, further curtailment of asylum seekers' rights occurred since the judgment: by 2019 anyone who is in an irregular situation and apprehended by the authorities anywhere in Hungary is by force taken to the Serbian side of the fence, with a view to approach the transit zone from there, in which a full procedure (not only a border procedure) is conducted and the asylum seeker is detained until the end of it including the court appeal phase.[16]

Ilias and Ahmed went beyond the earlier ECtHR judgments as it established a violation of Article 5 (4) as 'the applicants did not have at their disposal any 'proceedings

15 For a most detailed account of the legal developments in Hungary see: Boldizsar Nagy, 'From Reluctance to Total Denial. Asylum Policy in Hungary 2015-2018', in: Vladislava Stoyanova & Eleni Karageorgiou (eds), *The New Asylum and Transit Countries in Europe During and in the Aftermath of the 2015/2016 Crisis*, Leiden: Brill 2019, p. 17-65, and for an earlier account offering more detail of the same author: 'Hungarian Asylum Law and Policy in 2015-2016. Securitization Instead of Loyal Cooperation', 17(6) *German Law Journal* 2016, p. 1032-1081. The same story told by an outside observer in great detail: Ashley Binetti Armstrong, 'Chutes and Ladders: Non-refoulement and the Sisyphean Challenge of Seeking Asylum in Hungary', 50 *Columbia Human Rights Law Review* 2019, p. 46; for a very well documented review of the situation see: Daniel Gyollai, *Global Migration: Consequences and Responses,* RESPOND Working Paper 2018/05; Hungary Country Report: Legal & Policy Framework of Migration Governance, May 2018, Uppsala: Uppsala Universitet 2018, http://www.crs.uu.se/respond/working-paper-series/ (accessed: 15 June 2019).

16 When this regime was introduced in 2017 UNHCR made a statement in which it stressed 'that physical barriers and restrictive policies have resulted in effectively denying access to territory and asylum'. UNHCR, *UNHCR urges suspension of transfers of asylum-seekers to Hungary under EU Dublin regulation*, Geneva: UNHCR, 10 April 2017, https://www.unhcr.org/news/press/2017/4/58eb7e454/ unhcr-urges-suspension-transfers-asylum-seekers-hungary-under-dublin.html (accessed 15 June 2019).

by which the lawfulness of [their] detention [could have been] decided speedily by a court' ' (§ 76). The applicants' claim that the treatment in the transit zone amounted to a breach of Article 3 ECHR was rejected, but the ECtHR accepted that they 'did not have the benefit of effective guarantees which would have protected them from exposure to a real risk of being subjected to inhuman or degrading treatment in breach of Article 3 of the Convention' after expulsion to Serbia or further down their route of arrival.

The present system which is a generalised version, without time limits, of the border procedure declared illegal in *Ilias and Ahmed* will be tested in a case communicated to the Government on 30 August 2017 that concerns the confinement, in conditions which are allegedly inhuman, of an unaccompanied Afghan national minor to the Röszke transit zone and revolves around three questions:

- is the treatment in the transit zone contrary to Article 3,
- does the deprivation of liberty in the transit zone breach Article 5 (1),
- is there an effective procedure and remedy to challenge the detention and complaint against the treatment?[17]

The Strasbourg mirror painted a gloomy image of the Hungarian situation in the early 2010s in two Austrian cases, dealing with transfers to Hungary under the Dublin II regulation.[18] None of the judgments established that the concrete person ran the real and individual risk of ill treatment reaching the threshold of Article 3 in Hungary, nor that a possible return to Serbia would entail that, but especially *Mohammed v Austria* was critical:

> 'The Court notes the seemingly general practice of detaining asylum-seekers for a considerable time and partly under conditions that fell short of international and EU standards, which, in conjunction with the repeatedly reported deficiencies in review proceedings for administrative detention, depicted a situation raising serious concern. Note is further taken of the reports of abuse of detained asylum-seekers by officials and of forced medication.' (§ 103)

Two more cases against Austria[19], started in 2015, implicated the Hungarian conditions and the transfer under Dublin III regulation[20] but were concluded with an order as Austria quashed decisions on transferring the applicants to Hungary. That move may have been inspired by the invited intervention of the Council of Europe Commissioner

17 *I.A. v. Hungary*, application no. 38297/17.

18 *Mohammed v. Austria*, application no. 2283/12, judgment of 6 June 2013, and *Mohammadi v. Austria*, application No. 71932/12, judgment of 3 July 2014. Council Regulation (EC) No. 343/2003 of 18 February 2003 establishing the criteria and mechanisms for determining the Member State responsible for examining an asylum application lodged in one of the Member States by a third-country national, OJ 2003 L 50/1.

19 Applications No. 44825/15 and No. 44944/15, *S.O. v. Austria* and *A.A. v. Austria.*

20 Regulation (EU) No 604/2013 of the European Parliament and of the Council of 26 June 2013 establishing the criteria and mechanisms for determining the Member State responsible for examining an application for international protection lodged in one of the Member States by a third-country national or a stateless person (recast) (OJ 2013 L 180/96).

for Human Rights. As a third party[21] he gave a detailed account of the critical elements of the substantive law, of the procedure and of the detention regime, warned against the threat of chain *refoulement* as a consequence of returning persons to Serbia without examining their cases, even if transferred to Hungary under the Dublin regime and concluded that the authorities intention is to 'deter asylum seekers from entering the country and applying for asylum'.[22]

Much could be added on the role of other third party interveners in highlighting those elements of the Hungarian legal system that are incompatible with international standards, (UNHCR, Aire Centre, International Commission of Jurists), on the repeated calls of the Court not to treat asylum seekers as criminals and consider their individual circumstances, especially in cases of vulnerability and for offering substantive arguments, whether in detention cases or when qualifying another country as safe third, but space limitations require us to turn to other judges of Hungary: the CJEU.

The Court of Justice of the European Union: An Effort to Socialise the Antisocial

Hungarian courts were instrumental in clarifying important aspects of EU law by way of preliminary questions[23] – but they are not the subject of this study beyond noting that *F.* and *Shajin Ahmed* reflected the rigidity and alienation of the system. In the first case the authority wished to establish the credibility of the applicant with the help of a forensic psychologist's expert opinion based on projective personality tests, what – according to the CJEU – entailed an unjustified interference into private life. In the second case the 'severity' of a crime in the exclusion procedure was determined simply by a reference to the sole criterion of the penalty provided for it, which again was found

21 Council of Europe, Commissioner for Human Rights, Third Party Intervention by the Council of Europe Commissioner for Human Rights under Article 36 of the European Convention on Human Rights Applications No. 44825/15 and No. 44944/15, *S.O. v. Austria* and *A.A. v. Austria* 5-7 (Council of Europe, 17 December 2015).

22 *Ibid.*, p. 10

23 *Bolbol* (CJEU C-31/09, judgment of 17 June 2010) and *El Kott a.o.* (CJEU C-364/11, judgment of 19 Dec. 2012) contributed greatly to the interpretation of the Qualification Directive exclusion clause in Article 12 para 1 a, in case of Palestine applicants, *F.* (CJEU C-473/16, judgment of 25 Jan. 2018) on the available tools to examine sexual orientation, *Shajin Ahmed* (CJEU C-369/17, judgment of 13 Sep. 2018) clarified the meaning of 'serious crime' in Article 17 para 1 (b) in exclusion from subsidiary protection status, *L.H,* (Case C-564/18, pending in June 2019) will address whether states may add inadmissibility grounds to those listed in the Procedures Directive (in this case a watered down safe third country concept) and whether an eight day limit for the court to decide in the review procedure is compatible with the requirement of fair procedure and effective remedy. The *Alekszij Torubarov* (Case C-556/17 – pending) is asking if – based on Article 46(3) of the Procedures Directive in conjunction with Article 47 of the Charter of Fundamental Rights – the Hungarian courts have the power to amend administrative decisions of the competent asylum authority refusing international protection and also to grant such protection, notwithstanding that the law only gives them the right of annulment of the administrative decision. *PG* (Case C-406/18 – also pending) asks whether fair procedure and effective remedy are compatible with the Hungarian rule, according to which courts cannot amend decisions given in asylum procedures but may only annul them and order that a new procedure be conducted and with the single mandatory time limit of 60 days in total for judicial proceedings in asylum matters, irrespective of any individual circumstances and without regard to the particular features of the case.

to be incompatible with the requirement to assess the specific facts of each individual case and weigh them in the light of the nature of the act, its consequences, the practice of other states sentencing a similar act and other criteria.

Turning to the broader picture one may state that Hungary undermines the EU asylum system in two different ways: it rejects solidarity and the sharing of responsibility in providing protection and adopts rules and practice contradicting to the EU asylum acquis.[24]

Solidarity was not only rejected at the political level[25] and by the total refusal to participate in the relocation of asylum seekers from Greece and Italy in and after 2015 as well as in any form of resettlement, but also took the form of – just like Slovakia – seeking annulment of Council Decision (EU) 2015/1601 of 22 September 2015[26] which established provisional measures in the area of international protection for the benefit of Italy and Greece.[27] The court refused more than a dozen arguments by Hungary and Slovakia. It denied that the decision was (or had to be) a legislative act amending the Dublin Regulation, it saw no violation of the procedural rules governing a decision under Article 78 (3) TFEU and, finally found no basis to the material law claims related to proportionality, legal certainty, normative clarity and compatibility with the Geneva Convention relating to the Status of Refugees.[28]

From the point of view of solidarity para 293 of the judgment may be the most important, recalling that it was Hungary that opted against being a beneficiary of relocation – together with Greece and Italy – and in so

> 'the Council cannot be criticised, from the point of view of the principle of proportionality, for having concluded on the basis of the principle of solidarity and fair sharing of responsibility laid down in Article 80 TFEU that Hungary had to be allocated relocation quotas in the same way as all the other Member States that were not beneficiaries of the relocation mechanism.'[29]

The Commission did not wait until the judgment came out and started infringement procedures against the Czech Republic, Hungary and Poland for refusal to relocate.[30] As the three states did not act even after the judgment confirming the validity of the

---

24 For an elaboration of these ideas see: Boldizsár Nagy, 'Renegade in the club. Hungary's resistance to EU efforts in the asylum field', *Osteuroparecht, Fragen zur Rechtsentwicklung in Mittel- und Osteuropa sowie den GUS-Staaten*, 63. Jahrgang, Heft 4|2017 'Rechtsdurchsetzung durch die EU', p. 413-427.

25 The Hungarian Parliament adopted an Act on 17 November 2015, the preambular paragraphs of which reflect the tenor of the resistance: 'condemning the failed immigration policy of Brussels; rejecting the compulsory settling-in quota as the quota is senseless and dangerous, it would increase crime, spread terror and it endangers our culture; finding that no sovereign state may be forced to take over and examine applications for international protection submitted in another member State' and the operative part invites the government to initiate the annulment procedure in front of the CJEU. Act No CLXXV of 2015.

26 OJ 2015 L 248, p. 80.

27 Case C-643/15, *Slovak Republic v. Council of the European Union*, Case C-647/15, *Hungary v. Council of the European Union*, 2016 E.C.R 43.

28 Judgment of 6. 9. 2017 – joined cases C-643/15 and C-647/15, *Slovakia and Hungary v. Council of the European Union.*

29 Hungary was expected to take in 1294 of the 120 000 persons to be relocated in the course of two years.

30 IP/17/1607 Relocation: Commission launches infringement procedures against the Czech Republic, Hungary and Poland Brussels, 14 June 2017

relocation decision, the case was referred to the CJEU on 22 December 2017, where at it is still pending in June 2019.[31] The Commission is seeking a declaratory judgment confirming that Hungary had failed to fulfil its relocation obligations.

The second way of undermining the system includes laws and practices that are incompatible with the norms and the principles of the EU *acquis*. The number of problems identified in several infringement procedures against Hungary reflect their scope, especially as the Commission is known to use infringement procedures as a last resort.[32]

In 2013 an infringement procedure started[33] finding non-compliance with the Asylum Procedures Directive, the Reception Conditions Directive and Article 47 of the Charter. Its precise content was not made public and it did not make it to the court.

The construction of the fence and the drastic tightening of the applicants' procedural rights led to another infringement procedure[34] the scope of which was extended after the 2017 March changes that practically ended all regular asylum procedures. The press release reflecting the points of sustained disagreement lists the following:

- asylum applications can only be submitted within the transit zones
- only a limited number of persons are granted access to the two zones after excessively long waiting periods
- the border procedure implemented by Hungary is longer than the 4 weeks accepted as the maximum length of border procedures
- no special guarantees for vulnerable applicants exist,.
- effective access to asylum procedures is denied as irregular migrants are escorted back across the border, even if they wish to apply for asylum.
- indefinite detention of asylum seekers in transit zones without respecting the applicable procedural guarantees.[35]

A long dormant procedure concerning the transposition of the Qualification Directive[36] was revived in January 2019, when the Commission sent reasoned opinion on shortcomings of implementation (without adding details). On the same day it announced its reasoned opinion challenging the 2018 amendments[37] criminalisation of support to asylum applicants and the introduction of an additional non-admissibility ground for asylum applications not provided for by EU law, which essentially excludes anyone who has arrived to Hungary, from a country, where 'the appropriate level of protection' is secured (Asylum Act, 51§ (2) f).

31 C-718/17 *Commission v. Hungary*. Hearing was held on 15 May 2019

32 Olivier De Schutter, *Infringement proceedings as a tool for the enforcement of fundamental rights in the European Union Open Society*, Brussels: European Policy Institute 2017, p. 46-47.

33 2013/4062, dates 17 October 2013. No press release appeared and info on the content of the exchanges were denied to the Hungarian Helsinki Committee. (Ref. Ares(2014)521571 – 27/02/2014) The procedure was closed in November 2018 (http://ec.europa.eu/atwork/applying-eu-law/infringements-proceedings/infringement_decisions/index.cfm?lang_code=EN&typeOfSearch=true& active_only=0&noncom=2&r_dossier=&decision_date_from=01%2F05%2F2012&decision_date_to=20%2F06%2F2019&EM=HU&DG=HOME&DG=JLSE&title=&submit=Search (accessed 1 June 2019).

34 2015/2201, announced in IP/15/6228.

35 IP/18/4522 of 19 July 2018.

36 2014/0116.

37 IP/19/469 14 January 2019.

The CJEU is not engaged in a friendly dialogue with the Hungarian Government or the courts – beyond the Palestine refugee cases. In the preliminary question cases it tends to agree with the applicants and in the infringement cases with the Commission. In minor, technical issues the Commission or at least the Court is successful[38] but the in matters of solidarity or the deprivation of asylum seekers of fundamental rights no progress can be recorded.

Conclusion – The Broader Frame

The decisions of the two courts may have done justice to the victims or preserved the integrity of the relocation decision, but were incapable to stop the rapid destruction of the Hungarian asylum system. Filippo Grandi, the United Nations High Commissioner for Refugees, during his visit in Hungary in 2017 stated:

> When I was standing at the border fence today, I felt the entire system is designed to keep people, many of whom are fleeing war and persecution, out of the country and preventing many from making a legitimate asylum claim.[39]

The European Parliament's Proposal for a Council decision determining, pursuant to Article 7(1) of the Treaty on European Union, the existence of a clear risk of a serious breach by Hungary of the values on which the Union is founded[40] registers a long list of concerns related to the asylum system.[41]

Dunja Milatović, the Commissioner for Human Rights of the Council of Europe, in her 2019 May report on Hungary[42] observed that

> the notably negative stance against immigration and asylum seekers adopted by the Hungarian government since 2015 has resulted in a legislative framework which has undermined the reception and protection of asylum seekers and the integration of recognised refugees

and called upon the government to revoke the decreed 'crisis situation due to mass immigration' serving as the (il)legal basis of channelling all cases to the transit zone.[43]

The trend of liquidating the protection space in Hungary cannot be reversed by court action. The hole political system has to be changed, the rule of law and democracy restored. Pressure must come from inside as well as from outside.

Fight we must. If Elspeth is for us, who can be against us?

---

38 No longer may court secretaries proceed instead of judges, a few procedural deadlines have been extended.

39 UNHCR, *UNHCR Chief visits Hungary, calls for greater access to asylum, end to detention and more solidarity with refugees*, 12 September 2017, ttps://www.unhcr.org/news/press/2017/9/59b809d24/unhcr-chief-visits-hungary-calls-greater-access-asylum-end-detention-solidarity.html (accessed: 19 June 2019).

40 Annex to resolution P8_TA-PROV(2018)0340 (the so-called Sargentini report).

41 *Ibid.*, paras 62-72.

42 Commissioner for Human Rights of the Council of Europe Dunja Mijatović, Report Following her visit to Hungary from 4 to 8 February 2019, https://search.coe.int/commissioner/Pages/result_details.aspx?ObjectId=0900001680942f0d#_Toc6306514 (accessed: 19 June 2019).

43 *Ibid.*, point 37.

Activation versus Forced Inactivity
Government, Civil Society and the Promotion of Self-sufficiency of Asylum Seekers and Irregular Immigrants

*Ricky van Oers & Tetty Havinga**

Introduction

In 2015, the Netherlands, like many other European countries, was faced with the influx of larger numbers of refugees. 3,000 of these refugees were accommodated at Heumensoord, a temporary (October 2015-May 2016) reception centre consisting of tents in the woods near the campus of the Radboud University (RU) situated in Nijmegen, where they waited for their asylum procedures to commence. Almost immediately, more than 1,000 Nijmegen citizens volunteered to act as buddies for the asylum seekers. They received a letter from the Central Agency for the Reception of Asylum Seekers (COA), the government agency responsible for the reception of asylum seekers thanking them for their readiness and asking them to be patient. The 'working group for refugees', consisting of several University staff members, provided training for the volunteers to give language lessons to the people of Heumensoord and started a crowd funding campaign to buy books which could be used by the refugees to learn the Dutch language. The COA however did not allow the books to be distributed at Heumensoord. In doing so, the agency apparently followed the direction set out by the secretary of state for Security and Justice in a letter of 27 October 2015. In the letter, the secretary stated that it would be undesirable to offer language lessons to asylum seekers directly after arrival in the Netherlands, as this might 'create expectations' and the government should prevent the sending of contradictory signals.[1]

The activities of Radboud University's working group triggered Elspeth Guild to ask Ricky van Oers, the working group's secretary, to write an article about the group's experience of civil society engagement with asylum seekers for the European Journal of Migration and Law. The present contribution is a late acceptance of Guild's request.

As is demonstrated by the example given above, different actors involved in the integration of immigrants into the host society have different ideas on who is allowed to integrate and when the integration process should start. This contribution asks how different actors in the Netherlands approach the issue of immigrant integration, which is to be understood here as the promotion of self-sufficiency of immigrants in the host

* Ricky van Oers and Tetty Havinga, Radboud University, Nijmegen, the Netherlands. The authors thank Rian Ederveen and Marieke Aarts for their useful comments and suggestions.

1 *Kamerstukken II* 2015-2016, 19637, nr. 2073. After the publication by members of the working group of an op-ed in a national newspaper (Fernhout et al. 2015), the COA allowed the lessons to be given and the books to be distributed.

society.[2] More specifically, the article analyses to what extent the different actors aim at activating immigrants. We look at actors operating at three different levels: 1) central government, 2) the municipalities and 3) civil society, and two different groups of immigrants: 1) asylum seekers (either waiting for their procedure to start (the refugees of Heumensoord) as well as those who are 'in procedure') and 2) irregular immigrants (focusing on rejected asylum seekers).[3] We focus in particular on possibilities for employment, volunteer work and learning the Dutch language. By comparing the approaches taken by the different actors, we hope to provide insight into the question of how these actors interact when it comes to the integration of (rejected) asylum seekers, and to draw lessons from these insights.

Relation between Activation and Integration and Self- sufficiency

Research shows that activation and reception of immigrants is desirable, as it has a positive influence on their well-being (ACVZ 2013, Boersema et al. 2015, Ten Holder & De Boer 2012, Lintner & Elsen 2018, Winter et al. 2018). Additionally, for immigrants awaiting a decision on their asylum applications, activation will contribute to their self-sufficiency during the procedure and afterwards (ACVZ 2013, Ten Holder & De Boer 2012, De Lange et al. 2017, WRR 1989).

A common argument against activating asylum seekers is that offering language lessons and allowing or encouraging participation in volunteer work, training or employment, might give rise to unjustified expectations among asylum seekers and prevent the return of rejected asylum seekers.[4] Furthermore, activation is thought to obstruct the restrictive immigration policy applied by the Netherlands (De Lange et al. 2017:11). At the same time, however, forced idleness due to a lack of activities in governmental reception centres and a prohibition on working produces many negative effects which will stand in the way of a successful integration and participation in the host society after asylum has been granted. It contributes to stress, institutionalisation and passivity of asylum seekers (ACVZ 2013, Ten Holder & De Boer 2012, Kloosterboer 2009, Kramer et al. 2003, Kramer 2010). Institutionalisation refers to the harmful effects such as apathy and loss of independence arising from spending a long time in a so-called 'total institution'.[5] That is why a number of authoritative research institutes

---

2 This definition corresponds with Preamble 23 to Directive 2013/33/EU (Reception Conditions directive) which calls for clear rules regarding access to the labour market of applicants for international protection in order to promote self-sufficiency. The definition also corresponds to the explanatory memorandum to the Dutch Newcomers Integration Act of 1998, the first Dutch Act containing a legal obligation for immigrants to integrate, which stated that the goal of integration (*inburgering*) was to achieve educational, professional and social self-sufficiency (*Kamerstukken II* 1996-1997, 25114, nr. 3, p. 6).

3 The first group concerns immigrants whose asylum procedure has not yet finished or who are waiting for their procedure to start. The second group concerns those whose application for a residence permit has failed or whose permit has been withdrawn and who for that reason are undocumented immigrants who have no legal entitlement to reside in the Netherlands.

4 *Kamerstukken II* 2015-2016, 19637, nr. 2073.

5 Based on https://en.oxforddictionaries.com/definition/institutionalization. Some authors use the concept of hospitalisation to describe these processes.

and advisory bodies advised activating asylum seekers early in the asylum procedure (ACVZ 2013,, Engbersen et al. 2015).

Furthermore, many staff members of civil society shelter organisations and municipal officials are of the opinion that activation is a necessary condition for rejected asylum seekers to reflect on possible return to their home country (ACVZ 2013, Winter et al. 2018).[6] Moreover, it is not the policy applied regarding the (prevention of) activation of rejected asylum seekers, but the conditions in the country of origin that are most decisive for return migration. Return is unlikely when people do not have confidence in security in their country of origin and when they are afraid that they cannot build a life there (housing, work, medical care) (Black et al. 2004, Leerkes et al. 2010, 2014; Winter et al. 2018). UK research 'does not support the notion that restricting employment of asylum seekers in the UK increases the likelihood of return' (Black et al. 2004). Lastly, activation will contribute to the well-being of immigrants living in shelters (Viergever et al. 2018: 40). It is likely to contribute to increased independence and self-esteem, and will thereby decrease the risk of exploitation of irregular immigrants who often find themselves in disadvantaged positions. We first discuss options to participate in society for asylum seekers in the Netherlands. Subsequently, the situation of rejected asylum seekers in the Netherlands is analysed.

Asylum Seekers

Central Government

With the entry into force of the revised Aliens Act on 1 April 2001, the asylum procedure was altered with the aim of shortening its length.[7] On 1 July 2010, the abbreviated procedure was introduced.[8] This procedure lasts eight days and can be extended to fourteen days in cases where the minister so decides.[9] The shorter the procedure, the sooner the asylum seekers can participate in Dutch society, according to the explanatory memorandum to the bill amending the Aliens Act.[10] From this explanation the Dutch policy of discouraging asylum seekers from integrating into Dutch society as long as their procedure is in process becomes apparent. This policy was adopted in the early 1990s with the aim of controlling immigration and preventing the Netherlands

6 On the basis of available data, however, it cannot be concluded that activation and support increase return migration. This is shown both by an evaluation of a pilot project on activating residents at family locations in order to promote the voluntary return of residents of family locations to their countries of origin (Boersema et al. 2015) and from an investigation into state and municipal facilities for aliens who are obliged to leave the country (Winter et al. 2018).

7 In the 1990s, asylum seekers would spend years in reception locations (Ghorashi 2005; Weiler & Wijnkoop 2011).

8 Programme for the introduction of the Improved Asylum Procedure.

9 Article 3.110 Aliens decree. Should fourteen days not suffice for the Immigration and Naturalisation Service (IND) to decide on the asylum application, the asylum seeker will end up in the 'lengthened procedure', which will last six months at most, but which can be extended with another nine months in cases where research is required by third parties in order for the minister to decide on the request. Article 42 paragraphs 1 and 4 Aliens Act 2000.

10 *Kamerstukken II* 1998-1999, 26732, nr. 3.

from becoming too attractive (Ten Holder & De Boer 2012: 18). The policy of discouraging immigrants from integrating was supposed to support the restrictive immigration policy (De Lange et al. 2017: 2). It is inter alia reflected in the location of the reception centres, which are often situated in rural areas (Bakker et al. 2013: 435).[11] Furthermore, asylum seekers have only limited access to the labour market. Lastly, all aspects of life are conducted in the same place, and all activities are tightly scheduled and controlled, which means that privacy and autonomy are limited (Bakker et al. 2013: 435, De Haan & Althoff 2002). In this respect, Dutch reception centres can be regarded as 'total institutions'.

- *Language lessons*

The Dutch government's stance on the integration of asylum seekers also entailed that the government should not provide language lessons for them.[12] As mentioned above, the government re-emphasised this point of view in 2015, by stating that the provision of language lessons by the government could create false expectations and that the government should prevent sending mixed signals.[13]

At the end of 2016, the government however appeared to have changed its mind. In a letter of 17 November 2016, the minister for Social Affairs and Employment stated that 'a fast integration starts with learning the Dutch language. The government finds it important that those asylum seekers whose application will probably be granted should be able to start learning Dutch as quickly as possible'.[14] Since then, asylum seekers who have a high chance that their applications for asylum will be granted have been allowed to join the language lessons in the framework of the 'pre-integration' education (*voorinburgering*) taught by trained Dutch language teachers (not volunteers) provided by the government to refugees who have already been awarded a status but who are still living in a reception centre while waiting to be housed in a municipality.[15] The policy change has been triggered by the increased duration of the procedure which was caused partially by the increase in the number of asylum applications. This rise prompted a series of resolutions by several parliamentarians claiming – inter alia – that the long duration of the procedure offered justification for asylum seekers who were in procedure to start learning the language.[16] Furthermore, also following a series of

11 The reception centre of Heumensoord was an exception.

12 Asylum seekers would however be allowed to follow language lessons provided by volunteers.

13 *Kamerstukken II* 2015-2016, 32824, nr. 2073.

14 *Kamerstukken II* 2016-2017, 34334, nr. 23, p. 1.

15 Notably Eritreans and Syrians are considered as asylum seekers who have a high chance that their application for asylum will be granted. *Kamerstukken II* 2016-2017, 34334, nr. 23, p. 1. Since 1 January 2013, accepted asylum seekers living in reception centres have been able to participate in the programme '*Voorbereiding op inburgering*' (pre-integration education). This programme consists of language lessons, individual support, a training Knowledge of Dutch Society, and, since 1 January 2016, Orientation on the Dutch Employment Market.

16 According to the resolution of Sjoerdsma (D66 Liberal Democrats), the period asylum seekers in October 2015 had to wait for their procedure to start had risen to 4 months (*Kamerstukken II* 2015-2016, 19 637, nr. 2055). For other resolutions, see *Kamerstukken II* 2015-2016, 19 637, nr. 2057, *Kamerstukken II 2015-2016,* 32 824, nr. 119, *Kamerstukken II* 2016-2017, 34 550, nr. 12. In March of 2019, on average the asylum procedure took 23 weeks (https://ind.nl/Paginas/Doorlooptijden-asielprocedure.aspx, site accessed 1 May 2019).

resolutions by parliamentarians, in June 2016 the government had started training volunteers who would assist asylum seekers in learning the Dutch language.[17] Following these decisions, the COA had to take on a different role. Whereas it used to be an organisation focused solely on the reception of refugees, as of 2016 it was supposed to focus on their integration as well.

- *Employment*

Once a residence permit has been granted, refugees have free access to the labour market. Before that time, asylum seekers are only allowed to work if their application procedure lasts at least six months and the employer has been awarded a work permit.[18] Employers employing asylum seekers without having obtained the required permit are fined.[19] The work permit for asylum seekers is granted for a maximum period of 24 weeks.[20] The reason for the 24-week maximum is to prevent entitlement to unemployment benefits. Also, the government feared that allowing a longer period of 'unregulated' work would inspire other refugees to apply for asylum in the Netherlands (De Lange et al. 2017: 21).[21]

This fear of becoming too attractive to potential refugees is also the reason the government has not followed the advice of several advisory bodies to allow refugees to start working as early as two months after filing their application for a residence permit. Already in 1989, the Netherlands Scientific Council for Government Policy (WRR) stated that the policies aiming at the integration of immigrants pursued so far, failed to provide immigrants possibilities to become self-supporting by treating them too much as 'care categories' (WRR 1989). It advised allowing asylum seekers conditional access to the labour market after a period of two months. One of the arguments put forward by the government against this advice was the fear that asylum seekers whose future in the Netherlands was unsure would integrate into Dutch society and the increased difficulty of returning asylum seekers whose application would be denied.[22]

In their 2015 policy brief 'no time to lose; from reception to integration of asylum migrants' the WRR, the Netherlands Institute for Social Research (SCP) and the Research and Documentation Centre of the Ministry of Justice (WODC) concluded that

17 *Kamerstukken II* 2015-2016, 32824, 130, *Kamerstukken II* 2016-2017, 19637-2243. The resolutions concern *Kamerstukken II* 2015-2016, 19 637, nr. 2055; *Kamerstukken II* 2015-2016, 19 637, nr. 2057; *Kamerstukken II* 2013-2014, 32 824, nr. 109.

18 A work permit can be granted, if the employer can prove that there are no (suitable) candidates originating from the Netherlands, or an EU or EEA Member State, the so-called priority work force, available (Article 8(1)(a) Labour Act for Aliens). At the end of 2016, the average asylum procedure lasted less than six months. By the end of 2015, 605 asylum seekers were in a procedure for six months or longer. Therefore, most asylum seekers will not be awarded the right to work while in procedure (De Lange et al. 2017: 13).

19 Article 18 et seq. of the Labour Act for Aliens.

20 Article 8 paragraph 2 and Article 11 paragraphs 2 and 3 Labour Act for Aliens. Until 2008, the permit would be granted for a maximum period 12 weeks.

21 Some academics claim that by setting the 24 week maximum, the Netherlands infringes the obligation set out in Article 15 paragraph 3 of the Reception Conditions Directive which provides that 'access to the labour market shall not be withdrawn during appeals procedures'. T. de Lange & C. Rijken, 'Asielzoeker kan eerder aan de slag', Opinie *De Volkskrant* 12 januari 2016.

22 *Kamerstukken II* 1990-1991, 19637, nr. 76, De Lange et al. 2017: 23.

the position of asylum seekers in the Dutch labour market was poor. Factors such as the length of the procedure, the fact that asylum seekers were allowed to start working only after six months and the fact they would need a working permit which was valid for a maximum period of 24 weeks all contributed to a period of inactivity, according to the authors (Engbersen et al. 2015: 14). The Advisory Committee on Migration Affairs (ACVZ) for that reason referred to 'lost time' (ACVZ 2013). In the policy brief, WRR, SCP and WODC advised the government to consider changing the conditions under which asylum seekers 'in procedure' were allowed to work and to give municipalities more possibilities to experiment (Engbersen et al. 2015: 39). More recently, in October 2015, the municipality of Amsterdam called for a shortening of the six-month period and an extension of the maximum period of 24 weeks of validity of the work permit.[23] The Dutch government has until now not been willing to accept these recommendations for activating asylum seekers through work by changing the rules.

- *Volunteering*

Whereas the rules regarding access to the labour market for asylum seekers remained unaltered, the government lowered the barrier for asylum seekers to work on a voluntary basis.[24] According to the minister, engaging in volunteer work would allow asylum seekers the possibility to participate, be active, meet people and combat boredom and tensions.[25] As of mid-October 2016, organisations would be able to allow asylum seekers to work on a voluntary basis if they had filed for the required permit.[26] Previously, asylum seekers were only allowed to volunteer for organisations that had already disposed of the required permit.[27] Furthermore, in the spring of 2016, the central government and the municipalities agreed to stimulate volunteering by asylum seekers by improving the provision of information, by bringing together supply and demand and by stimulating associations and organisations to offer opportunities to volunteer.[28] In August of that year, the minister awarded one million euro to Pharos to carry out the project 'Let's get to work! Volunteering for asylum seekers and refugees with residence

23 Action plan entrepreneurship and work: opportunities for refugees, Letter of alderman Ollongren (Economy) to the municipal council of Amsterdam 2 October 2015, .https://praktijkvoorbeelden.vng.nl/databank/asiel-en-integratie/integratie-en-participatie/vluchtelingenbeleid-2015-2018.aspx, site accessed 27 March 2019

24 SZW, *Vrijwilligerswerk door asielzoekers en statushouders in de opvang. Tips en aandachtspunten voor maatschappelijke organisaties*, Den Haag: SZW,June 2016. An updated version of the brochure is downloadable from https://www.rijksoverheid.nl/documenten/brochures/2016/06/20/handreiking-vluchtelingen, site accessed 9 April 2019.

25 *Stcrt.* 2016, Nr. 57116.

26 *Stcrt.* 2016, Nr. 57116.

27 A volunteer permit is only required if the volunteers do not have free access to the labour market. Organisations offering volunteering opportunities to refugees who have been awarded a residence status hence do not require a volunteering permit, as refugees with a permit have unlimited access to the Dutch labour market.

28 *Kamerstukken II* 2016-2017, 19637 nr. 2243.

permits in reception centres'.[29] The ministry assigned the COA the new task of promoting volunteer work among the asylum seekers in the reception centres.[30] Before 2016, the COA was not allowed to stimulate activation and activities which were directed at the integration of asylum seekers into Dutch society, as this would diminish the likelihood of return (De Lange et al. 2017: 31). In 2018, the focus on volunteer work for asylum seekers in reception centres was evaluated. The researchers concluded that volunteering appeared to stimulate participation and integration (Bakker et al. 2018: 77).

- *The role of the COA*

For the volunteers to be able to provide language lessons and other types of activities to asylum seekers, cooperation from the COA is required. As we have seen in the introduction, the COA was not always inclined to allow language lessons by volunteers to be organised, even though asylum seekers have always been allowed to receive language training from volunteers. As the role of the COA has changed, starting in 2016, from being an organisation focused solely on the reception of asylum seekers to an organisation focusing on both reception and integration, local COA departments have adopted a more welcoming attitude towards volunteers organising activities for asylum seekers. The local COA department in Nijmegen has in any case made a switch. In 2016, the COA teamed up with the welfare foundation Interlokaal.[31] In that year, more than 130 activities were organised at Heumensoord each week in the area of sports, language and culture.[32] Volunteers were also welcomed at the reception centre in the city centre (Stieltjesstraat) which opened in February 2017. Also, the working group for refugees of the Radboud University was allowed to start a 'buddy project' aimed at matching asylum seekers living in the Stieltjesstraat with RU students and staff members with comparable interests. To name another example, in April of 2016, the COA department in the city of Alkmaar, in cooperation with the municipality and volunteer organisations developed a plan to provide a meaningful way for asylum seekers to spend the day. The plan claimed that this would benefit the well-being of the asylum seekers and would open up their minds to think about the future, including considering return to their home countries.[33]

---

29 '*Aan de slag! Vrijwilligerswerk voor asielzoekers en vergunninghouders in opvang.*' The project would last for 2.5 years and aimed at realising 14,000 matches from 25 COA reception centres. Pharos is the Dutch Centre of expertise on Health Disparities (www.pharos.nl).

30 In March 2019, around 23,500 asylum seekers stayed in reception centres, 4,500 of whom had already been granted a residence permit and were waiting to be relocated to a municipality (https://www.coa.nl/nl/over-coa/bezetting, site accessed 19 March 2019).

31 Municipality of Nijmegen and municipality of Heumen report 'Noodopvang Heumensoord. Een terugblik', Nijmegen: Gemeente Nijmegen & Gemeente Heumen 2016 (Emergency reception Heumensoord. Looking back), p. 21, https://www.ifv.nl/kennisplein/Documents/201605-Gemeente Nijmegen-Rapport-Heumensoord.pdf.

32 Interlokaal, *Jaarverslag 2016* (Interlokaal, Annual report 2016), Nijmegen: Het Inter-lokaal 2016, p. 14, http://www.inter-lokaal.nl/wp-content/uploads/2016/06/Het-Inter-lokaal-jaarverslag-2016-vs-def-17-07-03.pdf. Site accessed 27 March 2019.

33 Plan van aanpak activering, April 2016, https://www.alkmaar.nl/gemeente/webcms/site/gemeente/product/Plan%20van%20aanpak%20Activering%20mei%202016.pdf, site accessed 20 March 2019.

Municipalities

As we have seen above, until November 2016, the government would not provide language lessons for asylum seekers 'in procedure', who would depend on volunteers for their language lessons, and on the willingness of municipalities to take charge. Different municipalities adopted different strategies. The municipality of The Hague for instance invested 250,000 Euro to provide language lessons to asylum seekers in an 'emergency' reception centre which was open from October 2015 until 1 January 2016 (Vasterman 2015). In October 2015, the municipality of Amsterdam adopted an 'action plan entrepreneurship and work: opportunities for refugees'.[34] Starting language education as quickly as possible was one of the central elements of this plan. The municipality of Nijmegen did not invest in language lessons or other programmes aimed at activation for the people of Heumensoord. Kees Groenendijk concluded: 'whether a language project for asylum seekers succeeds or not depends on the local politicians and local COA-managers. And this should not be the case' (Vasterman 2015). The reluctant attitude of several municipalities can be explained by the fact that asylum seekers are the responsibility of the COA. The central government will not allocate money to the municipalities to organise language lessons or other activities for asylum seekers who happen to live there, but who are not registered as inhabitants.

Civil Society

As far as civil society is concerned, asylum seekers in reception centres will be dependent on what is offered in the vicinity of the reception centre, and this will differ from centre to centre (Ten Holder & De Boer 2012: 16). Furthermore, the fact that many reception centres are located in remote locations will possibly form a barrier for asylum seekers to engage in activities provided outside of the centre (Kloosterboer 2009).

In the case of Nijmegen, civil society organisations organised activities aimed at the activation of asylum seekers following the opening of new reception centres at Heumensoord and the Stieltjesstraat. On a more structural, and national, basis, the Dutch Council for Refugees lobbies for asylum seekers to start integrating as quickly as possible into Dutch society, at the latest six months after arrival.[35] According to the Council, while awaiting the decision on their asylum application, asylum seekers should be able to participate in society, for instance via volunteering, in order to prepare for the labour market in the Netherlands or the country of origin.[36] The Council does not engage in activities aimed at the employment of asylum seekers who are still awaiting the outcome of their procedures.

---

34 Letter of alderman Ollongren (Economy) to the municipal council of Amsterdam 2 October 2015, https://praktijkvoorbeelden.vng.nl/databank/asiel-en-integratie/integratie-en-participatie/vluchtelingenbeleid-2015-2018.aspx, site accessed 27 March 2019.

35 Visie vluchtelingenwerk op inburgering (https://www.vluchtelingenwerk.nl/sites/default/files/Vluchtelingenwerk/Webartikel/images/visie_in_het_kort_inburgering_def.pdf, site accessed 27 May 2019).

36 Visie vluchtelingenwerk op arbeidsparticipatie (https://www.vluchtelingenwerk.nl/sites/default/files/u895/visie_op_arbeidsparticipatie_in_het_kort_2016.pdf, site accessed 27 May 2019).

We did not find examples of civil society initiatives focused on making matches between asylum seekers and employment. The reason for this might be that the group of asylum seekers who are allowed to work is simply too small and the (administrative) conditions too unattractive for employers.[37] Employers might furthermore be deterred from hiring asylum seekers as the municipality where they will be housed when they leave the reception centre might be in a different part of the Netherlands than where the reception centre is located. Moreover, asylum seekers will often not sufficiently master the Dutch language to be able to take up employment. Lastly, asylum seekers themselves might be deterred from taking up paid employment as they are obliged to pay the COA a personal contribution of 75% of their wages to a maximum of € 185.

Rejected Asylum Seekers

Rejected asylum seekers and other irregular immigrants must leave the Netherlands. They are expected to organise their own departure and have 28 days to do this. During that period, the asylum seeker still receives money and accommodation from the government (COA). The Return and Departure Service (DT&V) can mediate to get a travel document. In 2018 14,882 aliens who were not allowed to stay in the Netherlands left the country (Onderzoekscommissie 2019: 51).[38] These are official statistics; only 42% of them have left demonstrably. Some persons who should leave in fact remain in the Netherlands for various reasons, such as inability to obtain the necessary travel documents, fear of imprisonment, honour killings, forced marriage or insufficient means of support after return From that moment they become part of the group of foreign nationals who do not have a residence status in the Netherlands. Reliable statistics are not available.[39] This paragraph is about this category.

Central Government

The central government policy for this group is primarily focused on their departure from the Netherlands.[40] To be eligible for some form of housing and assistance provided by the government, illegal residents need to work actively on their departure.[41] Asylum seekers must leave the 'ordinary' reception location (AZC) within 28 days after a court has upheld the rejection of their asylum application. If they have not left the Netherlands by this time, they may be transferred to restrictive accommodation to prepare their departure. They are required to cooperate fully with the investigation into

37 See above footnote 18.

38 This concerns not only rejected asylum seekers but also, for example, people who are staying in the Netherlands illegally and people whose permits are no longer valid.

39 It is estimated that in 2012-2013 between 22,881 and 48,179 people were living in the Netherlands without a residence permit (Snippe & Mennes 2018). Most of them manage somehow without help from the government and organisations (Koppes 2017: 7).

40 This is also the case in Austria and Sweden (Ataç 2019).

41 https://www.rijksoverheid.nl/onderwerpen/asielbeleid/vraag-en-antwoord/afgewezen-asielzoekers.

their nationality and identity.[42] Families with minor children receive shelter at a 'family location' until their departure or until the youngest child is 18 years old. The support and guidance at these locations is focused on return, including forced departure. It is strongly emphasized that the activities and services offered must not in any way give the impression that the foreign national may remain in the Netherlands.

Foreigners who are not lawfully residing in the Netherlands do not have legal opportunities to participate in society. They are not allowed to work, to register with an educational institution, to open a bank account or take out health insurance.[43] For years, the central government and the municipalities have disagreed about the reception of irregular immigrants. Municipalities advocate a bed-bath-bread arrangement (BBB) because they are confronted with homeless and often traumatized people as a result of a failing expulsion policy. The central government emphasizes that the safety net provided by municipalities undermines the deadlines and the obligation to cooperate on departure and therefore the return policy.[44] At the end of 2018, the government and the municipalities agreed on a pilot project of national reception facilities for foreigners without residence rights in five municipalities (LVV, see below).[45]

Municipalities

Municipalities have no specific legally defined tasks related to the reception of illegal immigrants.[46] Nevertheless, particular case law from the highest court in social security issues of 17 December 2014 induced several municipalities to provide some form of shelter.[47] In May 2017, 39 municipalities were offering some form of emergency shelter (Winter et al. 2018: 33). Municipalities refer to the need to offer shelter from the perspective of maintaining public order and for humanitarian reasons (Van der Leun & Bouter 2015: 145-146, Winter et al. 2018: 34). There are huge differences between municipalities in terms of the organisational structure and the facilities offered (Koppes 2017, Winter et al. 2018). Some offer exclusively shelter during the night, while others offer 24-hour shelter, whether or not in combination with support and guidance. Differences also exist in categories of irregular immigrants for whom shelter is provided. In some municipalities, only immigrants with some perspective on acquiring a legal residence status will be able to benefit from the municipal arrangements that are provided.

Many municipalities have not set up facilities themselves. Quite often existing initiatives from churches and local NGOs provide shelter or living allowance, fully or

---

42 https://english.dienstterugkeerenvertrek.nl/RepatriationandDeparture/Predepartureaccommodation/index.aspx. A person can be placed in a detention location in case disappearing in illegal life is suspected.

43 However, illegal aliens are entitled to medically necessary treatment and minors are entitled to education.

44 Letter of 21 November 2017 of the Secretary of State Dijkhoff to Parliament, 'Stand van zaken bestuursakkoord tussen rijk en gemeenten over uitgeprocedeerde vreemdelingen'.

45 Samenwerkingsafspraken Landelijke Vreemdelingen Voorziening (LVV) d.d. 29 november 2018, ministerie van Justitie en Veiligheid en Vereniging Nederlandse Gemeenten.

46 Terlouw & Böcker (in this volume) discuss how mayors in the Netherlands perceive and use their discretion in situations involving rejected asylum seekers or other migrants whom the national government considers to be 'unlawfully present aliens'.

47 ECLI:NL:CRVB:2014:4178 . The state lodged an appeal and the final verdict did not confirm this decision. See ECLI:NL:CRVB:2015:3803 and ECLI:NL:CRVB:2015:3834.

partially funded by the municipality. Municipalities were financially compensated by the central government from 2014-2017. Several municipalities use the so-called INLIA eligibility criteria, indicating three target groups for municipal shelter places: foreign nationals who are lawfully residing and who have no accommodation, no income and no insurance; foreign nationals who actively and controllably cooperate with their departure but cannot realise this within 28 days, and foreign nationals for whom it is unacceptable on humanitarian grounds for the municipality to have no reception (Winter et al 2018, 37-38).

Because of the high level of diversity of reception facilities commissioned by the municipalities, it is impossible to answer the question about activation in general. Instead we will just offer some examples. The municipality of Groningen is to be regarded as a frontrunner. Groningen has delegated the organisation and management of the shelter facilities to civil society organisation INLIA (Koppes 2017: 22, Winter et al. 2018: xxxiii-xxxvi). INLIA was founded in 1988 as a service desk for local church communities in all matters concerning refugees and provides assistance and shelter to asylum seekers in need.[48] The organisation runs two 'Bed-Bath-Bread+'-shelters in Groningen with 270 beds.[49] Residents receive shelter, money, and legal and social guidance to work on a safe return or a residence permit. Residents are responsible for cleaning and cooking and can participate in classes (including the Dutch language) and activities (Winter et al. 2018: xxxiv-xxxv). The municipality of Groningen pays the bill but is not involved in the content of reception and guidance.

The municipality of Eindhoven offers support and allowance for rejected asylum seekers who live within their own network (80-95 persons). Rejected asylum seekers without a social network who are working on a future perspective (return migration, legal residence or transit migration) may receive 24/7 shelter (20-30 persons). The reception and support of rejected asylum seekers are organised and managed by civil society organisation *Vluchtelingen in de knel.* This NGO provides legal guidance, training and coaching. It runs into legal restrictions when mediating for paid or voluntary work. The organisation receives an annual financial contribution from the municipality (Winter et al. 2018: xxvi-xxviii).

In 2019 the government started the pilot project LVV (National aliens' facility) in five municipalities.[50] This includes the existing BBB facilities in Groningen and Eindhoven. The facilities are meant to make all other municipal reception facilities for unlawfully residing immigrants redundant. The LVVs are supposed to offer guidance on self-employed return, further migration or if applicable, legalisation of residence. The LVVs operate under the joint responsibility of the municipal and central government and will be funded by state and municipal funds. At the time of writing (April 2019) it is unclear how this pilot will operate and how it will change the approach of for instance INLIA and Vluchtelingen in de Knel. The City of Amsterdam is planning to organise

48 https://www.inlia.nl/en, site accessed on 8 April 2019. INLIA stands for 'International Network of Local Initiatives with Asylumseekers'.

49 https://gemeente.groningen.nl/actueel/nieuws/groningse-bed-bad-brood-wordt-vanaf-1-april-landelijke-voorziening-voor-vreemdelingen, site accessed on 8 April 2019.

50 Samenwerkingsafspraken Landelijke Vreemdelingen Voorziening (LVV) d.d. 29 november 2018, ministerie van Justitie en Veiligheid en Vereniging Nederlandse Gemeenten, https://vng.nl/files/vng/brieven/2018/attachments/20181130_getekende-samenwerkingsafspraak-lvv.pdf site accessed on 27 May 2019 en *Kamerstukken II* 2018-2019, 19637, nr. 2445.

small-scale housing for 500 undocumented foreign citizens to implement the LVV agreement. Amsterdam did not provide 24/7 shelter before and the plans have met with resistance from neighbourhood citizens (Niemantsverdriet 2019). The future will show what consequences the implementation of LVVs has for reception and support facilities for irregular residents that do not fit into the eligibility criteria of the LVVs. In particular, the mandatory active cooperation to organise their return migration, is expected to deter many irregular immigrants from applying for a place to stay in a LVV. The Amsterdam City Council decided that Amsterdam will also offer shelter to so-called Dublin claimants (asylum seekers whose proceedings must be settled in another EU member state) and other irregular migrants who do not meet the LVV's eligibility criteria.[51]

Civil Society

On its website the foundation LOS lists 62 shelter organisations for irregular immigrants.[52] This list includes civil society initiatives funded by the municipality and/or by donations from churches, citizens or charity funds. As has been pointed out in the foregoing section, most municipal activities for rejected asylum seekers (and other irregular immigrants) are in fact organised and carried out by civil society organisations such as INLIA and Vluchtelingen in de knel. However, there are also organisations that provide support for rejected asylum seekers not on behalf of or funded by the municipality. We will list some examples below:

- *Wereldvrouwenhuis* in Nijmegen offers shelter for women for six months in combination with a training and guidance programme aimed at strengthening their self-reliance. This includes Dutch language lessons.[53]
- *De Vluchtmaat* is a former office building in Amsterdam, housing 40 irregular refugees from Eritrea and Ethiopia from the 'We are here' group. Foundation *Noodzaak* provides free shelter for irregular immigrants and rents part of the building to small companies to cover the costs.[54] *Noodzaak* does not organise training or activities.
- *STIL Utrecht* offers individual guidance to people without a residence permit and helps them to find a place to live. Occasionally, they find individuals and families who are willing to offer temporary shelter, for example for an asylum seeker with

51 https://www.binnenlandsbestuur.nl/sociaal/nieuws/akkoord-over-opvang-uitgeprocedeerden-groningen.9611390.lynkx.

52 Stichting LOS is the national knowledge center for people and organisations that provide assistance to irregular immigrants.=, http://www.stichtinglos.nl/noodopvang, site accessed 8-4-2019. The information provided for each organisation indicates that some offer accommodation, others mediate for accommodation or medical treatment, and/or provide legal assistance.

53 www.wereldvrouwenhuis.nl, site accessed 8 April 2019. Both authors are members of the Board of the Wereldvrouwenhuis Foundation. Wereldvrouwenhuis is supported by the municipality and it receives subsidy from the municipality, but it is an independent foundation not working on behalf of the municipality.

54 https://vluchtmaat.nl/, site accessed 10 May 2019.

a clear perspective on a new successful procedure after the waiting period of 18 months (Dublin claim) (Keulen 2019).[55]

Next to organisations providing or helping to find shelter, there are many other civil society organisations offering assistance to rejected asylum seekers and other irregular immigrants:

- Foundation *Solid Road* helps people without residence permits and (former) asylum seekers to prepare for voluntary return to their country of origin by providing vocational training and guidance in the country of origin.[56]
- The *Wereldhuis* (Worldhouse) Amsterdam is a centre for and run by irregular immigrants initiated by the *Diaconie* of Amsterdam and *Luthers* Amsterdam. The Worldhouse facilitates educational and recreational activities and offers. counselling, referrals to medical and judicial instances and a daily warm meal. [57]
- The Dutch Council for Refugees offers support to rejected asylum seekers in examining the available options. Practical assistance is only available for rejected asylum seekers who opt for return or transmigration.[58]
- Foundation *Gast* offers social activation and sports for undocumented refugees in Nijmegen, including Dutch language lessons (Stam 2017).

Civil society networks may assist irregular immigrants in getting paid or volunteer work through training and job placement. A civil society campaign to extend the opportunities to develop and participate in society for irregular refugees and migrants stresses the importance of meaningful activities such as education, paid and voluntary work.[59]

Although the central government policy towards rejected asylum seekers is focused on return migration only, the experiences in the reception facilities of the central government, municipalities and civil society organisations all show that only a small percentage of rejected asylum seekers actually return to their country of origin. It also shows that after some time quite a few manage to get a residence status or a new application (Boersema et al. 2015, Winter et al. 2018: 65-67).[60] Winter (2018: 67) concludes that about half of all rejected asylum seekers in municipal shelters get a permanent or temporary residence status or they have a right to reception in an asylum seekers' center. The responsible Utrecht alderman claims that Utrecht has succeeded in finding a solution for 9 out of 10 people over the past 15 years (Kuiper 2019).[61]

55 http://www.stil-utrecht.nl/, site accessed 8 April 2019. The Dublin Regulation implies that an asylum request will be dealt with by the state of first entrance. Asylum seekers who travel through Italy or Greece are not permitted an asylum procedure in the Netherlands, they are sent back to Italy or Greece. Filing a new asylum application is however possible after 18 months. Many people are searching for temporary shelter to bridge those 18 months.

56 http://www.solidroad.nl/, site accessed 30 April 2019.

57 http://wereldhuis.org/en/, site accessed 10 May 2019.

58 https://www.vluchtelingenwerk.nl/forrefugees/geen-verblijfsvergunning-wat-nu?language=en.

59 http://iedereen-aandeslag.nl/wp-content/uploads/2016/05/manifest-GB.pdf (1 May 2019).

60 See also LOS, http://www.stichtinglos.nl/content/resultaten-opvang-ongedocumenteerden.

61 Half of them get residence papers and 20% return to the country of origin. Such figures reflect the eligibility criteria of the shelter organisation. Some organisations only accept immigrants that have a high chance of getting a residence permit

Conclusions

In the above we investigated the perspectives of the central and municipal government, local COA departments and civil society organisations on integration through activation of (rejected) asylum seekers in Dutch society. What can we learn from this comparison?

As regards asylum seekers, we have seen that the Dutch government until recently applied a policy of discouraging asylum seekers from integrating into Dutch society as long as their procedure was in process. As a consequence, the asylum seeker was effectively placed outside society- due to the location of the reception centres not only figuratively but also literally speaking. In 2016, however, we noticed a remarkable change in the government's perspective on integration and activation of asylum seekers. The government started offering language lessons to asylum seekers whose applications had a high chance of being granted, invested in the promotion of volunteering by asylum seekers and assigned the COA a new role facilitating the integration of asylum seekers. However, steps towards facilitating the access of asylum seekers to the labour market have not been taken so far.

The change in perspective of the Dutch government can partially be explained by the role played by civil society. Following the large number of asylum applications in the Netherlands in 2015 and following years, these organisations exerted pressure from below by offering their services to the benefit of the asylum seekers. Furthermore, the Dutch parliament insisted on a policy change.

The policy towards rejected asylum seekers is still one of preventing integration and promoting departure. In course of time, the central government was pressed to accept that reception facilities for rejected asylum seekers were needed. However, the objective of the facilities run by the government is to promote rejected asylum seekers' departure from the Netherlands. Civil society organisations and some municipalities acknowledge that not all irregular migrants will leave and- unlike the central government- they are in favour of activation. It is hard to get a clear picture of what civil society organisations and municipalities actually do to activate the target group. Most seem to focus on arranging accommodation and legal assistance as these are the most pressing needs. Only after someone has a place to live can they release energy to reflect on the future, to learn a language or a profession or to consider how return could be safely possible.

The need for shelter by civil society varies greatly over time depending on the admission policy of the government (Koppes 2017: 8-10, Van der Leun & Bouter 2015: 144, 149). The above shows that, as a consequence, the state and civil society act as communicating vessels providing shelter for and activation of asylum seekers and irregular immigrants: in times where the state offers more shelter, guidance and perspectives for integration, civil society withdraws; when the state draws back, civil society organisations take over. The history of refugees in the Netherlands shows that this is not a new phenomenon. The reception of Belgian war refugees during the First World War, of Jewish refugees of the Nazi regime in the 1930s and of displaced persons after the Second World War was primarily the responsibility of private organisations, as the Dutch government did not take responsibility for this (Böcker et al. 1998; Böcker & Havinga 2011). For the past 50 years, it has been primarily the government that has taken responsibility for the reception of asylum seekers, leaving civil society organisations to organise additional support. Since the end of the 1980s, some rejected asylum seekers have sought help from churches and individuals and have been offered shelter and assistance by churches and individuals in an attempt to become recognized refugees (Koppes 2017).

As we have seen, the interaction between central government and civil society in the Netherlands in relation to the reception and activation of asylum seekers, has entered a new phase: the government has accepted more responsibility for rejected asylum seekers, but ties the right to shelter and guidance to the condition of the refugees' active cooperation towards return migration. The new policy is in no way focused on the activation of the rejected asylum seekers. As activation will have a positive effect on the physical and mental well-being of rejected asylum seekers and will decrease the risk of exploitation of irregular immigrants who often find themselves in a vulnerable position, from a humanitarian perspective the Dutch government would be wise to change perspective also for this group of immigrants.

References

Ataç, I. (2019) 'Deserving Shelter: Conditional Access to Accommodation for Rejected Asylum Seekers in Austria, the Netherlands, and Sweden', *Journal of Immigrant & Refugee Studies* 17, 1: 44-60.

ACVZ (2013) *Verloren tijd. Advies over dagbesteding in de opvang voor vreemdelingen.* Den Haag: Adviescommissie voor Vreemdelingenzaken.

Bakker, L., J. Dagevos & G. Engbersen (2013) 'The Importance of Resources and Security in Socio-Economic Integration of Refugees', *Journal of International Migration and Integration* 15, 3: 431-448.

Bakker, L., R. Bekkers, J. Reitsma, C. Sederel, P. Smets & Y. Younes (2018) *Vrijwilligerswerk: Stimulans voor tijdige participatie en integratie: Monitor- en evaluatie onderzoek vrijwilligerswerk door asielzoekers en statushouders die in de opvang verblijven*, Den Haag : Ministerie van Sociale Zaken en Werkgelegenheid.

Black, R., K. Koser, K. Munk, G. Atfield, L. D'Onofrio & R. Tiemoko (2004) *Understanding voluntary return.* Home Office Online Report 50/04

Böcker, A., C.A. Groenendijk & T. Havinga (1998) 'Oorlogsvluchtelingen in Nederland', in: Y. Buruma et al (eds.), *Recht door de eeuw, Opstellen ter gelegenheid van het 75-jarig bestaan van de Faculteit der Rechtsgeleerdheid van de Katholieke Universiteit Nijmegen*, Deventer: Kluwer, p. 51-68.

Böcker, A. & T. Havinga (2011) 'Een eeuw opvang van Europese oorlogsvluchtelingen in Nederland', in: A. Terlouw & K. Zwaan (red.), *Tijd en asiel. 60 jaar Vluchtelingenverdrag*, Deventer: Kluwer, p. 7-25.

Boersema, E., I.D.A. Sportel, M. Smit & A.S. Leerkes (2015) 'Als ik bezig ben, denk ik niet zo veel'. *Evaluatie van de pilot Activeren bewoners gezinslocaties,* Cahier 2015-6, Den Haag: Wetenschappelijk Onderzoek- en Documentatiecentrum.

Engbersen, G., J. Dagevos, R. Jennissen, L. Bakker en A. Leerkes m.m.v. J. Klaver en A. Odé (2015) *'Geen tijd verliezen: van opvang naar integratie van asielmigranten'*, WRR-Policy Brief 4, Den Haag: WRR.

Fernhout, R., C. Groenendijk, C. Kortmann & S. Kortmann (2015) 'Hoezo, geef geen les aan vluchtelingen?', *NRC* 3 December 2015.

Ghorashi, H. (2005), 'Agents of Change or Passive Victims: the Impact of Welfare States (the case of the Netherlands) on Refugees', *Journal of Refugee Studies*, 8(2): 181-198.

Haan, W. de & M. Althoff (2002). *Vreemd en verdacht. Een verkennend onderzoek naar criminaliteit in en om asielzoekerscentra.* Groningen: Rijksuniversiteit Groningen.

Holder, F. ten & M. de Boer (2012) *Kleine stappen van grote betekenis: een nieuw perspectief op humane opvang van asielzoekers,* Amsterdam: de Werkelijkheid.

INLIA (2018) *Inlia Works*, Groningen: INLIA.

Keulen, B. (2019) Moderne onderduikers. 'Het is beter om niet te veel te weten', *De Groene Amsterdammer* 18 maart 2019.

Kloosterboer, K. (2009) *Kind in het centrum: kinderrechten in asielzoekerscentra*, Den Haag: Unicef.

Koppes, S. (2017) *Valse hoop of bittere noodzaak. Opvang van mensen zonder verblijfsrecht*, Amsterdam: Amnesty International Nederland/Stichting LOS.

Kramer, S., J. Bala, R. van Dijk & F. Öry (2003) *Making sense of Experience*, Utrecht: USBO.

Kramer, S. (2010) *Zorg voor Asielzoekers met Psychische Problemen. Het Perspectief van de Asielzoeker (ZAPP)*, Amsterdam: ASKV/Steunpunt Vluchtelingen.

Kuiper, M. (2019) 'Reportage Noodopvang Utrecht. Een flatje en voor elke twee weken 110 Euro leefgeld', *NRC* 4 april 2019, p. 10-11.

Lange, T. de, E. Besselsen, S. Rahouti & C. Rijken (2017) *Van AZC naar een baan. De Nederlandse regelgeving over en praktijk van arbeidsmarktintegratie van vluchtelingen*, Amsterdam: Universiteit van Amsterdam.

Leerkes, A., M. Galloway & M. Kromhout (2010) *Kiezen tussen twee kwaden: Determinanten van terugkeerintenties onder (bijna) uitgeprocedeerde asielmigranten,* Cahier 2010-5, Den Haag: WODC.

Leerkes, A.S., E. Boersema, R.M.V. van Os, A.M. Galloway & M. van Londen (2014) *Afgewezen en uit Nederland vertrokken? Een onderzoek naar de achtergronden van variatie in zelfstandige terugkeer onder uitgeprocedeerde asielzoekers,* Cahier 2014-3, Den Haag: Wetenschappelijk Onderzoek- en Documentatiecentrum.

Leun, J. van der & H. Bouter (2015) 'Gimme Shelter: Inclusion and Exclusion of Irregular Immigrants in Dutch Civil Society', *Journal of Immigrant & Refugee Studies*, 13/2: 135-155, DOI: 10.1080/15562948.2015.1033507.

Lintner, C. & S. Elsen (2018) 'Getting out of the seclusion trap? Work as meaningful occupation for the subjective well-being of asylum seekers in South Tyrol, Italy', *Journal of Occupational Science*, 25/1: 76-86.

Niemantsverdriet, T. (2019) 'Uitgeprocedeerde asielzoekers. In de linkse hoofdstad zijn ze niet welkom', *NRC* 4 april 2019, p. 10.

Onderzoekscommissie Langdurig verblijvende vreemdelingen zonder bestendig verblijfsrecht (2019) *Rapport*, Den Haag: Rijksoverheid.

Snippe, J. & R. Mennes (2018) *Vooronderzoek data en methoden illegalenschatting*, Groningen: Breuer en Intraval Onderzoek & Advies.

Stam, K. (2017) *Sociale activering als participatie bevorderend proces binnen het bureaucratisch veld van de maatschappij met betrekking tot ongedocumenteerde vluchtelingen*, Deventer, Bachelor scriptie Saxion.

Vasterman, J. (2015) *'Pe-per-no-ten' leren, maar noem het geen inburgering*, *NRC* 3 oktober 2015.

Viergever, R., N. Thorogood, T. van Driel, J. Wolf & M. Durand (2018) *Facing forward. Nine stories about being a Survivor of Human Trafficking in a post-trafficking shelter in the Netherlands*, Amersfoort: CoMensha.

Weiler, R. & M. Wijnkoop (2011) 'Jullie hebben de klok, wij hebben de tijd. 60 jaar vluchtelingenbescherming en de Nederlandse praktijk', in: A. Terlouw & K. Zwaan (eds), *Tijd en asiel, 60 jaar Vluchtelingenverdrag*, Deventer: Kluwer, p. 81-109.

WRR (1989) *Allochtonenbeleid* (Immigrants' Policy), Den Haag: Sdu, https://english.wrr.nl/publications/reports/1989/05/09/immigrant-policy.

Winter, H., V.M. Bex-Reimert, B. Geertsema & E. Krol (2018) *Onderdak en opvang door Rijk en gemeenten van vertrekplichtige vreemdelingen en de invloed daarvan op terugkeer*. Groningen: Pro Facto.

The European Parliament: From a Human Rights Watchdog to a Responsible Decision Maker?

*Tineke Strik**

1. Introduction

Elspeth was already involved in the European asylum and migration policy before a legal basis was established in the Treaty of Amsterdam. With her commitment to the ILPA proposals,[1] she contributed to important principles that still guide European standards. I would like to reflect on twenty years EU asylum and migration policy from a point of view of democratic control. Since the beginning of this century, the European Union has been working towards common rules on legal migration for third country nationals and a European Common Asylum System. Now, two decades later, this process has resulted in an impressive number of first generation directives (and some regulations) and a number of additional or recast-directives in this field. During the negotiations on the Treaty of Amsterdam, where Member States decided to establish a legal basis for legislation on asylum and migration at the European level, they appeared quite hesitant to immediately give up their veto and to share their competences with the European Parliament. As a result, the first generation instruments were to be established by the consultation procedure, where unanimity was required in the Council and the European Parliament was left with a purely advisory role. This exceptional procedure, which also limited the competences of the Court of Justice, would last for a transition period of five years, after which the Council could decide by unanimity to apply the communitarian regime to this policy area.[2] The Parliament gained co-decision power in the field of irregular migration and border control in December 2004, one year later extended to the field of asylum. It is only since the entry into force of the Lisbon Treaty in December 2009 that the Parliament has to give its consent to legislation on regular migration.

During my PhD-research on the decision-making process of the first two directives in this field,[3] I found that the Parliament's direct influence on those instruments was very limited. It is to be expected that the impact of this procedural anomaly during the crucial first exercise of standardising, must have remained on the legislation adopted under co-decision, as new proposals built on the legislation it was kept out. In this contribution, I will briefly summarize my findings on the role of Parliament during the adoption of asylum and migration instruments during the consultation procedure. Af-

* Associate professor, Centre for Migration Law, Radboud University Nijmegen, the Netherlands. Since July 2019, Strik is an MEP for the Greens, member of the committees LIBE and AFET.

1 Immigration Law Practitioners Association (ILPA). For the proposals see: https://www.ilpa.org.uk/pages/publications.html.

2 Title IV of the EC-Treaty, Article 67and 68.

3 The Family Reunification Directive and the Asylum Procedures Directive.

terwards, I will analyse how the role of Parliament has changed over time, paying attention to its position as well as its strategy, using the Returns Directive as a case-study. While doing so, I will highlight how the shift from the Union towards the external dimension of asylum and migration policies, where intergovernmental cooperation revived, and how these policies impeded effective parliamentary control. This brings me to some final words on the way forward for a strong, transparent and rights-based European Parliament.

2. The Amsterdam Period: The Watchdog

In my dissertation, I analysed the formation process of the Family Reunification Directive and the Asylum Procedures Directive, which laid the foundation for an important part of the current EU migration legislation.[4] Both directives have been negotiated during the first years of this millennium, after the Treaty of Amsterdam had laid down the legal basis for asylum and migration legislation in May 1999.[5] On the Family Reunification Directive, the Council negotiated from the beginning of 2000 to September 2003.[6] After two years the Belgian Presidency concluded that the Council had reached a deadlock and asked the Commission to present a new proposal, including the compromises that had been achieved and solutions for the controversies.[7] The new proposal, which left more room for manoeuvre for the Member States, was accepted as a sound basis by the Member States.[8] Nevertheless it took more than a year to adopt the directive.[9] The process towards the adoption of the Asylum Procedures Directive had a similar pattern. More than a year after presentation of the first proposal in October 2000, the Belgian Presidency submitted a request to the Commission to draft a new proposal, accompanied by a number of principles that the proposal should adhere to.[10] After the Commission had presented its proposal mid-2002, the Council reached a political agreement on 30 April 2004, the day before the accession of ten new EU Member States.[11] As it unsuccessfully tried to reach a common list of safe countries of origin, it took until December 2005 before the Council decided to adopt the directive, which included a procedure for adopting a common list in the future.[12]

4 T. Strik, *Besluitvorming over asiel- en migratierichtlijnen. De wisselwerking tussen nationaal en Europees niveau*, Den Haag: Boom Juridische uitgevers 2011. More information on the study under 'Assessing the negotiation process: methodology'.

5 Treaty of Amsterdam amending the Treaty on European Union, the Treaties establishing the European Communities and certain related acts – Final Act, Official Journal *C 340, 10/11/1997 P. 0115.*

6 See the first proposal of the Commission, COM(1999)638, 1 December 1999 and the second, COM(2000)624, 10 October 2000, released after the European Parliament had adopted its resolution.

7 Presidency Conclusions – Laeken, 14 and 15 December 2001, SN 300/1/01.

8 COM(2002)225, 2 May 2002.

9 The Directive on the right to Family Reunification, 2003/86, OJ 3 October 2003, L 251/12.

10 See the first proposal, COM(2000)278, 24 October 2000 and Presidency Conclusion no. 41, Laeken, SN 300/1/01 REV 1.

11 See the revised proposal COM(2002)326, 18 June 2002; see the agreement 8771/04 ASILE 33, 30 April 2004.

12 Asylum Procedures Directive, 2005/85, OJ 13 December 2005, L 326/13.

Due to the limitations of the Treaty of Amsterdam, the decision making process concentrated around the Commission and Council.[13] The Commission took the initiative for the draft directives and acted as advisor and mediator during the negotiations at the Council.[14] The principle of unanimity in the Council on Justice and Home Affairs -matters and the limited role of the European Parliament paved the way for a dominant role for national interests. As every single Member State needed to give its consent, it had the power to insist on certain amendments, which often contradicted the interests of the Commission.[15] This intergovernmental approach impeded the institutionalisation of an EU migrant inclusion policy.[16] Whereas the Commission mainly defended the aim of harmonisation at a high protection level for migrants, the ministers of Interior or Justice in the Council primarily aimed for maintenance of their national legislation and preferably also their national sovereignty. Harmonisation as such was not recognised as being in their national interest, despite official declarations that claimed the opposite.[17] The negotiation table hence transformed into a 'market of optional provisions' for which the delegations' actions were mutually supportive. This exchange of amendments only functioned well regarding proposals which lowered the level of protection, as they did not imply any additional obligations for the Member States.

The influence of the European Parliament on the decision-making process had been minimal. As the Council had the final say, it drastically changed the proposals of the Commission by lowering the standards and creating more discretion for the Member States. The amendments of the European Parliament, which merely supported the Commission, were practically ignored. The Commission only accepted these amendments insofar as this did not undermine the support for its own proposal by the Member States. It therefore only accepted amendments, which narrowed the personal scope or did not lead to additional obligations for Member States. The Council did not make an effort to involve the Parliament or to take its amendments seriously. The gap in position between the Parliament and the Council was even broader than the one between the Commission and the Council. This made the Parliament use its competence to bring both directives to the Court of Justice, requesting it to annul certain provisions of the directives. In the case of the Family Reunification Directive, the judgment *Parliament against Council* has impacted the meaning of the directive. In that judgment, the Court showed the difference with Article 8 ECHR, by making clear that the right to family reunification leaves no discretion for the Member States regarding sponsors who

---

13 The legal basis for the Asylum Procedures Directive was Article 63 (1) (d) and the basis for the Family Reunification Directive was Article 63 (3) (a) EC-Treaty.

14 Most of the negotiations took place in the Working Group consisting of governmental experts. The next higher level was Scifa, consisting of the managers of the department involved, and the highest level of officials was COREPER, where the heads of the Permanent Representatives (PR) had to reach an agreement before it could be referred to the Council of Ministers. The Council could refer the text back to the JHA-Council, where experts of the PR solved the outstanding questions and problems of a more technical nature. These were the most informal meetings, without translators. See Strik 2011, p. 45-49.

15 Strik 2011, p. 391-393.

16 See also A. Geddes, 'Lobbying for migrant inclusion in the European Union: new opportunities for transnational advocacy?', 7:4 *JEPP* 2000, p. 632-649, at p. 634.

17 See for instance the Tampere conclusions of 1999, where the European Council expressed the objective of harmonisation of asylum and migration policy, Council document no. 200/1/99.

fulfill the conditions allowed by the directive. But even if these conditions are not fulfilled, they have to perform an individual assessment in the light of the Charter of Fundamental Rights, taking into account all relevant circumstances and interests.[18] In the case of the Asylum Procedures Directive, where the exclusive competence of the Council to adopt a common list of safe third countries was challenged, Parliament has made the establishment of common lists of safe third countries more difficult, as the Court decided that such list would need the consent of the Parliament in the framework of co-decision.[19] This impact is still relevant during the current negotiations on safe third country concepts and common lists in the framework of the Procedures Regulation.[20]

The limited impact of the Parliament also reduced the opportunities for the NGOs, as they exerted most influence during the preparation stage carried out by the Commission and the consultation stage involving the European Parliament. Certain provisions in the proposals of the Commission and opinions of the Parliament were identical to the proposals of the NGOs and UNHCR. The texts that the NGOs and UNHCR had successfully promoted towards the Commission and Parliament were however deleted or weakened by the Council, or transferred to the preamble of the directives. As the institutional context of that time had made the Council extremely powerful, the final outcome of the NGO lobbying was close to zero.[21] After adoption of both directives, the NGOs successfully advocated for an action for annulment by the European Parliament before the Court of Justice. Their lobbying activities hence resulted in some influence prior to and after the Council negotiations, but hardly any during the actual decisions taken by the Council.

3. The Lisbon Period

Fundamentalists versus Pragmatists

With the adoption of the Lisbon Treaty, co-decision procedures became the rule (with some exceptions) for JHA-legislation.[22] The switch from consultation to co-decision, combined with the abolishment of the right of veto for the Member States, has significantly changed the position of Parliament. As the Member States could no longer ignore the Parliament, member of Parliament (MEPs) suddenly became an object of lobby for the national representatives. But the new power also changed the approach of political groups. Before, the consultation procedure combined with the simple majority rule within Parliament had enabled the development of confrontational positions towards the Council, as the Parliament could disclaim any responsibility in the policy

18 CJEU 27 June 2006, C-540/03, *Parliament against Council.*

19 CJEU 6 May 2008, C-133/06, *Parliament against Council.*

20 On 13 July 2016, the Commission put forward a legislative proposal on the reform of the Asylum Procedures Directive. The Commission proposed to replace the Asylum Procedures Directive with a regulation COM (2016) 467 final.

21 Strik 2011, p. 402-405.

22 See Title V of the TFEU. With the Lisbon Treaty, this procedure is defined as the 'ordinary legislation procedure'.

outcomes.[23] Smaller political groups were more visible and more successful, as they managed to mobilise the entire LIBE committee (European Parliament's Committee on Civil Liberties, Justice and Home Affairs). Rather than a left-right division, Ripoll Servent observed a cleavage between those advocating liberty-oriented policies and those supporting the more security-oriented position of Commission and Council.[24] It resulted in a generally liberal voting record on irregular migration and asylum legislation. The shift towards co-decision worked out well for the moderate big parties: the conservative European People's Party (EPP), which often shared its position with the Council, became a key player in negotiations, necessary for reaching the required majorities. The group formed grand coalitions with the Socialists and Democrats Party (S&D), thus marginalizing smaller party groups. Their changing positions also seem closely linked to the increased authority and responsibility of the Parliament, which made the two groups realize that in order to be effective and not to run the risk that legislation would be dropped, it needed to propose amendments that were acceptable to the Council. The shift towards co-decision thus led to more restrictive positions of the Parliament on asylum and migration legislation.[25] Acosta criticized this 'all-to-eager acceptance of a deficient piece of legislation', referring to Parliament's position in the Returns Directive. The reasoning that it is better to have something rather than nothing at all, runs the risk that the power remains with the Council.[26] In that light, Acosta but also other authors point at the tendency of MEPs to aim at achieving an agreement with the Council in the first reading, which does not serve the interest of a more democratic and transparent European Union.[27] Yet, the role of the European Parliament is central to the criticism on the lack of democratic legitimacy and accountability of the EU, as Parliament is in the best position to address the democratic deficit through its role in the decision-making process.

Returns Directive: Putting the New Rule to the Test

The first acid test for the meaning of the new position of Parliament was formed by the negotiations on the Returns Directive, which has been comprehensively analysed by Lutz, representing the Commission in that process.[28] According to Lutz, this procedural change prevented the Member States from agreeing relatively easily on a watered down text with very limited added value.[29] The strengthened position of the Parliament made the achievement of an agreement significantly more difficult, but it also

23 A. Ripoll Servent, 'Playing the Co-Decision Game? Rules' Changes and institutional adaptation at the LIBE Committee', 34:1 *Journal of European Integration* 2012, p. 55-73.

24 A. Ripoll Servent, 'Playing the Co-Decision Game? Rules' Changes and institutional adaptation at the LIBE Committee', 34:1 *Journal of European Integration* 2012, p. 55-73, at p. 62.

25 E. Lopatin, 'The changing position of the European Parliament on irregular migration and asylum under co-decision', 51(4) *JCMS* 2013, p. 751-752.

26 D. Acosta, 'The Good, the Bad and the Ugly in EU Migration Law: is the European Parliament Becoming Bad and Ugly?', 11 *EJML* 2009, p. 38-39.

27 See also F. Trauner & A. Ripoll Servent, 'The Communitarization of the Area of Freedom, Security and Justice: Why Institutional Change does not Translate into Policy Change', 54(6) *JCMS* 2016, p. 1426; R. Parkes, 'Borders: EU Institutions Fail to Reconcile their Agendas Despite Communitarisation', in: F. Trauner & A. Ripoll Servent (eds), *Policy Change in the Area of Freedom, Security and Justice: How EU Institutions Matter*, London: Routledge, p. 65.

28 F. Lutz, *The Negotiations on the Return Directive*, Nijmegen: Wolf Legal Publishers 2010.

29 F. Lutz 2010.

allowed for qualitative improvements that would not have been made under the consultation procedure. Examples are the exceptions to the obligation to impose a re-entry ban, the obligation to provide for free legal aid, the individualized approach with regard to determining the risk of absconding, explicit references to the *non-refoulement* principle, the priority given to voluntary return, an express set of rights for illegally staying persons facing return, and special safeguards for minors and their families.

During the process of adopting amendments, the rapporteur and his shadow rapporteurs had an intensive debate in order to reach agreement on some principles which were known 'no-goes' for the Council, such as an absolute prohibition to remove minors, suspensive effect of appeals in all cases, a prohibition to return persons to countries of transit and an absolute prohibition to remove persons if that would worsen their medical treatment. Meanwhile, during the Council negotiations, the Member States moved towards the enlargement of national discretion and thus minimalizing the level of harmonisation. The complete absence of communication between the Council and the Parliament facilitated these parallel developments. This did not only delay the process but the premature fixing of positions also made it harder to achieve common ground. The European Parliament perceived council as 'repressive', whereas the Council criticized the European Parliament for a 'lack of realism'. In response to the request of Parliament rapporteur Weber to attend some meetings, referring to the presence of the Council and Commission representatives at the LIBE committee meetings, the Council refused access and continued the non-communication with the Parliament that it was used to during the previous consultation procedures.[30]

Lutz observed that under consultation the European Parliament tended to adopt ambitious and maximalist opinions, but under co-decision there was a division between MEPs who wanted to 'keep their hands clean' and those who wanted to accept compromises in order to avoid failure of negotiations, which would backfire to the Parliament as well.[31] This illustrates that the Parliament also had an institutional interest in achieving an agreement with the Council. Although these differences between the groups can indeed be observed, it must be noted that for members of the EPP and the Alliance of Liberals and Democrats for Europe (ALDE) it was more easy to accept compromises as these were close to their position anyhow. As for the left-winged politicians the gap between their ambitions and the Council positions was much more difficult to bridge, and the compromises thus had a higher cost.

4. Common European Asylum System

The ordinary legislation procedure also applied to the recast asylum instruments, which the Commission proposed as a step for further harmonisation in the framework of the Common European Asylum System.[32] The main function of the recast was diminishing the derogation clauses, which the Member States had managed to negotiate under the unanimity rule. As Parliament had not been able to influence the initial instruments,

---

30 Lutz 2010, p. 19-21.

31 Lutz 2010, p. 85.

32 The common European asylum system (CEAS) sets common standards for the treatment of all asylum seekers and applications across the EU.

which still constituted the pillars of the recast ones, the effect of co-decision on the instruments as a whole remained limited. Parliament had to satisfy itself with changes of secondary importance, however those changes implied more protection, procedural safeguards and solidarity, often supported by successful litigation before the European Courts.[33]

After the recast of most of the asylum instruments, there was a broad consensus that attention for a correct implementation would be the best way forward to reach harmonisation. However, the increasing numbers of asylum seekers in 2015 triggered the Commission and national political leaders to show they were in control. This led to a new wave of legislative proposals, distracting from the implementation process of the newly adopted measures. Ironically enough, the Member States could not agree on the content, which resulted in a deadlock at the end of the Juncker term. Disagreement on reforming the Dublin Regulation (with its relocation mechanism and the strengthened responsibility for the Member State of first entrance) and the proposed Asylum Procedures Regulation (with its concepts and list of safe third countries) are among the main hurdles. The European Parliament on the other hand, managed to adopt a mandate for negotiations with the Council on seven instruments. One of the strong elements of the Parliament's position, shared by Member States like Italy, Greece, Sweden and Hungary, was its condition that the instruments were negotiated as a package, which prevented the Member States from cherry picking.[34] If this requirement would not have been applied by the Parliament, it would have risked that repressive tools would have been adopted, but that the refugee-friendly instruments such as the resettlement Regulation would have been left out. But it would also have meant that the disagreement on the most divisive legislation, namely the Dublin Regulation continues, which would prevent the EU from achieving a genuine harmonisation. Here the Parliament shows that it is able to use its power and leverage in a strategic way, in favour of reaching harmonisation. Political groups in the new Parliament have already expressed their will to continue its 'package approach', and to stick to the positions taken by the previous Parliament in order not to create an avenue for re-opening the package. This will force the Member States to reach agreement instead of asking the Commission to present new proposals.

5. The External Dimension

Where Member States are not able to agree on the internal EU asylum policy, they find each other in focussing on externalising asylum policies through cooperation with third countries. In exchange for benefits to those countries, the EU seduces them to strengthen their border controls and visa rules and to readmit migrants and refugees who crossed their territory. The Partnership Framework, presented by the Commission in

33 F. Trauner & A. Ripoll Servent, 'The Communitarization of the Area of Freedom, Security and Justice: Why Institutional Change does not Translate into Policy Change', 54(6) *JCMS* 2016, p. 1426-1429. See also the briefing of the Parliament, 'European Parliament's positions on key issues related to asylum and migration', High-Level Conference on Migration Management, 21 June 2017, PE 583.160.

34 L. Rasche, 'Breaking the deadlock on the EU asylum front?' Policy Position 20, December 2018, Berlin: Jacques Delors Institute 2018.

2016, aims to adopt tailor made 'compacts' with priority partner countries, in which all instruments, tools and leverage are put together, 'to better manage migration in full respect of our humanitarian and human rights obligations'.[35] Here the principle of conditionality has been put to the centre of the policy, implying that the economic support of third countries depends on their performances on readmission and border control. The 'more for more' principle would therefore be complemented with the 'less for less' principle and strengthened by the use of all EU policy areas, with the exception of humanitarian aid.

The external dimension of EU migration and asylum policies is not only complementary to the Common European Asylum System, but also steers the content of its legislation. Perhaps the most visible example is the safe third country concept in the Asylum Procedures Directive, which is currently discussed in the framework of the draft Procedures Regulation. On 22-23 June 2017, the European Council agreed that:

> 'in order to enhance cooperation with third countries and prevent new crises, the "safe third country" concept should be aligned with the effective requirements arising from the Geneva Convention and EU primary law, while respecting the competences of the EU and the Member States under the Treaties. In this context, the European Council calls for work on an EU list of safe third countries to be taken forward (...). The European Council invites the Council to continue negotiations on this basis and amend the legislative proposals as necessary, with the active help of the Commission.'[36]

The expected watering down of the criteria for the designation of a safe third country, will further pave the way for the adoption of the EU-Turkey model to other countries with even less safeguards for protection, reception and access to society.[37] Political leaders have clearly shown an interest in concluding similar agreements with Tunisia, but also other countries of interest have their attention.

Apart from these internal legislative elements of the external dimension, it remains very difficult for the Parliament to get grip on the externalisation process itself. The main cause for that is the weak role of Parliament in foreign policies, where the Council acts on the basis of unanimity and is not bound by any position Parliament takes. The Lisbon Treaty granted European Parliament explicit competence in the field of readmission, as readmission agreements require parliamentary approval. Reslow notes that Parliament already exercised influence before, especially by criticising the lack of references to human rights instruments in the European Readmission Agreements (EURA's).[38] The policy on visa, an important incentive in external cooperation, is also governed by formal agreements subject to Parliament's consent. More influence on the external cooperation on migration could make a difference, as Parliament's narrative is

35 Commission, 'Communication on establishing a new Partnership Framework with third countries under the European Agenda on Migration', COM (2016) 385; T, Strik, 'Migration deals and responsibility sharing: can the two go together?', in: S. Carrera, T. Strik, J. Santos Vara, *Constitutionalising the External Dimensions of EU Migration Policies in Times of Crisis*, Cheltenham: Edward Elgar Publishing 2019.

36 European Council, 'Meeting of 22-23 June' (Council document EUCO 8/17, 23 June 2017), Conclusion no. 23.

37 European Council, 'EU-Turkey statement, 18 March 2016', Press release 144/16.

38 N. Reslow, *Crisis, Change and Continuity: The Role of the European Parliament in EU External Migration Policy*, paper prepared for the ECPR conference, Hamburg, 22-25 August 2018.

based on human rights, whereas the Council is rather led by security concerns.[39] This is illustrated by Parliament's 2017 resolution on the role of EU external action in addressing migration, in which Parliament emphasised the need for a human rights approach and stipulated that the external action should be guided by the principles on which the EU is based, such as democracy and human rights.[40] However, I see two reasons why this expectation should be tempered. First, due to the tendency towards more restrictive positions, a dominant human rights approach by Parliament cannot be taken for granted. It approved for instance the EU-Turkey readmission agreement despite pleas from NGOs not to adopt it until the rights of migrants could be guaranteed.[41] Second, most of the instruments concluded with third countries in the framework of migration cooperation lack the formal status of an international agreement, which sidelines the European Parliament. EURAs and Visa Facilitation Agreements are the formal elements of a much broader, more comprehensive set of agreements with a significant impact despite its legally non-binding nature. The consent of Parliament only relates to the more technical outcome of this cooperation, and not to the whole EU approach and the reciprocation by the third countries. Parliament has no voice in Mobility Partnerships with third countries, although the conditionality principle (cooperation on irregular migration in exchange for legal migration) clearly relates to Parliament's competences on visa and return. It is also not involved in bilateral, regional and multilateral dialogues on migration, such as the African, Caribbean and Pacific (ACP)-EU migration dialogue, the Rabat Process or the Prague Process, in which the Commission and the Member States participate.[42] The European Parliament however decided to take an active role during the negotiations on the Global Compacts on Safe, Orderly and Regular Migration and on Refugees, which may reveal an increasing awareness of the need for parliamentary involvement in international migration policies.[43]

Parliamentary Scrutiny of the External Dimension

Since the large arrival of asylum seekers in 2015, the gap between Council and Parliament has further widened in this area. The Member States increased their intergovernmental cooperation in order to tackle the irregular migration through the so-called 'Balkan-route'. The General Court of the EU ruled that 'neither the European Council nor

39 A. Maricut, 'Different narratives, one area without internal frontiers: why EU institutions cannot agree on the refugee crisis', 19(2) *National Identities* 2017, p. 161-177.

40 See for instance the European Parliament resolutions, 'Addressing refugee and migrant movements: the role of EU external action', P_TA(2017)0124 and 'The situation in the Mediterranean and the need for a holistic EU approach to migration' P8_TA(2016)0102; N. Reslow, *Crisis, Change and Continuity: The Role of the European Parliament in EU External Migration Policy*, paper prepared for the ECPR conference, Hamburg, 22-25 August 2018.

41 Euro-Mediterranean Human Rights Network, 'European Parliament: do not vote on favour of an EU-Turkey readmission agreement!', Brussels: EMHRN 2014, http://www.migreurop.org/article2476.html?lang=fr.

42 N. Reslow, *Crisis, Change and Continuity: The Role of the European Parliament in EU External Migration Policy*, paper prepared for the ECPR conference, Hamburg, 22-25 August 2018; see for an overview P. García Andrade, P. Martín & S. Mananashvili, *EU cooperation with third countries in the field of migration*, Study for the LIBE Committee, PE 536.469, Brussels: European Parliament 2015.

43 European Parliament resolution of 18 April 2018 on progress on the UN Global Compacts for Safe, Orderly and Regular Migration and on Refugees, P8_TA(2018)0118.

any other institution of the EU decided to conclude an agreement with the Turkish government on the subject of the migration crisis'.[44] The European Parliament expressed its concerns about 'outsourcing the refugee crisis to Turkey', as it is 'not a credible long-term solution to the problem'.[45] It also expressed its criticism to the form and content of the deal.[46] The Court approved of this strategy to use the intergovernmental framework by denying its competence to rule on the EU-Turkey Statement, despite the heavy involvement of the Commission, the Council president and the use of EU funds and EU policies as incentives for Turkey to sign the Statement.[47] The circumvention of the institutional framework of the EU, clearly affecting the necessary checks and balances, has not only consequences for the democratic legitimacy but also for the level of accountability, including access to justice and fundamental rights.[48] These interests beg for more competences and scrutiny by the European Parliament. Preferably those international instruments, with names like 'compacts', 'the Joint Way Forward' or 'Memoranda of Understanding', would have the status of a treaty. But even if this informal cooperation continues, Parliament could use its whole 'toolkit' in order to get involved in this external cooperation. The most logical strategy is to use its formal power to become involved in non-legislative instruments. In some instances, Parliament managed to create political linkage of the Return Fund to the Returns Directive. In Spring 2007, Parliament planned not to release the budget for the first year of the European Return Fund in 2008, which created pressure on the Council to agree with certain procedural safeguards for a humane and dignified treatment of returnees in order to achieve an agreement with the Parliament.[49] It would be very logical to refrain from approving a EURA or Visa-Facilitation Agreement as long as the more comprehensive cooperation arrangement with that specific third country has not been discussed and agreed upon by Parliament. But with the same purpose, it could also freeze negotiations on secondary legislation in case of linkage with the external dimension. This could create leverage to demand an ex-ante evaluation of the human rights impact of a migration

44 General Court of the European Union, case nos T-193/16, NG, ECLI:EU:T:2017:129 and T-257/16, *NM*, ECLI:EU:T:2017:130; on 12 September 2018 CJEU declared the appeals against the decisions *manifestly inadmissible*, see C-208/17.
'The General Court declares that it lacks jurisdiction to hear and determine the actions brought by three asylum seekers against the EU-Turkey statement which seeks to resolve the migration crisis', https://curia.europa.eu/jcms/upload/docs/application/pdf/2017-02/cp170019en.pdf.

45 European Parliament, *2015 Report on Turkey*, P8_TA(2016)0133, Brussel: European Parliament 2015; see N. Reslow, *Crisis, Change and Continuity: The Role of the European Parliament in EU External Migration Policy*, paper prepared for the ECPR conference, Hamburg, 22-25 August 2018.

46 European Parliament, 'MEPs demand details of the EU-Turkey deal and compliance with international law', Brussels: European Parliament 2016, http://www.europarl.europa.eu/news/en/press-room/20160303IPR16928/meps-demand-details-of-the-eu-turkey-deal-and-compliance-with-international-law.

47 Commission, 'EU-Turkey Joint Action Plan – Implementation Report', http://ec.europa.eu/dgs/home-affairs/what-we-do/policies/european-agenda-migration/background-information/docs/managing_the_refugee_crisis_-_eu-turkey_join_action_plan_implementation_report_20160210_en.pdf, accessed 9 November 2017. European Council, 'EU-Turkey statement, 18 March 2016', Press release 144/16.

48 See also J.-P. Cassarino, 'Informalising Readmission Agreements in the EU Neighbourhood', 42(4) *The International Spectator* 2007, p. 179-196.

49 See Lutz 2010, p. 22.

deal, combined with the establishment of an independent monitoring system. Parliament could come up with a set of human rights criteria for such impact assessment and monitoring. Using its power of consent to gain influence on external cooperation on migration would also be a way to compensate for the absence of a right to initiative, which is currently impeding an effective performance. In 2018, the Parliament managed to agree on the need for humanitarian visa, in order to create safe and legal channels for refugees.[50] The ever increasing externalisation, which prevents refugees from getting access to the EU territory, strengthens the need for such channels. However , the Commission and Council could afford not to respond to this resolution. Den Hartog and Reslow also point at the scrutiny role of Parliament regarding Funds, observing that its budgetary authority has been affected by the emergency mechanisms.[51] The Refugee Facility For Turkey was adopted as a Commission decision, and the EU Emergency Trust Fund for Africa (EUTF) has been established through the adoption of a constitutive agreement between Commission and some Member States only. Although the EUTF is framed as an emergency instrument, most of its resources consist of Official Development Assistance (ODA), which is intended to fund long-term development programmes. In their analyses of the implementation of the Fund, OECD and the European Court of Auditors observed that migration control is often prioritized above development goals, which underlines the importance of parliamentary scrutiny.[52] The increase of the budget for Asylum, Migration and Integration Fund (AMIF) and Internal Security Fund (ISF) was accompanied by parliamentary scrutiny, but the process of adoption happened in a rush, followed by a request from the Commission for urgent approval. The marginal role of Parliament contradicts to its traditionally strong position on the budget, for instance regarding the Multiannual Financial Framework. As with other EU programmes, the implementation of these funds requires transparency, monitoring and evaluation, accountability mechanisms, as well as preliminary and ongoing assessments of their impact on fundamental rights. Another weakness of the Parliament is that its scrutiny role is divided among different committees, whereas the external dimension encompasses all policy areas. That the role of Parliament is different at every policy area, makes an effective scrutiny extra challenging. As migration control is the main objective of the external dimension, LIBE committee would be best placed to play a central role in establishing requirements for the cooperation, assessing the agreements and monitoring their implementation.

50 European Parliament resolution of 11 December 2018 with recommendations to the Commission on Humanitarian Visas, P8_TA(2018)0494.

51 N. Reslow, *Crisis, Change and Continuity: The Role of the European Parliament in EU External Migration Policy*, paper prepared for the ECPR conference, Hamburg, 22-25 August 2018; L. den Hertog, *Money Talks. Mapping the funding for EU external migration policy*, CEPS Papers in Liberty and Security in Europe no. 95, Brussels: CEPS 2016; L. den Hertog, *EU Budgetary Responses to the 'Refugee Crisis'. Reconfiguring the Funding Landscape*, Papers in Liberty and Security in Europe no. 93, Brussels: CEPS 2016.

52 OECD Development Co-operation Peer Reviews: European Union 2018, December 2018; European Court of Auditors, *European Union Emergency Trust Fund for Africa: Flexible but lacking focus*, special report no. 32, Luxembourg: European Court of Auditors 2018.

6. Conclusion

Although the role of the European Parliament on asylum and migration legislation has strengthened since the entry into force of the Lisbon Treaty, it still struggles to safeguard democratic control on European asylum and migration policy in general. The choice of Member States to adopt the first generation asylum and migration instruments in a consultation procedure, has created a significant disadvantage for the Parliament. This has its effect up until now, as the subsequent recasts are based on the instruments negotiated among the Member States. Another main factor is that Member States tend to pursue their aims through intergovernmental cooperation, especially in the external cooperation, where the European Parliament has a much weaker position. Their tendency to circumvent the institutional framework has its repercussions for the democratic legitimacy and accountability of the EU. Another factor affecting effective control is that where the Commission previously shared the human rights approach of Parliament, it seems to prioritise the objectives of the Member States. Yet, the failing of a right to initiative makes Parliament depend on the acceptance of their proposals by the Commission. In order to compensate the lack of checks and balances, the Parliament needs to be creative as well. It can use its legislative and budgetary powers as a leverage to demand involvement and influence on the asylum and migration policies. A more comprehensive approach through which all relevant committees cooperate in establishing an integral position on the external cooperation, would not only avoid fragmented control or the possibility to be played off against each other, but also enhance coherence of the EU's foreign policy. Lastly, the European Parliament could also strengthen democratic control by creating more transparency of the decision making process. Apart from urging the Council to grant public access to its working documents (in line with the CJEU jurisprudence), it could also create more openness in the trilogue process, for instance by opting for a second reading more frequently. More openness would enable civil society to be informed and become a player in the decision making process. Taking into account all current hurdles, it is amazing that Elspeth always manages to respond timely and thoroughly to new developments, and to be so influential in this way.

Dear Elspeth, I am sure that I will benefit from you closely watching EU decision making in this field. You are a great source of inspiration to me. Thanks a lot for our cooperation at the Radboud University, and I hope we find ample opportunities to continue it.

Mayors' Discretion in Decisions about Rejected Asylum Seekers

*Ashley Terlouw & Anita Böcker**

1. Introduction

In October 2018, the mayor of Riace, a small Italian town in southern Italy, was put under house arrest over claims that he had set up an illegal operation to prevent asylum seekers being deported. In the years before his arrest, Mayor Domenico Lucano had gained international fame for welcoming hundreds of refugees to Riace. Prosecutors issued a statement saying that their investigation had brought to light 'the unscrupulousness of Mr Lucano, despite his institutional role', in organising marriages of convenience between Riace citizens and asylum seekers, to secure the latter's stay in Italy. Civil society organisations expressed concern about the arrest, and anti-mafia writer Roberto Saviano wrote in a Facebook post that the goal of Lucano's actions was 'not profit, but civil disobedience' and that this was 'the only weapon we have to defend not only the rights of migrants, but everyone's'.[1] Another writer, Gioacchino Criaco, said Lucano was an honest man but that the 'rules on the reception and management of migrants are too tangled, and administrators often find themselves caught in a dilemma between a humanitarian choice and a legal one'.[2]

During her long and extremely productive academic career, Elspeth Guild has published on law and law making processes in the field of migration and asylum at a variety of levels and in a variety of arenas, critically examining the role of a wide variety of actors – state and non-state, national, supranational and intergovernmental actors – involved in these processes. In this contribution, we will focus on an actor which, as far as we have been able to establish, has more or less escaped Elspeth Guild's attention. We will examine how mayors in the Netherlands perceive and use their discretion in situations involving rejected asylum seekers or other migrants whom the national government considers to be 'unlawfully present aliens'.

In several European countries, mayors have stood up for (rejected) asylum seekers. The position of mayors in different countries differs and so do their formal and informal powers and competences. In Italy, mayors are elected and enjoy large autonomy and independence. In the Netherlands, mayors are appointed by the national government. They are not as autonomous and independent vis-à-vis the national government as elected mayors. However, they too may be required to decide about offering support to rejected asylum seekers.

---

* Radboud University Nijmegen, the Netherlands.

1 Ylenia Gostoli, 'Italy's pro-refugee mayor Domenico Lucano arrested', *Al Jazeera News*, 2 October 2018. Retrieved from https://www.aljazeera.com.

2 'Pro-refugee Italian mayor arrested for "aiding illegal migration"', *The Guardian* 2 October 2018. Retrieved from https://www.theguardian.com.

> In 2018, the expulsion of Afghan asylum seekers to their country of origin led to societal unrest in Tytsjerksteradiel, a village in the north of the Netherlands and the location of a reception centre for rejected asylum seekers. The municipal council and several NGOs urged the mayor to refuse to cooperate with the expulsions. Mayor Jeroen Gebben responded that he would be exceeding or abusing his discretion if he did so, because the matter fell within the competence of the national government.[3]

There have also been cases where mayors in the Netherlands helped rejected asylum seekers to go into hiding to prevent their expulsion, or where they instructed the police not to cooperate in an expulsion.

> In 2012, Mayor Els Boot (Giessenlanden) instructed the police not to provide assistance in the expulsion of an Afghan asylum seeker. She said she feared disastrous consequences for his wife and children if the man was expelled. 'As a mayor, I am bound by my duty of care for every resident in my municipality. I cannot stand by and watch the drama unfold if I can prevent it', she stated.

Mayors apparently have different perceptions of their discretion or, in terms of Dworkin's hole-in-the-doughnut analogy, different ideas about the content and tightness of the 'belt of restriction' surrounding their discretion. In this contribution, we will examine how mayors in the Netherlands have responded to two types of situations involving rejected asylum seekers or other unlawfully present migrants:

1. Mayors may be asked (by local actors like members of the municipal council, NGOs or individual citizens) to resist the expulsion of unlawfully present migrants. This often concerns (families with) children who have grown up in the Netherlands.
2. Mayors may be asked to provide shelter and other forms of support to unlawfully present migrants who cannot be expelled and who have been found living on the street or causing a public nuisance.

In both situations, mayors are asked to act against or depart from the policies of the national government. How do they respond? Do they take action, and if yes, what types of action, and how do they justify their responses? Do they consider them as falling within their discretionary space? In brief, how do mayors perceive, define and use their discretion? As we are interested in how mayors perceive their discretion, we do not distinguish beforehand between weak and strong discretion, or between discretion and autonomy.[4] To use once more Dworkin's hole-in-the-doughnut analogy, we assume

---

3 'Wat kan de gemeente doen tegen uitzettingen van afgewezen asielzoekers?', *Friesch Dagblad* 18 August 2018. Retrieved from https://frieschdagblad.nl.

4 The concept discretion has been defined in different ways. According to Van Leeuwen, Tummers & Van der Walle (2017, p. 2), 'discretion can be broadly conceptualized as decision-making power over sort, quantity, and quality of sanctions and rewards during policy implementation'. According to Evans & Harris (2004, p. 871, 881), 'discretion should be regarded as a series of gradations of freedom to make decisions'. See also Eule (2014, p. 57), commenting on Lipsky's (1980, 2010) distinction between discretion and autonomy.

that mayors may have different ideas about both the content (they may refer to different sets of rules) and the tightness (they may see more or less room for manoeuvre) of the 'belt of restriction' surrounding their discretion.

To answer the above questions, we analysed newspaper reports of local cases that occurred in the years 2011-2018. We conducted a search of all Dutch news in *Lexis Nexis*, an online database of newspaper articles, using the search terms *burgemeester** AND *uitgeprocedeerd**. This yielded 551 results. After excluding double hits[5], we had 361 results left. Further selection was done by reading the articles: 295 articles turned out to be relevant. Next, 16 more relevant articles were found by way of the snowball method and a Google search.[6] All in all, we analysed 311 newspaper articles. Moreover, we interviewed four mayors. One of them had also been chair of the committee for asylum affairs of the Association of Netherlands Municipalities. Another one had also been the responsible minister for some years.

2. Backgrounds

In the Netherlands, mayors (*burgemeesters*) are the head of the municipal government. There are 355 municipalities in the Netherlands. They are responsible for various public services. The mayor chairs both the municipal council, whose members are elected by the general populace, and the council of mayor and aldermen (*College van B&W*), which is the executive board of the municipality. The members of this executive all have their own portfolio. The mayor's portfolio always includes public order and safety. Whereas the aldermen are elected and can be voted out by the municipal council, the mayor is appointed by the national government and therefore cannot be removed from his office by the municipal council. Nearly all mayors are members of political parties, but they are expected to be impartial. Mayors are responsible for public order and safety in the municipality. For this purpose, they have authority over the police. They cannot be instructed about the use of their powers in this respect by the municipal council, they can only be called to account about their actions afterwards.[7]

Although there has been a trend toward decentralising powers from the national government to the municipalities, powers and competences in the field of migration and asylum law have remained with the national government. Over the past decades, the treatment of rejected asylum seekers has been a continuous matter of debate between the national government and municipalities. Under the Aliens Act 2000, rejected asylum seekers are obliged to leave the country and their entitlement to reception ends four weeks after their asylum application has been turned down. In practice, however, many do not voluntarily leave and are not forcibly expelled either. Some of them end up on the streets in municipalities. Municipalities are responsible for providing social support, but the so-called Linking Act, which entered into force in 1998, prohibits them from providing support to unlawfully present aliens.[8] The municipalities (through

5 If the same article was published in different newspapers with joint editorial offices, we selected the article in the main journal. When an article with the same title was published twice in the same newspaper, we selected the longest version.

6 We thank Mienke de Wilde for searching and selecting relevant articles.

7 Voermans & Waling 2018, p. 106.

8 Pluymen 2008, p. 36.

the Association of Netherlands Municipalities, of which all municipalities are members, and LOGO, a platform of municipalities which offer shelter to rejected asylum seekers) argue that rejected asylum seekers should be offered reception facilities until their departure or expulsion, to prevent problems in the field of public order and safety and public health. Moreover, they argue that if the national government does not take its responsibility in this respect, municipalities are allowed or even obliged to provide at least a minimal form of shelter, often referred to as 'bed, bath and bread'.[9] The national government wants the municipalities to stop providing shelter as it will encourage rejected asylum seekers to stay in the country unlawfully.[10]

Another disagreement concerned the authority over the police in relation to expulsions of rejected asylum seekers. Whereas the national government took the position that the authority lies with the minister of Justice and Security, many mayors thought they could instruct the police not to provide assistance with an expulsion to prevent public unrest in their municipality.[11] In 2012, forty mayors signed a letter in which they supported the refusal of Mayor Els Boot to call in the police for the expulsion of an Afghan asylum seeker.[12] The mayors argued that the minister's interpretation of the Police Act was incorrect. The minister then commissioned an expert opinion from legal scholars. They concluded that the authority over the police in relation to expulsions lay exclusively with the minister, and that save in very exceptional circumstances, mayors could not forbid the police to assist with expulsions.[13]

The municipalities also called for a regularisation scheme for asylum seekers who had been in the country for many years. In 2007, after years of discussion, the national government agreed to a one-off regularisation scheme, the so-called *Pardonregeling* (amnesty scheme), on condition that the municipalities would stop offering shelter to rejected asylum seekers who did not fulfil the conditions of the scheme. In 2013, again under pressure from, among others, municipalities, the national government agreed to a special regularisation scheme for long-term resident children, the *Kinderpardon* (children's amnesty scheme). In January 2019, the government agreed to loosen the conditions of the scheme.

The municipalities have thus achieved some successes. However, the problem of rejected asylum seekers ending up on the streets in municipalities has not been solved; it has remained a bone of contention between the national government and municipalities. The national government has used a variety of means and arguments to persuade municipalities to stop providing shelter to rejected asylum seekers, from emphasising the importance of uniform government action and denying mayors' discretionary powers in these matters to threatening municipalities with financial penalties.

The national government does not exclude rejected asylum seekers entirely from reception facilities. An exception is made for families with minor children. They are

---

9 Cf. Kos, Maussen & Doomernik 2015, p. 9.

10 ACVZ 2012, 2018; Winter et. al. 2018.

11 ACVZ 2012.

12 Rob Pietersen, 'Burgemeester belet uitzetting Afghaan', *Trouw* 27 March 2012. Retrieved from https://www.trouw.nl; '40 burgemeesters tegen uitzetten', *Binnenlands Bestuur* 1 April 201). Retrieved from https://www.binnenlandsbestuur.nl.

13 Advies van prof. mr. dr. J.G. Brouwer en prof. mr. dr. A.E. Schilder inzake 'het gezag over de politie bij uitzetting van vreemdelingen' van 24 september 2012 (bijlage bij 19637, nr.1588). Retrieved from https://zoek.officielebekendmakingen.nl/blg-191055. See also Brouwer & Schilder 2012.

entitled to reception in special family centres. Other rejected asylum seekers are offered reception in a special centre, with a freedom-restricting regime, for a maximum of twelve weeks, under the condition that they cooperate with their expulsion. In 2014, the European Committee for Social Rights (ECSR) ruled that the Dutch government had violated its obligations under the European Social Charter by refusing reception facilities to rejected asylum seekers and other unlawfully present migrants.[14] According to the ECSR, the provision of emergency assistance could not be made conditional upon the willingness of the persons concerned to cooperate in the organisation of their own expulsion. This judgment led to a period of legal uncertainty, as the government indicated that it would not comply with the ruling and the Committee of Ministers of the ECSR was vague about whether unlawfully present migrants fell within the scope of the Charter. In 2015, the two highest administrative courts in the Netherlands ruled that the government might make the provision of reception facilities to rejected asylum seekers conditional upon their cooperation with their expulsion.[15] In 2016, another judgment was passed by the Judicial Division of the Council of State, stating that municipalities had no specific power to provide shelter to unlawfully present migrants and that there was no legal or international duty upon municipalities to do so. The highest administrative court thus departed from the ECSR.[16]

In the meantime, deliberations between the national government and the municipalities continued, and in November 2018, a new agreement was reached. In five large municipalities, reception facilities for rejected asylum seekers will be opened. The results will be evaluated after three years and if the reception facilities lead to more voluntary departures, another three facilities will be opened. Both the national government and the municipalities will contribute financially.

3. Legal and Moral Arguments for Taking Action on Issues Involving Rejected Asylum Seekers

Municipalities are a decentralised tier of the government, and as heads of these decentralised governments, mayors are bound to follow the laws and policies of the national government. It is the national government, more specifically the state secretary of Justice and Security, that decides whether a country is safe to return to for migrants who are not allowed to stay in the Netherlands. Mayors are expected to follow the national government in this regard. As Kos et al. pointed out, from the viewpoint of the national government, municipalities are formally a 'chain partner' or a 'cooperation partner' when they provide space or land for the reception centres that are owned and run by the national government, but 'they are expected to be 'cooperative' when it comes to other aspects of policy implementation for which they take no formal responsibility'.[17]

---

14 *Conference of European Churches (CEC) v. the Netherlands (decisions on the merits)*, Complaint No. 90/2013, Council of Europe: European Committee of Social Rights, 10 November 2014.

15 CRvB 26 November 2015, ECLI:NL:CRVB:2015:3834; ABRvS 26 November 2015, ECLI:NL:RVS:2015:3415. See also Terlouw 2016, p. 4.

16 ABRvS 29 juni 2016, ECLI:NL:RVS:2016:1782 and ECLI:NL:RVS:2016:1783.

17 Kos, Maussen & Doomernik 2015, p. 362.

The Dutch aliens law grants hardly any discretion to mayors when it comes to providing police assistance in cases of expulsion and refusing shelter to unlawfully present migrants. Nevertheless, mayors could in theory find at least three types of arguments in the law to argue that it falls within their discretion to refuse police assistance or to (continue to) provide shelter:

- Firstly, mayors could argue that the municipality's duty of care toward vulnerable people, as laid down in the Social Support Act (*Wet maatschappelijke ondersteuning*), and their responsibility for public order and safety allows or even obliges them to act.[18] Particularly with regard to offering shelter, mayors could argue that they exercise their powers in the field of public order and security reasonably if offering shelter prevents people from wandering around, destitute, on the streets.[19]
- Secondly, mayors could argue that they have an independent responsibility to protect human rights as laid down in international treaties, such as the right to human dignity in Art. 1 of the EU Charter of Fundamental Rights and the right of *non-refoulement* of Art. 33 of the Refugee Convention. In 2012, the Association of Netherlands Municipalities together with the Dutch section of Amnesty International published a brochure on the meaning of human rights for municipalities. According to this brochure, both national and local governments and individual government officials have the responsibility to respect, protect and promote human rights as formulated in human rights treaties and the Constitution. Moreover, the Netherlands has a monist system: Arts. 93 and 94 of the Dutch Constitution determine that international law provisions have preference above national laws.[20]
- Thirdly, mayors could refer to inconsistent jurisprudence. For example, with regard to offering shelter, there was a period of diverging case law after the judgment of the European Committee for Social Rights. Mayors who decided to support unlawfully present migrants, could thus argue that they were not acting *contra legem,* but in conformity with legal obligations resting on them.

Our newspaper search and interviews with mayors did not yield clear examples of mayors using the latter two arguments. Of course, these arguments may well have been used in, e.g., letters to the state secretary, but we did not find them in interviews given to journalists. Among the four mayors we interviewed, one mayor did refer to 'fundamental human rights' and 'people's right to a dignified treatment', but he had doubts about using them as a basis for concrete action.[21]

We did find many examples of the first argument, i.e. mayors arguing that their responsibility for public order and safety allowed or obliged them to act.

> In 2015, Mayor Frits Naafs (Utrechtse Heuvelrug) claimed that he had the authority to offer shelter to rejected asylum seekers – to prevent them falling into anonymity, illegality and criminality – as the reception of homeless people fell within his competence. This would not be necessary if the national government ensured that rejected asylum seekers did not stay here unlawfully, he stated.[22]

---

18 Zwaan & Minderhoud 2016, p. 897; De Jong et. al. 2017.

19 ACVZ 2018, Bijlage 1; ACVZ 2012.

20 *Goed bezig. De betekenis van mensenrechten voor gemeenten* 2012.

21 Interview M2 (2018, November 23).

22 Naafs blijft asielzoekers steunen (2015, April 30). Retrieved from https://nieuwsbladdekaap.nl.

All four mayors we interviewed stated that their responsibility for public order and safety gave them discretion to take action for rejected asylum seekers. However, two of them added that this discretion was sometimes misused or improperly used by colleagues. The first mayor considered refusing police assistance for expulsions to be 'improper use of the powers mayors have for the purpose of protecting public order, in cases when the public order is not at stake'.[23] The second mayor stated that mayors sometimes 'choose the easy route' by supporting protests against an asylum seeker's expulsion, as the final decision did not lie with them, but with the state secretary. In this respondent's view, 'it is easy to claim that you have discretion if the final responsibility for the bigger issue does not lie with you'.[24] The third mayor stated that nearly all laws and regulations contained 'a safety net', i.e. provisions that made it possible to deviate from the letter of the law if the spirit of the law required it.[25] The mayors talked about their discretionary space in a rather loose way, without referring to specific provisions or laws or regulations. The fourth mayor explained that he thought he had a large discretionary space but would rather not know if it was not as large as he thought, and that he would use it anyway.[26]

Some mayors are prepared to act (or accept that they may act) *contra legem* when supporting rejected asylum seekers. These mayors invoke different arguments. Our newspaper search yielded examples of four types of arguments.

- Mayors may experience the legal norms as unjust or in contradiction with moral norms such as the right to have rights,[27] or religious norms such as 'love your neighbour like you love yourself'.
- They may regard national policies vis-à-vis rejected asylum seekers as failing and argue they have to step in where the national government fails to take responsibility. They may also think that municipalities are best aware of and best equipped to solve problematic situations involving rejected asylum seekers.
- They may feel they have a special responsibility toward rejected asylum seekers in their municipality, which may be strengthened by pleas from schools, neighbours, football clubs, etcetera, that claim that the migrants concerned have become part of the community.
- They may not agree with the decision that was made in the refugee status determination procedure and/or with the expulsion decision.

The first three arguments are most common and they are often combined. The following example is interesting because the mayor concerned differentiated between law and policy.

> In the context of the debate on reception facilities for rejected asylum seekers, Mayor Annemarie Penn-te Strake (Maastricht) said she did not have a problem with acting contrary to national policies 'if the interest of the person concerned serves a higher purpose than the implementation of policies that lead to distressing situations. That is the space I take, it is not my job to look

23 Interview M1 (2018, November 19).
24 Interview M2 (2018, November 23).
25 Interview M3 (2018, November 28).
26 Interview M4 (2019, February 15).
27 Arendt 1968, p. 177.

> away', she said. However, she differentiated between law and policies. She would not be prepared to break the law, except in the extreme case that by doing so she could save a human life, and she would resign immediately afterward.[28]
>
> In 2016, Mayor Jos Heijmans (Weert) helped a Syrian asylum seeker and her four young children to hide in a monastery to prevent their expulsion to Germany (and prevent them being separated from relatives in the Netherlands). 'I let my heart prevail over the rules', he explained, and: 'As a mayor, you have to intervene when people fall victim to the rules.'[29]

All four mayors we interviewed were of the opinion that there are situations where it might be necessary to exceed one's discretionary powers and/or to break the law. 'Necessity knows no law', the first respondent said, and: 'Conscience, not law, is the highest norm for me.' However, he added that he would go that far only in 'cases of life and death'.[30] The second respondent referred to 'fundamental human rights' and 'people's right to a dignified treatment'.[31] The third respondent said that mayors often acted without formal power or authority, 'because as a mayor, you want to solve problems'. He did not feel the need to justify his actions by referring to the law: 'I feel I'm authorised to do what I deem necessary if the national government does not perform its duties properly.' In his view, if people were not granted a residence permit they should be expelled, and if they could not be expelled they should be granted reception. 'You cannot just accept that people fall between two stools. That is inhuman.'[32] The fourth respondent likewise described himself as a problem solver, but he also referred to the Second World War to explain why he felt authorised to do what he deemed necessary to prevent people from living on the streets.[33]

4. Choices and Justifications

In our newspaper search, we found a large variety of actions taken by mayors to support rejected asylum seekers. With regard to resisting deportations, actions taken ranged from writing letters to the state secretary to withholding police assistance for removing rejected asylum seekers from their houses and helping families to hide. With regard to offering shelter, we found a series of joint (public) lobbying activities by mayors, aimed at changing national policies. But we also found a range of actions to support rejected asylum seekers in the municipality concerned, for example by providing shelter to specific groups of vulnerable rejected asylum seekers; providing shelter for a specific period of time (e.g., one month or in wintertime); permitting a tent camp

---

28 Marten Muskee (2018, June 1). Burgemeester Annemarie Penn-te Strake van Maastricht: 'We mogen soms wel iets dapperder zijn'. Retrieved from https://vng.nl.

29 Burgemeester Weert: 'Onderduiken hielp voor Syrisch gezin' (2018, September 3). Retrieved from https://www.nporadio1.nl.

30 Interview M1 (2018, November 19).

31 Interview M2 (2018, November 23).

32 Interview M3 (2018, November 28).

33 Interview M4 (2019, February 15).

and offering bins and mobile toilets;[34] terminating reception facilities but offering money to the migrants concerned;[35] providing financial support to NGOs that offered shelter.

Mayors make different choices with regard to what actions to take. Some mayors offer actual support to rejected asylum seekers, others try to convince the state secretary to use his discretionary power. Some participate in joint (public) lobbying efforts aimed at changing policies, others prefer to conduct silent diplomacy for asylum seekers in their municipality.[36]

> Mayor Jeroen Gebben (Tytsjerksteradiel) said he used 'silent diplomacy' to prevent the expulsion of Afghan asylum seekers. However, going against the policy of the national government was not his style: 'This mayor will not resort to administrative disobedience, I have been appointed by the government.'[37]

> In 2014, Mayor Harald Bergmann (Middelburg) asked the state secretary to grant residence permits to an asylum seeker family with children. The family's application for residence permits under the children's regularisation scheme had been rejected. The same mayor had refused to sign a letter in which (over 300) mayors had urged the state secretary to extend the children's regularisation scheme.[38] The mayor explained that signing that letter would have been a political act which did not suit a mayor.[39]

If mayors are prepared to take action in individual cases, their choices with regard to whom to support do not differ that much. Proximity plays a role in the sense that mayors may feel they have a special responsibility toward rejected asylum seekers in their own municipality. Political philosophers have pointed to the arbitrariness of proximity as an argument for responsibility (of states for refugees), but they hold that migrants must be offered the opportunities of citizenship once they have been taken in. Presence on the territory is regarded by them as a basis for membership of the community.[40] In actual life, whether rejected asylum seekers in a municipality are regarded as members (or as deserving membership) of the community depends on their integration.

---

34 In 2013, Mayor Eberhard van der Laan (Amsterdam) legitimised his decision to permit a tent camp by stating that he regarded it as a demonstration; the decision to provide bins and mobile toilets was legitimised referring to public health and public order.

35 Hanne Obink, '225 euro rijker, maar opnieuw op straat', *Trouw* 31 May 2013. Retrieved from https://advance.lexis.com/api/document?collection=news&id=urn:contentItem:58J5-D9F1-JC8W-Y00H-00000-00&context=1516831.

36 Cf. Van der Leun & Bouter 2015, p. 149.

37 'Wat kan de gemeente doen tegen uitzettingen van afgewezen asielzoekers?', *Friesch Dagblad* 18 August 2018. Retrieved from https://frieschdagblad.nl.

38 'Oproep burgemeesters aan staatssecretaris Teeven' (2014, May 21). Retrieved from http://www.logo-gemeenten.nl/dossier-kinderpardon.

39 'Burgemeester op de bres voor asielzoekersgezin' (2014, June 6). Retrieved from https://www.omroepzeeland.nl.

40 Walzer (1983, p. 62) states that 'every new immigrant, every refugee taken in, every resident and worker must be offered the opportunities of citizenship.' Miller (2016, p. 83-84) sees proximity (presence on the territory) as one of the bases for responsibility for refugees. See also Gibney (2004, p. 31) on membership and identity.

> This is illustrated by the aforementioned letter of appeal, in which over 300 mayors had urged the state secretary to extend the children's regularisation scheme. The concluding sentence was: 'For the municipalities, these children already are well integrated citizens of their town or village. It would be good to formalise this by granting real residence permits.'[41]

Cases of children who grew up in the Netherlands (the Dutch speak of them as being 'rooted') have also been prominent in the media. In several cases, the state secretary ultimately decided to use his discretionary power and grant residence permits. More generally, visibility and the circumstance of a neighbourhood, school, community standing up for the migrants concerned, may help to prevent their expulsion.[42]

All four mayors we interviewed had written letters to the state secretary for rejected asylum seekers in their municipality, in most or some cases with success, they said. One respondent explained that he only wrote such letters for asylum seekers who were well integrated, working or studying and participating in the local society. Moreover, they had to be of irreproachable conduct. Later on he added that he also found it relevant if people were traumatised and vulnerable.[43] Another respondent explained that he had once made his support conditional on the migrant concerned improving his Dutch language proficiency, because otherwise he could not credibly argue that the migrant (who had been living in the municipality for eighteen years) was well integrated in the community.[44] The third respondent explained that he had to be convinced that the decision deserved reconsideration because there were special circumstances that had not been taken into account when the asylum application was rejected. The same respondent was critical about 'some colleagues who too easily say yes when they are asked to write a letter', thereby shirking their responsibility and passing the buck to the secretary of state. However, he also thought that mayors should get a larger say in decision-making processes about rejected asylum seekers. He called it 'completely ridiculous' that the national government claimed to be in a better position to assess the situation of a rejected asylum seeker who was living in a municipality than the municipality concerned.[45] The fourth mayor described one situation in which he would have liked to have had the state secretary's discretionary power. It concerned a vulnerable rejected asylum seeker who had lived for years with a private person, an inhabitant of the town who had offered him shelter.[46]

---

41 'Oproep burgemeesters aan staatssecretaris Teeven' (2014, May 21). Retrieved from http://www.logo-gemeenten.nl/dossier-kinderpardon.

42 Schrover (2018, p. 459) speaks of a 'restrictionist paradox': voters vote for a restrictive policy, but protest against deportations of those who have been given a face.

43 Interview M3 (2018, November 28).

44 Interview M4 (2019, February 15).

45 Interview M2 (2018, November 19). This was also proposed by the Advisory Committee on Aliens Affairs (ACVZ) in 2011. The committee pointed at the German example of the *Härtefall Kommissionen*, which consisted of representatives from the relevant state ministries, local authorities, regional and local civil society organisations and a single independent member. The ACVZ advised setting up a similar advisory body in the Netherlands, to examine from various perspectives cases in which the use of discretionary powers was requested on the basis of exceptional circumstances (ACVZ 2011, p. 65).

46 Interview M1 (2018, November 19).

5. Concluding Remarks

Mayors can, to a certain extent, be compared to street-level bureaucrats. Like street-level bureaucrats, they have more proximity than the policymakers at the national level to the people targeted by the policies. Like them, they have a certain amount of discretion and they may select between 'deserving' and 'undeserving' rejected asylum seekers. However, unlike street-level bureaucrats, mayors do not implement law and policies as a primary task. Moreover, they do not have the task of applying rules to individual cases.

Many mayors are confronted with rejected asylum seekers living in their municipality, and with requests to support them. Dutch aliens law gives mayors little or no formal discretion as regards resisting expulsions or offering shelter, but they can derive room for manoeuvre from other national laws, in particular the Municipalities Act (*Gemeentewet*) and the Social Support Act, and international human rights law. Mayors who refer to the law and their formal discretion, mostly refer to their responsibility for public order in their municipality as laid down in the Municipalities Act. Other mayors (or the same mayors in different situations) accept that they may be exceeding their discretion when supporting rejected asylum seekers. The vague nature of what mayors' discretion exactly entails explains partly why we see differences between mayors in their approaches to problems involving unlawfully present migrants and in their perceived discretion in this regard.

Another explanation can be found in the specificities and complexities of the policy domain concerned. Expulsion sometimes proves to be hardly possible. The idea that people whose claim for a residence status has been rejected will leave the country is largely a fiction and it is the municipalities (and mayors) who are confronted with the consequences of the failing expulsion policy. In addition, both expulsion and refusing reception touch upon basic human rights, which makes the issue very sensitive. Mayors can therefore hardly stay neutral, and doing nothing is also a decision. Moreover, quite a few mayors disagree with national policies especially when it concerns the expulsion of children who were born and raised in the Netherlands, or refusing shelter to people who have not been deported.

References

ACVZ (2011). *Om het maatschappelijk belang. Advies over het betrekken van het lokale bestuur en de lokale bevolking bij het toepassen van de discretionaire bevoegdheid*, Den Haag: ACVZ.

ACVZ (2012). *Recht op een menswaardig bestaan. Advies over opvang en bijstand voor niet rechtmatig verblijvende vreemdelingen en rechtmatig verblijvende vreemdelingen zonder recht op voorzieningen*, Den Haag: ACVZ.

ACVZ (2018). *Bijlage 1 bij brief ACVZ over bed, bad, brood (ACVZ/ADV/2018/004)*, Den Haag: ACVZ.

Arendt, H. (1968). *The origins of totalitarianism*, New York: Harcourt, Brace & World.

Brouwer, J. & J. Schilder (2012). Betwist gezag bij uitzetting van asielzoekers. Wie is de baas over de politie?, *Ars Aequi*, November 2012, p. 803-810.

Bruquetas Callejo, M. (2014). *Mind the gap! Policies and practices of educational reception in Rotterdam and Barcelona*, Amsterdam: Amsterdam University Press.

De Jong, M.A.D.W., W. van der Woude, W.S Zorg, J.L.W. Broeksteeg, R. Nehmelman, I.U. Tappenier & H.R.B.M. Kummeling (2017). *Orde in de openbare orde. Een onderzoek naar verbetering van de toepasbaarheid en inzichtelijkheid van het openbare-orderecht*, Deventer: Kluwer.

Dworkin, R. (1977). *Taking rights seriously*, Cambridge: Harvard University Press.

Eule, T.G. (2014). *Inside immigration law. Migration management and policy application in Germany*, Farnham: Ashgate.

Evans, T. & J. Harris (2004). Street-level bureaucracy, social work and the (exaggerated) death of discretion, *British Journal of Social Work* 34(6), p. 871-895.

Gibney, M.J. (2004). *The ethics and politics of asylum*, Cambridge: Cambridge University Press.

Goed bezig. De betekenis van mensenrechten voor gemeenten (2012). Den Haag/Amsterdam: VNG/Amnesty International Nederland.

Kos, S., M. Maussen & J. Doomernik (2016). Policies of exclusion and practices of inclusion: How municipal governments negotiate asylum policies in the Netherlands, *Territory, Politics, Governance* 4(3), p. 354-374.

Miller, D. (2016). *Strangers in our midst: The political philosophy of immigration*, Harvard: Harvard University Press.

Pluymen, M. (2008). *Niet toelaten betekent uitsluiten. Een rechtssociologisch onderzoek naar rechtvaardigingen en praktijk van uitsluiting van vreemdelingen van voorzieningen,* Den Haag: Boom juridische uitgevers.

Schrover, M. (2018). Wie mag er blijven, *Asiel &Migrantenrecht* 2018/9, p. 459.

Van Leeuwen, M.J., L.G. Tummers & S. van der Walle (2017). *Street-level bureaucrat discretion: A systematic literature review*, Working paper in preparation of PMRC 2017. Retrieved from https://swoogo.s3.amazonaws.com/uploads/47221-59286a1bd983b.pdf.

Van der Leun, J. & H. Bouter (2015). Gimme shelter: Inclusion and exclusion of irregular immigrants in Dutch civil society, *Journal of Immigrant & Refugee Studies*, 13(2), p. 135-155.

Voermans, W. & G. Waling (2018). *Gemeente in de genen. Tradities en toekomst van de lokale democratie in Nederland*, Amsterdam: Prometheus.

Walzer, M. (1983). *Spheres of justice. A defense of pluralism and equality*, Oxford: Basil Blackwell.

Winter, H., V. Bex-Reimert, B. Geertsema & E. Krol (2018), *Onderdak en opvang door Rijk en gemeenten van vertrekplichtige vreemdelingen en de invloed daarvan op terugkeer*, Groningen: Pro facto.

Zwaan, K. & P. Minderhoud (2016). Bed-bad-brood: Vrijheidsbeperking niet in strijd met verplichting om opvang te bieden?, *Gemeentestem* 2016/165.

The Aznar Protocol: Diminishing the Geography of Refugee Protection in Europe

*Karin Zwaan**

1. Introduction

The Aznar Protocol No. 24 is a protocol to the Treaty of the European Union (it became part of the EU treaties in 1999). The Aznar Protocol was an initiative of Spain. Spain was dissatisfied with the way Belgium and France dealt with asylum request from and offered protection to Spanish citizens who had committed or were suspected to have committed terrorist activities for the ETA.[1] At first, Spain proposed to exclude EU-citizens from the right to seek asylum within the EU as follows: 'Every citizen of the Union shall be regarded, for all legal and judicial purposes connected with the granting of refugee status and matters relating to asylum, as a national of the Member State in which he is seeking asylum. Consequently, no State of the Union shall agree to process an application for asylum submitted by a national of another State of the Union.'[2] The text that finally was adopted is 'less' far reaching.

The Aznar Protocol contains one single Article stating in short that Member States do not grant asylum to citizens of another Member State.[3] The reason for this is, according to the text of the Protocol, the level of protection of fundamental rights and freedoms by the Member States of the European Union. This level is such that: 'Member States shall be regarded as constituting safe countries of origin in respect of each other for all legal and practical purposes in relation to asylum matters. Accordingly, any application for asylum made by a national of a Member State may not be taken into consideration or declared admissible for processing by another Member State'. Belgium is the only EU country that has made a separate declaration, emphasizing the conditioning of the application of the Protocol.[4] Subsequently, specifically enumerated exceptions are listed. An asylum application by an EU citizen may be taken into consideration or declared admissible by another Member State only in the following cases:

> '(a) if the Member State of which the applicant is a national proceeds after the entry into force of the Treaty of Amsterdam, availing itself of the provisions of Article 15 of the European Convention for the Protection of Human Rights and Fundamental Freedoms, to take measures derogating in its territory from its obligations under that Convention;

---

* Researcher, Centre for Migration Law, Radboud University Nijmegen

1 ETA is an acronym of Euskadi Ta Askatasuna, 'Basque Homeland and Freedom', an armed Basque nationalist and separatist organisation.

2 Conference of the Representatives of the Governments of the Member States, Discussion Paper, Brussels, 4 February 1997. SN/507/97 (C 8), para. 1.

3 This contribution is partly based on an unpublished paper: A. Terlouw, C. Grütters and K. Zwaan, Implementation of the Aznar Protocol, March 2014.

4 OJ C340, 10.11.1997, p. 1-144; 'Declarations the conference took note of', Declaration 5 to Protocol 24.

(b) if the procedure referred to Article 7(1) of the Treaty on European Union has been initiated and until the Council, or, where appropriate, the European Council, takes a decision in respect thereof with regard to the Member State of which the applicant is a national;
(c) if the Council has adopted a decision in accordance with Article 7(1) of the Treaty on European Union in respect of the Member State of which the applicant is a national or if the European Council has adopted a decision in accordance with Article 7(2) of that Treaty in respect of the Member State of which the applicant is a national;
(d) if a Member State should so decide unilaterally in respect of the application of a national of another Member State; in that case the Council shall be immediately informed; the application shall be dealt with on the basis of the presumption that it is manifestly unfounded without affecting in any way, whatever the cases may be, the decision-making power of the Member State.'

What does this imply for an asylum seeker having well-founded fear for persecution coming from an EU Member State? In principle his country of origin will be considered to be a safe country, able and willing to protect, meaning that the asylum claim will be rejected. There are a few exceptions. Only if the country of origin of the asylum seeker has formally derogated from its human rights obligations, or if that has been determined through a political process that this Member State is a serious and persistent violator of human rights, an asylum application can be dealt with by another EU Member State. In any other circumstances, an asylum request can only be received if there is a unilateral Member States decision, which is communicated to a political organ of the EU, the Council.[5] The preamble justifies the protocol on the following grounds: The TEU recognizes rights, freedoms and principles as set out in the EU Charter of Fundamental Rights and as guaranteed by the ECHR; The Court of Justice of the EU has the power to ensure fundamental rights are respected within the scope of EU law; The TEU provides that membership of the EU is only open to states which comply with European fundamental rights and a mechanism for sanction exists against states which fail to live up to their commitments; EU citizens are entitled to a special status and have the right to move and reside freely across the territory of the Member States in an area without internal frontiers; and finally The institution of asylum should not be used for purposes alien to those for which it was intended.

In this contribution the consequences of the Aznar protocol will be analysed, and special attention will be given to the 'protection' gap that exists due to this Protocol

5 Compare K. Landgren, Deflecting international protection by treaty: bilateral and multilateral accords on extradition, readmission and the inadmissibility of asylum requests, New Issues in Refugee Research, Working paper No. 10, June 1999, p. 9.

for specific categories of EU-citizens.[6] Also Elspeth Guild in her work has given much attention to this 'Geography of Refugee Protection'.[7]

2. Mutual Trust?

The Aznar Protocol is based on the idea of mutual trust between EU Member States. The principle of mutual trust is based on Article 2 TEU: 'The Union is founded on the values of respect for human dignity, freedom, democracy, equality and the rule of law and respect for human rights, including the rights of persons belonging to minorities. These values are common to the Member States in a society in which pluralism, non-discrimination, tolerance, justice, solidarity and equality between women and men prevail'. The presumption of the Aznar protocol is that EU-citizens come from safe countries of origin.[8] There is no general sovereignty clause in the Protocol and the exceptions to the mutual trust of the Aznar system are rather restrictive and require from a Member State that wants to examine an application of an EU-citizen on the substance at least to inform the Commission but preferable to consult other Member States. This restriction of the sovereignty can be understood by the character of a decision to grant a refugee states to an asylum seeker fleeing from another EU Member State. Although granting asylum officially always has been seen as a matter to be viewed separately from criticism of the country of origin, and as a peaceful and humanitarian act[9], protection against persecution by other states, is based upon distrust or disapproval of other states or on a judgment that this other State has abused its authority. Granting asylum to an EU-citizen therefore is an implicit statement that this Member State is persecuting its citizens or failing to offer protection.

---

6 In this contribution the question whether the right of free movement is an alternative for refugee protection will not be dealt with. See on this C.A. Groenendijk, Kunnen Unieburgers nog vluchten? Bescherming van Roma door het Vluchtelingenverdrag en het vrij verkeer in de EU, in A. Terlouw en K. Zwaan (red.), Tijd en Asiel. 60 jaar Vluchtelingenverdrag, Oisterwijk: WLP 2011, pp. 59-81, P.R. Rodrigues, 'Vrij verkeer van Roma in Frankrijk' in K. Groenendijk (red.) Issues that matter, Mensenrechten, minderheden en migranten. Oisterwijk: WLP 2013, pp. 87-97; D. Mahoney, 'Expulsion of the Roma; is France Violating EU Freedom of Movement and Playing by French Rules or can it proceed with collective Roma Expulsions Free of Charge', *Brooklyn Journal of International Law*, Vol. 37, 2, 2012, pp. 649-682.

7 E. Guild, Examining the European Geography of Refugee Protection. Exclusions, Limitations and Exceptions from the 1967 Protocol to the Present, Nijmegen Migration Law Working Paper Series 2012/03; E. Guild and K.M. Zwaan, Does Europe still create Refugees? Examining the Situation of Roma, *Queens Law Journal*, vol. 40, iss. 1, (2015), pp. 142-164; E. Guild, Does the EU need a European Migration and Protection Agency? *International Journal of Refugee Law*, vol. 28, iss. 4 (2016), pp. 585-600; S. Carrera and E. Guild, EU Borders and Their Controls. Preventing Unwanted Movement of People in Europe?, CEPS 2013.

8 G. Noll, Negotiating Asylum: The EU Acquis, Extraterritorial Protection and the Common Market of Deflection, Dordrecht: Martinus Nijhoff 2000.

9 Declaration on Territorial Asylum, GA res. 2312 (XXII), 22 U.N. GAOR Supp. (No. 16) at 81, U.N. Doc. A/6716 (1967) and B.P. Vermeulen et al., *Persecution by Third Parties*, Commissioned by the Research and Documentation Centre of the Ministry of Justice of the Netherlands, Nijmegen: Centre for Migration Law, May 1998.

The landmark cases *M.S.S.* by the ECtHR[10] and *N.S.* by the CJEU[11] have shown that non-rebuttable trust is not allowed when this would jeopardise the protection of the fundamental rights of the individual.[12] Moreover, the mutual trust principle is set-aside in cases of unaccompanied minors.[13] Relevant for the mutual trust which forms the basis of the Aznar protocol is that these Court decisions make clear that an escape to blind trust is necessary even if it concerns trust between EU-countries. The CJEU has not reviewed a case regarding asylum seekers, who are EU nationals yet.. So far, the closest-related case to the problematics of the Aznar Protocol in the jurisprudence of CJEU is the *N.S.* and *M.E.* case, concerning the possibility of rebuttal of mutual trust in cases of risk of ill-treatment of asylum seekers under the Dublin system.[14] But the absoluteness of mutual trust was confirmed in Opinion 2/13 of the CJEU which emphasized the fundamental importance of mutual trust.[15]

It can be concluded that there is at least a tension between the Aznar Protocol, and international obligations that are incorporated in the Refugee Convention, the Convention Against Torture, and the ECHR.[16] It can have as a consequence that asylum requests are not dealt with, that refugees are not recognised as such, and that asylum seekers are returned to a country where they have to fear for persecution (in this case an EU Member State). In this regard it is interesting to refer to the *Kadi* case, in which

---

10 ECtHR, 21 January 2011, appl. no. 30696/09, para. 345: 'The Court must therefore now consider whether the Belgian authorities should have regarded as rebutted the presumption that the Greek authorities would respect their international obligations in asylum matters, in spite of the K.R.S. case-law, which the Government claimed the administrative and judicial authorities had wanted to follow in the instant case.', *M.S.S. v Belgium and Greece*, m.nt. Spijkerboer *A&MR* 2011, nr. 1 p. 32/33 and m.nt Battjes *A&MR* 2011, 2, p. 66-74.

11 CJEU 21 December 2011, NS v SSHD, C-411/10, para. 83: 'At issue here is the raison d'être of the European Union and the creation of an area of freedom, security and justice and, in particular, the Common European Asylum System, based on mutual confidence and a presumption of compliance, by other Member States, with European Union law and, in particular, fundamental rights.' CJEU 21 December 2011, N.S., C-493/10, and M.E et al. C-411/10.

12 C. Costello, 'Dublin-case NS/ME: Finally, an end to blind trust across the EU?', *A&MR*, 2012 no. 2, p. 83-92; V. Moreno-Lax, 'Dismantling the Dublin System: M.S.S. v. Belgium and Greece', *European Journal of Migration and Law*, 2012, 14, p. 1-31; P. Brown, P. Dwyer, & L. Scullion, The Limits of Inclusion? Exploring the views of Roma and Non-Roma in six European Union Member States, Manchester: University of Salford 2013.

13 CJEU 6 June 2013, C-648/11, *MA and Others v Secretary of State for the Home Department, England and Wales.*

14 Regulation (EU) No 604/2013 of the European Parliament and of the Council of 26 June 2013 establishing the criteria and mechanisms for determining the Member State responsible for examining an application for international protection lodged in one of the Member States by a third-country national or a stateless person, OJ L 180, 29.6.2013, p. 31–59.

15 Opinion of the Court (Full Court) of 18 December 2014, Accession of the European Union to the European Convention for the Protection of Human Rights and Fundamental Freedoms, Case Opinion 2/13.

16 A. Hurwitz, The Collective Responsibility of States to Protect Refugees, Oxford: Oxford University Press 2009; V. Moreno Lax, 'Must EU Borders Have Doors for Refugees? On the Compatibility of Schengen Visas and Carrier Sanctions with EU Member States' Obligations to Provide International Protection to Refugees', *European Journal of Migration and Law 2008*, pp. 315-364.

the CJEU judged that the protection of fundamental rights forms part of the very foundations of the Union legal order.[17] Accordingly, all Union measures must be compatible with fundamental rights.

While Article 33(1) of the Refugee Convention provides that 'No Contracting Party shall expel or return (*'refouler'*) a refugee in any manner whatsoever to the frontiers of territories where his life or freedom would be threatened on account of his race, religion, nationality, membership of a particular social ground or political opinion', the Aznar Protocol permits a Member State to limit its obligations to a refugee where his/her state of origin is a Member State of the EU. The principle set out in the Aznar Protocol of the exclusion of nationals of the Member States from international protection in another Member State has been reflected in the other instruments forming part of the secondary legislation of the EU on asylum, the personal scope of which is limited to third country nationals – that is persons who are not nationals of the Member States.[18]

The fundamental role of the mutual trust principle has an impact on both extradition law and asylum law, as well as on the intersection between asylum and extradition in political offence cases like that of Puigdemont.[19] Carles Puigdemont is a Catalan pro-independence politician and journalist from Spain, currently living in Belgium. On 6–7 September 2017, he approved laws for permitting an independence referendum, and the juridical transition and foundation of a Republic, a new constitution for Catalonia that would be in place if the referendum supported independence. On 30 October 2017 charges of rebellion, sedition and misuse of public funds were brought against Puigdemont and other members of the Puigdemont Government. Puigdemont, along with others, fled to Belgium. However, the application of mutual trust to asylum and extradition does not have an extensive theoretical basis. Just the contrary: The reason for the introduction of mutual trust to asylum and extradition of political offenders in the EU legislation can be narrowed down to one single case, as also the case of Puigdemont shows.

International protection may be needed for EU nationals in another Member State. Seeking and being granted asylum on the grounds of political opinion or cumulative discrimination is very unlikely in the EU, but, as the Puigdemont and Roma cases[20] (see next paragraph 3) indicate – not an impossibility. Puigdemont has become the face of a very uneasy problem the EU is confronted with upholding mutual trust for the sake of long-term cooperation, while facing an asylum claim.

While Carles Puigdemont, whose potential asylum application has not been filed, is the sole EU national with a public face and a specified name, to illustrate the norm-

17 CJEU 3 September 2008, C–402/05P and C–415/05P, *Kadi and Al Barakaat International Foundation v. Council and Commission*, ECR I–6351.

18 See e.g. the Qualification Directive, Directive 2011/95/EU on standards for the qualification of third-country nationals or stateless persons as beneficiaries of international protection, for a uniform status for refugees or for persons eligible for subsidiary protection, and for the content of the protection granted (recast), OJ L 337/9-26, Art. 1.

19 See Dace Winther, Extradition, Asylum and Mutual Trust in the European Union One man's terrorist is another man's freedom fighter, yet another man's asylum seeker, yet another man's fugitive, Master Thesis Spring 2018.

20 See e.g. the fact sheet of the ECtHR on Roma and Travellers, april 2019, https://www.echr.coe.int/Documents/FS_Roma_ENG.pdf

conflict in the Aznar Protocol, he is far from being the only individual whose rights are concerned.[21]

3. Asylum Applications of EU-citizens in EU Member States and non-EU Member States

First some data on asylum applications by citizens of EU Member States in other Member States will be presented (Table 1). The ratio behind this is the hypothesis that probably the main social group or minority in Europe that may have in certain regions a well-founded fear of persecution, are Roma. If that is a correct assumption, the majority of asylum applications that are made by EU citizens in an EU Member State could be Roma.[22]

The available data over the period 2000-2018 show that most EU Member States do not 'produce' asylum seekers, or if they do, the relevant numbers are very small, e.g. less than five. These asylum requests therefore can be labelled as incidental. There are, however, a few Member States that have 'produced' on a more 'regular' basis larger numbers of asylum seekers who have applied for asylum in one of the EU Member States. In the following the focus is on the asylum applications from citizens of these states. These states are: Bulgaria, the Czech Republic, Hungary, Romania and Slovakia. As is listed in Table 1, the estimated total population of Roma in these 5 Southeast- and Central European (SEE) countries is 3 million, which is roughly one fourth of the total population of Roma in Europe.[23]

All of these countries have become a Member State of the EU in the last decade. The Czech Republic, Hungary, and Slovakia joined the EU in 2004, whereas Bulgaria and Romania became a Member State in 2007. This implies that the data that will be provided in the following graphs reflect asylum applications, partly by citizens from non-EU states, and partly by citizens from EU Member States, depending on the reference point in time. However, this may also illustrate the possible quantitative effect of becoming a Member State of the EU on the number of asylum applications submitted by citizens of these new Member States in other Member States.[24]

21 https://www.ejiltalk.org/the-european-arrest-warrant-against-puigdemont-a-feeling-of-deja-vu/

22 See also E. Guild and K.M. Zwaan, Does Europe still create Refugees? Examining the Situation of Roma , *Queens Law Journal*, vol. 40, iss. 1, (2015), pp. 142-164.

23 H. O'Nions, 'Roma Expulsions and Discriminations: The Elephant in Brussels', *European Journal of Migration and Law*, 13:4,2011, pp. 361-388.

24 ERRC fact sheet, Mob Justice: Collective Punishment against Roma in Europe, https://issuu.com/romarightsjournal/docs/mob-justice-collective-punishment-a.

Table 1.[25] *Total # first instance decisions on asylum applications in EU 28 of citizens from Bulgaria, Czechia, Hungary, Romania, Slovakia*

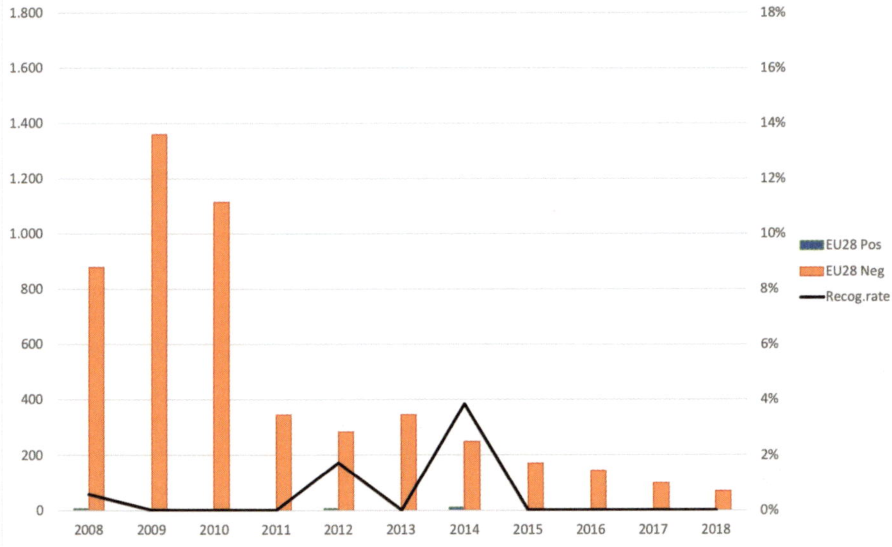

Although the Aznar Protocol is not implemented in the national legislation in every Member State, applications from EU-citizens are in one way or another rejected and in some EU Member States not even processed or registered.[26]

If the assumption is correct that the Aznar Protocol does prevent EU citizens, such as Roma, from applying for asylum in one of the EU Member States, it might be relevant to look at other countries of asylum outside the EU. The first option is in Europe. Nearby and not bound to EU regulations: Switzerland and Norway. From Table 2 it shows, that even though it is only in very rare cases that asylum is actually granted to an EU national in another EU Member State, asylum claims have indeed been filed by EU nationals both inside and outside the EU. In the past decade asylum outside the European Union has been granted to nationals from nearly every EU Member State. Incomparably more positive decisions on granting asylum have been made outside the EU, comparing to inside of the EU.[27]

25 Tables 1 and 2 made by mr.dr.C. Grütters on the basis of Eurostat data.

26 See also Report on the evaluation of the EU Framework for National Roma Integration Strategies up to 2020, COM (2018) 785 final.

27 R. Allveri, EU Accession to the ECHR and the Stumbling block of Asylum Protocol 24, *Ankara Law Review* 2012, pp. 175-194.

Table 2. Total # first instance decisions on asylum applications in Norway and Switzerland of citizens from Bulgaria, Czechia, Hungary Romania, Slovakia

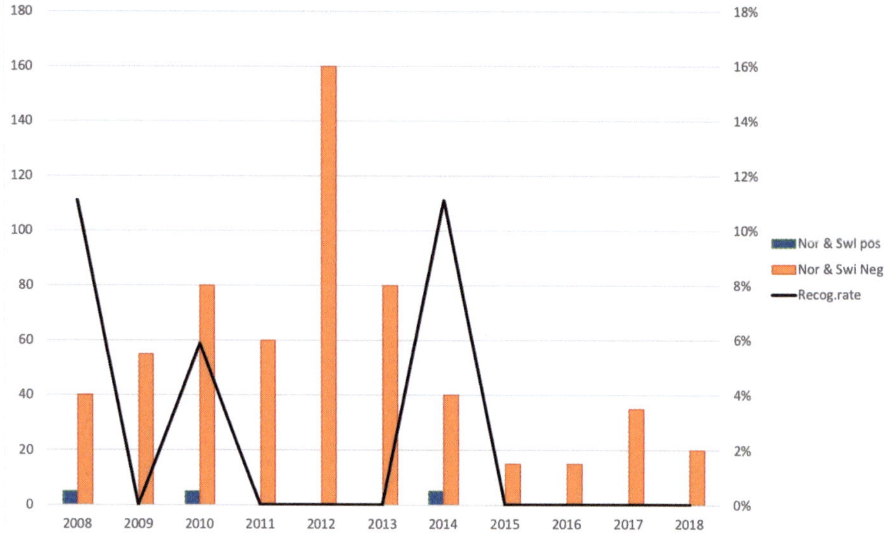

In most countries it is possible to rebut the presumption of safety of EU Member States that no well-founded fear exists, but the burden of proof is heavy or the time pressure of the accelerated procedure is high. In the details there are important differences between the different EU countries. The asylum seeker for example may have difficulties in rebutting the presumption if no interview on the merits takes place. Also if his appeal has no suspensive effect, or if he cannot benefit from reception measures, he may encounter problems to rebut the presumption of safety.

A far more interesting picture comes up if the asylum applications of EU-citizens in Canada are analysed. The recognition rates of Canada prove that EU-citizens can be refugees and as such can fall under the scope of the Refugee Convention[28], Article 3 ECHR, Article 3 Convention Against Torture and Article 18 EU Charter of Fundamental Rights. Rules with regard to the qualification as refugees and on asylum procedures must pursuant to Article 78(1) TFEU first clause be in accordance with the Refugee Convention and relevant international law. Moreover, Article 52(3) of the Charter provides that, in so far as the Charter contains rights which correspond to rights guaranteed by the ECHR, 'the meaning and the scope of those rights shall be the same as those laid down by the said Convention.' The meaning and the scope of the guaranteed rights are determined not only by the text of the ECHR, but also by case law of the ECtHR and by the Court of Justice of the EU.[29] The explanations state that 'in any

28 J. Tóth, 'Czech and Hungarian Roma Exodus to Canada: how to distinguish between Unbearable Destitution and Unbearable Persecution', in: D. Bigo, S. Carrera and E. Guild,, *Foreigners, refugees or minorities?: rethinking people in the context of border controls and visas*, Ashgate: Farnham 2013, pp. 39-54.

29 A.M. Reneman, *EU asylum procedures and the right to an effective remedy* (diss. Leiden), Leiden: Uitgeverij BOXPress 2012, p. 54.

event, the level of protection afforded by the Charter may never be lower than that guaranteed by the ECHR.'[30]

The circumstances in asylum cases must always be judged on an individual basis. Therefore the provisions of the Aznar Protocol create an exceptionally high threshold for an asylum claim by an EU national in another EU Member State.

4. Concluding Remarks

Landgren takes a strong view:

> 'The purpose of the Protocol is radically to reduce, or to remove, asylum possibilities within the EU for Union-citizens. It violates the letter and the spirit of the 1951 Refugee Convention, as well as other human rights instruments and principles in five broad areas. It makes asylum decisions subject to a political process, which includes the alleged violator state; it does not (as a general principle) examine the individual grounds for fear of persecution; it restricts access to any form of status determination procedures; it discriminates on the basis of nationality, and it evades international obligations through reliance on the obligations of another state.'[31]

This contribution argues that there are at least tensions between the Aznar Protocol and international obligations laid down in the Refugee Convention, the Convention Against Torture, the ECHR and the EU Charter of Fundamental Rights. The Aznar Protocol and the exclusion of EU-asylum seekers from the EU asylum acquis can have as a consequence that asylum requests are not dealt with, that refugees are not recognised as such and that they are returned to a country where they have a well-founded fear of being persecuted. In this regard this situation is comparable to the one in the *Kadi* case, in which the CJEU judged that the protection of fundamental rights forms part of the very foundations of the Union legal order.[32] Accordingly, all Union measures must be compatible with fundamental rights.

Apparently, there is a protection gap for EU-citizens who have a well-founded fear of persecution. In most EU countries they cannot apply for asylum or their applications are rejected in accelerated procedures. A possibility to rebut the presumption of safety of their country of origin is not always foreseen or realistic. All Member States are presumed to respect freedom, democracy, the rule of law and human rights, based on the principle of mutual trust. That is why it is particularly complicated to grant asylum to a refugee from another Member State. The fact that asylum claims by EU nationals – from EU-Roma and from those comparable to Puigdemont- would have to be treated as 'manifestly unfounded', shows that the threshold set in the Aznar Protocol is very high. Mutual trust prevails.

---

30 Explanations relating to the Charter of Fundamental Rights (2007/C 303/02), OJ 14 December 2007, C 303/33.

31 K. Landgren, Deflecting international protection by treaty: bilateral and multilateral accords on extradition, readmission and the inadmissibility of asylum requests, New Issues in Refugee Research, Working paper No. 10, June 1999, p. 13.

32 CJEU 3 September 2008, C–402/05P and C–415/05P, *Kadi and Al Barakaat International Foundation v. Council and Commission.*

Global Compact

The Global Compact for Safe, Orderly and Regular Migration: What now with Standards?

*Ryszard Cholewinski**

1. Introduction

The Global Compact for Safe, Orderly and Regular Migration (GCM), adopted by the United Nations (UN) General Assembly, on 19 December 2018,[1] has been heralded as the first comprehensive global framework addressing all aspects of international migration.[2] 152 UN Member States voted in favour of the GCM, with five voting against and 12 abstaining.[3] A number of those Member States which voted against the GCM have taken the view that the GCM risks undermining national sovereignty by encouraging more open borders and irregular migration. While the GCM is explicitly presented as a 'non-legally binding cooperative framework',[4] there are also concerns in some quarters that it could generate binding international customary law.[5]

The controversies surrounding the GCM are nothing new when it comes to agreement and adoption of global or regional negotiated outcomes on migration, whether legally binding or non-binding, or indeed to the application of international human rights and labour standards to migrants.

But the wide-ranging international support for the GCM in a climate of growing populism and challenges to multilateralism can on the whole be viewed as a success. Its adoption comes in the wake of the UN Summit on Addressing Large Movements of Refugees and Migrants in September 2016,[6] the subsequent New York Declaration for Refugees and Migrants,[7] and the parallel work undertaken on the Global Compact for Refugees under auspices of the UN High Commissioner for Refugees (UNHCR).[8]

---

* International Labour Organization (ILO) Regional Office for Arab States, Beirut. The views expressed in this article are solely those of the author and do not necessarily represent the views of the ILO or its tripartite constituents.

1 UN General Assembly (UNGA), 73rd Session, *Global Compact for Safe, Orderly and Regular Migration (GCM)*, A/RES/73/195 (11 January 2019).

2 See e.g. K. Newland, *Global Governance of International Migration 2.0: What Lies Ahead*, Washington, D.C.: Migration Policy Institute 2019, p. 2.

3 The Czech Republic, Hungary, Israel, Poland, and the United States voted against the GCM, and the following countries abstained: Algeria, Australia, Austria, Bulgaria, Chile, Italy, Latvia, Libya, Liechtenstein, Romania, Singapore, Switzerland.

4 UNGA 2019 (note 1), para. 7.

5 See *National Statement of the United States of America on the Adoption of the Global Compact for Safe, Orderly and Regular Migration*, 7 December 2018: 'The United States … is concerned that Compact supporters, recognizing the lack of widespread support for a legally-binding international migration convention, seek to use the Compact and its outcomes and objectives as a long-term means of building customary international law or so-called 'soft law' in the area of migration'.

6 UNGA, 70th Session, *In safety and dignity: addressing large movements of refugees and migrants*, Report of the Secretary-General, A/70/59 (21 April 2016).

7 UNGA, 71st Session, *New York Declaration for Refugees and Migrants*, A/RES/71/1 (3 October 2016).

8 UNGA, 73rd Session, *Report of the United Nations High Commissioner for Refugees. Part II: Global compact on refugees*, A/73/12 (Part II).

Moreover, the GCM itself observes that it is 'rooted' in the 2030 Agenda for Sustainable Development,[9] which recognizes the positive contribution of migrants for inclusive growth and sustainable development, commits to devoting special attention to vulnerable population groups by pledging that no one will be left behind,[10] and references migration in a number of Sustainable Development Goals (SDGs), with particular attention given to combatting trafficking and modern slavery, protection of the labour rights of migrant workers, implementation of well-managed migration policies, and disaggregation of data by migratory status.[11] The need to lower the costs of migration, and particularly the costs relating to the recruitment process, is also identified as an important enabler of sustainable development in the 2030 Agenda.[12]

This context to the GCM arguably strengthens its significance as the 'go-to' global guidance tool for migration governance, confirming also the desires of many migrant destination country governments to frame migration governance within a non-binding policy realm. This naturally gives rise to the question whether the binding legal obligations governments have entered into in respect of migration – whether in core human rights instruments and international labour standards, or in the specific international treaties concluded to protect migrant workers, who continue to represent the large majority of international migrants today[13] – have been somehow weakened by the adoption of the GCM. Or can the GCM also be viewed as a means of reinforcing the legally binding standards on which it is stated to rest?

This chapter attempts to address these questions in several ways. First, on a more general level, it juxtaposes the GCM with legally binding standards and explains that there continue to be significant differences between the two frameworks as well as complementarities. Second, it examines selective points of tension in the GCM, focusing on the rights of migrants in an irregular situation and access of migrants to social rights, to see if the provisions in question, while non-binding, could undermine the more favourable provisions in international standards or their interpretation. Third, the GCM will stand and fall in relation to how effectively it will be applied at the national level, and therefore there is a need to examine whether the mechanisms envisaged for its implementation have any advantage over the supervisory systems currently in place for the application of international human rights and labour standards.

9 UNGA 2019 (note 1), para. 6.

10 UNGA, 70th Session, *Transforming our world: the 2030 Agenda for Sustainable Development*, adopted on 25 September 2015, UN doc. A/RES/70/71 (21 October 2015), paras. 29 and 4.

11 SDG targets 5.2, 8.7, 8.8, 10.7, 16.2 and 17.18.

12 See SDG indicator 10.7.1 (Recruitment cost borne by employee as a proportion of monthly income earned in country of destination) and UNGA, 69th Session, Addis Ababa Action Agenda of the Third International Conference on Financing for Development, A/RES/69/313 (17 August 2015), para. 111.

13 According to recent ILO global estimates on international migrant workers, 164 million people are migrant workers (including refugees who work), 96 million men and 68 million women, out of the total population of 258 million international migrants globally. International Labour Office, *ILO Global Estimates on International Migrant Workers: Results and Methodology*, 2nd ed. (reference year 2017), Executive Summary, Geneva: ILO 2018, p. ix.

2. The GCM and International Standards

As a non-legally binding framework, the GCM purports to align itself with the international legally-binding framework. It is stated to rest on the purposes and principles of the UN Charter and other international law instruments.[14] In this regard, it explicitly mentions the Universal Declaration of Human Rights, the International Covenant on Civil and Political Rights (ICCPR), and the International Covenant on Economic, Social and Cultural Rights (ICESCR),[15] and references in a footnote the remaining seven core international human rights instruments, including the International Convention on the Protection of the Rights of All Migrant Workers and Members of their Families (ICRMW).[16] It also cites in the main text to the two Palermo Protocols concerned with trafficking in persons and migrant smuggling,[17] and footnotes a number of International Labour Organization (ILO) conventions, including the two legally binding instruments on migrant workers, namely the ILO Migration for Employment Convention (Revised), 1949 (No. 97) (C97) and the Migrant Workers (Supplementary Provisions) Convention, 1975 (No. 143) (C143), as well as the Domestic Workers Convention, 2011 (No. 189) (C189).[18] The relegation to footnotes of the three specific international instruments on migrant workers, however, is telling and also reflects the desire of a number of governments to downplay their relevance, in comparison with the more widely ratified Protocols on trafficking and smuggling, which appear openly in the body of the GCM text and in respect of which there are explicit calls to promote their ratification, accession and implementation.[19] Nonetheless, the inclusion of these three instruments in the GCM indicates that the legally-binding framework on migrant workers cannot be ignored, and indeed should be a source of inspiration and play an important role in informing the understanding of some of the GCM's provisions, which, as noted in the next section, fail to reflect fully the interpretation of relevant human rights and labour standards by bodies operating under the respective supervisory systems.

In addition to referencing specific instruments, the GCM is also based on a set of cross-cutting and interdependent guiding principles, including that it is people-centred, recognizes respect for the rule of law and due process, is based on international human rights law, is gender-responsive and child-sensitive, and promotes 'whole of government' and 'whole of society' approaches,[20] which all resonate well with the spirit of the legally-binding standards and their application.

These complementarities between the GCM and international standards, however, cannot hide their significant differences. As noted above, the GCM does not impose

14 UNGA 2019 (note 1), paras. 1 and 2.

15 UNGA Resolution 217 A (III) of 10 December 1948; UNGA Resolution 2200A (XXI) of 16 December 1966; UNGA Resolution 2200A (XXI) of 16 December 1966.

16 UNGA Resolution 45/158 of 18 December 1990.

17 Protocol to Prevent, Suppress and Punish Trafficking in Persons, Especially Women and Children, UN, *Treaty Series*, vol. 2237, No. 39574; Protocol against the Smuggling of Migrants by Land, Sea and Air, UN, *Treaty Series*, vol. 2241, No. 39574.

18 The texts of these and other ILO Conventions are available from ILO NORMLEX – Information System on International Labour Standards.

19 UNGA 2019 (note 1), paras. 25(a) and 26(a).

20 UNGA 2019 (note 1), para. 15. The remaining guiding principles refer to international cooperation, national sovereignty and sustainable development.

any legally-binding commitments on UN Member States despite the concerns expressed by some of them that it may lay the groundwork for the development of international customary law. It would appear also that GCM provisions are largely optional and leave a wide margin of discretion to Member States.[21] The GCM's core structure outlines commitments to 23 objectives supported by actions for the realization of the commitments, but these actions are selective and can arguably be applied at different times. Although the GCM is supposed to be aligned to the 2030 Agenda, there is no organized framework of goals, targets and indicators, as with the SDGs, which sets timelines for the achievement of the actions specified.[22]

While the scope of the GCM is also covered by the framework of international human rights and labour standards, its content applies to nearly all aspects of migration, with the possible exception of mixed migration,[23] and is thus considerably broader in scope to that of the legally-binding specific migration instruments, which focus on regulating the labour migration process and protection of migrant workers and their families. Indeed, the GCM addresses one particular area which is essentially refuted by these instruments, namely the need to make available more flexible pathways for the admission of regular migrants for the purposes of employment, family reunion and study, which is articulated by its objective 5.[24] Contrary to views in some quarters, however, the ICRMW, C97 and C143, do not interfere with the state sovereign prerogative to regulate the admission of foreigners into the territory. Even where the question of regularization of migrants in an irregular situation is raised in these instruments, States parties are only encouraged to give consideration to this possibility.[25] Arguably, in addition to its overall non-legally binding nature, the GCM does not undertake anything similar in objective 5, although this position continued to be expressed by some governments, namely that the GCM poses a threat to the sovereign right of States to enforce their immigration laws and to secure their borders, and even that it would create a human right to immigration.[26]

---

21 See also S. Carrera et al., *Some EU governments leaving the UN Global Compact on Migration: A contradiction in terms?*, Centre for European Policy Studies (CEPS) Policy Insights, No. 2018/15, Brussels: CEPS 2018, p. 3.

22 Indeed, such a framework was proposed as a model for the GCM by the former UN Special Rapporteur on the human rights of migrants. See UNGA, Human Rights Council, 35th Session, *Report of the Special Rapporteur on the human rights of migrants on a 2035 agenda for facilitating human mobility*, A/HRC/35/25 (28 April 2017).

23 The *Mixed Migration Centre* provides a working definition of mixed migration: 'Mixed migration refers to cross-border movements of people including refugees fleeing persecution and conflict, victims of trafficking and people seeking better lives and opportunities. Motivated to move by a multiplicity of factors, people in mixed flows have different legal statuses as well as a variety of vulnerabilities. Although entitled to protection under international human rights law, they are exposed to multiple rights violations along their journey. Those in mixed migration flows travel along similar routes, using similar means of travel – often travelling irregularly and wholly or partially assisted by migrant smugglers'.

24 GCM Objective 5: Enhance availability and flexibility of pathways for regular migration, para. 21.

25 For example, see ICRMW, Art. 69(1), 'States Parties shall, when there are migrant workers and members of their families within their territory in an irregular situation, take appropriate measures to ensure that such a situation does not persist', and C143, Art. 9(4), 'Nothing in this Convention shall prevent Members from giving persons who are illegally residing or working within the country the right to stay and to take up legal employment.'

26 Carrera et al. 2018, p. 1, 6-7.

Another significant difference between the GCM and legally-binding international standards relates to the modalities for their implementation and the mechanisms envisaged to review such implementation, and this is addressed in Section 4 below.

3. Points of Tension

There were several points of tension during the consultations and negotiations on the GCM. One of these relating to opening up more flexible pathways for regular migration has already been mentioned above. Others concerned the cost of recruitment and the extent to which workers could be expected to pay recruitment fees. During the negotiations, one of the earlier draft texts of objective 6 of the GCM referred to prohibiting recruiters from 'charging *disproportionate or hidden fees* as well as related costs to the migrant worker',[27] which implied that workers could be charged reasonable fees or related costs, but due to the resistance of a number of governments and international agencies, including the ILO, this eventually gave way to the application of the principle that workers should not pay recruitment fees or related costs,[28] in line with ILO standards,[29] articulated in the ILO General Principles and Operational Guidelines for Fair Recruitment, approved by the ILO Governing Body in November 2016, and which have recently been supplemented by the Definition of Recruitment Fees and Related Costs, approved by the ILO Governing Body in March 2019.[30] Another bone of contention, which was probably the most sensitive issue in the adoption of the New York Declaration for Refugees and Migrants, concerned immigration detention, and particularly the detention of children.[31] Neither document ends immigration detention for children, as advocated by a number of international and civil society organizations, although the GCM commits Member States to work 'to end the practice of child detention in the context of international migration'.[32]

However, the two points of tension that have historically concerned governments when discussing migration governance relate to irregular migration and how best to address it, and the degree to which migrants, and particularly migrants in an irregular situation, should have access to social rights.

3.1. Irregular Migration

While the GCM recognizes that irregular migration is a phenomenon, which impacts negatively on migration governance, and should therefore be addressed, it avoids an

27 GCM, Draft Rev. 2, 28 May 2018, para. 21(d). Emphasis added.

28 The wording in the final version of the GCM reads: 'prohibit recruiters and employers from charging or shifting recruitment fees or related costs to migrant workers'. UNGA 2019 (note 1), para. 22(c).

29 See in particular the ILO Private Employment Convention, 1997 (No. 181), Article 7(1): 'Private employment agencies shall not charge directly or indirectly, in whole or in part, any fees or costs to workers.'

30 *ILO General principles and operational guidelines for fair recruitment and definition of recruitment fees and related costs*, General Principle 7.

31 See *New York Declaration for Refugees and Migrants* (note 7), para. 33, and UNGA 2019 (note 1), objective 13.

32 UNGA 2019 (note 1), para. 29(h).

approach that is based exclusively on security considerations by declaring that all migrants, regardless of their migration status, are also entitled to enjoyment of their human rights.[33] In this sense, it echoes the New York Declaration for Refugees and Migrants,[34] the 2013 UN General Assembly Declaration of the High-level Dialogue on International Migration and Development,[35] as well as the approach taken to irregular migration in the three specific instruments on migrant workers, which is probably best articulated in the following preambular paragraph of the ICRMW:

> Bearing in mind that the human problems involved in migration are even more serious in the case of irregular migration and convinced therefore that appropriate action should be encouraged in order to prevent and eliminate clandestine movements and trafficking in migrant workers, while at the same time assuring the protection of their fundamental human rights.[36]

In reviewing the landscape of international human rights law, the UN Special Rapporteur on the human rights of migrants has argued that all migrants, without discrimination are protected under this framework and that there are only a few and narrowly defined exceptions to this, including the right to vote and to be elected and the right to enter and stay in a country.[37] And even in the latter case, the Human Rights Committee, which supervises the application of the ICCPR, has qualified this restriction and interpreted the right to enter one's own country as applying also to a country's long-term or permanent residents.[38]

With regard to migrants in an irregular situation, the picture is somewhat more complex. Fundamental human rights and labour standards should also apply to them without discrimination, and this has been reiterated by the treaty bodies supervising the implementation by State parties of human rights instruments,[39] as well as by the independent ILO Committee of Experts on the Application of Conventions and Recommendations, with reference in particular to the eight ILO conventions addressing fundamental rights and principles at work.[40] On the other hand, the ICRMW, C97 and

33 See in particular UNGA 2019 (note 1), paras. 11 and 27.

34 *New York Declaration for Refugees and Migrants* (note 7), para. 41: 'We are committed to protecting the safety, dignity and human rights and fundamental freedoms of all migrants, regardless of their migratory status, at all times'.

35 UNGA, 68th Session, *Declaration of the High-level Dialogue on International Migration and Development*, A/RES/68/4 (21 January 2014), para. 10: 'Reaffirm the need to promote and protect effectively the human rights and fundamental freedoms of all migrants, regardless of their migration status …'.

36 ICRMW (note 25), Preamble, para. 12.

37 UNGA, 68th Session, *Report of the Special Rapporteur on the human rights of migrants: A human rights framework for global migration governance*, A/68/283 (7 August 2013), para. 28.

38 UN, Human Rights Committee, *General Comment No. 27: Freedom of movement (article 12)*, CCPR/C/21/Rev.1/Add.9 (1 November 1999), para. 20.

39 See e.g. UN, Economic and Social Council, Committee on Economic, Social and Cultural Rights (CESCR), *General Comment No. 20: Non-discrimination in economic, social and cultural rights (art. 2, para. 2, of the ICESCR)*, E/C.12/GC/20 (2 July 2009), para. 30: 'The Covenant rights apply to everyone including non-nationals, such as refugees, asylum-seekers, stateless persons, migrant workers and victims of international trafficking, regardless of legal status and documentation'.

40 ILO, *Promoting Fair Migration, General Survey concerning the migrant worker instruments, Report of the Committee of Experts on the Application of Conventions and Recommendations (CEACR), Report III (Part 1B)*, International Labour Conference, 105th Session, Geneva: International Labour Office 2016, p. 90, para. 276.

C143 present a more nuanced picture. C97 was adopted in 1949 when irregular migration was not considered to be a significant phenomenon and thus its focus is to regulate regular migration for employment and ensure non-discrimination and equality of treatment between migrant workers in a regular situation and nationals. While C143 contains a very important provision in Article 1 requiring Members 'to respect the basic human rights of all migrant workers', which the ILO Committee of Experts has clearly linked to the eight ILO fundamental conventions and the nine core international human rights instruments, including the ICRMW,[41] and Part I on migrations in abusive conditions applies to all migrant workers, it affords a wider range of rights to those in a regular situation in Part II on equality of opportunity and treatment. A similar approach is taken in the ICRMW, in the division between Parts III and IV, which distinguish between the rights afforded all migrant workers and their families, including those in irregular status, to those afforded regular migrants.[42] As such, rights to free choice of employment, and family reunion, for example, which are both qualified,[43] are not afforded migrant workers in an irregular situation. On the other hand, these three instruments, when considered together, do not generally make distinctions between other economic and social rights, such as equality of treatment in respect of wages and working conditions, access to health care and other branches of social security, and education.

The specific GCM provisions expose further tensions in this area. A provision that attracted considerable attention during the negotiations concerned paragraph 22(i) in objective 6, which commits UN Member States to facilitate fair and ethical recruitment and safeguard conditions that ensure decent work:

> Provide migrant workers engaged in remunerated and contractual labour with the same labour rights and protections extended to all workers in the respective sector, such as the rights to just and favourable conditions of work, to equal pay for work of equal value, to freedom of peaceful assembly and association, and to the highest attainable standard of physical and mental health, including through wage protection mechanisms, social dialogue and membership in trade unions.

On its face, this provision would appear to afford basic labour rights, which are also clearly recognized human rights, such as the right to freedom of association, only to workers holding formal employment contracts, which could exclude many migrant workers in the informal economy, including those in an irregular situation. While the reference to 'contractual labour' is rather ambiguous, the above narrow interpretation would not be in accordance with human rights and labour standards, including the three specific instruments on migrant workers discussed above. This is an evident example, therefore, of an important area where human rights and labour standards can assist in the application of the GCM to ensure that it is compatible with international law on which it is supposed to rest.

---

41 ILO 2016 (note 40), p. 90, paras. 276-277.

42 UN, Committee on the Protection of the Rights of All Migrant Workers and Members of Their Families, *General Comment No. 2 on the rights of migrant workers in an irregular situation and members of their families*, CMW/C/GC/2 (28 August 2013), paras. 6 and 8.

43 ICRMW (note 25), Arts. 44(2) and Arts. 52 and 53.

3.2. Social Rights for Migrants

As discussed above, international human rights instruments, have not explicitly made any distinctions on the basis of nationality or immigration status, with some minor exceptions. This includes the ICESCR, which applies to everyone, including non-nationals, regardless of legal status.[44] Subsequent interpretation of the ICESCR's provisions by the Committee on Economic, Social and Cultural Rights has strengthened this position in a number of general comments, including those relating to the human rights to health and just and favourable conditions of work.[45] While the position in international law, therefore, is relatively clear, despite the resistance to these interpretations by some States, application of these rights to migrants in an irregular situation in practice is much more challenging. One proposal in recent times has been to argue for the imposition of 'firewalls' between the roles of enforcement authorities charged with immigration control and social, health and service providers.[46] In the employment context, this would require labour inspectors to focus on protecting the rights and interests of all workers, and improving working conditions, rather than checking on their immigration status and enforcement of immigration law, a position endorsed by the ILO Committee of Experts in the application of ILO Labour Inspection Convention, 1947 (No. 81).[47]

While the GCM recognizes the tension between enjoyment of basic social rights by migrants in an irregular situation and the need by immigration authorities to address irregular migration, the final text in objective 15 has been considerably diluted from previous versions:

> Ensure that cooperation between service providers and immigration authorities does not exacerbate vulnerabilities of irregular migrants by compromising their safe access to basic services or unlawfully infringing upon the human rights to privacy, liberty and security of person at places of basic service delivery.[48]

Depending therefore on how this action is interpreted by governments, this may once again call into question the extent to which application of the GCM in this area is in conformity with international law.

---

44 CESCR (note 39), para. 30. However, there is an exception in respect of developing countries and the extent of enjoyment by non-nationals of economic rights. See Article 2(3) of the ICESCR: 'Developing countries, with due regard to human rights and their national economy, may determine to what extent they would guarantee the economic rights recognized in the present Covenant to non-nationals'.

45 UN, Economic and Social Council (ECOSOC), CESCR, *General Comment No. 14: The right to the highest attainable standard of health (article 12 of the ICESCR)*, E/C.12/2000/4 (11 August 2001), para. 34, and UN, ECOSOC, CESCR, *General Comment No. 23 (2016) on the right to just and favourable conditions of work (article 7 of the ICESCR)*, paras. 5, 11 and 47(e).

46 See e.g. European Commission against Racism and Intolerance (ECRI), *General Policy Recommendation No. 16 on Safeguarding Irregularly Present Migrants from Discrimination*, 16 March 2016, Strasbourg: Council of Europe 2016, para. 3.

47 ILO 2016 (note 40), p. 153, para. 482.

48 UNGA 2019 (note 1), para. 31(b).

4. Implementation and Enforcement

Perhaps the biggest difference between the GCM and the application of legally-binding standards to migrants relates to implementation and enforcement.

The supervisory system set up to monitor the application of international instruments ratified by UN Member States is longstanding and well developed. All of the core international human rights instruments have set up treaty-based bodies to supervise the application of these instruments by State parties, which are based on the submission and consideration of periodic reports and the possibility for individual and inter-state complaints. Moreover, the treaty bodies provide authoritative interpretations of the instruments' provisions by issuing general comments or recommendations. They can also conduct country visits. Supervision of the application of human rights is complemented by a system of review under the UN Charter under the auspices of the Human Rights Council, the two main mechanisms being the Universal Periodic Review and the Special Procedures of the Council, which include the thematic mandate of the UN Special Rapporteur on the human rights of migrants.[49]

The ILO has also established an elaborate supervisory system to monitor the application of ILO Conventions, based on reports submitted to the ILO Committee of Experts, which issues observations and direct requests to States parties. A select number of observations are subsequently discussed by the Committee on the Application of Standards at the annual International Labour Conference, to which the governments concerned are required to respond, and which often result in follow-up action by the ILO. In addition, the ILO Constitution provides for a system of complaints and representations that can be brought against individual States by ILO tripartite constituents of governments, workers' and employers' organizations in the ILO Governing Body.[50] It is through this mechanism that a complaint was made against Qatar under the ILO Forced Labour Convention, 1930 (No. 29) and the Labour Inspection Convention, 1947 (No. 81), both ratified by Qatar.[51] The outcome of this complaint was an agreement to establish the ILO-Qatar technical cooperation programme, which aims to make improvements to the situation of migrant workers in that country with reference to five key focus areas.[52]

In contrast, the GCM envisages a much looser and flexible system for its implementation, follow-up and review.[53] While States remain the primary vehicle for this,

---

49 See UN Office of the High Commissioner for Human Rights (OHCHR), *Human Rights Bodies*, Geneva: OHCHR 1996-2019, at https://www.ohchr.org/EN/HRBodies/Pages/HumanRightsBodies.aspx.

50 See ILO, *Rules of the Game: A brief introduction to International Labour Standards*, Revised Edition, Geneva: International Labour Office 2014.

51 ILO, *Complaint concerning non-observance by Qatar of the Forced Labour Convention, 1930 (No. 29), and the Labour Inspection Convention, 1947 (No. 81), made by delegates to the 103rd Session (2014) of the International Labour Conference under article 26 of the ILO Constitution*, ILO Governing Body, 331st Session, 26 October-9 November 2017, GB.331/INS/13(Rev.) (31 October), Geneva: ILO 2017.

52 (1) Improvement in the payment of wages; (2) Enhanced labour inspection and Occupational Safety and Health systems; (3) A contractual system established to replace *Kafala*, and improved employment conditions and labour recruitment procedures; (4) Increased prevention, protection and prosecution against forced labour; and (5) Promotion of workers' voice. See: https://www.ilo.org/beirut/projects/qatar-office/lang--en/index.htm.

53 UNGA 2019 (note 1), paras. 40-54.

the GCM welcomes the decision of the UN Secretary-General to establish a UN Network on Migration, which is tasked 'to ensure effective and coherent system-wide support' for implementation, follow-up and review of the GCM,[54] and is coordinated by the International Organization for Migration (IOM), which also provides for its Secretariat.[55] The Network brings together 38 UN agencies and comprises an Executive Committee of eight agencies,[56] which takes decisions by consensus. The Network formally commenced its operations in October 2018 and at the first Principals' meeting of its Executive Committee in May 2019 launched a Migration Multi-Partner Trust Fund, which is a component of the capacity-building mechanism established by the GCM,[57] and which will pool donor contributions that can then be channelled to support Member States' implementation of the GCM.[58] In addition to assigning this support role to the UN Network on Migration, the GCM also provides for an International Migration Review Forum, which repurposes and renames the previous High-level Dialogue on International Migration and Development. This Forum will be held at the UN General Assembly every four years beginning in 2022 and 'serve as the primary intergovernmental global platform for Member States to discuss and share progress on the implementation of all aspects of the Global Compact, including as it relates to the 2030 Agenda for Sustainable Development, and with the participation of all relevant stakeholders'. Each edition of the Forum will result in 'an intergovernmentally agreed Progress Declaration'.[59] The GCM also invites relevant subregional, regional and cross-regional processes, platforms and organizations, including UN regional economic commissions or regional consultative processes (RCPs) on migration to review GCM implementation in respective regions, starting in 2020.[60] Other intergovernmental dialogues on migration taking place among States, such as the Global Forum on Migration and Development (GFMD), are also requested to provide a space for annual informal exchange on GCM implementation and to contribute to the International Migration Review Forum.[61] The GCM encourages all UN Member States 'to develop, as soon as practicable, ambitious national responses for the implementation of the Global Compact, and to conduct regular and inclusive reviews of progress at the national level, such as through the voluntary elaboration and use of a national implementation plan'.[62] While the modalities for the International Migration Review Forum and review at the regional level are under discussion,[63] it is difficult to see the development of processes of review that are anything but voluntary, or to subject any voluntary reporting by UN Member States to independent scrutiny, given the stated non-legally binding nature of the GCM.

---

54 UNGA 2019 (note 1),1,para. 45.

55 UNGA 2019 (note 1),1,para. 45(a).

56 Department of Economic and Social Affairs (DESA), ILO, IOM, OHCHR, United Nations Development Programme (UNDP), UNHCR, UN Children's Fund (UNICEF), UN Office on Drugs and Crime (UNODC).

57 UNGA 2019 (note 1),1,para. 43(b).

58 See UN DESA Voice, *UN establishes pioneering trust fund for cooperation on safe, orderly and regular migration*, 9 May 2019, New York: UN.

59 UNGA 2019 (note 1), para. 49.

60 UNGA 2019 (note 1), para. 50.

61 UNGA 2019 (note 1), paras. 51 and 52.

62 UNGA 2019 (note 1), para. 53.

63 IISD, *States Share Views on International Migration Review Forum Modalities*', SDG Knowledge Hub, 21 March, Geneva: IISD 2019.

5. Conclusion

This chapter has provided a comparative snapshot of the GCM juxtaposed with the international law framework on which it rests, with particular reference to relevant human rights and labour standards. In the first part of the GCM, strong statements are made purporting to align the GCM with these standards and the 2030 Agenda for Sustainable Development, by listing a number of key international instruments and referring to cross-cutting and interdependent guiding principles. Conformity with these standards, however, becomes less clear when some of the more detailed actionable paragraphs under the GCM's 23 objectives are examined, particularly in sensitive areas of migration governance such as addressing irregular migration and affording migrants access to basic social rights. In this sense, it is unfortunate that more care was not taken to ensure fuller alignment with human rights and labour standards in the core part of the GCM.[64]

The GCM, however, will stand and fall, on the extent to which it is implemented at the national level. In some parts of the world, such as in Asia and the Middle East, where the level of acceptance of international human rights instruments and labour standards is generally lower than in Africa, Europe and Latin America, the GCM can serve as an important policy framework for change to improve migration governance and the life and work of migrants based in those regions. Given that UN Member States are very likely to opt for a less formal and more voluntary mechanism for implementation, review and follow-up of the GCM, it is important that such a mechanism takes account of and speaks to the more established systems of supervision set up under the auspices of the Human Rights Council, treaty-based bodies and the ILO. Otherwise, there is a further risk of divergence and fragmentation, which will only undermine the rule of law in respect of the governance of migration.

64 Indeed, in an academic paper published in January 2017 before the start of the GCM negotiations, the authors urged negotiators to pay more attention to this question: 'Before the negotiations towards the Global Compact move forward in a substantive manner it is critical that the negotiators are fully aware of the existing obligations applicable to states. It would be a grave error if the Compact process failed to build on the existing standards as a starting point. A subsequent review of outcomes in light of human rights obligations is never satisfactory in this type of negotiation'. E. Guild & S. Grant, *Migration Governance in the UN: What is the Global Compact and What does it mean?,* School of Law Legal Studies Research Paper No. 252/2017, 8 January, London: Queen Mary University of London, 2017, p. 16.

Challenges to the Human Rights Principle of Non-Discrimination in Implementation of the Global Compact for Safe, Orderly and Regular Migration?

*Bjarney Friðriksdóttir**

> '.....the relationship of security and insecurity is a continuum which permits insecurity to follow the subject – the foreigner, the immigrant – even though the individuals concerned are completely different, have separate trajectories and objectives.'[1]

The Global Compact for Safe, Orderly and Regular Migration

The Global Compact for Safe, Orderly and Regular Migration (the Compact), was formally adopted by the General Assembly of the United Nations on December 19, 2018. In the preamble to the Compact it is stated that it 'presents a non-legally binding, cooperative framework' based on commitments agreed upon by Member States in the New York Declaration for Refugees and Migrants that was adopted by the General Assembly in 2016. That the Compact 'fosters international cooperation among all relevant actors in migration, acknowledging that no State can address migration alone, and upholds the sovereignty of States and their obligations under international law.'[2] Furthermore, that the Compact rests upon the purposes and principles of the Charter of the United Nations, as well as the Universal Declaration of Human Rights and the nine core United Nations Human Rights Treaties.[3]

The Compact is based on a set of ten cross-cutting and interdependent guiding principles, for the issues addressed herein, the following three are of most relevance:

(a) *People-centred.* The Global Compact carries a strong human dimension, inherent to the migration experience itself. It promotes the well-being of migrants and the members of communities in countries of origin, transit and destination. As a result, the Global Compact places individuals at its core.[4]

(c) *National sovereignty.* The Global Compact reaffirms the sovereign right of States to determine their national migration policy and their prerogative to govern migration within their jurisdiction, in conformity with international law. Within their sovereign jurisdiction, Sates may distinguish between regular and irregular migration status, including as they determine their legislative and policy measures for the implementation of the Global Compact, taking into account different national realities,

---

* Human Rights Officer on Migration Issues, OHCHR Regional Office for the Middle East and North Africa.

1 E. Guild, *Security and Migration in the 21st Century*, Cambridge: Polity Press 2009, p.191.

2 United Nations General Assembly, Resolution adopted by the General Assembly – Global Compact on Safe, Orderly and Regular Migration, UN DOC A/RES/73/195. New York: United Nations 2018, paragraph 7.

3 *Ibid.*, paragraph 1 and 2.

4 *Ibid.*, paragraph 15(a).

policies, priorities and requirements for entry, residence and work, in accordance with international law.[5]

(f) *Human rights*. The Global Compact is based on international human rights law and upholds the principle of non-regression and non-discrimination. By implementing the Global Compact, we ensure effective respect for and protection and fulfilment of the human rights of all migrants, regardless of their migration status, across all stages of the migration cycle. We also reaffirm the commitment to eliminate all forms of discrimination, including racism, xenophobia and intolerance, against migrants and their families.[6]

The Right of States to Distinguish Between Irregular and Regular Migrants in their Reading and Implementation of the Compact

In the adoption of the Compact by the General Assembly, European States distinguished themselves from States in other regions of the world in the number of States that abstained from voting on it and those that voted against it. Out of five States that voted against it, three are European. Seven of the twelve States that abstained from voting are European. In addition, the majority of European States that gave an explanation of their vote, stood out from other Member States in the emphasis they set on differentiation between irregular and regular migrants in their reading and implementation of the Compact.

In its explanation of vote against adopting the Compact, the Czech Republic provided that some of their 'crucial concerns remained unresolved or were not reflected in the final text' of the Compact, those most importantly, concerned 'the issues of distinction, or rather the lack of any distinction, between legal and illegal migration and more broadly, of unclear definitions of terms used in the Compact.'[7] Similarly, Poland stated in its vote against the Compact, that as it 'fails to distinguish sufficiently between regular and irregular migration, Poland would face significant difficulties in implementing some of the commitments arising from the Compact's provisions, particularly including identity cards, the decriminalization of irregular migration and national child detention standards.'[8] Austria which abstained from voting, provided in its explanation of its vote that a 'human right to migrate is unknown in Austria's legal system', that it 'rejects the creation of a category of migrants, which does not exist under international law' and that it 'draws a clear distinction between legal and illegal immigration, and is opposed to watering it down, which would result from the Global Compact.'[9]

5 *Ibid.*, paragraph 15(c).

6 *Ibid.*, paragraph 15(f).

7 United Nations General Assembly, 60th Plenary Meeting Wednesday 19 December 2018, UN DOC A/73/PV.60, New York: United Nations 2018, p. 16.

8 *Ibid.*, p. 16.

9 *Ibid.*, p. 18.

From the European States that voted for adopting the Compact, Croatia,[10] France,[11] Lithuania,[12] Slovenia,[13] Turkey[14] and the United Kingdom[15] gave similar statements in the explanations of their votes, that they intended to apply the distinction between irregular and regular migrants in the reading and/or implementation of the Compact. Croatia for example, stated that it will 'continue to legally and practically differentiate between refugees and migrants, as well as between regular and irregular migration, and invest all necessary efforts in combating irregular migration, especially smugglers and traffickers in human beings.' Furthermore, that while 'recognizing the universality of human rights and fundamental freedoms, which belong equally to migrants and all other human beings, the Compact does not create any new legal category or associated benefits, nor does it establish a human right to migrate.'[16] Similarly, Turkey provided that it 'will make a clear distinction between the objectives and commitments in the Compact regarding regular migrants and those regarding irregular migrants.'[17]

Denmark made a statement on behalf of Iceland, Lithuania, Malta and the Netherlands which was supported by Norway[18] and Estonia.[19] The explanation of the vote on behalf of these States provided their assessment of the obligation undertaken in regard to the implementation of the Compact including in the following:

> 'The Compact is a non-legally binding framework. It does not in any way create legal obligations for States, nor does it seek to establish international customary law or further interpret national obligations under existing treaties. It respects States' sovereignty and affirms their sovereign right to determine their national immigration policies and laws. It recognizes the universality of human rights and fundamental freedoms and emphasizes that all migrants are entitled to the same rights as any individual born into this world. It creates no new legal categories of migrants or associated benefits and does not establish a human right to migrate. It considers it essential to ensure that borders are managed for the security of States, communities and migrants.'

Furthermore, that they 'welcome the clear principle in the Compact that States have the sole authority to distinguish between regular and irregular migratory status within their sovereign jurisdiction. That distinction could have been more clearly mainstreamed throughout the Compact. We emphasize that in our reading of the Compact we will apply a clear distinction between regular and irregular migrants.'[20]

10 United Nations General Assembly, 61st Plenary Meeting Wednesday 19 December 2018, UN DOC A/73/PV.61, New York: United Nations 2018, p. 5.
11 UN DOC A/73/PV.61, p. 8.
12 UN DOC A/73/PV.61, p. 10.
13 UN DOC A/73/PV.60, p. 21.
14 UN DOC A/73/PV.60, p. 27.
15 UN DOC A/73/PV.60, p. 22.
16 UN DOC A/73/PV.61, p. 5.
17 UN DOC A/73/PV.60, p. 27.
18 UN DOC A/73/PV.60, p. 24.
19 UN DOC A/73/PV.61, p. 2.
20 UN DOC A/73/PV.60, p. 24.

The Principle of Non-Discrimination Related to Nationality and Migration Status in International Human Rights Law

There is no universally accepted definition of 'irregular' or 'regular' migrant. In relation to the implementation of the Compact at the national level, the lack of distinction between the two should not be an obstacle to fully respect the cross-cutting guiding principle of the Compact related to human rights, whereas the commitment of the States that adopted it is to 'ensure effective respect for and protection and fulfilment of the human rights of all migrants, regardless of their migration status across all stages of the migration cycle.'[21] The principle of non-discrimination based on nationality and migration status is one of the most important principles of international human rights laws in regard to protection of the human rights of persons present as foreign nationals in States other than their own. In relation to that, it is important to recall how the principle of non-discrimination has been interpreted as regards nationality and migration status by the Treaty Bodies of three of the nine core United Nations human rights treaties.

The International Convention on the Elimination of All forms of Racial Discrimination (ICERD) Article 1, defines racial discrimination as any distinction, exclusion, restriction or preference based on race, colour, descent, or national or ethnic origin which has the purpose or the effect of nullifying or impairing the recognition, enjoyment or exercise, on an equal footing, of human rights and fundamental freedoms in the political, economic, social, cultural or any other field of public life. Furthermore, it provides that the Convention shall not apply to distinction, exclusion, restrictions or preferences made by a State party between citizens and non-citizens and that nothing in the Convention may be interpreted as affecting in any way the legal provisions of States parties concerning nationality, citizenship or naturalization, provided that such provisions do not discriminate against any particular nationality. This construction of what can be considered justifiable distinctions based on nationality under the Convention provides important safeguards in cases where discrimination that is in fact based on race or a particular nationality is being justified as legitimate discrimination based on nationality or citizenship.

The Committee on the Elimination of Racial Discrimination (the Committee) has provided some clarification regarding the scope of this non-discrimination clause in the Convention and its relation to discrimination based on nationality in declaring that it excepts from the definition of discrimination provided therein 'actions by a State party which differentiate between citizens and non-citizens,' that this exemption is however qualified by 'declaring that, among non-citizens, States may not discriminate against any particular nationality.'[22] In relation to this formulation, the Committee stated that the exemption of actions that differentiate between citizens and non-citizens 'must not be interpreted to detract in any way from the rights and freedoms recognized and enunciated in other instruments, especially the Universal Declaration of Human Rights, the International Covenant on Economic, Social and Cultural Rights and the

---

21 United Nations General Assembly, Resolution adopted by the General Assembly – Global Compact on Safe, Orderly and Regular Migration, UN DOC A/RES/73/195, New York: United Nations 2018, paragraph 15(f).

22 Committee on the Elimination of Racial Discrimination, *General Recommendation No. XI on non-citizens*, New York: United Nations 1993, paragraph 1.

International Covenant on Civil and Political Rights.[23] In General Recommendation No. 30 on discrimination against non-citizens, the Committee elaborates on differential treatment based on citizenship or immigration status and concludes that such treatment 'will constitute discrimination if the criteria for such differentiation, judged in the light of the objectives and purposes of the Convention, are not applied pursuant to a legitimate aim, and are not proportional to the achievement of this aim'.[24] The Committee also encourages States to ensure that immigration policies do not have the effect of discriminating against persons on the basis of race, colour, descent, or national or ethnic origin,[25] as well as safeguarding that 'legislative guarantees against racial discrimination apply to non-citizens regardless of their immigration status, and that the implementation of legislation does not have a discriminatory effect on non-citizens'.[26] The issue the Committee is addressing in these recommendations, where it outlines the possible intersection between legitimate differences in treatment based on nationality on the one hand, in particular with regard to immigration control, and discrimination based on race on the other hand, is to clarify that when discrimination based on nationality is used as a proxy for discrimination based on race or certain selected nationalities, that such conduct will constitute unjustifiable discrimination under the Convention.

The International Covenant on Economic, Social and Cultural Rights (ICESCR), provides in Article 2(2) that the States parties undertake to guarantee that the rights enshrined in the Covenant will be exercised without discrimination of any kind as to race, colour, sex, language, religion, political or other opinion, national or social origin, property, birth or other status.

In *General Comment No. 20* addressing non-discrimination in economic, social and cultural rights, the Committee on Economic, Social and Cultural Rights (the Committee), discussed the grounds of discrimination prohibited by the ICESCR. In reviewing and commenting on these various grounds, the Committee observed that national and social origin are among the express grounds found in the Covenant and that nationality is listed in a grouping of 'other status', that is additional grounds which 'are commonly recognized when they reflect the experience of social groups that are vulnerable and have suffered and continue to suffer marginalization'.[27] The Committee interprets 'national origin' as referring 'to a person's State, nation, or place of origin,' and notes that 'individuals may face systematic discrimination in both the public and the private sphere in the exercise of the Covenant rights',[28] due to these factors or personal circumstances. In addressing the personal scope of the Covenant in relation to non-nationals, the Committee established that the Covenant 'applies to everyone including non-nationals, such as refugees, asylum-seekers, stateless persons, migrant workers and victims of international trafficking, regardless of legal status and documentation'.[29]

23 *Ibid.*, paragraph 3.

24 Committee on the Elimination of Racial Discrimination, *General Recommendation No. 30 on discrimination against non-citizens*, New York: United Nations 2004, paragraph 4.

25 *Ibid.*, paragraph 9.

26 *Ibid.*, paragraph 7.

27 Committee on Economic, Social and Cultural Rights, *General Comment No. 20, Non-discrimination in economic, social and cultural rights*, New York: United Nations 2009, paragraph 20.

28 *Ibid.*, paragraph 24.

29 *Ibid.*, paragraph 30.

The personal scope of the International Covenant on Civil and Political Rights (ICCPR) extends to everyone within the territory of a State party. In Article 2(1) it is stipulated that each State party undertakes to respect and to ensure to all individuals within its territory and subject to its jurisdiction the rights recognized in the Covenant, without distinction of any kind, such as race, colour, sex, language, religion, political or other opinion, national or social origin, property, birth or other status. The Covenant does not include a definition of what constitutes discrimination, but the Human Rights Committee (the Committee), provided a definition in *General Comment No. 18* on non-discrimination, that is largely based on the definition of discrimination in the ICERD. It provides that the term 'discrimination' as 'used in the Covenant should be understood to imply any distinction, exclusion, restriction or preference which is based on any ground such as race, colour, sex, language, religion, political or other opinion, national or social origin, property, birth or other status, and which has the purpose or effect of nullifying or impairing the recognition, enjoyment or exercise by all persons, on equal footing, of all rights and freedoms'.[30] In its *General Comment No. 15* on the position of aliens[31] under the Covenant, the Committee has provided an interpretation of the principle of non-discrimination as it relates to non-citizens. Referring to Article 2(1) on the personal scope of the Covenant, the Committee established that 'the general rule is that each one of the rights of the Covenant must be guaranteed without discrimination between citizens and aliens,' and that aliens 'receive the benefit of the general requirement of non-discrimination in respect of the rights guaranteed in the Covenant'.[32] In relation to the fact that although the Covenant does not 'recognize the rights of aliens to enter or reside in the territory of a State party', the Committee has reiterated that however, 'once aliens are allowed to enter the territory of a State party they are entitled to the rights set out in the Covenant'.[33]

The ICCPR contains some exceptions to the general rule of the fully inclusive personal scope. These are for example found in Article 12 which restricts the right to liberty of movement and freedom to choose own residence to those lawfully within the territory of a State and Article 25 which limits to citizens, the right to take part in public affairs, to vote and be elected and have equal access to public services. The Committee in its *General Comment No. 25*, stated that Article 25, while it protects the rights of 'every citizen', is in 'contrast with other rights and freedoms recognized by the Covenant (which are ensured to all individuals within the territory and subject to the jurisdiction of the State)'.[34] With respect to the personal scope of Article 12, the Committee proclaimed that 'once an alien is lawfully within a territory, his freedom of movement within the territory and his right to leave that territory may only be restricted' if such restrictions are provided by law, are necessary to protect national security, public order,

30 Human Rights Committee, *General Comment No. 18, Non-Discrimination*, New York: United Nations 1998, paragraph 7.

31 The Human Rights Committee uses the term 'alien' in its *General Comments*, this term is however not used in the Covenant itself or other UN human rights instruments.

32 Human Rights Committee, *General Comment No. 15, The Position of Aliens under the Covenant*, New York: United Nations 1986, paragraph 2.

33 *Ibid.*, paragraphs 5 and 6.

34 Human Rights Committee, *General Comment No. 25, Participation in public affairs and the right to vote*, New York: United Nations 1996, paragraph 3.

public health or morals or the rights and freedoms of others. Additionally, that 'differences in treatment in this regard between aliens and nationals, or between different categories of aliens, need to be justified' in accordance with the above.[35]

In addition to the general non-discrimination clause, the ICCPR contains a provision on equality before the law in Article 26 which provides that all persons are equal before the law and entitled to the equal protection of the law without any discrimination. In the explanation of the Committee on the meaning of Article 26, it stated that it 'not only entitles all persons to equality before the law as well as equal protection of the law but also prohibits any discrimination under the law and guarantees to all persons equal and effective protection against discrimination' on the grounds enumerated in the Covenant's non-discrimination clause.[36] Article 26 is regarded as complimentary to the principle of non-discrimination which 'together with equality before the law and equal protection of the law without any discrimination, constitute a basic and general principle relating to the protection of human rights'.[37] The Committee provides further that Article 26 does not merely duplicate the guarantee already provided for in Article 2 but provides in itself an autonomous right, while it 'prohibits discrimination in law or in fact in any field regulated and protected by public authorities.' Article 26 thereby addresses 'the obligations imposed on State parties in regard to their legislation and the application thereof. Thus, when legislation is adopted by a State party, it must comply with the requirement of Article 26 that its content should not be discriminatory.'[38]

National Sovereignty and Duties of Sovereign States in the Implementation of the Global Compact for Safe, Orderly and Regular Migration

Having regard to the interpretation of the principle of non-discrimination as it relates to nationality and migration status outlined in the above, it is clear that although States are free to distinguish between irregular and regular migrants in determination of the administrative status of migrants, that States have a duty to protect the human rights of all migrants. The differentiation that can be made between migrants based on their administrative status as regards human rights protection is limited to rights related to political participation and freedom of movement. For the Compact to be implemented with respect for the three cross-cutting and interdependent governing principles addressing a *People Centred* approach, *National Sovereignty* and *Human rights*, States have to have equal regard to their sovereign right to govern their borders and protect their community and their sovereign duty to fulfil the human rights obligations they have voluntarily undertaken by ratifying international human rights law. In order to reach the stated 'intention' of the Compact 'to reduce the risks and vulnerabilities migrants face at different stages of migration by respecting, protecting and fulfilling their human

35 Human Rights Committee, *General Comment No. 15, The Position of Aliens under the Covenant*, New York: United Nations 1986, paragraph 8.

36 Human Rights Committee, *General Comment No. 18, Non-Discrimination*, New York: United Nations 1989, paragraph 1.

37 *Ibid.*

38 *Ibid.*, paragraph 12.

rights and providing them with care and assistance',[39] individual migrants and their personal security must be at the core,[40] of the policies set forth and actions taken in implementation of the Compact.

References

Committee on Economic, Social and Cultural Rights, General Comment No. 20, *Non-discrimination in economic, social and cultural rights (Art. 2(2)),* UN Doc E/C.12/ GC/20, New York: United Nations 2009.

Committee on the Elimination of Racial Discrimination, *General Recommendation No. XI on non-citizens*, UN Doc HRI/GEN/1/Rev.9 (Vol II), New York: United Nations 2008, p. 275-276.

Committee on the Elimination of Racial Discrimination, *General Recommendation No. 30, on discrimination against non-citizens*, UN Doc CERD/C/64/Misc.11/Rev 3. New York: United Nations 2004.

Guild, E., *Security and Migration in the 21st Century*. Cambridge: Polity Press 2009.

Human Rights Committee, *General Comment No. 25, Participation in public affairs and the right to vote,* UN Doc HRI/GEN/1/Rev.9 (Vol I), New York: United Nations 2008, p. 217-222.

Human Rights Committee, *General Comment No. 18, Non-discrimination.* UN Doc HRI/GEN/1/Rev.9 (Vol I), New York: United Nations 2008, p. 195-198.

Human Rights Committee, *General Comment No. 15, The Position of Aliens under the Covenant.* UN Doc HRI/GEN/1/Rev.9 (Vol I), New York: United Nations, 2008, p. 189-191.

Human Rights Committee, *General Comment No. 25, Participation in public affairs and the right to vote*, New York: United Nations 1996.

International Convention on the Elimination of All forms of Racial Discrimination, UN General Assembly resolution 2106 (XX), 21 December 1965, United Nations, *Treaty Series*, vol. 660, 195.

International Covenant on Civil and Political Rights, UN General Assembly Resolution 2200A (XXI), 16 December 1966, United Nations, *Treaty Series*, vol. 999, no. 14668.

International Covenant on Economic, Social and Cultural Rights, UN General Assembly Resolution 2200A (XXI), 16 December 1966, United Nations, *Treaty Series*, vol. 993, no. 14531.

United Nations General Assembly, 61st Plenary Meeting Wednesday 19 December 2018, UN DOC A/73/PV.61. New York: United Nations 2018.

United Nations General Assembly, 60th Plenary Meeting Wednesday 19 December 2018, UN DOC A/73/PV.60. New York: United Nations 2018.

United Nations General Assembly, Resolution adopted by the General Assembly – Global Compact on Safe, Orderly and Regular Migration, UN DOC A/RES/ 73/195. New York: United Nations 2018.

39 United Nations General Assembly, Resolution adopted by the General Assembly – Global Compact on Safe, Orderly and Regular Migration, UN DOC A/RES/73/195. New York: United Nations 2018, paragraph 12.

40 *Ibid.*, paragraph 15.

The Normative Potential of the Migration Compact

*Jens Vedsted-Hansen**

1. Political Distortion – Legal Confusion?

As the scheduled adoption of the UN Global Compact for Safe, Orderly and Regular Migration[1] came closer, the negotiation process attracted significant attention in a number of countries across Europe and beyond. While the political background and organisational framing of the Migration Compact were directed towards improving international cooperation on forced displacement and irregular migration with a view to preventing irregular migration and alleviating the plight of refugees and migrants, including those in irregular situations,[2] the process and its purpose became subject to interventions with quite different purposes. The general tenor of many such interventions was extremist and anti-immigrant with more or less clear xenophobic assumptions, and the underlying agenda seems to have been presenting the UN process towards the adoption of the Migration Compact as yet another attempt from politically correct policy makers and the international community to limit the sovereign powers of states and national authorities.

There were strong indications that the anti-Compact campaign was orchestrated by a covert, and perhaps somewhat incidental, alliance of anti-immigrant groups and political extremists from nationalist circles, some of which having the wider purpose of destabilising international organisations and political institutions, not least the United Nations and the European Union. Be that as it may, the campaign was in all circumstances guided by lack of clarity concerning the legal nature of the Migration Compact and its normative effects. In this context, the Migration Compact appears to have been targeted far more than the Global Compact on Refugees.[3] Notably, the campaign itself contributed significantly to such lack of clarity by misrepresenting legal effects and impose obligations on states to accept more migrants with more demanding standards for their treatment. Thus, legal confusion seems to have been part of the strategy for political distortion of the Migration Compact process.

Against this background, it was not surprising that governments as well as legal experts responding to the anti-Compact campaign's assertions emphasised the legally non-binding nature of the Migration Compact. As a clear example, the Danish government prepared a well-argued memorandum outlining the contents of the Migration Compact and analysing its legal nature in order to explain to the Parliament that it

---

* Aarhus University, Denmark.

1 Global Compact for Safe, Orderly and Regular Migration, Annex to Resolution 73/195, adopted by the General Assembly 19 December 2018, UN doc. A/Res/73/195 (hereinafter GCM or Migration Compact).

2 See the New York Declaration for Refugees and Migrants, Resolution 71/1, adopted by the General Assembly 19 September 2016, UN doc. A/Res/71/1.

3 Global Compact on Refugees, Part II of the Annual Report of the UN High Commissioner for Refugees, adopted by the General Assembly 17 December 2018, UN doc. A/Res/73/151.

would have no legal effects.[4] While in themselves convincing, such legal assessments may have been somewhat counter-productive in the sense that they might risk detracting attention from the actual object and purpose of the Migration Compact, thus potentially jeopardising its full implementation. It is therefore timely to consider the extent to which this international instrument can in fact become relevant to future efforts of international organisations and national authorities not only by way of guiding their policy decisions, but also through normative influence that may ultimately be of legal, or at least quasi-legal, nature.

2. The Legal Status of GCM Commitments: Various Approaches

In the first place, it is to be noted that the GCM itself explicitly states the absence of any legally binding effects of its adoption in two partly identical paragraphs:

> This Global Compact presents a *non-legally binding, cooperative framework* that builds on the commitments agreed upon by Member States in the New York Declaration for Refugees and Migrants. It fosters international cooperation among all relevant actors on migration, acknowledging that no State can address migration alone, and upholds the *sovereignty* of States and their *obligations under international law.*[5]

Notably, the clarification of the non-legally binding nature of the GCM itself is here combined with the emphasis on state sovereignty and, at the same time, their obligations under international law. The impact of state sovereignty in the migration context is further highlighted in that the GCM 'reaffirms the sovereign right of States to determine their national migration policy and their prerogative to govern migration within their jurisdiction, in conformity with international law'.[6] Importantly, the GCM links the absence of legally binding effects with the need for international cooperation by providing for a cooperative framework:

> The Global Compact is a *non-legally binding cooperative framework* that recognizes that no State can address migration on its own because of the inherently transnational nature of the phenomenon. It *requires international, regional and bilateral cooperation and dialogue.* Its authority rests on its consensual nature, credibility, collective ownership, joint implementation, follow-up and review.[7]

The non-legally binding nature of the GCM and its respect for state sovereignty thus seem to be qualified in two different respects. First, the GCM has to be seen in the light of states' already existing international obligations. This is actually made clear from the very outset as the GCM, according to the Preamble, is resting on the purposes and principles of the UN Charter and on the Universal Declaration of Human Rights, the

4 Legal memorandum on the UN Global Compact for Safe, Orderly and Regular Migration, prepared by the Danish Ministry of Foreign Affairs, Ministry of Justice and Ministry of Immigration and Integration, 3 December 2018, Parliament Committee doc. UUI Alm.del – Bilag 57.

5 GCM para. 7 (italics added).

6 GCM para. 15 (c).

7 GCM para. 15 (b) (italics added).

two UN Covenants and the other seven core international human rights treaties as well as a number of additional UN Conventions.[8] Furthermore, the Preamble recognises that '[r]efugees and migrants are entitled to the same universal human rights and fundamental freedoms, which must be respected, protected and fulfilled at all times', whereas 'migrants and refugees are distinct groups governed by separate legal frameworks' under which only refugees are entitled to the specific protection as defined by international refugee law.[9] Finally, among its guiding principles the GCM refers specifically to human rights by stating:

> The Global Compact is based on international human rights law and upholds the principles of *non-regression* and *non-discrimination*. By implementing the Global Compact, we ensure effective respect for and protection and fulfilment of the *human rights of all migrants, regardless of their migration status*, across all stages of the migration cycle. We also reaffirm the commitment to eliminate all forms of discrimination, including racism, xenophobia and intolerance, against migrants and their families.[10]

Second, the non-legally binding nature of the GCM does not detract from the explicit recognition of the need for international cooperation which is operationalised in the final parts dealing with Implementation, Follow-up and Review.[11] The commitment to review the implementation of the GCM may ultimately imply that some of the non-legal commitments undertaken by the UN and member states adopting the GCM can be expected to have certain normative powers in the wider sense of the term. While not legally binding by virtue of the adoption of the GCM *per se*, those commitments may acquire legal nature as a result of the pre-existing human rights obligations that are recognised in the GCM and whose implementation will be included in such reviews. In addition, some of the GCM commitments might appear suitable to serve as normative sources in the development of these human rights obligations by way of interpreting the existing legal norms or developing standards for the actual application of such norms.[12]

As regards the question of more precise ways in which the normative effects of the GCM could possibly materialise over time, the answer depends on the precise meaning of the concept that the GCM is 'based' on international human rights law and 'rests' on the Univeral Declaration and the various human rights treaties. Insofar as the GCM is reflecting already existing human rights treaty standards, its connection to legally binding obligations would seem to be rather straightforward as the GCM can be seen as merely restating such treaty standards. If the link between the GCM and treaty obligations is less direct and therefore depending on interpretive choices concerning the

8 GCM paras. 1 and 2, listing the specific instruments in footnotes 3-17.

9 GCM para. 4.

10 GCM para. 15 (f).

11 GCM paras. 40-47 and 48-54, respectively.

12 For a distinction between norm-creating and norm-filling roles of the Global Compact on Refugees, see T. Gammeltoft-Hansen, 'The Normative Impact of the Global Compact on Refugees', 30(4) *International Journal of Refugee Law* 2018, p. 605-610. While there are indeed similarities in the analyses of the normative impacts of the GCM and the Global Compact on Refugees, the contents of the latter as well as substantive and structural aspects of its implementation seem rather different from those characterising the GCM.

treaty norms pertaining to the GCM objectives or commitments, various legal avenues may be relevant.

One option for construing the treaty provisions in question so as to reflect the GCM could be the methods of treaty interpretation in the light of subsequent developments as laid down in article 31(3) of the Vienna Convention on the Law of Treaties. However, the *subsequent agreement* referred to in article 31(3)(a) presupposes the consent of (almost) all the parties to the treaty in question, a requirement that is quite unlikely to be met given the fact that a number of states decided not to endorse the GCM or actively distanced themselves from its contents. The adoption of the GCM does not in itself constitute a *subsequent practice* as defined in article 31(3)(b), and even when such practice might occur in line with the GCM commitments, it will probably fail to meet the requirement of establishing the agreement of the treaty parties regarding its interpretation. The *integrative interpretation method* drawing on 'relevant rules of international law' in accordance with article 31(3)(c) might be likely to provide another basis of interpreting treaty norms in line with the GCM, yet here again there will be problems in that the GCM may not be considered as 'relevant rules' and certainly not such that are applicable in the relations between all the parties of the relevant human rights treaty.

While traditional interpretation methods thus do not seem to provide any clear answer as to how to consider the GCM commitments from a legal perspective, an alternative approach could be to consider those commitments as sources of soft law evidencing the existing or emerging *consensus* among the states that actually supported the adoption of the GCM. In this connection it could also be relevant to examine the potential of some of the GCM commitments as giving evidence of *opinio juris* for the purpose of establishing norms of customary international law, provided that all the additional requirements for the creation of such customary norms be fulfilled. The following section is going to pursue the former alternative by examining the potential of GCM commitments to inform the decision making of regional human rights bodies.[13] Focus will here be on the European system for the protection of human rights which seems to be of particular relevance in this context.

3. Making Law Softly: European Human Rights Bodies

It is a widely observed phenomenon that the European Court of Human Rights frequently refers to other sources of European and international law than the European Convention on Human Rights (ECHR) when it is to decide on yet unsettled issues of interpretation or application of the Convention. As the Court has explained, the Convention

> 'cannot be interpreted in a vacuum but must be interpreted in harmony with the general principles of international law. Account should be taken, as indicated in Article 31 § 3 (c) of the Vienna Convention on the Law of Treaties of 1969, of "any relevant rules of international law

13 Cf. GCM para. 50, specifically mentioning regional organisations among those invited to review the implementation of the Migration Compact within the respective regions.

applicable in the relations between the parties", and in particular the rules concerning the international protection of human rights'.[14]

Importantly, the Court has made references to international instruments beyond those strictly following from this provision of the Vienna Convention, often applying a kind of double-comparative method of referring to relevant norms of European and international law as well as domestic legal developments showing (emerging) consensus among the member states of the Council of Europe being parties to the ECHR.[15]

The other bodies dealing with human rights within the framework of the Council of Europe obviously have a primary role in guiding or informing the Court, including the Committee of Ministers, the Parliamentary Assembly, the European Committee of Social Rights, the Commissioner for Human Rights, the European Committee for the Prevention of Torture (CPT) and the European Commission against Racism and Intolerance (ECRI). While the sources emanating from the former three bodies, and in some instances also those from the Commissioner and ECRI, typically have the form of soft law such as resolutions or recommendations on the human rights issues that are pending before the Court,[16] the Court's references to the CPT, the Commissioner for Human Rights and ECRI often serve the purpose of providing or confirming information on factual matters such as the conditions of detention in situations where the applicant is unable to establish all the facts complained of with the requisite certainty or country findings on discrimination.[17]

Not only sources from the Council of Europe, but also EU sources and international instruments may be of relevance to the European Court of Human Rights, as illustrated in judgments on so diverse issues as the right to freedom of association,[18] the right of postoperative transsexuals to respect for private life and conclusion of marriage,[19] and the right to reunification between child and parent in cases of transnational child abduction.[20] Importantly, the Court has been basing its reasoning not only

14 *Neulinger and Shuruk v. Switzerland*, ECtHR judgment 6 July 2010, para. 131.

15 Cf. I.E. Koch & J. Vedsted-Hansen, 'International Human Rights and National Legislatures – Conflict or Balance?', 75 *Nordic Journal of International Law* 2006, p. 3-28, at p. 11 ff.

16 Cf. *Sigurjónsson v. Iceland*, ECtHR judgment 30 June 1993, para. 35, *Gebremedhin v. France*, ECtHR judgment 26 April 2007, paras. 36-38, and *M.S.S. v. Belgium and Greece*, ECtHR judgment 21 January 2011, para. 87.

17 See, as examples, *Dougoz v. Greece*, ECtHR judgment 6 March 2001, paras. 40 and 46-48, *S.D. v. Greece*, ECtHR judgment 11 June 2009, paras. 38 and 51, and *M.S.S. v. Belgium and Greece*, ECtHR judgment 21 January 2011, paras. 160, 163-164, 187, 190, 212, 227, 229, 244, 255, 281-282, 300, 304, 318, 320 and 348. As regards ECRI, see *Annual Report on ECRI's Activities covering the period from 1 January to 31 December 2018*, Strasbourg: Council of Europe 2019, p. 15, para. 30 with references to ECtHR caselaw.

18 Cf. *Sigurjónsson v. Iceland*, ECtHR judgment 30 June 1993, para. 35 with references to the Universal Declaration of Human Rights, decisions of the Freedom of Association Committee of the ILO and the European Community Charter of the Fundamental Social Rights of Workers.

19 Cf. *Christine Goodwin v. UK*, ECtHR judgment 11 July 2002, paras. 58, 81 and 100 with references to the EU Charter of Fundamental Rights and the International Classification of Diseases issued by WHO.

20 Cf. *Neulinger and Shuruk v. Switzerland*, ECtHR judgment 6 July 2010, paras. 48, 50, 52, 53, 55, 56, 57, 66-67, 99-105 and 132-138 with references to the UN Convention on the Rights of the Child, the UN Convention on the Elimination of Discrimination against Women, General Comments from the UN

on binding international treaties and EU legislation, but also on non-binding instruments having the legal nature of *soft law* emanating from international organisations and the EU. Thus, the normative relevance is not necessarily contingent on the legally binding nature of an instrument if it is considered relevant to the case in substantive terms.

This may in turn prove relevant to the implementation of the GCM if or when cases should arise before the European Court of Human Rights that might affect migrant rights issues that have been dealt with in the GCM. It is not excluded in principle that the Court might refer directly to standards laid down in the GCM, given the fact that the GCM Objectives and the commitments for their realisation have been endorsed by the UN General Assembly. As an example, GCM Objective 12 on certainty and predictability in migration procedures would seem to be relevant in cases concerning article 13 ECHR, taken together with substantive migration-related rights such as that of respect for private and family life under article 8 ECHR, in order to emphasise the centrality of effective domestic remedies that would contribute to realising this commitment:

> We commit to increase legal certainty and predictability of migration procedures by developing and strengthening *effective and human-rights based mechanisms* for the adequate and timely screening and individual assessment of all migrants for the purpose of identifying and facilitating *access to the appropriate referral procedures*, in accordance with international law.[21]

As an indirect source of inspiration for the European Court of Human Rights it would be conceivable that GCM commitments might first be addressed by some of the other Council of Europe bodies following which the Court might in turn include the relevant sources from such European human rights bodies into its reasoning. Pertinent examples concerning the treatment of migrants could be found in the work of the European Commission against Racism and Intolerance (ECRI) which has, as mentioned above, been quoted quite frequently by the European Court of Human Rights.

In its General Policy Recommendation (GPR) on irregular migrants ECRI stresses that all migrants, including those irregularly present, have human rights, recalling that international law establishes minimum standards in this respect, and consequently recommends that governments respect the fundamental human rights of irregularly present migrants, inter alia in the fields of education, health care, housing, social security and assistance, labour protection and justice.[22] This recommendation is well in line with the commitments under GCM Objective 15 on access to basic services for migrants:

We commit to ensure that all migrants, regardless of their migration status, can exercise their human rights through safe access to basic services. We further commit to strengthen

---

Human Rights Committee, UNHCR guidelines, the EU Charter of Fundamental Rights and, in particular, the Hague Convention on the Civil Aspects of International Child Abduction and related instruments.

21 GCM para. 28 (italics added). For a critical account of the drafting and substance of Objective 12, see B. Nagy, Objective 12', in: E. Guild & Tugba Basaran (eds), *The UN's Global Compact for Safe, Orderly and Regular Migration, Refugee Law Initiative*, London: University of London 2018, p. 35-37.

22 ECRI General Policy Recommendation (GPR) No. 16 on safeguarding irregularly present migrants from discrimination, 2016, recital 4 and para. 2.

migrant-inclusive service delivery systems, notwithstanding that nationals and regular migrants may be entitled to more comprehensive service provision, while ensuring that any differential treatment must be based on law, be proportionate and pursue a legitimate aim, in accordance with international human rights law.[23]

Interestingly, two particular aspects of the GCM must be considered as more vague and less protective of migrant rights than the ECRI recommendation. Objective 15 does not specify the various types of services as comprehensively as the latter, whether that should be seen as reflecting a narrow GCM delimitation of 'basic services' or it is due to a political desire during the UN negotiation process to keep the GCM commitments vague and, at the same time, potentially open-ended in this regard.[24] In addition, the GCM does not exclude cooperation between service providers and immigration authorities, but merely suggests that it should be ensured that such cooperation does not exacerbate vulnerabilities of irregular migrants by 'compromising their safe access to basic services or unlawfully infringing upon the human rights to privacy, liberty and security of person'.[25] By contrast, ECRI explicitly recommends that governments decouple immigration control and enforcement from the provision of services and assurance of rights of irregularly present migrants within their jurisdiction in order to ensure that those rights are guaranteed to such migrants and that authorities with other primary responsibilities be relieved from interference by immigration enforcement institutions.[26] Nonetheless, since the GCM commitments do not substantively deviate from the ECRI recommendation, the GCM could well serve as generally reinforcing the regional standard previously adopted by ECRI.

Yet other examples could be mentioned, reflecting the fact that ECRI's mandate in general and its recommendations in GPR No. 16 in particular have important similarities with commitments laid down in the Migration Compact. Thus, GCM Objective 17 on the elimination of all forms of discrimination and countering of expressions, acts and manifestations of racism, racial discrimination, violence, xenophobia and related intolerance against all migrants in conformity with international human rights law has clear overlaps with ECRI's mandate.[27] To the contrary, certain GCM commitments may, despite the existence of parallel ECRI recommendations, be difficult to include into rulings on the European Convention on Human Rights because they deal with human rights issues only weakly protected or even beyond the scope of the ECHR.[28]

23 GCM para. 31.

24 Cf. the concrete actions towards realising this commitment in GCM para. 31, litras (a)-(f) that are less specific than those listed in ECRI GPR No. 16, para. 2, and further elaborated in paras. 11-33. See B. Hastie, 'Objective 15', in E. Guild & Tugba Basaran (eds), *The UN's Global Compact for Safe, Orderly and Regular Migration, Refugee Law Initiative*, London: University of London 2018, p. 44.

25 GCM para. 31 (b). For a critical account of the absence of 'firewall' language and changes of this commitment during the GCM negotiations, see Hastie 2018 (n. 21), p. 43: 'As a result, the final text regarding cooperation with immigration authorities renders much of the remaining recommendations of the objective impractical, as cooperation with immigration authorities is known to be one of the most significant deterrents for migrants to seek out and access services.'

26 ECRI GPR No. 16, para. 3.

27 GCM para. 33, cf. ECRI's mandate laid down in Resolution Res(2002)8 of the Committee of Ministers of the Council of Europe on the Statute of the European Commission against Racism and Intolerance.

28 As an example, see GCM Objective 22 on portability of social security entitlements, cf. E. Guild, 'GCM Indicators: Implementation, Follow-up and Review', in: E. Guild & Tugba Basaran (eds), *The UN's Global Compact for Safe, Orderly and Regular Migration, Refugee Law Initiative*, London: University of

4. Distortion or Adoption of the GCM in EU Law?

The combination of political distortion and legal confusion was not brought to an end with the adoption of the GCM in December 2018. A rather peculiar example of continued focus on imagined impacts of the GCM occurred in March 2019 as a document providing the opinion of the European Commission's Legal Service was made public and soon came to form the basis of allegations that the EU was in the course of secretly making the Migration Compact a legally binding instrument.

Indeed, the Note from the Legal Service purported to analyse the legal effects of the formal adoption of the GCM. And it was undoubtedly controversial to some EU Member States by highlighting those Member States that had either decided not to attend the Intergovernmental Conference in Marrakech adopting the GCM, been absent from the UN General Assembly when adopting the GCM Resolution, or voted against or abstained from voting on the Resolution endorsing the GCM.[29] However, the analytical focus of the Note was limited to assessing the legal effects of the GCM on EU development cooperation under article 208(1) TFEU in the light of the UN Agenda for Sustainable Development. Without going into any detail of the legal reasoning, it would seem that the conclusion of the Note from the Legal Service – according to which the EU shall promote multilateral solutions elaborated in the framework of the GCM, the GCM is an integral part of the EU positions in development cooperation, and Member States should facilitate the achievement of EU objectives including the implementation of the GCM in accordance with the principle of loyal cooperation[30] – is not particularly controversial in general terms.

In any event, it is hardly incidental that the allegations raised against the Commission and its Legal Service were fuelled by members of the Hungarian and Austrian governments, promoted by extremist political parties in France and Belgium, and futher circulated by the US newssite *Breitbart* and media connected to *Generation Identitaire*.[31] The future research and follow up of this will therefore be confronting interesting challenges with a need to combine analytical precision as regards the legal nature of the GCM as a UN instrument *per se* on the one hand, and clarification of the legal and political impact of the principles of loyal cooperation not only within the EU, but indeed also at the global level and in the UN implementation process, on the other.

London 2018, p. 63-64. While there is a similar recommendation in ECRI GPR No. 16, para. 31, upholding these standards may seem uncertain in the light of current case law under article 14 ECHR.

29 European Commission Legal Service, *Note on the legal effects of the adoption of the Global Compact for Safe, Orderly and Regular Migration by the UN General Assembly*, 1 February 2019, Brussels: European Commission 2019.

30 *Ibid.*, paras. 52-53.

31 Cf. 'Hemmeligt dokument, der ikke er hemmeligt, binder ikke EU til migrationsaftale', fact check in Danish web-magazine *Altinget*, 2 May 2019.

Publications of Elspeth Guild 1997-2018

2018

Grütters, C.A.F.M., E. Guild, P.E. Minderhoud, R. van Oers & M.H.A. Strik, *Brexit and Migration. Civil Liberties, Justice And Home Affairs. Study for the LIBE committee,* (external report), Brussels: European Parliament.

Grütters, C.A.F.M. & E. Guild, Introduction, in C.A.F.M. Grütters & D. Dzananovic (Eds.), *Migration and Religious Freedom. Essays on the interaction between religious duty and migration law*, Nijmegen: Wolf Legal Publishers, p. 15-19.

Guild, E., In Honour of Ted Badoux. Making migration safer and more orderly, in: A.M. van Melle (Ed.), *Liber amoricum Ted L. Badoux*, Den Haag: Sdu, p. 19-35.

Guild, E., *A Shared EU Fixation on Third Country National Family Members?* (external report, Nijmegen Migration Law Working Papers Series, no. 2018/04), Nijmegen: Radboud University Nijmegen.

Guild, E. & K. Vowden, BREXIT and the Fate of EU Citizens. Substantial Insecurity, *Asiel & Migrantenrecht, 9* (6/7), p. 303-313.

Guild, E., Unsafe, Disorderly, and Irregular Migration? Examining the Assumptions Underlying the United Nations' New York Declaration. *Peace Research. The Canadian Journal of Peace and Conflict Studies, 50* (1), p. 53-75.

Guild, E., Concluding Remarks, in: C.A.F.M. Grütters & D. Dzananovic (Eds.), *Migration and Religious Freedom. Essays on the interaction between religious duty and migration law*, Nijmegen: Wolf Legal Publishers, p. 251-254.

Guild, E., Intra-Corporate Transferees. Between the Directive and the EU's International Obligations, in: P.E. Minderhoud & T. de Lange (Eds.), *The Intra Corporate Transferee Directive. Central Themes, Problem Issues and Implementation in Selected Member States*, Oisterwijk: Wolf Legal Publishers, p. 55-66.

Guild, E., W. Sandholtz & C. A. Whytock (Eds.), Research Handbooks on the Politics of International Law [Bespreking van het boek *Research Handbooks on the Politics of International Law*], *European Review of International Studies, 5*(1), p. 135-138.

2017

Carrera, S., A. Geddes, E. Guild & M. Stefan, Conclusions and recommendations. Towards a fair EU agenda, in: S. Carrera, A. Geddes, E. Guild & M. Stefan (Eds.), *Pathways towards legal Migration into the EU. Reappraising concepts, trajectories and policies*, Brussels: CEPS, p. 183-209.

Carrera, S., A. Geddes, E. Guild & M. Stefan, Introduction, in: S. Carrera, A. Geddes, E. Guild & M. Stefan (Eds.), *Pathways towards legal Migration into the EU. Reappraising concepts, trajectories and policies*, Brussels: CEPS, p. 1-6.

Carrera, S., A. Geddes, E. Guild & M. Stefan (Eds.), *Pathways towards legal Migration into the EU. Reappraising concepts, trajectories and policies.* Brussels: CEPS, 231 p.

Gammeltoft-Hansen, T., E. Guild, V. Moreno-Lax, M. Panizzon & I. Roele, *What is a Compact? Migrants' Rights and State Responsibilities Regarding the Design of the UN Global Compact for Safe, Orderly and Regular Migration,* (external report, Raoul Wallenberg Institute Working Paper), Raoul Wallenberg Institute.

Guild, E., S. Grant & C.A. Groenendijk, *Human Rights of Migrants in the 21st Century,* London: Routledge, 96 p.

Guild, E., Can the EU use trade agreements to facilitate regular migration?, in: S. Carrera, A. Geddes, E. Guild & M. Stefan (Eds.), *Pathways towards legal Migration into the EU. Reappraising concepts, trajectories and policies*, Brussels: CEPS, p. 157-162.

Guild, E., EU Inclusion and Exclusion. From Workers to Citizens to People, in: C.A.F.M. Grütters, S.A. Mantu & P.E. Minderhoud (Eds.), *Migration on the Move. Essays on the Dynamics of Migration*, Leiden: Brill, p. 197-224.

Guild, E., Questioning temporary migration schemes in the EU, in: S. Carrera, A. Geddes, E. Guild & M. Stefan (Eds.), *Pathways towards legal Migration into the EU. Reappraising concepts, trajectories and policies*, Brussels: CEPS, p. 42-48.

Guild, E., *Border Controls, Surveillance and Counter Terrorism* (external report, Nijmegen Migration Law Working Papers Series, no 2017/03), Nijmegen: Radboud University Nijmegen.

Guild, E., S. Grant & C.A. Groenendijk, *IOM and the UN. Unfinished Business* (external report, Queen Mary School of Law Legal Studies Research Paper, no. 255/2017), London: Queen Mary School of Law.

Guild, E. & S. Grant, *Migration Governance in the UN. What is the Global Compact and What Does it Mean?* (external report, Queen Mary School of Law Legal Studies Research Paper, no. 252/2017), London: Queen Mary University of London.

Guild, E., The UN's Search for a Global Compact on Safe, Orderly and Regular Migration, *German Law Journal, 18* (7), p. 1780-1797.

Guild, E., S. Grant & C.A. Groenendijk, Introduction, in: E. Guild, S. Grant & C.A. Groenendijk (Eds.), *Human Rights of Migrants in the 21st Century,* London: Routledge, p. 1-15.

2016

Bard, P., S. Carrera, E. Guild & D. Kochenov, *An EU Mechanism on Democracy, the Rule of Law and Fundamental Rights* (external report, CEPS Liberty and Security in Europe, no. 91), Brussels: CEPS.

Bard, P., S. Carrera & E. Guild, *An EU Mechanism on Democracy, the Rule of Law and Fundamental Rights. Annex II Assessing the Need and Possibilities for the Establishment of an EU Scoreboard on Democracy, the Rule of Law and Fundamental Rights* (external report, European Parliament Research Paper, no. PE 579328), Brussels: European Parliament.

Bigo, D., S. Carrera & E. Guild, *The EU and the 2016 Terrorist Attacks in Brussels. Better instead of more information sharing,* Brussels: CEPS Commentary (last update: 6 April 2016).

Carrera, S., E. Guild & L. Vosyliūtė, *The Cost of Non-Europe in the Area of Organised Crime* (external report, CEPS Liberty and Security in Europe, no. 90), Brussels: CEPS.

Carrera, S. & E. Guild, *EU-Turkey plan for handling refugees is fraught with legal and procedural challenges,* Brussels: CEPS Commentary (last update: 10 March 2016).

Carrera, S. & E. Guild, E. *Rethinking asylum distribution in the EU. Shall we start with the facts?*, Brussels: CEPS Commentary (last update: 17 June 2016).

Carrera, S., E. Guild & N. Chun Luk, *What does Brexit mean for the EU's Area of Freedom, Security and Justice,* Brussels: CEPS Commentary (last update: 11 July 2016).

Carrera, S. & E. Guild, Addressing Irregular Migration, Facilitation and Human Trafficking. The EU's Approach, in: S. Carrera & E. Guild (Eds.), *Irregular Migration, Trafficking and Smuggling of Human Beings. Policy Dilemmas in the EU*, Brussels: Centre for European Policy Studies, p. 1-9.

Carrera, S. & E. Guild, Migrant Smuggling In The EU. What Do The Facts Tell Us?, in: S. Carrera & E. Guild (Eds.), *Irregular Migration, Trafficking and Smuggling of Human Beings. Policy Dilemmas in the EU*, Brussels: Centre for European Policy Studies, p. 11-16.

Carrera, S. & E. Guild (Eds.), *Irregular Migration, Trafficking and Smuggling of Human Beings. Policy Dilemmas in the EU,* Brussels: Centre for European Policy Studies (114 p.).

Guild, E., *BREXIT and its Consequences for UK and EU Citizenship or Monstrous Citizenship,* Leiden: Brill (XII, 90 p.).

Guild, E., EU Citizenship, in: D. Patterson & A. Sodersten (Eds.), *A Companion to European Union Law and International Law*, Chichester: Wiley-Blackwell, p. 491-505.

Guild, E. & T. Basaran, Mobilities, ruptures, transitions, in: T. Basaran, D. Bigo et al. (Eds.), *International Political Sociology. Transversal Lines*, New York: Routledge, p. 272-285.

Guild, E., Seguridad. Terrorismo y asilo en el espacio Schengen, in: J. Arango & R. Mahia (Eds.), *El año de los refugiados. Anuario CIDOB de la Inmigración 2015-2016* (Anuario CIDOB de la Immigración), Barcelona: Edicions Bellaterra, S.L., p. 59-78.

Guild, E., The Complex Relationship of Asylum and Border Controls in the European Union, in: V. Chetail, P. De Bruycker & F. Maiani (Eds.), *Reforming the Common European Asylum System. The New European Refugee Law*, Leiden: Brill, p. 39-54.

Guild, E., The Dark Side of Globalisation. Do EU border controls contribute to death in the Mediterranean?, in: T. Gammeltoft-Hansen & J. Vedsted-Hansen (Eds.), *Human Rights and the Dark Side of Globalisation. Transnational law enforcement and migration control*, New York: Routledge, p. 314-331.

Guild, E., Understanding Immigration Detention in the UK and Europe, in: M.J. Guia, R. Koulish & V. Mitsilegas (Eds.), *Immigration Detention, Risk and Human Rights. Studies on Immigration and Crime*, Cham: Springer, p. 141-155.

Guild, E., C.A. Groenendijk et al. *Internal border controls in the Schengen area. Is Schengen crisis-proof?* (external report), Brussels: CEPS.

Guild, E., *Brexit and Social Security in the EU,* Brussels: CEPS Commentary (last update: 17 November 2016).

Guild, E., *Rethinking Migration Distribution in the EU. Shall we start with the facts?*, Brussels: CEPS Essay (last update: 22 January 2016).

Guild, E., Does the EU need a European Migration and Protection Agency?, *International Journal of Refugee Law, 28* (4), p. 585-600.

Vries, L., E. Guild & S. Carrera, *Documenting the Migration Crisis in the Mediterranean Spaces of Transit, Migration Management and Migrant Agency* (external report, CEPS Liberty and Security in Europe, no 94), Brussels: CEPS.

2015

Bigo, D., S. Carrera, E. Guild & R. Radescu, *A Question for accountability? EU and Member State inquiries into the CIA rendition and secret detention programme* (external report), Brussels: European Parliament LIBE Committee.

Carrera, S., G.G. Fuster, E. Guild & V. Mitsilegas, *Access to Electronic Data by Third-Country Law Enforcement Authorities. Challenges to EU Rule of Law and Fundamental Rights* (external report), Brussels: CEPS.

Carrera, S., E. Guild & K. Eisele, *No Move without Free Movement. The EU-Swiss controversy over quotas for free movement of persons* (external report, CEPS Policy Briefs, no. 331), Brussel: CEPS

Didier, B. & E. Guild, *The EU Counter-Terrorism Policy Responses to the Attacks in Paris. Towards an EU Security and Liberty Agenda* (external report, CEPS Paper in Liberty and Security in Europe, no 81), Brussels: CEPS.

Guild, E., Aliens and Terrorism, in: G. Lennon & C. Walker (Eds.), *Routledge Handbook of Law and Terrorism*, London: Routledge, p. 251-265.

Guild, E., The Asylum Seeker's Right to Free Legal Assistance and/or Representation, in: R. Plender (Ed.), *Issues in International Migration Law*, Leiden: Brill, p. 261-284.

Guild, E., C. Costello, M. Garlick, V. Moreno-Lax & M. Mouzourakis, *New Approaches, Alternative Avenues and Means of Access to Asylum Procedures for Persons Seeking International Protection* (external report, CEPS Paper in Liberty and Security in Europe, no. 77), Brussels: CEPS.

Guild, E., E.R. Brouwer, C.A. Groenendijk & S. Carrera, *What is happening to the Schengen Borders?* (external report, CEPS Paper in Liberty and Security in Europe, no. 86), Brussels: CEPS.

Guild, E. & K.M. Zwaan, Does Europe still create Refugees? Examining the Situation of Roma, *Queen's Law Journal, 40* (1), p. 142-164.

Peers, S., V. Moreno-Lax, E. Guild & M.V. Garlick, *EU Immigration and Asylum Law: (Text and Commentary). Vol. 3 EU Asylum Law* (Immigration and Asylum Law and Policy in Europe), Leiden: Brill (VIII, 674 p.)

2014

Bauman, Z., D. Bigo, P. Esteves, E. Guild & V. Jabri, After Snowden. Rethinking the Impact of Surveillance. *International Political Sociology, 8* (2), p. 121-144, doi: 10.1111/ips.12048.

Carrera, S., E. Guild & J. Parkin, *Who will monitor the spies?* (external report, CEPS Commentaries), Brussels: CEPS.

Guild, E., S. Carrera & K. Eisele, *Rethinking the attractiveness of the EU Labour Market. Comparative perspectives on the EU, US and Canada,* Brussel: CEPS (160 p.).

Guild, E., S. Peers & J. Tomkin, *The EU Citizenship Directive. A Commentary,* New York: Oxford University Press (XXIII, 334 p.).

Guild, E., C.J. Gortázar Rotaeche & D. Kostakopoulou, *The Reconceptualizing of European Union Citizenship* (Immigration and Asylum Law and Policy in Europe, 33), Leiden: Brill Nijhoff (XVII, 405 p.).

Guild, E., Labour migration and the European Union, in: V. Chetail & C. Bauloz (Eds.), *Research Handbook on International Law and Migration*, Cheltenham: Edward Elgar, p. 368-389.

Guild, E. & S. Carrera, *The Political and Judicial Life of Metadata. Digital Rights Ireland and the Trail of the Data Retention Directive* (external report, CEPS Paper in Liberty and Security in Europe, no. 65), Brussels: CEPS.

Guild, E., S. Carrera & J. Parkin, *What role for migration policy in the Ukraine crisis?* (external report, CEPS Commentaries), Brussels: CEPS.

Guild, E., Immigration Regulation as a Battleground. The European Union's Anxiety over Federalism, in: S. Baglay & D. Nakache (Eds.), *Immigration Regulation in Federal States* (International perspectives on migration, 9), Dordrecht: Springer, p. 223-244.

Guild, E., The EU's Internal Market and the Fragmentary Nature of EU Labour Migration, in: C. Costello & M. Freedland (Eds.), *Migrants at work. Immigration and vulnerability in labour law*, Oxford: Oxford University Press, p. 98-118.

Guild, E., Article 19. Protection in the Event of Removal, Expulsion or Extradition, in: S. Peers & T. Hervey (Eds.), *The EU Charter of Fundamental Rights. A Commentary*, Oxford: Hart Publishing, p. 543-562.

Guild, E., *Does European Human Rights Law Capture War on Terror Activity? On whose evidence?* (external report, Nijmegen Migration Law Working Papers Series, no. 2014/09), Nijmegen: Radboud University Nijmegen.

2013

Carrera, S., E. Guild & N. Hernanz, *The Triangular Relationship between Fundamental Rights, Democracy and the Rule of Law in the EU Towards an EU Copenhagen Mechanism.* (CEPS paperbacks), Brussels: Centre for European Policy Studies (101 p.).

Carrera, S., E. Guild & N. Hernanz, *Europe's most wanted? Recalibrating Trust in the European Arrest Warrant System* (external report, CEPS Special Report, no. 76), Brussels: Centre for European Policy Studies.

Carrera, S., E. Guild & N. Hernanz, *Rule of Law or Rule of Thumb? A New Copenhagen Mechanism for the EU* (external report, CEPS Policy Briefs, no. 303), Brussels: Centre for European Policy Studies.

Groenendijk, C.A., E. Guild, R. Cholewinski, P.E. Minderhoud, H. Oosterom & S.A. Mantu, *European Report on the Free Movement of Workers in 27 EU Member States in 2012-2013* (external report), Nijmegen: Centre for Migration Law.

Groenendijk, C.A., E. Guild, S.A. Mantu, P.E. Minderhoud, A.B. Terlouw & K.M. Zwaan (Eds.), *Issues that matter. Mensenrechten, minderheden en migranten. Liber Amicorum prof. mr. R. Fernhout,* Oisterwijk: Wolf Legal Publishers (VIII, 384 p.).

Grütters, C.A.F.M., E. Guild & S. de Groot, *Assessment of Credibility by Judges in Asylum Cases in the EU,* Oisterwijk: Wolf Legal Publishers (219 p.).

Grütters, C.A.F.M. & E. Guild, Introduction, in: C.A.F.M. Grütters, E. Guild & S. de Groot (Eds.), *Assessment of Credibility by judges in Asylum Cases in the EU*, Oisterwijk: Wolf Legal Publishers, p. 7-8.

Guild, E., S. Carrera & K. Eisele, *Social Benefits and Migration. A Contested Relationship and Policy Challenge in the EU*, Brussels: Centre for European Policy Studies (XII, 152 p.).

Guild, E., Does European Human Rights Law Capture War on Terror Activity?, in: C.A. Groenendijk, E. Guild, S.A. Mantu, P.E. Minderhoud, A.B. Terlouw & K.M. Zwaan (Eds.), *Issues that matter. Mensenrechten, minderheden en migranten*, Oisterwijk: Wolf Legal Publishers, p. 189-201.

Guild, E. & V. Moreno-Lax, *Current Challenges regarding the International Refugee Law with focus on EU Policies and EU Co-operation with UNHCR* (external report, Centre for European Policy Studies Liberty and Security in Europe Paper, no. 59), Brussels: Centre for European Policy Studies.

Guild, E. & S. Carrera, *EU Borders and Their Controls. Preventing Unwanted Movement of People in Europe?* (external report, CEPS Essays, no. 6), Brussels: Centre for European Policy Studies.

Guild, E., D. Bigo & S. Carrera, *Foreigners, Refugees or Minorities? Rethinking People in the Context of Border Controls and Visas*, Farnham: Ashgate (XIV, 258 p.).

Guild, E., EU Immigration in the new Treaty Framework, in: S.S. Juss (Ed.), *Ashgate Research Companion to Migration Law, Theory and Policy*, Farnham: Ashgate, p. 43-61.

Mantu, S.A. & E. Guild, E. (2013)., in: E.F. Isin & M. Saward (Eds.), *Enacting European Citizenship*, Cambridge: Cambridge University Press, p. 111-132.

2012

Groenendijk, C.A., E. Guild, R. Cholewinski, P.E. Minderhoud, H. Oosterom & S.A. Mantu, *European Report on the Free Movement of Workers in 27 EU Member States in 2011-2012* (external report), Nijmegen: Centre for Migration Law.

Guild, E., P.E. Minderhoud & R. Cholewinski, Preface to the First Decade of EU Migration and Asylum Law, in: E. Guild & P.E. Minderhoud (Eds.), *First Decade of EU Migration and Asylum Law* (Immigration and Asylum Law and Policy in Europe, 24), Leiden: Martinus Nijhoff, p. VII-XVI.

Guild, E., Who is a Migrant? EU Law and the Categorisation of People, in: P. Xuereb (Ed.), *Migration and Asylum in Malta and the European Union. Rights and Realities 2002 to 2011*, Msida: Malta University Press, p. 279-294.

Guild, E., The European Geography of Refugee Protection. Exclusions, Limitations and Exceptions from the 1967 Protocol to the Present, *European Human Rights Law Review, 17* (4), p. 413-426.

Guild, E., The Evolution of the Concept of Union Citizenship after the Lisbon Treaty, in: S. Morano-Foadi & M. Malena (Eds.), *Integration for Third Country Nationals in the European Union. The Equality Challenge*, Cheltenham: Edward Elgar, p. 3-15.

Guild, E., *Examining the European Geography of Refugee Protection Exclusions, Limitations and Exceptions from the 1967 Protocol to the Present* (external report, Nijmegen Migration Law Working Papers Series, no. 2012/03), Nijmegen: Radboud University Nijmegen.

Guild, E., *From Persecution to Management of Populations. Governmentality and the Common European Asylum System* (external report, Nijmegen Migration Law Working Papers Series, no. 2012/04), Nijmegen: Radboud University Nijmegen.

Minderhoud, P.E. & E. Guild, *The First Decade of EU Migration and Asylum Law* (Immigration and Asylum Law and Policy in Europe, 24), Leiden: Martinus Nijhoff (XVI, 485 p.).

Peers, S., E. Guild & J. Tomkin, *EU Immigration and Asylum Law: (Text and Commentary). Vol. 1 Visas and Border Controls* (Immigration and Asylum Law and Policy in Europe, 27), Leiden: Nijhoff (VIII, 411 p.).

Peers, S., E. Guild, D. Acosta Arcarazo, C.A. Groenendijk & V. Moreno-Lax, *EU Immigration and Asylum Law: (Text and Commentary). Vol. 2 EU Immigration Law* (Immigration and Asylum Law and Policy in Europe, 28), Leiden: Nijhoff (VIII, 589 p.).

2011

Groenendijk, C.A., E. Guild, R. Cholewinski, P.E. Minderhoud & H. Oosterom, *European Report on the Free Movement of Workers in 27 EU Member States in 2010-2011* (external report), Nijmegen: Centre for Migration Law.

Groenendijk, C.A. & E. Guild, *Visa policy of Member States and the EU towards Turkish nationals after Soysal* (external report, Economic Development Foundation Publications, no. 249), Istanbul: Economic Development Foundation.

Guild, E., From Persecution to Management of Populations. Governmentality and the Common European Asylum System, *Tidsskriftet Politik, 14* (4), p. 13-26.

Guild, E., Quem E o Imigrante? O Direito Europeu e a Categorizacao das Pessoas na Uniao Europeia, *Contexto Internacional, 33* (1), p. 19-46.

Guild, E., Financing Terrorism. The Struggle for Dominance Between the Political and judicial in EU and National Settings, in: P. Burgess & S. Gutwirth (Eds.), *A Threat Against Europe. Security, Migration and Integration*, Brussels: VUB Press, p. 75-92.

Guild, E., The Lisbon Treaty, the Stockholm Programme and data transfers in the new AFSJ. Where are the limits?, in: S. Wolff, F. Goudappel & J. de Zwaan (Eds.), *Freedom, Security and justice after Lisbon and Stockholm*, The Hague: T.M.C. Asser Press, p. 195-212.

Guild, E., Equivocal Claims? Ambivalent Controls? Labour Migration regimes in the European Union, in: E. Guild & S.A. Mantu (Eds.), *Constructing and Imagining Labour Migration. Perspectives of control from five continents*, Farnham: Ashgate, p. 207-228.

Guild, E. & S.A. Mantu, *Constructing and Imagining Labour Migration. Perspectives of Control from five Continents,* Farnham: Ashgate (334 p.).

2010

Bigo, D., S. Carrera, E. Guild & R.B.J. Walker, *Europe's 21st Century Challenge,* Farnham: Ashgate (352 p.).

Groenendijk, C.A., E. Guild, R. Cholewinski, P.E. Minderhoud & H. Oosterom, *European Report on the Free Movement of Workers in 27 EU Member States in 2009-2010* (external report), Nijmegen: Centre for Migration Law.

Groenendijk, C.A. & E. Guild, *Visa policy of Member States and the EU towards Turkish nationals after Soysal* (external report, Economic Development Foundation Publications, no. 232), Istanbul: Economic Development Foundation.

Groenendijk, C.A. & E. Guild, *Visa Policy of Member States and the EU towards Turkish Nationals after Soysal* (external report, Nijmegen Migration Law Working Papers Series, no. 2010/02), Nijmegen: Radboud University Nijmegen.

Guild, E. & M. Garlick, Refugee Protection, Counter-terrorism and Exclusion in the European Union, *Refugee Survey Quarterly, 29* (4), p. 63-82.

Guild, E., E.R. Brouwer, P.E. Minderhoud & R. van Oers, Securitization, Liberty and Law. The EU's 21st Century, in: D. Bigo, S. Carrera & E. Guild (Eds.), *Europe's 21st Century Challenge*, Farnham: Ashgate, p. 217-233.

Guild, E., *Securitization, Liberty and Rule of Law, the EU's 21st Century* (external report), New Orleans: ISA.

Guild, E., When even Machiavelli's Prince needs a Visa – Migration, Euro-Mediterranean Relations and Intercultural Dialogue, *European Foreign Affairs Review, 15* (3), p. 367-384.

Guild, E., Asymmetrical Sovereignty and the Refugee: Diplomatic Assurances and the Failure of due Process. *Agiza v Sweden and Alzery v Sweden*, in: J. Simeon (Ed.), *Critical Issues in International Refugee Law. Strategies Toward Interpretative Harmony*, Cambridge: Cambridge University Press, p. 119-142.

Guild, E., *Equivocal Claims? Ambivalent Controls? Labour Migration Regimes in the European Union* (external report, Nijmegen Migration Law Working Papers Series, no. 2010/05). Nijmegen: Radboud University Nijmegen.

2009

Groenendijk, C.A., E. Guild, R. Fernhout, R. Cholewinski, H. Oosterom & P.E. Minderhoud, *European Report on the Free Movement of Workers in 27 EU Member States in 2008* (external report), Nijmegen: Centre for Migration Law.

Guild, E., C.A. Groenendijk & S. Carrera, *Illiberal Liberal States. Immigration, Citizenship and Integration in the EU*, Farnham: Ashgate (436 p.).

Guild, E., *Security and Migration in the 21st Century*, Cambridge: Polity (216 p.).

Guild, E. & L. Marin, *Still not Resolved? Constitutional Issues of the European Arrest Warrant*, Nijmegen: Wolf Legal Publishers (X, 308 p.),.

Guild, E., *War or Crime? National Legal Challenges in Europe to the War in Iraq*, Nijmegen: Wolf Legal Publishers (X, 743 p.).

Guild, E., La migration, un défi pour la souveraineté nationale. Le cas de l'Europe, in: F. Crépeau, D. Nakache & I. Atak (Eds.), *Les migrations internationales contemporaines. Une dynamique complexe au cœur de la globalisation*, Montreal: Les Presses de l'Université de Montréal. p. 100-123.

Guild, E. & C.A. Groenendijk, Understanding the Contest of Community. Illiberal Practices in the EU?, in: E. Guild, C.A. Groenendijk & S. Carrera (Eds.), *Illiberal Liberal States. Immigration, Citizenship and Integration in the EU*, Farnham: Ashgate, p. 1-28.

Guild, E., *Mikor Bűncselekmény a Háború? = Security and European human rights. Protecting individual rights in times of exception and military action. Vertaald in het Hongaars door Majtényi Balázs en Pap András László*, Boedapest: L'Harmattan Kiadó (136 p.).

2008

Groenendijk, C.A., E. Guild, R. Fernhout, R. Cholewinski, P.E. Minderhoud & P. Boeles, *European Report on the Free Movement of Workers in 27 EU Member States in 2007* (external report), Nijmegen: Centre for Migration Law.

Guild, E. & F. Geyer, *Security versus Justice? Police and Judicial Cooperation in the European Union*, Aldershot: Ashgate (XVI, 336 p.).

Guild, E., Borders or Order? Borders or Disorder? Between the State and the Citizen, in: A. Böcker, T. Havinga, P. Minderhoud, H. van Put, L. de Groot-van Leeuwen, B. de Hart, A. Jettinghoff & K. Zwaan (Eds.), *Migratierecht en rechtssociologie, gebundeld in Kees' studies. Migration Law and Sociology of Law, Collected Essays in honour of Kees Groenendijk*, Nijmegen: Wolf Legal Publishers, p. 331-338.

Guild, E. & D. Bigo, Un espace en tension. Entre sécurité et liberté. Un tournant sécuritaire de l'Union européenne?, in : J. de Maillard & A. Wyvekens (Eds.), *L'Europe de la sécurité intérieure* (Problèmes politiques et sociaux: articles et documents d'actualité mondiale, 945), Paris: La documentation Française, p. 83-85.

Guild, E., The Uses and Abuses of Counter-terrorism Policies in Europe. The Case of the "Terrorist lists"', *Journal of Common Market Studies, 46* (1), p. 173-193.

Guild, E., S. Carrera & F. Geyer, The Commission's New Border Package. Does it Take Us one Step Closer to a 'Cyber-Fortress Europe'?, *Ceps Policy Brief,* 2008 (154), p. 1-6, doi: 10.1007/978-3-642-15708-0_1.

Guild, E., D. Bigo & S. Carrera, What Future for the Area of Freedom, Security and Justice? Recommendations on EU Migration and Borders Policies in a Globalising World, *Ceps Policy Brief,* (156), p. 1-4. doi: 10.1007/978-3-642-15708-0_1.

2007

Baldaccini, A., E. Guild & H. Toner, *Whose freedom, security and justice? EU immigration and asylum law and policy* (Essays in European law), Oxford: Hart (XXXI, 550 p.).

Groenendijk, C.A., E. Guild, R. Fernhout, R. Cholewinski & P.E. Minderhoud, *European Report on the Free Movement of Workers in 25 EU Member States in 2006* (external report), Nijmegen: Centre for Migration Law.

Guild, E., EU Policy on Labour Migration. A First Look at the Commission's Blue Card Initiative, *Ceps Policy Brief,* (145), p. 1-8. doi: 10.1007/978-3-642-14828-6.

Guild, E., *Security and European human rights. Protecting individual rights in times of exception and military action*, Nijmegen: Wolf Legal Publishers (IX, 82 p.).

Guild, E. & A. Baldaccini, *Terrorism and the foreigner. A decade of tension around the rule of law in Europe* (Immigration and asylum law and policy in Europe, 11), Leiden: Nijhoff (XXII, 431 p.).

Guild, E., Citizens without a Constitution, Borders without a State. EU Free Movement of Persons, in: A. Baldaccini, E. Guild & H. Toner, *Whose freedom, security and justice? EU immigration and asylum law and policy*, Oxford: Hart, p. 25-56.

Guild, E., The Foreigner in the Security Continuum. Judicial Resistance in the United Kingdom, in: P.K. Rajaram & C. Grundy-Warr (Eds.), *Borderscapes. Hidden Geographies and Politics at Territory's Edge* (Borderlines, 29), Minneapolis: University of Minnesota Press, p. 65-90.

Guild, E., Inside Out or Outside in? Examining Human Rights in Situations of Armed Conflict, *International Community Law Review*, p. 33-58.

Guild, E. & S. Carrera, An EU Framework on Sanctions against Employers of Irregular Immigrants. Some Reflections on the Scope, Features and Added Value, *Ceps Policy Brief,* (140), p. 1-11, doi: 10.1007/978-3-642-14828-6.

Guild, E., Inquiry into the EU-US Passenger Name Record Agreement, *Ceps Policy Brief,* (125), p. 1-4, doi: 10.1007/978-3-642-14828-6.

Guild, E., Making the Citizen's Agenda Work. *Ceps Policy Brief,* (122), p. 1-5, doi: 10.1007/978-3-642-14828-6.

Guild, E., Merging security from the Two-Level Game. Inserting the Treaty of Prüm into EU Law? *Ceps Policy Brief,* (124), p. 1-3, doi: 10.1007/978-3-642-14828-.6

Guild, E., La Union Europea y los limites de la soberania, in: *Inmigrantes. El continente móvil* (Vanguardia dossier, 22), Barcelona: Grupo Godó.

2006

Apap, J., L.F.M. Besselink, S. Carrera, C.A. Groenendijk, G.R. de Groot, E. Guild, J. Niessen & S. Pratt, *The Nexus between Immigration, Integration and Citizenship in the EU* (external report, Collective Conference Volume, April 2006). Brussels: CEPS.

Balzacq, T., D. Bigo, S. Carrera & E. Guild, *Security and the Two-Level Game: the Treaty of Prüm, the EU and the Management of Threats* (external report, CEPS Working Document, no. 234), Brussels: CEPS.

Brouwer, E.R. & E. Guild, The Political Life of Data. The ECJ Decision on the PNR Agreement between the EU and the US, *Ceps Policy Brief,* (109), p. 1-6.

Carlier, J.Y. & E. Guild, *The Future of Free Movement of Persons in the EU,* Brussels: Bruylant (322 p.).

Groenendijk, C.A., E. Guild, R. Fernhout, R. Cholewinski & P.E. Minderhoud, *European Report on the Free Movement of Workers in 25 EU Member States in 2005.* (external report), Nijmegen: Centre for Migration Law.

Guild, E., *Constitutional Challenges to the European Arrest Warrant: a Challenge for European Law. The Merging of Internal and External Security*, Nijmegen: Wolf Legal Publishers (X, 272 p.)

Guild, E. & A. Baldaccini, *Terrorism and the Foreigner: A Decade of Tension around the Rule of Law in Europe* (Immigration and Asylum Law and Policy in Europe, 11), The Hague: Martinus Nijhoff (XXII, 431 p.).

Guild, E., Citizenship and Fundamental Rights, in: J.Y. Carlier & E. Guild (Eds.), *The Future of Free Movement of Persons in the EU*, Brussels: Bruylant, p. 45-65.

Guild, E., Danger: Borders under Construction. Assessing the first five Years of Border Policy in an Area of Freedom, Security and Justice, in: J. de Zwaan & F. Goudappel (Eds.), *Freedom, Security and Justice in the European Union. Implementation of the Hague Programme*, The Hague: Asser Press, p. 45-72.

Guild, E., The Judicialisation of Armed Conflict: Transforming the Twenty-first Century, in: J. Huysmans, A. Dobson & R. Prokhovnik (Eds.), *The Politics of Protection*, London: Routledge, p. 122-135.

Guild, E. & P.E. Minderhoud (Eds.), *Immigration and Criminal Law in the European Union: the Legal Measures and Social Consequences of Criminal Law in Member States on Trafficking and Smuggling in Human Beings*, Leiden: Martinus Nijhoff Publishers (VI, 424 p.).

Toyota, M., A.G.M. Böcker & E. Guild, Pensioners on the Move: Social Security and Transborder Retirement Migration in Asia and Europe, *IIAS Newsletter/International Institute for Asian Studies,* (40), p. 30.

2005

Groenendijk, C.A., R. Cholewinski, E. Guild & P.E. Minderhoud, *European Report on the Free Movement of Workers in 25 EU Member States in 2004* (external report), Nijmegen: Centre for Migration Law.

Guild, E., The Legal Framework of EU Migration, in: M. Bommes, K. Hoesch, U. Hunger & H. Kolb (Eds.), *Organisational Recruitment and Patterns of Migration. Interdependencies in an Integrating Europe*, Special Issue, Vol. 25, *Imis-Beiträge*, Osnabrück: Universität Osnabrück, IMIS.

Guild, E., B. Andrees & M.H. van der Linden, *Human Trafficking and Forced Labour Exploitation: Guidance for Legislation and Law Enforcement*, Geneva: International Labour Office (70 p.).

Guild, E. & S. Carrera, *No Constitutional Treaty? Implications for the Area of Freedom, Security and Justice* (CEPS Working Documents, 231), Brussels: CEPS (28 p.).

Guild, E., The Legal Framework. Who is Entitled to Move?, in: E. Guild & D. Bigo (Eds.), *Controlling Frontiers. Free Movement into and within Europe*, Aldershot: Ashgate, p. 14-48.

Guild, E., Who is Entitled to Work and Who is in Charge?, in: E. Guild & D. Bigo (Eds.), *Controlling Frontiers. Free Movement into and within Europe*, Aldershot: Ashgate, p. 100-139.

Guild, E. & D. Bigo (Eds.), *Controlling Frontiers. Free Movement into and within Europe.* Aldershot: Ashgate (VII, 283 p.).

Guild, E. & J. van Selm (Eds.), *International Migration and Security. Opportunities and Challenges* (Routledge research in transnationalism, 18), London: Routledge (XVI, 280 p.).

Guild, E., Borderline Personalities. A Comparison of EU and UK five year strategies reveals increased compliance by the UK except in the thorny area of border controls, *European Lawyer,* (June 2005), p. 44-45.

2004

Groenendijk, C.A., E. Guild & P.E. Minderhoud, European report on the free movement of workers in 15 EU member states in 2002 and 2003, in: *Observatory on free movement of workers with the European Union. Report 2002 and 2003*, Nijmegen: Centre for Migration Law, p. 8-43.

Groenendijk, C.A., P.E. Minderhoud & E. Guild (Eds.), *European Report on the Free Movement of Workers in 15 EU Member States in 2002-2003.* Nijmegen: Centre for Migration Law (40 p.).

Guild, E., Crime and the EU's Constitutional Future in an Area of Freedom, Security and Justice, *European Law Journal, 10* (2), p. 218-234.

Guild, E., Seeking Asylum: storm clouds between international commitments and EU legislative measures, *European Law Review, 29* (2), p. 198-218.

Guild, E., The Borders of the European Union: Visas and carrier sanctions, *Politik: Tidsskriftet Politik, 7* (3), p. 34-43.

Guild, E., The Variable Subject of the EU Constitution, Civil Liberties and Human Rights, *European Journal of Migration and Law, 6* (4), p. 381-395, doi: 10.1163/1571816044088809.

Guild, E., *The Legal Elements of European Identity: EU Citizenship and Migration Law* (Kluwer European law library, 1), The Hague: Kluwer Law International (265 p.).

Guild, E., Jurisprudence of the European Court of Human Rights: Lessons for the EU Asylum Policy, in: C. Dias Urbano de Sousa & P. de Bruycker (Eds.), *The Emergence of a European Asylum Policy* (Collection de la Faculté de droit de l'Université libre de Bruxelles), Brussels: Bruylant, p. 329-342.

Guild, E., Mechanisms of Exclusion: Labour Migration in the European Union, in: J. Apap (Ed.), *Justice and Home Affairs in the EU*, Cheltenham: Edward Elgar, p. 211-223.

2003

Brouwer, E.R., P. Catz & E. Guild, *Immigration, Asylum and Terrorism. A Changing Dynamic in European Law* (Reeks Recht & Samenleving, 19), Nijmegen: KU Nijmegen (202 p.).

Groenendijk, C.A. & E. Guild, The Western Balkan and the European Union, Liberalising Movement of Persons, *Immigration Law Practitioners' Association Update*, p. 1-7.

Groenendijk, C.A., E. Guild & P.E. Minderhoud (Eds.), *In Search of Europe's Borders.* The Hague, London: Kluwer Law International (294 p.).

Guild, E., Economic and Social Challenges of Member and Accession States: Social Security in the Europe Agreements, *European Journal of Social Security*, 4 (1), p. 55-66.

Guild, E., Exceptionalism and Transnationalism: UK Judicial Control of the Detention of Foreign "International terrorists"', *Cultures et Conflits*, 28 (4), p. 491-515.

Guild, E., International Terrorism and EU Immigration, Asylum and Borders Policy: The Unexpected Victims of 11 September 2001, *European Foreign Affairs Review*, 8 (3), p. 331-346.

Guild, E. & D. Bigo, La mise a l'écart des étrangers: la logique du visa Schengen, *Cultures et Conflits*, p. 445-447.

Guild, E., The Concept of Refugee in the EU Asylum Policy with Special Reference to EU Practice, *Revue des Affaires Européennes/Law & European Affairs*, p. 559-569.

Guild, E., *Memorandum on Europol's Role in Fighting Crime*, House of Lords Select Committee on the European Union, 5th Report, Session 2002/3, London: House of Lords.

Guild, E., Citizens Immigrants Terrorists and others, in: A. Ward & S. Peers (Eds.), *The EU Charter of Fundamental Rights: Politics, Law and Policy*, Oxford: Hart, p. 246-321.

Guild, E., Immigration, Asylum, Borders and Terrorism: The Unexpected Victims, in: B. Gokay & R.B.J. Walker (Eds.), *11 September 2001, War, Terror and Judgement*, London: Frank Cass, p. 176-194.

Guild, E., The Border Abroad – Visas and Border Controls, in: K. Groenendijk, E. Guild & P.E. Minderhoud (Eds.), *In Search of Europe's Borders*, Deventer: Kluwer, p. 87-105.

Guild, E., The Face of Securitas: Redefining the Relationship of Security and Foreigners in Europe. Essays in Honour of Carol Harlow, in: P. Craig & R. Rawlings (Eds.), *Law and Administration in Europe*, Oxford: Oxford University Press, p. 139-153.

Guild, E., E.R. Brouwer & P. Catz (Eds.), *Asylum and Terrorism: a Changing Dynamic in European Law* (Reeks Recht & Samenleving, 19). Nijmegen: GNI (202 p.).

2002

Böcker, A.G.M. & E. Guild, *Implementation of the Europe Agreements in France, Germany, the Netherlands and the UK: Movement of Persons*, London: Platinium (XVIII, 219 p.).

Guild, E., The Borders of Legal Orders: Challenging the Exclusion of Foreigners, *Roma Rights Quarterly*, p. 28-33.

Guild, E., Comparative Legal Study on Subsidiary Protection – United Kingdom, in: D. Bouteillet-Paquet (Ed.), *Subsidiary Protection of Refugees in the European Union: Complementing the Geneva Convention?*, Brussels: Bruylant, p. 787-839.

Guild, E. & D. Bigo, The Legal Mechanisms – Collectively Specifying the Individual: The Schengen Border System and Enlargement, in: M. Anderson & J. Apap (Eds.), *Police and Justice Co-operation and the New European Borders*, The Hague: Kluwer Law International, p. 121-138.

Guild, E., The Single Market, Movement of Persons and Borders, in: J. Scoot & C. Barnard (Eds.), *The Law of the Single European Market*, Oxford: Hart Publishing, p. 295-310.

Guild, E., Workers, in: A. Ott & K. Inglis (Eds.), *Handbook on European Enlargement: A Commentary on the Enlargement Process*, The Hague: TMC Asser Press, p. 427-447.

Guild, E., Noot bij: EHRM 20 juni 2002 (*Al Nashif*), *JV* 2002-, p. 720-740.

2001

Groenendijk, C.A. & E. Guild, Converging Criteria: Creating an Area of Security of Residence for Europe's Third Country Nationals, *European Journal of Migration and Law*, p. 37-59.

Groenendijk, C.A., E. Guild & R. Barzilay, *The Legal Status of Third Country Nationals who are Long Term Residents in a Member State of the European Union*, Brussels: Office for Official Publications of the European Commission (113 p.).

Guild, E., In and Out: the UK and third country nationals and Community law, *Charities Appeals Supplement*, p. 1543-1545.

Guild, E., Whose Model? The Commission's Proposal on Access to Employment and Self Employed Migration Immigration, *Immigration and Nationality Law & Practice, 15* (3), p. 142-150.

Guild, E., *Immigration Law in the European Community,* The Hague: Kluwer Law International (240 p.).

Guild, E. & C. Harlow, *Implementing Amsterdam: Immigration and Asylum rights in EC Law*, Oxford: Hart Publishing (250 p.).

Guild, E. & P.E. Minderhoud, *Security of Residence and Expulsion: Protection of Aliens in Europe*, The Hague: Kluwer Law International (256 p.).

Guild, E., Between Persecution and Protection – Refugees and the New European Asylum Policy, in: A. Dashwood, J. Spencer, A. Ward & C. Hillion (Eds.), *The Cambridge Yearbook of European Legal Studies*, Oxford: Hart Publishing, p. 169-199.

Guild, E. & R. Cholewinski, Expulsion and Detention of Aliens in the UK, in: B. Nascimbene (Ed.), *Expulsion and Detention of Aliens in the European Union Countries*, Milan: Guiffrè Editore, p. 497-530.

Guild, E., Free Movement and Same Sex Relationships: Existing EC Law and Article 13 EC, in: R. Wintemute & M. Andenas (Eds.), *Legal Recognition of Same-Sex Partnerships*, Oxford: Hart Publishing, p. 677-289.

Guild, E., Free Movement of Workers, in: P. Goulding (Ed.), *European Employment Law and the UK* (loose-leaf), London: Sweet & Maxwell, p. 450-500.

Guild, E., The Case Law of the Dublin Convention in the UK. Between Reality and Aspirations, in: C. Faria (Ed.), *The Dublin Convention on Asylum*, Maastricht: European Institute of Public Administration, p. 149-172.

Guild, E., *Moving the Borders of Europe*, Publicaties van de faculteit der Rechtsgeleerdheid 14, Nijmegen: CPO (72 p.).

2000

Bunyan, T., H. Busch, E. Guild & S. Peers, *The Impact of the Amsterdam Treaty on Justice and Home Affairs Issues*, European Parliament Civil Liberties Series, nr. 3. Brussels: European Parliament.

Groenendijk, C.A., E. Guild & R. Barzilay, *The Legal Status of Third Country Nationals who are Long Term Residents in a Member State of the European Union. Rapport voor Europese Commissie*, Nijmegen: Centre For Migration Law (116 p.).

Groenendijk, C.A., S. Peers, E. Guild & R, Barzilay, *The legal status of persons admitted for family reunion. A comparative study of Law and Practice in some European states*, Community Relations Series, Strasbourg: Council of Europe (78 p.).

Groenendijk, C.A., E. Guild & R. Barzilay, *The Legal Status of Third Country Nationals who are Long Term Residents in a Member State of the European Union. Rapport voor Europese Commissie* (external report, Nijmegen Migration Law Working Papers Series, no 2000/01), Nijmegen: Radboud University Nijmegen.

Guild, E., *European Community Law from a Migrant's Perspective*, dissertation KU Nijmegen, Nijmegen: GNI (xiv + 341 p.).

Guild, E., De Europese gemeenschap uit het perspectief van migranten, *Migrantenrecht*, p. 151-159.

Guild, E., Entry into the UK: the changing nature of national borders, *Immigration and Nationality Law & Practice*, 14 (4), p. 227-238.

Guild, E., *Thirty years of free movement of workers in Europe*, in: J-Y Carlier & M. Verwilghen (Eds.), *Thirty years of free movement of workers in the European Union*, Luxembourg/The Hague: Office for official publications of the European Communities/Kluwer Law International, p. 61ff.

Guild, E., Identification of Legal Elements for a Successful Integration Policy, in: Council of Europe, *Strategies for Implementing Integration Policies*, Strasbourg: Council of Europe.

Guild, E., Security of Residence and Expulsion of Foreigners: European Community Law, in: E Guild & P. Minderhoud (Eds.), *Security of Residence and Expulsion: Protection of Aliens in Europe*, The Hague: Kluwer Law International, p. 59-80.

Guild, E., The European Union and Article 13 of the Treaty establishing the European Community, in: G Moon (Ed.), *Race Discrimination: Developing and Using a New Legal Framework*, Oxford: Hart Publishing, p. 65-79.

Guild, E., The United Kingdom: Kosovar Albanian refugees, in: Joanne van Selm (Ed.), *Kosovo's Refugees in the European Union*, London: Pinter, p. 67-90.

Guild, E., The regularisation of illegal immigrants in the United Kingdom, in: P. de Bruycker (Ed.), *Les régularisations des étrangers illégaux dans l'Union Européenne*, Brussels: Bruylant, p. 211-230.

Guild, E., What right of residence, Summary Report. Proceedings of the conference Brussels 17-19 December, in: J-Y Carlier & M. Verwilghen (Eds.), *Thirty years of free movement of workers in the European Union*, Luxembourg/The Hague: Office for official publications of the European Communities/Kluwer Law International, p. 161-165.

1999

Barth, P. & E. Guild, Globalisation and GATS: Movement of natural persons: a UK Perspective and European Dilemmas, *European Foreign Affairs Review*, p. 395-415.

Groenendijk, K., E. Guild & H. Dogan, *Security of Residence of Long Term Migrants: A Comparative Study of Law and Practice in European Countries*, Strasbourg: Council of Europe.

Guild, E., *The European Convention on the Legal Status of Migrant Workers (1977): an analysis of its scope and benefits*, Strasbourg: Council of Europe.

Guild, E., The Impetus to Harmonise: asylum policy in the European Union, in: F. Nicholson & P. Twomey (Eds.), *Refugee Rights and Realities, Evolving International Concepts and Regimes*, Cambridge: Campbridge University Press, p. 313-335.

Guild, E., How Can Social Protection Survive EMU? A United Kingdom Perspective, *ELRev*, 25(1), p. 22-37.

Guild, E., Adjudicating Schengen: National Judicial Control in France, *European Journal of Migration and Law*, 1(4), p. 419-439.

Guild, E., The European Community and the Movement of Key Personnel, *Texas Transnational Law Quarterly*, June 1999, p. 3-11.

Guild, E., Free movement of persons in Europe: the Amsterdam Treaty and its implications for the UK, *I&NL&P*, 13(4), p. 127-131.

Guild, E., Free Movement of Business People, *Perspectives on European Business Law*, p. 3-5.

Guild, E., Discretion, Competence and Migration in the European Union, *European Journal of Migration and Law*, 1(1), p. 61-87.

1998

Guild, E., Competence, discretion and third country nationals: the European Union's legal struggle with migration, *Journal of Ethnic and Migration Studies, 24* (4), p. 613-625.

Guild, E., Waltzing Towards Accession: the case of the Central and Eastern European countries, *European Business Law Review, 9* (3-4), p. 92-99.

Guild, E., C.A. Groenendijk & H. Dogan, *Security of Residence of Long Term Migrants: . a comparative study of law and practice in European countries*, Strasbourg: Council of Europe (117 p.).

Guild, E., *Security of Residence of Long Term Migrants: a comparative study of law and practice in European countries*, Strasbourg: Council of Europe

Guild, E. & G. Lesieur, *The European Court of Justice on the European Convention on Human Rights. Who Said What When*, The Hague: Kluwer Law International (440 p.).

Guild, E., Consequences of the Schengen Agreements on the Baltic and East European countries, in: K. Hakola (Ed.), *Migration and Refugee Policy on the Eastern Border of the EU*, University of Jyväskylä, p. 75-83.

Guild, E., The Constitutional Consequences of Lawmaking in the Third Pillar of the European Union, in: P. Craig & C. Harlow (Eds.), *Lawmaking in the European Union*, Dordrecht: Springer, p, 65-88.

Guild, E., The Europe Agreements: the Right of Establishment in the Central and Eastern European Agreements, in: J-Y Carlier & M. Verwilghen (Eds.), *Thirty years of free movement of workers in the European Union*, Luxembourg/The Hague: Office for official publications of the European Communities/Kluwer Law International, p. 128ff.

Guild, E., The European Agreements, in: Yves Jorens, Bernd Schulte, B. Van Maydell (Eds.), *European Social Security Law and Third Country Nationals*. Brussels: Die Keure.

Guild, E., Competence, discretion and third country nationals: the European Union's legal struggle with migration, *Journal of Ethnic and Migration Studies*, p. 613-625.

Guild, E., Waltzing Towards Accession: the case of the Central and Eastern European countries, *European Business Law Review, 9* (3/4), p. 92-99.

Guild, E., *Report on the Slovenian Law on Asylum* (external report), Nijmegen: Centre for Migration Law.

1997

Guild, E., Employer Sanctions: a UK own goal in Europe?, *Charities Appeals Supplement, 147* (6793).

Guild, E., EC Law and the means to combat Racism and Xenophobia, in: A Dashwood & S. O'Leary (Eds.), *The Principles of Equal Treatment in EC Law*, London: Sweet en Maxwell.

Guild, E., The Schengen Agreement: A Study in the Legitimacy of Identity and Separation, in: R Giuseppin & W.A.M. Jansen (Eds.), *Het Akkoord van Schengen en vreemdelingen, Een ongecontroleerde grens tussen recht en beleid?*, Utrecht: NCB.

Dissertations Nijmegen with Elspeth Guild as Promotor

Anoeshka Gehring
Pensioners on the Move. A Socio-legal Study on Retirement Migration from the Netherlands to Spain and Turkey
diss. Nijmegen 11 February 2019, Enschede: Ipskamp
promotores: Elspeth Guild & Anita Böcker

Bjarney Friðriksdóttir
What Happened to Equality? The Construction of the Right to Equal Treatment of Third-Country Nationals in European Union Law on Labour Migration
diss. Nijmegen 21 November 2016, Enschede: Ipskamp
promotores: Elspeth Guild & Paul Minderhoud

Madeline Garlick
Solidarity Under Strain, Solidarity and Fair Sharing of the Responsibility for the International Protection of Refugees in the European Union
diss. Nijmegen 19 September 2016, Mont-St-Guibert, Belgium: MC Plan
promotores: Elspeth Guild & Roel Fernhout

Simon Tans
Service Provision and Migration. EU and WTO service trade liberalization and their impact on Dutch and UK immigration rules
diss. Nijmegen 30 November 2015, Deventer: Ipskamp
promotores: Elspeth Guild & Paul Minderhoud

Sandra Mantu
Contingent citizenship. The law and practice of citizenship deprivation in international, European and national perspectives
diss. Nijmegen 19 June 2014, Deventer: Ipskamp
promotores: Elspeth Guild & Paul Minderhoud

Claude Cahn
Sovereignty, autonomy and right. Human rights law and the international effort to seek justice for Romani women coercively sterilized in the Czech and Slovak Republics
diss. Nijmegen 14 January 2014, Nijmegen: Wolf Legal Publishers
promotores: Kees Groenendijk & Elspeth Guild

Dana Baldinger
Rigorous scrutiny versus Marginal review. Standards on judicial scrutiny and evidence in international and European asylum law
diss. Nijmegen 16 April 2013, Oisterwijk: Wolf Legal Publishers
promotores: Elspeth Guild & Kees Groenendijk

Daniel Wilsher
The Liberty of Foreigners: a History, Law and Politics of Immigration Detention
diss. Nijmegen 9 March 2009, Nijmegen: Wolf Legal Publishers
promotor: Elspeth Guild

Evelien Brouwer
Digital Borders and Real Rights : Effective Remedies for Third-country Nationals in the Schengen Information System
diss. Nijmegen 1 October 2007, Nijmegen: Wolf Legal Publishers
promotores: Elspeth Guild & Kees Groenendijk